Twitching
by numbers

A birder's account of his hectic life as he chases
rare species across Britain and Ireland

Written and illustrated by

Garry Bagnell

Twitching by numbers

Contents

INTRODUCTION
ACKNOWLEDGEMENTS

Contents

INTRODUCTION
ACKNOWLEDGEMENTS

INTRODUCTION

This book covers the last 24 years of my twitching escapades with bite-size chunks about my family, friends, and employment. It should give readers a deeper understanding of the journey I'm taking you on. I believe that if all four of the ingredients mentioned above are in harmony, the hobby can transform your life and help improve your mental health.

Each twitch is a series of frozen moments in time, from the time you hear about a bird, how you organise how you're going to see it and who you'll go with, the moment you leave home and the arrival, the search, the wait for the bird, seeing it for the first time, watching it, who else was there, then the craic afterwards and the journey home. I have shared my own frozen moments in time in Chapters 1 to 24. In the early chapters I only have space to briefly mention the rarest birds seen. From Chapter 8 onwards the opportunities for new birds become fewer and fewer, and this gives me more space to detail the adventures. Some write-ups are more eventful than others, and on occasion guest writers have kindly filled the gaps.

Twitching birds in Britain and Ireland is the main story of the book, but I've also mentioned the odd European twitch. If any of these birds ever appeared over here, thousands of twitchers throughout Britain would arrive within 24 hours.

Chapter 11 mentions the filming of a BBC4 documentary called "Twitchers, a Very British Obsession". Many were interviewed for the programme and I was proud to be selected. I think the programme put our crazy hobby in a good light.

Chapter 23 mentions the formation of the Casual Twitcher WhatsApp group, designed to help twitchers to rally enough individuals to help facilitate boat charters to remote islands at the drop of a hat. Now the group is a year old with 200+ members and all profits go to charities.

Chapter 25 shows tables depicting number of miles driven, number of boats and planes and the money spent on seeing all these wonderful birds I've written about. This chapter is a bit stat heavy, but I think it's necessary to bring together the facts mentioned throughout the book.

I've regularly mentioned how many records there have been for Britain and Ireland. Please note these totals are only using records since 1950. Records before would have made it difficult to calculate stats used from Chapter 8.

At the back of the book is a full list of every bird I've seen in Britain and Ireland, and a list of birds I haven't.

If you are into birds, I hope you find this book useful and motivating.

Thanks for reading

Garry Bagnell

28th November 2022

ACKNOWLEDGEMENTS

The first person I want to thank is my wonderful wife, Kim. This book could have easily never happened, as I cancelled our first date and decided to drive to Scotland for a Corncrake instead. Fortunately, she gave me a second chance and twenty years later I'm proud to say that we have a family consisting of our daughter Georgie, two dogs, Barney and Pepper, and two cats, Poppy and Midge. Over the last year, household projects have been put on hold to free up time to write the book. Now it's finished our bedroom is going to get its first lick of paint in six years. I'm so grateful to have a well-balanced wife at the centre of my universe, she's a gift from God. Love you dearly.

Secondly, I'd like to thank Georgie for being a kind and thoughtful daughter. I've embarrassed her in front of numerous friends, boyfriends, schoolteachers, and anybody else you care to mention. She forgives me, and even though I'm on the so called "spectrum", I'm proud she calls me Dad.

I promise to be a better Dad to Barney and Pepper – they too have been neglected during the book writing.

Over the twenty-four years many different birdwatching companions have come and gone.

However, one individual hasn't. This is ex-BBC sports commentator John Lees. We did our first twitch together back in 2005 and have remained friends ever since. John has rung me about many birds to get my initial reaction "Nah, I can't be bothered" and then ask, "What time are you getting here?" John and his partner Liz have got to know my family very well and I now consider them part of my family.

My big list wouldn't have been possible if it wasn't for my understanding employers. I want to thank my current manager, Philip Moores from Rapiscan, for all the short notice leave he provides me. Before him, I got similar treatment from Beverley Gasson, David Fairchild, Colin Huckwell, Trevor Purfield, Dennis Gregg, and Phil Parker whilst working at Colas.

The standard of write-ups from Ewan Urqhart, Justin Taylor, Cliff Smith, Brian McCloskey, and Vic Caschera has really enhanced the book. Thank you, gents.

I would like to thank Lee Evans, Birdguides, Rare Bird Alert, British Birds, Birding World and Birdwatching for providing such quality publications, which helped me to provide statistical information surrounding the birds I've seen.

CHAPTER 1

1999

During my first 33 years of life, I always had serious hobbies. Birdwatching was my first hobby from age 10 to 15 and then plane spotting from 15 to 33. Plane spotting was supplemented by other hobbies. These included playing competitive chess for Crawley and Coulsdon, mobile DJ work and British stamp collecting. Each of my hobbies had me hooked for around five years.

Why I am so keen on hobbies? There was no income for me in any of them. DJ-ing could have been a money spinner, but I was spending all my takings in buying fancy record decks, light screens, thousands of vinyl records and dating women. My devotion to these hobbies has produced serious side effects. Most people put career/work first, but the more I think about it, the more I realise I've always put my hobbies first.

During all this time I was a cigarette smoker. I remember buying a packet of cigarettes from the Virgin Atlantic vending machines in the morning for about 50p for a packet of 20 and then by the afternoon I was usually buying another packet. I was in my early 20s and cigarettes were regularly being left to burn in an ashtray whilst I was called away by another department. Plus, my Cornish boss, Michael, didn't help. He never had any money and was always on the scrounge for a fag. The number of times I would light a cigarette and then look down at the ashtray and see another burning away indicated I needed help.

During my time at Virgin Atlantic Airways, I tried my hand at studying accountancy. I was studying CIMA (Chartered Institute of Management Accountants) between 1989 to 1996 and successfully managed to pass 12 papers and become a part-qualified accountant. This wasn't good enough in a 7-year period, as most people would have been fully qualified in the same period and able to get more senior jobs to earn the big bucks.

I met an English-born Pakistan lady called Zainab at Virgin. We initially moved into my parents' Crawley home, and after a year we got an endowment mortgage for a one-bedroom house in Worth, West Sussex.

The plane spotting all started in 1981 when my school friend Martin Arter invited me to spend a day with him at Gatwick Airport overlooking the planes from the spectators' section of the airport. We went on a Saturday, which was Gatwick's busiest day with seven Russian flights and many big, colourful planes arriving from America. They were all big jumbo jets. There was a big orange one owned by Braniff, while Northwest Orient ones had big red tails and Transamerican had a light green tail. These beautiful liveries were mesmerising, I spent the day noting down all the registrations I could see and quickly became hooked. My aviation knowledge probably helped me get my post at Virgin Atlantic.

The plane-spotting hobby got me into having exotic holidays. I only left airports when it was time to go to bed or eat. Seeing and ticking off many planes in my aviation books created annoying gaps. These 'gap fillers' I longed to see, and this made the hobby all-consuming. Most of my jobs after leaving Virgin in October 1991 were temporary assignments. The periods in between jobs allowed me to spend my hard-earned money in the USA trying to see Gulfstreams, JetStars, Learjets etc.

My obsession with planes was not fun for Zainab. She occasionally came on these trips, but she had no interest in planes and spent her time reading books whilst sitting in hire cars around airport perimeters or driving between airports.

Zainab and I got slightly into arrears with our mortgage payments, and we were paid a visit by a Nationwide debt collector called Nigel Driver. Nigel is a keen Sussex birdwatcher and whilst visiting my house he remarked on how many Greenfinches were feeding in our small garden. I think we use to have 10 dispensers up at the back of the garden, and we had constant finch and tit traffic.

Big relief came in 1999 when the arrears got paid off and I managed to secure a one-year contract at National Grid plc in Leatherhead. I got a job as a Budget Accountant working for a South African guy called TC and an English guy called Martin. Both my bosses were based in Coventry, and I did have to make periodic visits to meet them. They were both nice guys. TC had a short temper, but as long as you got your work done on time, he was happy. Martin was the sort of the bloke you'd go to the pub and get drunk with. He had been at National Grid for many years, and he managed to change departments every time the company went through a restructuring.

On the 10th of May 1999, I got a phone call from Crawley Hospital, who informed me that I should come down immediately as my dad was not very well. I got permission to leave work and when I arrived at hospital, I found my mum with her daughter Linda at his bedside, looking very upset. The bed was empty. He had died from leukaemia, even before the hospital phone call. I felt devastated. My dad was my role model, and he was never going to make me laugh again.

The hospital staff allowed us to see him resting in another room. This was the first dead body I'd ever seen and when I reached out and touched his cold body, I collapsed into uncontrollable bouts of crying and screaming.

My dad had told me he had cancer back in 1997. I remember being at home when he rang me to give this devastating news. I'm so glad I managed to buy a video camera before he died, I spent a few hours filming him. One day I was videoing him at Tilgate shops. He loved jellied eels, and every Saturday a mobile shop appeared at the parade. Whilst I was videoing him, a customer in the queue asked, 'Is this guy famous?' I said, 'oh yes, he's very famous, he's my dad'.

I should have guessed he didn't have long to live. When he was admitted to hospital in early April, the doctor said, 'He's going to have his own private room and stay there as long as he wants'. He didn't have much of an appetite at hospital, but on the 3rd May I remember visiting him with Zainab and he craved a Kentucky Fried Chicken. I instantly drove to the nearest KFC and bought back a big family bucket of chicken pieces. He really enjoyed it, but the next day he lost his appetite again.

My mum was now left at home with her Yorkshire terrier, Pip. Zainab and I asked if we could move back in, and she agreed that was a good idea. We quickly found tenants for our house. Our new bedroom desperately needed a facelift. I got Carpetright to fit a luxury carpet, whilst we made a visit to Collingwood Batchelor in Horley and ordered a pine wardrobe, chest of drawers, bedside cabinet, and a new bed. The old furniture was predominantly made from chipboard, and this all got taken to the tip when new furniture arrived.

My mum's house was kept warm by two portable Calor gas heaters. This was an expensive way to keep the house warm, and my mum really needed central heating, something my dad and mum could fully justify in the past. I was determined to improve my mum's lifestyle, so we invited a plumber around the house, and he quoted circa £4,000 to get gas central heating in every room with a combi boiler fitted in the kitchen. It sounded expensive, but we agreed to pay half each.

Living with my mum and wife in the same house created an unusual atmosphere. My mum left Zainab to do the evening meal for us two. I'm sure this was agreed behind my back, as my mum had always been the main chef in the house. After dinner was eaten and the washing-up was put away, Zainab wanted to retreat to our bedroom and either read or watch TV. I wanted to spend some time talking with my mum, but also felt I couldn't be too long downstairs as Zainab also wanted to spend time talking to me. Weird how I got on with my mum and wife, but it certainly felt like an awkward atmosphere was building between the two ladies in the house.

Whilst working at National Grid in Dorking, I got talking to a birdwatcher called Neil Howes. Neil was a buyer, and one day he brought his birding notebook into work. His notebook was crammed full of rare birds he had encountered on British twitches, and had colour illustrations of the birds he had seen. I was blown away. One day he was in Cornwall, next twitch he was in Scotland, then in Yorkshire. I had never been to Scotland or Cornwall, and he had just done these humungous drives to see a bird. In fact, this was the first time I had met a proper twitcher.

I did some twitching myself between 1992 and 1997, but mostly I only travelled to the counties covered by Birdline Southeast. The rarest birds I had seen during this period included Pied-billed Grebe, Long-billed Dowitcher, Penduline Tit, Desert Wheatear, Hume's Warbler, American Coot, Lesser Scaup, White-winged Black Tern and Red-rumped Swallow. None of these were new for Neil. My British list totalled 244 and somehow he had seen nearly 200 more than that. His list was on 428 on 7th July 1999, using a checklist supplied by the UK400 Club. I felt very insignificant and thought maybe I should ditch the plane spotting pronto and see some proper rare birds. The rate new aircraft were being built meant you needed to keep spending money on visiting the same prolific countries or visiting various production lines just to keep on top. I was ready for a new hobby.

Neil had recently just seen a Baillons Crake

at Grove Ferry and suggested we both go down after work for it. We drove in separate cars and parked near the Grove Ferry inn. Just has we got out of the car and entered the site; we could hear the distinctive purring of a Turtle Dove and a few minutes later we heard a frog croaking. Neil said, 'No, It's not a frog, that the Baillon's Crake'. I started tingling with excitement and I was now determined to video it. Seeing it was hard, but occasionally you would catch a brief glimpse as it would speed-walk between clumps of reeds. It was constantly calling, so you generally knew where it was, but seeing it was impossible unless it came out of the reeds. I managed some video footage and it felt amazing to add a new bird to my British life list. First one since 1997.

Once I got home, I looked at my camcorder playback and zooming in on the Crake made the image very pixellated. I felt a bit cheated as I should have studied it through my bins.

National Grid also had another twitcher working there. Tucked away in the storeroom was little John Benham. John had only just started twitching in the last year; he had spent most of his spare time fishing or entering fishing competitions. He was completely content giving up angling, and now committed to spending his hard-earned money seeing birds.

Neil was a walking, talking encyclopaedia of rare British birds. Very useful to John, especially when he was planning on which direction to point the car at weekends. Mentoring is useful to a novice twitcher. You could spend 24 hours driving to Aberdeen and back for say a Whiskered Tern, but Whiskered Tern is an annual visitor to Britain and some years in good numbers. If you are prepared to wait a couple of years, you'll get the chance to see one closer to home. Every new bird can get your pulse racing, but not all of them

are gettable. Neil understood the rarity value of birds and what chances you had of seeing a bird today or tomorrow. He had experience of different sites and a plethora of birding contacts throughout Britain. Remember we did not yet have the internet, therefore no smartphones, so bird information was courtesy of a little grey plastic box called a pager.

Pagers were game changing devices; a rare bird could be found anywhere in the country. As soon as the information was known by Birdline, Rare Bird Alert or Birdnet, the information was broadcast instantly. Neil was a member of Rare Birds Alert and his pager was constantly beeping and flashing when bird news was received. This instant news is important if you can drop things and go. I could only go twitching at weekends, but Neil sold it to me that I really needed a pager if I was serious about twitching. I found the Birdnet pager was slightly cheaper than Rare Bird Alert, so being an accountant who liked value for money, I decided to get a year's contract with Birdnet. Once I had the pager, I could finally call myself a twitcher.

My first lifer via the pager was a Leach's Petrel at Shoreham beach. It was originally broadcast as a Storm Petrel, and I saw it by the skin of my teeth. Luckily, when I arrived at Shoreham, Sussex-born Andrew Wickham gave me directions and I just saw it in my collapsible Mirador telescope before it went west past the harbour arm. I really wanted to get another view, so Andrew jumped into my car and navigated me to another vantage point in the harbour. Sadly, we didn't see the Petrel again, but it was nice that a stranger was prepared to help me.

Over the next few weeks, lifers were being seen on a weekly basis. I got flight views of a Blyth's Pipit at Happisburgh in Norfolk. This place is pronounced 'haze-bruh' – worth remembering, as Norfolk folk take great pleasure in correcting people who get it wrong. I did manage to see it on the ground for 10 seconds, which felt like a bit of success after umpteen poor flight views.

I was advised that Stubb's Mill is a good place to end a day's birding in Norfolk. It has a good watchpoint where you can see raptors coming in to roost and more importantly the possibility of another lifer for the day; Common Crane. The Common Cranes established a small breeding population in the Norfolk Broads from the late 70s. If you follow signs to Hickling village and then to the nature reserve, you can park your car at the visitor centre and then walk for about 15 minutes to get to Stubbs Mill. I managed to see five Marsh Harriers and a Merlin. Then just before dusk I watched 3 Common Cranes fly distantly in formation for over a minute as they found a distant reed bed to land in. Such an iconic sight, long straight neck and long trailing legs as they fly effortlessly in a perfect straight line.

The Mirador telescope was a must-have bit of kit for a plane spotter. It was light and powerful and made it very easy to watch aeroplanes coming in to land and taking off. Originally purchased as a 32x 80mm draw tube spotting scope with rubber armour, it had a circular tripod mount. This fell off at some airport perimeter. I managed to get a custom-built metal bracket clamp for the scope with a screw thread. I was able to connect it to a tripod carried over my shoulder, but compared to other birders with fixed body scopes that sit tightly on a tripod, I was certainly hindering myself. Enough is enough, I made a visit to Kay Optical in Morden and came back with a Kowa TSN823 angled scope with 2 eyepieces, 32x and 50x, with stay-on Skua case. Birdnet were advertising a second-hand pair Leica 10 x 42 binoculars, so one phone call and these too were bought.

October was here and the pager was getting very busy with vagrants being found. Neil Howes was having a holiday on the Scillies with his birding chums and arrived too late to see the 2-day Baltimore Oriole on Bryher. I was busy doing the month end at work and over the next few days my pager was making loud buzzing sounds. On Tuesday 4th a buzz from the box and this time it was a male Siberian Thrush, found on Gugh, Scilly Isles. Later messages indicated that it was elusive and there was going to be an organised flush. Next day, the Siberian Thrush was still there and more organised flushes were advertised. A mega alert sounded again and this time a White's Thrush was found on St. Agnes. A few in the office, including Diane, Tracy, Guy and Sean, could also hear the strange beeping, and I kept them in the picture of what was happening. Thursday 7th we got 2 mega alerts and surprise, surprise both on the Scillies again. This time there was an Upland Sandpiper at St. Mary's and a first for Britain in the shape of a Short-toed Eagle.

I decided to go off birding for the weekend, not to the Scillies but to try and see a juvenile Baird's Sandpiper at Cantley Beet Factory. It was seen in the morning, but by the time I arrived it had gone missing. I hung around all day with no joy. Best bird of the day was a Barn Owl and I felt a little disappointed with no lifers, so I decided to take my trusty Volvo 440 on its furthest journey north. I had already done 166 miles, so another 163 miles wouldn't hurt it. I drove up to Blacktoft Sands RSPB on the River Humber near Hull and spent the night sleeping in the car. The next morning, I bumped into Brian Abdullah and Neville Wilson and we spent many hours chatting whilst we enjoyed watching a 1st winter Wilson's Phalarope. The phalarope was mainly swimming, but its long fine black bill, grey upperparts and white underparts really made it stand out in the crowd. Brian and Neville were friendly lads and gave me their addresses and telephone number and suggested meeting up in the future, when they could guarantee me rare sea birds including Sooty Shearwaters.

Back at work on Monday 11th, the mega alert was still making those beeping noises. This time a Swainson's Thrush had been found on Garnish Point in Cork and the Scillies Upland Sandpiper was joined by a second. The following day Scilly was back in the action with a Yellow-billed Cuckoo being found on Tresco. Wednesday 13th and Berkshire-based Chris Heard finds a Veery on St. Levan in Cornwall. The pager was now advertising a helicopter day return from St. Marys to Penzance for the Veery. Neil was still on Scilly, and I guessed he would be smiling like a Cheshire cat when I saw him next. Thursday 14th arrived and Scilly got another mega, this time a male Blue Rock Thrush. There was no point me spending this weekend driving to another location on the mainland – I needed to be going to Scilly.

The Blue Rock Thrush had last been seen on the Friday and Zainab and I set out for a 6-hour drive to Cornwall. En route we popped in at Titchfield Haven in Hampshire and saw a Temminck's Stint. We opted for a luxury B&B just off the A30 before arriving in Penzance. We had a great night's sleep and made sure we got to Penzance Harbour before the ticket office opened. Lots of birders were also planning on getting the *Scillonian III* across. The whole process of queuing with other birders to board the boat felt quite surreal.

It was nice to see my old Crawley birding friend Mushaq Ahmed in Penzance. Last time I saw him was in 1981 when were both school kids. He was now a fully established professional bird watcher running Birdline Southwest and now known as one of the most knowledgeable people in Britain on gulls. Known as 'Mush' for short, he offered

me a ticket on Skybus which would get me from nearby Lands End to St. Mary's in 15-20 minutes. Zainab and I were quite happy to get the 9:15am sea crossing and arrive around midday.

News was coming through that there was now no sign of the Blue Rock Thrush. This was a massive blow for most people on the boat but for me personally I wasn't bothered. Scilly still had some many good birds on offer. Getting off the boat felt amazing, such a beautiful island, and it was teeming with birders carrying bins and telescopes, and some had CB radios. The walk to B&B was 10 minutes and I helped carry the bags and I decided I would nip over to the airfield whilst Zainab unpacked. The airfield didn't disappoint – I managed to get three ticks in three minutes: 2 Upland Sandpipers, a Short-toed Lark and a Richards Pipit. I was starting to fall in love with the Scillies.

There was an advert on the pager about a special boat to Tresco leaving the quay shortly. I rang Zainab and said, 'Are you ready to walk quickly to the harbour?' We got there in time and climbed down the vertical metal ladder into a small boat with around 100 excited birders. Everybody was squeezed in like sardines in a tin can hoping to see the Yellow-billed Cuckoo. I really didn't know where to walk on Tresco, so we just followed the pack. The bird was very elusive. Every tree it was being claimed from was quickly surrounded by the birders. I managed to get a quick view of it in somebody else's scope, but the view was poor, you could only see its tail and breast above the foliage.

I offered Sussex birder Chris Glanfield, who was standing nearby, a view through this kind gentleman's scope. But as soon as he got a peek in the scope the crowd were shouting that the Cuckoo had hopped up higher in the tree. Chris was a fraction of a second too late to see it, and I felt bad for him, but there was plenty of daylight left to see it again. At this stage I guess around 50% of the crowd saw the cuckoo but most people hung around to the last sailing back to St. Marys. No further view for me of the Yellow-billed Cuckoo, and Chris also failed to see it.

On the boat back, it transpired that Chris and his friends were staying in the same B&B as us in Church Road. I had only met Chris once before, at St. Margaret's Bay, where we successfully both saw a Red-breasted Flycatcher, a Yellow-browed Warbler and a Firecrest. We got back with a bit of daylight and Chris was going to try and see the Radde's Warbler at Watermill Cottage. We shared a taxi and the Radde's was hopping around the floor when we arrived.

It suddenly dawned on me this was turning out to be a prolific lifer day – five in one day. To celebrate, Zainab and I dined with Chris and his friends in Hugh town. After the meal, we went to the log call run by Dick Filby. The log call is an opportunity to shout what birds you've seen when they systematically go through what birds have been seen on the island. They are generally interested in migrants, but if there was a large flock of Woodpigeon, that would also get mentioned. Photographers were also selling their bird images. Mike McDonnell, Tony Collinson, George Reszetter and Rob Wilson all had tables with their beautiful images displayed. I was drawn to Mike McDonnell's table. Mikes lives in Kent and he was sharing a table with Tony Collinson. I couldn't resist buying 6 by 4 prints of Short-toed Lark, Richards Pipit, Upland Sandpiper and Raddes Warbler. By this time in the evening Mike was a bit drunk, but some of the pictures I've bought from in the past have been slightly out of focus. However I'm not into perfection and he's probably one of the friendliest photographers you will ever meet.

The social scene on Scillies seemed to be amazing, likeminded people blown away by the amazing bunch of rare birds this autumn. I was under the impression Scilly was going to be like this every year.

The next day, Zainab and I decided to get the boat to St. Agnes to see the White's Thrush. So many horror stories were being told of how hard this bird was to see. One guy had visited St. Agnes every day since it arrived and still had not seen it. I thought my chance was very slim, but in fact I managed to watch it for a whole 20 seconds in my scope as it was walking low through a field. I was looking with a few others who managed to get their scopes wedged between narrow fence posts. Not everybody had a successful gap in the fence to view from. The guy who originally called out he could see it was not willing to share his scope view. I had never really encountered this selfish behaviour before. So glad that I chose the right gap to scan – some people managed to see it only by trespassing on private land.

I finished the day wandering around St. Mary's looking unsuccessfully for the Common Rosefinch or the Ortolan. In the evening we met Nick Tanner from London. A few pints later, Nick was discussing Asian warbler identification. Impressively, he was reeling off features you needed to see to decide whether it was a Greenish or Arctic, Dusky or Raddes, Olivaceous or Booted, Icterine or Melodious etc. He was right, there are more species pairs: Chiffchaff and Willow Warbler, Marsh and Reed Warbler and so on.

Monday was our last day and straight after breakfast I was out birding. I'd dipped Ring Ouzel at Beachy Head and Cuckmere Valley in the past, but there were a few mentioned on last night's log call. I wandered around Peninnis Head and bingo, I saw one in flight. I followed it to a bramble bush.

It was a male with a large white crescent across the breast and scaly underparts. Nice.

Getting new birds on Scilly and with a pager is so much easier than ringing the birdlines. My list is now on about 258, 15 new birds since Neil took me to the Baillons Crake.

Talking of Neil, I managed to see him wandering around Scilly. He looked really happy, he had 6 ticks there: Siberian Thrush, Veery, Blue Rock Thrush, Short-toed Eagle, Upland Sandpiper and Siberian Stonechat. He didn't even need the Yellow-billed Cuckoo (St. Mary's 1995) or White's Thrush (Lewis 1998) – what a guy.

More wandering around and I'm pretty sure I found an Ortolan Bunting (too brief to tick) and at Juliet's Café I found a Richard's Pipit. Just as I was walking back to the pier I bumped into Lee Evans, a big name in the birding world – much more of Lee later in the book. I had never spoken to him before, so I introduced myself and mentioned where I had seen the Ortolan and Richard's Pipit. Then off he went.

All goods things must come to an end, so Zainab and I boarded the *Scillonian III*. The crossing was calm, and it didn't take long before I saw a Manx Shearwater shearing at the side of the boat. A shout went out for a Great Skua at the back of the boat. I had such a poor view that I decided it wasn't tickable. I was on 8 ticks for the trip and Nick Tanner planted a seed by saying he wouldn't mind seeing a Red-flanked Bluetail at Rame before he went home. He was booked to head back home on the train to London, and Zainab and I were due back at work on Tuesday. Nick said the Red-flanked Bluetail used to be a rare bird in Britain. There had only been 24 records for Britain and 4 of them had turned up in the last few days.

Zainab wasn't in a rush to go back to work, so we decided to stay the night in Cornwall and offer Nick a lift back home. The Red-flanked Bluetail was found at Rame Church on the 17th October and our little black box confirmed it was still there on the 19th. We watched this colourful bird for a good 20 minutes as it was hopping around on gravestones. Nick mentioned he had seen Dippers in the past on the River Bovey. This would make it a 10th new trip bird for me, and sure enough we connected.

My new hobby was gradually removing all my aircraft chasing tendencies, but had I really wasted the last 20 years of my life? I'd been to the United States over 30 times. If I was there now, I would do a bit of birdwatching, but I would still want to see some sought-after aircraft. The Grumman Gulfstream Two was an aeroplane I was passionate to see. They built 256 between 1967 and 1980 and I managed to see 246 of them. Some of the Gulfstream Twos involved me visiting exotic locations including Japan, Venezuela, and Mexico. Sadly, six had been written off and would never be seen again, but I still had a chance of seeing three owned by North American companies and one owned by Libyan Arab Airlines that had visited Malta in the last few years.

Travel had not featured much in my mum's life. Whilst my dad was alive, the furthest she had ever travelled was Cornwall, and that was when she was evacuated during World War II. I seem to remember she had only once left the mainland, and that was crossing the Solent to visit the Isle of Wight. My late father had perforated eardrums and his doctors advised him never to go on an aeroplane, which I guess is the main reason they didn't go far. Since my father died, my mum had started catching the coach to Dover and hopping across the Channel to see my sister Chantal and her family in Northern France. Before my dad died, he asked me to try and visit Chantal. I said I would, but I've never been in a happy enough place to make this happen. My relationship with Zainab had been up and down and I had threatened to leave her many times, but when push came to shove, I always changed my mind and stayed. I had only met Chantal once, when Zainab, Mum and Dad, Linda and her two kids rendezvoused in Folkestone.

To clarify, I was adopted by my grandparents, and I will always refer to them as Mum and Dad. Linda is my real mum and I first met her when I was fifteen years old. She had spent several years living in a drug rehabilitation centre in Kent, until my dad reluctantly allowed her to move back into the family home. My real father was named Andre and died from a heroin overdose when he was 21 years old. I don't believe I ever met him. Linda originally had three children with Andre: Chantal, Andre and me. Linda only lived with my mum and dad for a year or so before she moved into a council house in Bewbush, Crawley, when she met Jack. Together they had three children and named them Leanne, Sasha and Jack. Father Jack was, surprise surprise, another drug addict. My dad had disowned Linda for the first 15 years of my life and disowned her again when he found out Jack was into drugs. Linda had never been honest to mum, dad, or me about many things. When we made the car trip to Folkestone, we were under the impression that she was a single parent.

I'd always wanted my mum to experience a nice holiday and that December, Zainab and I booked a holiday for all three of us, a week in Cyprus.

October 24 got me embarking on my longest car twitch. I went to Greatham Creek in Cleveland for a Short-billed Dowitcher. This juvenile bird was a first for Britain and originally found at Rosehearty, Aberdeenshire. It was there from 11th to 24th September and then relocated to Grenabella Marsh and Greatham Creek on the 29th September. It was jointly found by Bernie Beck and R.C. Taylor.

Bernie had now found both species of Dowitcher in Britain, which is an incredible feat. I watched this diagnostic juvenile from 8:10 to 8:30am. The main features to look for are the axillary feathers and flanks. The SBD is more heavily barred on the axillaries and flanks than the LBD. Also, this bird had a noticeably pale tail.

On 31st October I teamed up with some of Chris Glanfield's friends for a drive to Cornwall. Chris couldn't make it, but the trip was a success. We managed to see a Booted Eagle initially at Drift reservoir and then at Tremmick Cross. The white morph eagle was hovering up and down over a small wood. This eagle was quite distinctive with pale panels on the upper wings and two pale panels on the back. It had extensive white underparts with darker feathers on underwing and tail. The Booted Eagle is native to parts of southern and eastern Europe and Africa.

This bird was originally found on 5th March at Rogerstown (Dublin). Over the next six months it was also seen at Dungarvan (Waterford), Broadway (Wexford), Kilinick (Wexford), Bangor (Down), Lady Island (Wexford), Lambay Island (Dublin) and Rathlin Island (Antrim). Then it was found at St. Margaret's Bay (Kent) on 28th September and next in Cornwall from 25th October. It was the first record for Britain and Ireland.

Other good birds seen during the day included a Red-backed Shrike at RAF Culdrose and a Pacific Golden Plover amongst 50+ Golden Plovers at Helston. This bird was originally thought to be an American Golden Plover but our passenger Richard Kemp, who had previous experience with this species, was keen to look at the primary extension (PE), the length of the primary wing feathers compared to the secondaries. A Golden Plover with a PE clearly less than half the bill length should be a Pacific Golden Plover, whereas if the PE is equal or greater than the bill length it should be an American Golden Plover (Reference Marin Reid). Our summer plumaged plover was much smaller than the accompanying Golden Plover. I had no experience of American or Pacific Golden Plover up to then, so when an American Golden Plover turned up at Normandy Marsh (Hampshire) on the 7th November, I went.

So many good birds kept being found during November. I dipped a Two-barred Crossbill at New Forest on 13th November but instead got a spectacular flypast of a Goshawk. The following day I went for a Canvasback at Abberton Reservoir (Essex). This bird had been found at Abberton over the previous two winters in 1997 and 1998. It was mainly asleep with Northern Pochard but over the two hours I was present, it would lift its head from it back and reveal its sloping forehead and long black bill forming a perfect ski slope.

In the afternoon I searched for several hours for a Forster's Tern at Tollesbury, and noted 27 different species but nothing resembling a tern. Kent photographer Mike McDonnell said to me, 'Don't be disheartened, keep trying for it. When this birds finally goes, you never know if there will ever be another gettable one'.

This advice inspired me to come back a couple more times. On Sunday 5th December after a long walk, I could finally see a tern flying along the circular marsh. This was an exciting moment for me – you start to disbelieve a bird is really there. I watched this winter-plumaged stunner from 11:30 to 11:50am. It made a couple of unsuccessful dives in the channel but I noted the black triangle pattern around each eye, red feet, black bill on an all-white ghost-like appearance with a touch of light grey connecting mask and upperparts. I felt totally inspired and was now looking forward to our flight to Cyprus in four days' time.

Zainab, Mum and I stayed in the Coral Beach Hotel and resort, a stunning five-star hotel overlooking a partly sandy beach. Short walks from the hotel produced Red-throated Pipits, Sardinian Warblers and Fan-tailed Warblers. I managed to get a car for five days and we drove to Cape Grekko and saw Finsch's Wheatear, Crested Lark and Chukars. Pafos Beach had Greater Sandplovers and Kentish Plovers. I saw some Spanish Sparrows at Mandria and a pair of Black Francolins flew across the road and vanished.

I'm not a fan of heights, but I did manage a trip to Aspredremmos Dam. Such an impressive place with a distant Bonelli's Eagle flying over, and eventually I got a glimpse of a Moustached Warbler. I'm pretty sure we saw a Cyprus Warbler at Mavrokolympos Dam. The breast barring was not as distinctive as the book illustrations but very faint.

My mum was fine flying, and the highlight of our holiday was the karaoke night. Not many people braved the singing, but I did do one duo with the karaoke man. His voice was much better than mine, but that didn't put me off and I then spent the whole night trying to sing Elvis Presley, Donna Summer and Buddy Holly classics. Next morning all three of us entered the restaurant for breakfast and I'm pretty sure the hotel guests remembered me from last night. People started smiling and loudly clapping the whole time from arrival to sitting at our dining table. Sounds like my voice amused and enriched people's holidays.

An Ivory Gull was found at Aldeburgh in Suffolk on 7th December. Surely this bird wouldn't still be Suffolk when we flew back on the 16th? It sure was. I dropped off Zainab, mum and suitcases and made my way to Suffolk, where the bird was easily seen on the beach and allowed a really close approach.

To end the year, Zainab and I spent four days over Christmas on Anglesey. South Stack didn't disappoint with a couple of Chough on Boxing Day and on the way home a drake American Wigeon, with 30 Red Kite at Cors Caron.

SUMMARY – 1999

During 1999, I travelled 6,282 miles in Britain in the pursuit of new birds and managed to increase my list by 34 new BOU species, which took my British life list to 274. The Official British List now stood at 551 species, which meant I was almost halfway there with 49.7%. 1999 had three firsts for Britain: Short-toed Eagle, Short-billed Dowitcher and Booted Eagle. I would add these to the Official British List when they were accepted by BOURC and BBRC.

I really didn't try prioritising what birds to go for; my birdwatching activities were mostly after work and weekends. Nearly every weekend there was a new bird somewhere for me. Next year I hoped to see some of the seven Scottish specialities (Golden Eagle, Capercaillie, Black Grouse, Red Grouse, Ptarmigan, Crested Tit and Corncrake).

No doubt Scilly did well this autumn and if work allowed it would have been amazing to be there for first two weeks of October. Unsurprisingly my favourite bird of 1999 was the Scillies White's Thrush, the 52nd accepted record for Britain. It seems like a lot of records, but White's Thrushes are normally only seen in the Northern Isles. To get one as far down as Scilly was a real treat for the many birders staying on Scilly.

WHITE'S THRUSH
Zoothera aurea
St. Agnes. Scilly Isles
17th October 1999
G. BAGNELL

11

CHAPTER 2

2000

The Lady Amherst's Pheasant has a small population in Bedfordshire and could be extinct soon. Neil advised me that Lee Evans was advertising trips to see them on his RBA pager. I made a note of Lee's number and decided to ring him after work. Lee explained to me that the price for success would be £10 and failure would be half price. The next trip was planned on 21st January. I was uneasy about paying a fee to see a bird, but I guessed this was one of the ways Lee made his living and agreed to go.

Around 30 people turned up and we headed in separate cars to a place called Buttermilk Wood in Woburn. A male Lady Amherst's Pheasant came out onto the track, which had been seeded 8:40am and fed for about 10 minutes. Such a beautiful pheasant. It has a silver shawl with black tips to each individual mantle feather and a long black and silver tail with a bright red nape patch.

After the trip was finished Lee and Les Holiwell took me to see 20 Mandarin Ducks at Stock Grove Country Park and then onto stone barges at Rainham to see 5 Water Pipits and 5 Scandinavian Rock Pipits. We ended the day at Hanningfield Reservoir with a female Smew. Lee was very keen to get to know me, and was curious how many birds I had seen. He runs the UK400 Club, which lists every birder in Britain who has seen over 400 species in Britain and Ireland. I felt I wanted to join this organisation, but with a life list total of 288 species I was unsure if I was welcome. Lee said he had many members with lists lower than 400, and anyone could join as long as they paid the annual fee. I was sold hook, line and sinker. I was handed a previous newsletter and a copy of The Birds of Norfolk. There was no doubt about it, Lee had a good writing style and certainly could be a useful contact for me.

To complete the rare pheasant set, Lee was planning a trip to see Golden Pheasant on 22nd January. This time I was due to meet him at Junction 18 on the M25 at 6am. Whilst I was waiting, a police car drove up beside me and wound the window down and asked. 'What are you doing?'

I replied, 'Waiting for Lee Evans'. They chuckled and enquired 'The comedian?' I laughed and said, 'No the famous birdwatcher from Little Chalfont'. They hadn't heard of him. As soon as he arrived, we drove to Essex to pick up Les Holiwell.

Today the day was all about year ticks, which was fine with me as some would be lifers. First stop Wayland Wood, and we saw two male Golden Pheasant at 9am for about a minute in total before they dived back into cover. I didn't see the tail section well but I did catch the distinctive golden-yellow back and orange-red breast.

After a drive 38 miles north we saw Sammy the Black-winged Stilt at Titchwell RSPB on the brackish marsh. Sammy the Stilt was first found on 31st July 1993 at Druridge Bay, Northumberland. Two days later it arrived at Titchwell and stayed to 21st May 2005. It's estimated 1.5 million people visited Titchwell during those 12 years and seen it. No other rarity in Britain has been seen by more people).

Next we drove to Brancaster and saw 2500 Pinkfoot Geese and 1 Barnacle, then 120 Brambling at Barrow Common. A juvenile Rough-legged Buzzard was nice to see at Great Massingham. Holkham didn't disappoint with a good bundle of birds including 30 Twite, 20 Shorelark and 1 Snow Bunting.

Lee worked most Sundays at a car boot sale selling music CDs but got me in touch with a Watford-based twitcher called Geoff Goater. Geoff was a friendly guy who had an infectious smile. Geoff wasn't a car driver but worked in a café and was always keen to go birding on his two days off. He was free every week on Thursdays and Sundays.

On the 18th January a Sora, a member of the rail family, was found at Stover Country Park by B. Heasman. This was only the 9th record for Britain and it was still present on the 22nd. Geoff and I decided to head down the next day. We got onto

site around 8am and it took 50 minutes before the bird showed in the open. The most obvious features were the yellow bill, brown cap and no upper breast streaking, which ruled out Spotted Crake.

The rest of the day everything went wrong. We failed to connect with Little Auk at Goodrington, Black Duck at Slapton Lee, Cirl Bunting at Exminster and Pale-bellied Brents at Langton Herring, but I got on well with Geoff and could see us doing many twitches in the future.

National Grid Plc had employed me for nearly a year now. It originally started as a 3-month assignment to prepare budgets for a division with annual turnover of around £250 million, but more work, and more varied, was given to me over the year and there was a good chance I was going to be asked to stay past April. During April one of most friendly accountants you could ever wish to meet left to go on to bigger and better things – his name was Guy. He was the friendliest person in Leatherhead Finance. Guy was a people's person, and everybody liked him. His departure was going to create a completely different atmosphere within the team.

My home life was getting worse. Zainab and I had been living together now for almost 10 years and I think her not wanting kids and being two-faced to my poor widowed mum was the straw that broke the camel's back. We were arguing about everything. When we went shopping together, other Pakistani families would stare at Zainab as if she was an alien. I felt really trapped in the relationship and it was making me feel generally miserable in everything I did.

Zainab lost her father at an early age; her mum was still alive and living with her was Zainab's brother. Her mum spoke very little English, and she was not keen on me, or any white people for that matter. Zainab also had an older sister who lived with her partner in Croydon. She was a talented lady with a senior government job. Zainab's mum had a favourite person, and that was her son. Zainab knew that one day the family house would pass to the son, without either of the girls getting a share. Our mortgage was in joint names and I promised Zainab that if we ever split up, I would just sign over my share of the house to her for free. I was due to inherit my mum's house one day and Zainab was financially capable of paying the whole mortgage and household bills, if she wasn't burdened with any other debts.

I didn't want to part with Zainab until after I finished the exams. The first big decision I made was leave to National Grid plc.

Studying for my final level accounts exams started in August 1999. It took me to end of March to read four hefty 500-page A4 sized study texts. This was my first attempt at studying since 1996. I booked a week's Financial Training Company (FTC) revision course in Islington, London for £1,400 from 13th May to 19th May. My exams were due on 23rd and 25th May and I kept telling myself to stay focused on studying and to take a break from twitching to after exams, but unfortunately I couldn't I was under a twitching curse.

On Friday 5th May news broke of two adult Slender-billed Gulls at Cley. I arrived at 3pm and my luck was in – the two birds were still loafing around on Arnolds Marsh. These birds have downcurved red bills, pink flush to overall white breast and light grey wings and mantle, red legs and black primary tips with white leading edge and a red eye ring. One was asleep and the other had a distinctive feeding action. It plunged half its body into the water to grab a stickleback, then walked back to the beach to eat it whole. I admired these birds with Dave Johnson until 4pm. They represent the 7th and 8th record for Britain and Ireland since 1950 and were found by Mr & Mrs Brownswood and B. Dawson.

We watched the gulls for about an hour and saw a summer-plumaged Ruff, Green-winged Teal and 2 Temminck's Stints on site. Whilst driving home, it transpired that the gulls had flown off high at 7:30pm, never to be seen again. Surprisingly, the 3rd and 4th British records involved a pair at Cley in 1987.

On May 8th I travelled to Spurn to see an Asian Desert Warbler on its 2nd day. I arrived at 1:30pm and saw it straight away, perched in a bush 2 metres from the path, after which it decided to fly to a bush slighter further away. African and Asian can be separated by colour of eye and tail colour – the Asian has a red tail whereas the African's is brown. I clearly saw its reddish tail, large yellow eye, bill, milky brown back and white belly, white triangular undertail covert and white outer tail feathers. I saw the bird for about 15 minutes in total. This was only the 11th for Britain, found by M. Finn, A. Paullis and M. E. Stoyle, and it became a landmark bird for me. It was my 300th different bird for Britain. So thank you lads, for finding a great bird for me to twitch.

I popped up the road to Filey and enjoyed a male Red-spotted Bluethroat and a few seabirds, 9 Puffin, Guillemot and Razorbill and then off to see a Great Grey Shrike and male Garganey at Southfield reservoir.

My revision classes started on the 13th May. I took the train from Three Bridges to Kings Cross & St Pancras for the short walk to Islington. The classroom was big – there must have been 40 students in the room. Each desk had space for two students, and I was sitting next to an East End girl called Sian.

During the lunch breaks a big gang of us

used to walk down the street and eat generally at McDonalds. The lectures were good, but I could see I was surrounded by a lot of people who understood the syllabus better than me. I don't think all the recent twitches was helping to focus my mind on study.

On 14th May a female Blue Rock Thrush was found at Geevor, Pendeen in Cornwall. The plan was to go after my last day of revision on the 19th but this wasn't meant to be, because the Blue Rock Thrush decided to leave the night before.

On 20th May I drove to Hengistbury head for a Zitting Cisticola. This was only the 4th British record. This or another was originally seen at Portland Bill between 15-17th May. I arrived at 1pm and only ever saw the Zitting Cisticola in song flight. It flew at 1:20pm over my head between reeds and a shrub, then back to the reeds a few minutes later. At 2pm it flew back to shrub and gave its distinctive 'Zit' call. It was impossible to get a better view, so I decided to head up to Dawlish Warren for a Broad-billed Sandpiper.

I arrived around 5pm and went straight to the hide. It took an hour to find the bird. The most obvious feature was the black crown strip with white strip either side and then joining the supercilium just on the lores (the area behind the base of the bill). This feature is known as a split supercilium. They have a white belly, speckled breast and 2 tram lines on the back, a decurved bill, short legs and size between a Dunlin and a Ringed Plover. I saw it in total for about 25 minutes.

I travelled to Fairfield Halls in Croydon on 23rd and 25th May for my final CIMA exams. To celebrate the end of college we stayed the night in Sian's pub in Gravesend.

The next day I rang my mum and asked if I could move back in with her. She said, 'It's up to you'. Now it was time to have a proper conversation face to face with Zainab. After a long, hard conversation we agreed to go our separate ways, so I decided to move back into Mum's. I kept my promise and agreed to sign the house and rest of the contents to her. The house was a one-bedroom terraced house with an extension. It was bought just after the housing market crash in 1991 for only £49,000. In those days no deposits were needed, and we arranged an endowment mortgage. 9 years later this house was now worth in the region of £150,000, and the endowment policy still had 16 years to run.

I loaded my car, a white N reg Volvo 440, with clothes, bird books, plane books, chess set and tools and drove to my mum's. My 10-year relationship was finally over and to me there was no turning back. I felt like a free man leaving the prison gates. I wanted a completely new start, although for years I'd never really been able to my put my finger on exactly what had made me unhappy. Surely smoking wasn't a problem, but I also decided to give up on my 20-year addiction, which started at secondary school. I hung around with the tough guys and being part of this club involved being a smoker.

I think my problems started (mildly) whilst I working with Zainab at Virgin Atlantic Airways. I was at my all-time worst when I was working for a sportswear company called Converse back in 1992. Shoes were being sold to another company at a very low price and became even cheaper when a credit note was issued for damaged or missing shoes. This pattern of events was happening on a regular basis and the U.S. parent company suspected malpractice. I left in October 1992 and got interviewed by phone by the fraud squad. Later I heard that two of the UK directors had gone to prison.

Over the 10-year period I had been with Zainab I had suffered from various bouts of depression and anxiety. For quite a few months I had some private psychotherapy sessions in Brighton. The sessions lasted an hour and were once a week. Psychotherapists are convinced that all problems stem back to childhood. I just couldn't find a problem back then; my grandparents brought me up and showed me incredible love.

Eventually I concluded that I was wasting money on psychotherapists and went back to my general practitioner. The easy answer was to put me on various anti-depressant drugs. Prozac seemed to be the best. It takes the body a month to build up to the correct level in your bloodstream, then you become fearless towards life's anxieties.

Doctors are reluctant to keep you on anti-depressant drugs for too long and the next course of action was joining a self-help group. The idea behind these groups is that you find friends with similar issues and by sharing your problems, the group helps you find solutions that improve your self-confidence.

My mum was happy for me to live rent free until I found work. One good thing about being an accountant is that it's very easy to find temporary work. I got fixed up with a temporary role to start with AIG Ltd in Croydon on Monday 5th June, but before then I did a week's twitching.

On the 2nd June, Chris Sharratt found a male summer-plumaged Blackpoll Warbler at Seaforth. At 7pm that evening I was due to be in Little Chalfont for a Lee Evans-organised minibus tour to Scotland to see the Scottish specialities. I thought I would have time to see the Blackpoll Warbler first. I got to the M6 and hit bad traffic and Lee rang and said, 'I've seen the Blackpoll but you will never get back in time for the start of the trip'. I agreed with him and turned back. Lee had gone for the Blackpoll Warbler when the news broke at 10am. I got to Lee's before 7pm and felt a bit miserable that I had abandoned the warbler.

Lee had more people booked on the minibus than it could possibly take, so he persuaded a guy called Bill to take his car and follow the minibus. Lee placed James Lees, Geoff Goater and me in Bill's car. The minibus crew included Dave Johnson, Des McKenzie, John Broadbent, David & Matthew Roberts, Nick Montigriffo and Lee.

The route to Scotland was M1, M6, M42(N), M6, A74(M), M74, M73, M80, M9 etc. On the journey north all I could think about was the Warbler, so I persuaded Bill to drive to Seaforth. We got to the site around 10:30pm and we got talking to some drunken local girls who invited us to a house party. We had one drink at the party and decided that this was utter madness. It was a starlit sky, so the chances of the Blackpoll Warbler being there in the morning were low. We left the party and tried our best to catch up with the minibus. Thinking back on this trip now, I could have seen the Blackpoll Warbler if Lee had allowed me to meet the minibus or car en route.

Just after 6:30am we met the minibus at the Loch of Lowes, a regular breeding site for Ospreys. They have been coming there for over twenty years and birds are present from late April until late August. There is a hide overlooking the eyrie. We enjoyed views of a pair of Osprey on a nest and also heard a Wood Warbler. Just before we met up with the minibus, Lee's group did manage to see a Black Grouse in a lek at Braco Moor at 4am. Lee said he had another Black Grouse at Moulin Moor. This site is on the A925 just east of Pitlochry. We arrived around 8:15am, but there was no sign of the Black Grouse. There would probably would have been more chance if we had arrived between 4:30 and 7:00am.

Lee wanted to move on, so we headed north towards the Isle of Skye. At Inverness we started seeing Hooded Crows. As we approached the Kyle of Lochalsh on the A87 there is an area where you can pull off the road, just before you enter the town. From here you can look down to the harbour and the loch. At 8:15am we enjoyed watching 3 Black Guillemot, 20 Arctic Terns and a Grey Seal. Once over the Skye Bridge we headed up the A87 towards Kyleakin. Here Lee quickly found a Golden Eagle. There are estimated to be 560-600 pairs in the Western Isles and Highlands. At 1:30pm we arrived in Torvaig on the A855 north of Portree to look for White-tailed Sea Eagle. Here Lee had a long sleep. He really needed it, after doing a return trip to Seaforth and then almost immediately driving non-stop to Skye whilst the rest of us were scanning the stretch of sea towards Raasay.

White-tailed Sea Eagles were originally part of a successful re-introduction scheme that started in 1975. 100 Norwegian birds have been released on Rum since then. During the 2 hours on site, we managed to see 2 adult White-tailed Eagles, Black Guillemot and Shag. Lee woke up just as the eagles were showing.

From here we headed north and stopped at a little tea shop at Linicro around 5:15pm. Some stopped for a tea, but Geoff and I went on the wander and heard the repeated 'crex crex' call of a Corncrake, though we couldn't see it in the long grass. Pure Rock Doves could finally be ticked, with a nearby Whinchat perched on a fence post. We stayed about an hour then made our way to Grantown on Spey, checking into the digs around 10:30pm.

The next morning one of Lee's passengers, John Broadbent, decided to make his own way home. He wasn't happy with the busy itinerary and lack of the sleep all round. We had all witnessed a nasty crash on the A9 the previous when two cars collided, and he didn't want to risk being in a potential accident in the minibus.

Grantown on Spey produced a breeding Common Sandpiper as we drove to the car park. Once we were all out, we saw 7 Scottish Crossbills and a red squirrel. 12 miles down the road we went to Loch Vaa and saw a pair of breeding Slavonian Grebes. Loch Garten held a pair of Ospreys. Moormore Picnic site held 3 Crested Tits and a Spotted Flycatcher. We saw a Dipper on the River Avon and then drove a further 67 miles to Glenshee in the Cairngorms. The target bird to see here was Ptarmigan, but the visibility wasn't brilliant so we had to settle for some Red Grouse and 2 Ring Ouzel.

The last site of the trip was the Forth Road Bridge, quite a tricky place to find – you take M90 junction 1 and follow B981 towards North Queensferry, then take the next right to a substation and park directly under the north tower. Here there is a colony of Common Terns and we luckily saw one of the Roseate Terns. I could say I had now been to Scotland.

Six ticks under my belt and I was ready to start at AIG.

The first person I met at AIG was the receptionist, Carole. She was a very confident girl, whose bubbly personality was not a quality you find too often in accountancy offices. The job seemed fine, but being temporary gives the employer or employee the opportunity to quit at a moment's notice.

The next day at work Carole suggested I go on date with her best friend Louise. I thought brilliant, although I had no idea what she looked like as in 2000 there was no internet and no pictures displayed on mobile phones, which were only used for making calls or sending text messages. Carole later rang Louise and managed to fix us for a date the following evening.

I met up with Louise in a bar in Carshalton. She was drop dead gorgeous; God knows what she was going to see in me. She was 5'6' tall and very slim with light brown shoulder-length hair. She was half Italian and mother to two teenage boys with different fathers. Both her sons lived with her in Carshalton. I found it easy to make her laugh and we made plans to meet up at the weekend.

The first Saturday in July I was trying to see a Savi's Warbler and Golden Orioles at Lakenheath. We failed with both but did see a male Montagu's harrier in Norfolk. News broke midday of an unfamiliar grey and white warbler in Martin Cade's mist net in Portland. This turned out to be Britain's 3rd Sykes Warbler. It was going to take 6 hours to get there, and Syke's Warbler was then only a sub-species. I was due to meet Louise that evening and our date was more important than seeing this. Over 200 people saw the possible Sykes in the afternoon and apparently it became less elusive towards the end of the evening. Lars Svenson confirmed the measurements and photograph as typical H. rama. It was not seen the following day.

My evening with Louise was superb. Her boys were away for the night, so we decided to order a Chinese takeaway with a couple of bottles of wine. I was too tipsy to drive home, and she allowed me to stay over. Louise was the prettiest girl I had ever dated. She loved going to the gym and this showed.

From then on, Louise invited me over to her house twice a week. I got to meet her boys and they accepted me as her boyfriend.

At the end of Friday 21st, I got a call from the agency who said, 'AIG have decided to let you go'. No reason was given, and my agency was still prepared to help me find work. I felt devastated and told Louise the bad news when I got to hers that night. She wasn't happy and said that if I couldn't hold down a job, how viable was our relationship? On the Saturday her son Adam was going on about a £120 pair of trainers he wanted. Louise said no to him, but I took him to Croydon and bought him

the trainers. When we got back Louise went mad and said she would have to reimburse me for them.

We drove to West Wittering beach for the afternoon, and I met Louise's mum and brother for the first time. Her brother was a black belt in karate, and he was showing me the various karate kicks he could do. We had a nice day out, but Louise's mum said to me, 'My daughter doesn't always know what she wants in life'. I wasn't sure what she was referring to, but the next day Louise decided to end our relationship.

I felt devastated and then to make things even worse, I open my CIMA results letter and discovered that I had failed all four of my exams. To make matters worse I rang up all of the students in my revision class and found out they had all passed.

My Birdnet membership was now a year old and I had the option to renew. Most birders were using the Rare Bird Alert pagers with the dedicated local channel. I was especially going to miss talking to Birdnet operative Dave Morgan, who would go above and beyond helping me when I rang him. Sadly, for them, my mind was up and I went over to Rare Bird Alert.

Saturday 20th August I took my mum to Cornwall for a few days. We left Crawley at 9am and headed down to Penzance. My mum had not been to Cornwall since she was 12 years old. During World War 2, 1.5 million children were evacuated to places to escape the high risk of aerial bombing on cities. This was called Operation Pied Piper, and it began on 1st September 1939. At the time my mum was living in Walthamstow, London and without that manoeuvre I guess I wouldn't be here today.

We stayed at a B&B that I knew. The following day the *Scillonian III* was taking birders on the annual pelagic. I seem to recall I had to be at the harbour around 5am. My mum wasn't coming on the pelagic and was happy to potter around in Penzance for the day. We ate in Penzance and when my mum returned to the B&B, I went to a drum and bass club for the night, no sleep, and just caught the *Scillonian* in time. There must have been 400 birders on the boat and a heavy chumming session soon started. Chumming is the practice of luring various animals, usually fish such as sharks, by throwing in, chum, bait consisting of fish parts, bone, and blood which attract fish, particularly sharks. During the cruise we saw 10 Great Skuas, 3 Sooty Shearwaters , 1 adult Sabine's Gull , 40+ Storm Petrels, 5 Great Shearwaters , 1 Grey Phalarope, 1 Wilson's Storm Petrel and 3 Arctic Skuas.

The *Scillonian* pelagic had been an annual event for several years. Nearly every year you could almost guarantee getting a Wilson's Storm Petrel. 1989 produced 500 Great Shearwaters and not only birds – people were regularly seeing Blue Sharks, turtles, Sunfish, whales, and dolphins. The main downside is that the pelagic lasts 15 ½ hours and generally there is no way to escape once vomit is flying all over the place. Even the guys with the good sea legs were having to clear it from their ears, hair, and clothes.

The pelagic got me most shearwaters you can expect, but with a few missing I decided on doing some sea watching. I went to Porthgwarra on Monday from midday and saw 11 Mediterranean Shearwater, 2 Great Shearwater and 1 Sooty over a 6-hour period. The next day at Porthgwarra from 8:30am I saw 3 Cory's Shearwater, 3 Mediterranean Shearwater and 1 Storm Petrel over a 7-hour period. Sea watching is not something I really enjoy, but seeing the big shearwaters at Porthgwarra was an amazing experience. Getting 8 lifers in 3 days took my British List to 333.

Saturday 16th September saw me pairing up with the very entertaining Matthew Rosser for an overnight drive to Aberdeen. We stopped for a bite to eat in Aberdeen, and got chatting to two very drunk lasses. They conned me into giving them a lift home. One of them wanted me to open the sunroof, so I did, and she stood up and started singing through the sunroof. God knows what would have happened if the police had stopped us.

Next day we watched an Eastern Olivaceous Warbler four times between 9am and 1pm. The view at 1pm was incredible. We watched it for a whole minute as it sat in one of the two Sycamores in the small garden, then flicked across to a willow tree. We heard the 'tack' call a lot and once saw the tail pumping. It spent most of time with a showy Lesser Whitethroat. The warbler was only the 14th record for Britain and Ireland, found by P. Baxter and P.S. Crockett.

On Friday 29th September I had a decision to make – should I head down for the Cliff Swallow on the Scillies (John Higginson found it on the 28th and it was still present) or go for a different Cliff Swallow found at the Verne, Portland, by D.J. Chown on the 29th? If I went to Portland, I could kiss goodbye to getting to Scilly the same day.

Fortunately, both birds stayed to the Saturday, and I went for the cheap option of driving to Portland. I drove over up to the high advantage point of the Verne at 11:15am. The gathered twitchers had seen it just before I had arrived. One guy said 'Don't worry, you'll soon see it'. I waited 30 minutes and finally saw the Cliff Swallow show. I guess it was flying a wide circuit around the whole island. I noted that it had shorter wings than a House Martin. It had a dark square tail with no fork, dark head, white belly, dark brown back and pink rump. At 1:45pm it left the island for good, and many latecomers dipped. It was only the 8th record for Britain and Ireland.

Lee Evans and his partner Carmel booked accommodation on Scilly for two weeks from 7th to 21st October and at this time I was on working as a temp with lots of days/weeks with no work. I agreed to take a room and share the costs. Shortly after paying over the money, I got a offered a month's temporary job working for a guy called Mike Yearwood at Prismo. They wanted me from 2nd October and I happily accepted. Prismo were a white lining road business that were originally part of the Colas group. Mike was working as a Financial Director for Colas before the split occurred, and his employment moved to the newly formed Prismo. The Prismo office was in Chichester and the job was all about help Mike reconcile the accounts payable, accounts receivable and bank accounts. My two-week holiday to Scilly was now in jeopardy.

M. Collier found a Swainson's Thrush on Thursday 12th October at Porthellick House on St. Mary's. This American Catharus thrush is only the 21st record of Swainson's in Britain. Everybody knows American birds are exciting from a British listing point of view, so I warned Lee I would be staying at the accommodation for a couple of nights.

I flew from Lands End to St. Marys on the Saturday 15th and made my way to Porthelick house. So many birders were trying to peer into the garden from the entrance. When the bird was seen, an organised queuing system was in place, and I got into the garden at 9:40am and enjoyed good views of the Swainson's Thrush for 80 minutes. I spent the rest of the day wandering around Scilly, seeing Red-breasted Flycatcher, Red-backed Shrike, Jack Snipe, Yellow-browed Warbler, 2 Great Northern Divers – and then all hell broke loose when a Spectacled Warbler was found on Tresco. There

was a stampede to Hugh Town quay, and four boats must have been filled in minutes.

On the sail across news, broke of a Common Nighthawk on Bryher. That was all it took for all four boats to ignore Tresco and make their way to Bryher instead. The capacity of each boat was 80 people, so that meant 320 passengers disembarked at Bryher and formed a long human chain to Shipman Head. The whole crowd went deadly silent when a kestrel flew over, but after a good hour we had seen absolutely nowt. To make matters worse, the Spectacled Warbler was still showing on Tresco and there was not enough daylight left to get there.

Next morning boats were lined up at Hugh Town quay, going to Tresco at first light. I got off the boat at Tresco and tried to follow the super-fit Will Wagstaff to Middle Down. I was on site for 3 hours and only saw the Spectacled Warbler for 3 minutes in total. It was seen well on a gorse bush and vanished whilst dropping to the ground to feed. I grilled the bird to satisfy myself it wasn't a Common Whitethroat. The main difference to look out for was size. The Spectacled is 1.5cm smaller, with a shorter tail and primary projection and greater coverts, rusty all over (dark cantered in whitethroat). This was only the 4th record for Britain and Ireland, found by Steve Broyd, and it stayed to the 21st October.

After leaving the warbler I spent some time watching 3 Ring-necked Ducks and a sleeping female Blue-winged Teal on the Great Pool. Due to a weather problem on Saturday I managed to get a rare flight off of St. Marys back to Lands End the next day, which was perfect considering the work situation.

In my third week at Prismo, my agency managed to get me an interview at Colas in Rowfant. I guess my job working for Mike Yearwood gave me a massive advantage in the interview. That evening, my agency told me Colas were prepared to offer me a three-month contract that could turn permanent if I was successful with a trial. The job was for a Management Accountant for the Surface Dressing and Coating Roadstone division. The chance of a permanent job was something I hadn't had for years, and I agreed a mutually convenient date in early November when I could leave Prismo and start at Colas.

SUMMARY - 2000

During 2000, I travelled 22,475 miles in Britain in the pursuit of new birds and managed to increase my list by 73 BOU species, taking my British life list to 347. Unsurprisingly with so many new birds I also managed to see/hear 323 different species for my year list.

The official list now stood at 554 species, with four additions since 1999. These were Green-winged Teal (split), Short-toed Eagle (1999), Iberian Chiffchaff (split) and Common Redpoll (Now 3 species - Common, Lesser & Arctic). I had now seen 61.6% of The Official British List.

From last year's target, I had managed to see three of the seven Scottish species: Golden Eagle, Red Grouse and Crested Tit. The other four species, Capercaillie, Black Grouse, Ptarmigan and Corncrake, would now be 2001 targets. 2001 should be an interesting year. After leaving my partner Zainab in May, would I find love again?

The most important birds I saw during 2000 were Norfolk's two Slender-billed Gulls. The nearest birds to Britain are from the Mediterranean and surprisingly as they have only been seen in Britain 6 times before. Twitching Gulls in Britain is a very stressful sport. They don't wait to nightfall to migrate and an 8-hour round trip can very easily be for nothing.

CHAPTER 3

2001

The Colas office overlooked a large section of Rowfant forest, and it was not unusual to watch Bullfinches feeding in the nearby Silver Birches. The trees were 2-3 metres from our windows, and I remained invisible watching them as the windows were tinted. I shared an office with a friendly chap called Keith Ollett. 50% of my job was looking after the Surface Dressing division. This process involved a spray tanker, chipping lorry and roller. The spray tanker sprayed hot bitumen onto the old road surface, the chipping lorry was directly behind dropping chippings into the bitumen and the roller then pushed them firmly into the bitumen. Surface Dressing is the cheapest form of road repair and operates 6-8 months of the year in dry weather.

Dave Fairchild was the manager for this division. Dave lived in Exeter and was a keen trainspotter. Every month he would visit the estimator, Keith Ollett, to agree the cost and values, which would then be passed to me, and I would use my accounting knowledge to turn this and other data into the monthly management accounts. Dave had worked his way up from the tools to being the manager of the process. Dave called a spade a spade, and I could see early on that he was going to understand my passion for birdwatching.

My other manager was Colin Huckwell, who was based at Stanwell Moor near Heathrow Airport. Colin managed the Coating Plant business. The only product that was being manufactured at Stanwell was blacktop, the material they lay on motorways and major roads. It lasts a lot longer than surface dressing. The staff at Stanwell Moor included two sales staff (Ginnie and Denise), three lorry drivers, two plant operators (Terry and Reg), a laboratory technician (Jenny) and a shovel driver (David). The first person I met when I visited Stanwell Moor was shovel driver David Browne, an ultra-friendly lad who liked chatting. He told me his life story as I parked my car and walked across the yard to enter the Portakabins to meet the office staff. Colin was at one end of the Portakabin and Ginnie and Denise at the other.

It came across that Colin was very laid back and was technically minded, but he was a people person and a natural leader.

I had to visit Stanwell once a week to deliver invoices. These were matched to delivery notes and authorised for payment. Once a month I had to calculate the stocks of granite, limestone and bitumen. The coated roadstone business had its own manual accounts system, which I learnt and prepared the monthly management accounts.

My good working relationships were obviously fed back to Richard Weddle (Finance Head) and Steward Struthers (Business Manager of Products and Processes) and during February I was offered a permanent position. My decision was easy. I was working in beautiful countryside with laid-back managers, a subsided canteen and Weirwood Reservoir only a 15-minute drive away. I accepted.

Lunch breaks were an hour long and the nearby Europa Hotel had a fully equipped gym, indoor heated pool, sauna, steam room and spa pool that was only £20 per month. I was single and felt I needed to improve my fitness, so this was a place I decided to join and do a workout during some lunch breaks. Most Friday lunchtimes, various departments would descend on one of the nearby pubs. The Hillside Inn did excellent food and was the best place to go for leaving dos, whereas the White Knight pub was great for a few pints and game of pool.

Lee Evans had another of his Scottish minibus bird tours arranged. Hopefully this time, I would tick off the remaining Scottish specialities. I left Little Chalfont on Thursday 12th April and got to Braco Moor at first light the next day. Five Black Grouse were seen displaying at the lek, plus 3 Red Grouse nearby. At Glen Quaich we managed to see a further 7 Black Grouse including 3 females sitting in the larches. Scotston Farm had another 6 Black Grouse and 2 Red Grouse. Yep, I could definitely tick Black Grouse now. I think Lee was showing off after the last Scottish trip.

We gave Glenshee another go. This time we decided to walk up it. Glenshee is a 650m mountain with some pretty steep gradients in places. Now I thought I was fit, but John Pegden was walking up the mountain like it was a flight of stairs. He never stopped to catch his breath. I eventually caught him up and the whole group and we enjoyed 3 summer plumaged Ptarmigan. If these birds were in white winter plumage, I'm not so sure they would have been that easy.

The next day we visited Loch Garten and saw 2 Crested Tits on the feeders and an Osprey from the centre. At Kingston-on-Spey we caught up with a beautiful male King Eider in full summer plumage and 12 stonking summer-plumaged Long-tailed Ducks. We managed to flush a Capercaillie from a pine tree in Grantown on Spey. Lee probably had the best view, but I'm willing to wait for a better view before I add this elusive species to my list. Findhorn Valley provided a close view of a Scottish Crossbill. Aviemore had a nice flock of 44 Waxwing and the last stop was Ruddons Point, where we watched a splendid male Surf Scoter.

My RBA pager announce a presumed Iberian Chiffchaff at Dungeness Long Pit on Sunday 15th April. Presumed? Was it worth going? I rang up RBA and Andrew Raine told me Andy Wraithmell (the Dungeness warden) had found it and sound-recorded it and it would only be a matter of time before it was confirmed. I drove down and saw the presumed Iberian Chiffchaff in the company of photographer Mike McDonald. We heard its 'seep' call. The legs appeared dark brown, flared yellow supercilium past eye, bold yellow alula (a small projection at the front of the wing), white belly, and brown back with some olive tones in bright sunlight. To me it was in between a Willow Warbler and Chiffchaff, and the features certainly stood out once scrutinised. This bird's distinctive song is the most reliable feature. It was accepted and became the 7th record for Britain.

One of the places I used to visit was the Grasshopper Inn at Westerham. In my twenties I was once hired to be the DJ on a Saturday night for a private function there. This place has a large dance floor with table and chairs overlooking the dance floor and the DJ booth was slightly higher than the dance floor and all sealed off. On Sunday evenings it turned into a nightclub for over 30s. Ages varied up to people in their 60s. I felt like one of the youngest at 33. They played a couple of sets of slow music, where gentlemen would ask ladies for a dance.

I initially went down there by myself and was mesmerised by a guy who danced like John Travolta. He wore a white suit and was frequently doing the splits on the dance floor. I became friends with him, and he introduced me to his mate Gary. Russell was often down there; he always had a tan and was about 6 ft 3 and built like a brick sh*thouse. He had big hands and wore a lot of gold rings. Russell generally came with Dave and their scouser mate Chris. Chris was the pauper out of the three as Dave and Russell had their own businesses. Retired British Airways employee Eddie Myer usually went down too, I had known Eddie for many years, and I don't remember him ever having a lady friend despite always being on the lookout. All the cars in the car park had one thing in common, they were very expensive. Knowing that I couldn't afford any of these cars made me feel I was not worthy of being in the club.

Joking aside, in early May I decided it was time for a new car. My mum and I thumbed through Autotrader, and we found a garage in Burgess Hill that had a Ford Probe 2.2 litre. Like a fool, I fell in love with it as soon as I saw it. The car was all white, three doors with leather interior and the way the headlamp moved out of the bonnet was the deal breaker. The garage was happy to offer me part exchange of N reg Volvo plus £5k for an L reg Ford Probe. Good deal? Well let's find out.

On Saturday 26th May I took my new Ford Probe out for a spin. I picked up my friend Sean, a fellow chess player from our club in Coulsdon, Surrey. He wanted to experience what it was like to do a twitch. I'm not sure what time the Little Swift broke at Netherfield lagoon in Notts, but that seemed like a nice bird to show Sean. Then a Collared Pratincole was also found, closer to home at Siddlesham Ferry pool. I was suddenly in a dilemma over what to do, as both birds were new for me, but the Pratincole had the added incentive of being a Sussex County tick. Equally, both birds could fly off at any stage. There had been 54 Collared Pratincoles in Britain and only 17 Little Swifts, so the swift got my vote.

I wanted to see how fast my car can go. The handbook said 130 mph and I don't think it lied. En route the pager messages indicated that both birds were disappearing for long periods. In previous years I had been prone to doing a U-turn, but my mind was made up. I was going to ignore the messages and just get to Notts as quick as possible.

We arrived at Netherfield early afternoon, and it hadn't showed for a while. Two hours went by and still no sign. Naturally the Collared Pratincole kept coming on the pager to make matters worse. Then suddenly people started getting excited and quite rightly so, because at around 5pm the Little Swift appeared. This bird is slightly smaller than our Swift with a huge white rump and a square tail. It flew low, just missing my head, on two occasions.

What an amazing moment to witness.

Having a non-birder with me, I didn't outstay my welcome and we left at 5:45pm and headed back. The satnav calculated we would get to Siddlesham around 9:22pm. Again, I opened up the car a couple of times and poor old Sean almost shat himself and closed his eyes.

We got to Siddlesham at 9pm and the Collared Pratincole was sitting in a field with only its head showing above two wooden stumps. At 9:15pm, it decided to hawk above the ferry pool. It was flying very fast over the top half of the pool, and it landed on the spit for 1 minute. I watched it till 9:30pm and light was fading fast. I noted forked tail and white rump but couldn't really see the white trailing edge on both wings. The access to the bird was always going to be a problem because of the 2001 outbreak of foot and mouth disease, a huge tragedy that cost the lives of 6 million cows and sheep which had to be destroyed in a successful attempt to halt the disease. By the end of October 2001 this outbreak damaged the tourist industry and cost the British taxpayer £8bn.

The Little Swift was found by T. Lister and A. Przesnak and it stayed to the 29th May and roosted three nights under the railway bridge that crossed the lagoon.

On Tuesday 29th May I was allowed to work through my lunchbreak and leave an hour earlier to try to see a Marmora's Warbler. I got to Sizewell at 7pm to find a patch of gorse bushes with 200 birders forming a large circle round the bushes. Lee Evans was sitting between the circle of birders and the bushes on arrival. I was very happy to get a brief view of the warbler at 7:20pm, but more importantly I had a prolonged view at 7:40pm. This sylvia warbler was the same size as a Dartford Warbler, slatey bluish-grey all over with a red eye ring and iris with a long cocked tail. It was mostly perched for the whole 10 minutes and then flew off to roost. The bird, found by J. Davies, A. Miller and C. Powell, was only seen for a day. This was only the 5th record for Britain and the bird might have been the same one as the 4th record, at Scolt Head between 12th to 18th May.

David Browne was now regularly sleeping in Mum's third bedroom on Saturday nights. David had three children with his ex-wife, but they had parted when he found out she was sleeping with his best friend. David was becoming my best mate and he loved visiting Brannigans in Crawley, a cross between a bar and a nightclub with two bars, a restaurant, dance floor, stage, and a large screen TV. The walk from mum's house to Brannigans was about 20 minutes and Dave and I would walk down there and regularly meet up with Clinton, Lorenzo, Graham and Lee (cabin crew). The DJ was amazing and often played music that got my heart pumping. Lorenzo and I loved showing off our dancing skills on the stage. I used to try breakdancing, body popping and moon walking whenever the music allowed. I was constantly getting sweaty and making journeys to dry off clothes with the gent's hand drier. Brannigans felt like my second home. I got to know all bouncers, bar staff and use the VIP suite whenever I wanted.

David and I both met girls in Brannigans. He fell in love with a girl called Nicki and I was equally besotted by an Irish girl, Susan Tarrush. I would probably have married Susan if she had let me. I loved everything about the girl, her accent, her face, her personality, her figure. She really was a 10/10, but she was working for Monarch Airlines as a cabin crew hostess and was about to embark in a career in Dubai with Emirates Airlines.

That year, 2001, I regretted not going on the

Scillonian pelagic. Ex-Sussex birder Dave Flumm whetted my appetite by telling me what happened. *On Sunday 12th August, Dave, Royston Wilkins and Brian Mellows boarded the Scillonian III for the 5am pelagic trip with 267 birders boarded. The DMS (dimethyl sulfide) was brought down by Sara and Ted Griffiths from Plymouth. DMS is used in the chum mix. Only a small amount is added but seabirds are attracted because it's an indicator of high ocean food productivity, being produced naturally by zooplankton/phytoplankton interactions. Dave Flumm was wearing his wife's scarf laced in her favourite perfume whilst mixing the DMS and chum, but by midday he was feeling sick and took a break. He found a Wilson's Petrel in the afternoon and shouted out, but nobody came, because at 2:35pm Steve Rogers and Brian Mellow had found a Fea's type Petrel. This bird gave terrific views as it flew around the boat. It appeared off the stern but luckily it returned so all 267 birders could admire it. It spent nearly an hour flying up, down and around the Scillonian.*

At 3:30pm the boat turned around and headed back towards Penzance. The Fea's type Petrel changed direction and carried on following for a further 25 minutes. This whole amazing observation lasted to 3:55pm, 1 hour and 20 minutes. Other notable birds seen on this trip were 2 Great Shearwater, 1 Sooty Shearwater, 12 Bonxies and 2 adult Sabines Gull, before we finally docked at Penzance at 8:30pm.

Tim McKinney explained that dimethyl sulfide or methylthiomethane is an organosulfur compound with the formulae: $(CH_3)_2S$. Dimethyl sulfide is a flammable liquid that boils at 37 °C and has a characteristic disagreeable odor. It is a component of the smell produced from cooking of certain vegetables, notably maize, cabbage, beetroot, and seafoods. It is also an indication of bacterial contamination in malt production and brewing. It is a breakdown product of dimethylsulfoniopropionate, and is also produced by the bacterial metabolism of methanethiol.

On 14th September, Britain's 3rd Thick-billed Warbler was found on Out Skerries. Lee Evans acted quickly and managed to hire a plane from Highland Airways. The thought of chartering a plane to see a bird was very exciting. The main problem was that we had to get to Inverness Airport next morning. Lee had it all under control. He hired a minibus and filled it with Chris Heard, John Pedgen, Tony Shepherd, Neil Howes, Neil Glenn, James Hanlon and me. James picked the short straw and had to lie on the minibus floor for the 10 hours, all the way to Inverness. This was the first time I had met Chris Heard, who was ranked 3rd highest lister in Britain. Chris was an incredible bird finder who had found rarities including Tennessee Warbler, American Buff-Bellied Pipit, Veery and Brunnich's Guillemot, among others.

Once at Inverness, Lee checked in with the airline to make sure everything was still good to go. The bad news was starting to filter through that the Thick-billed Warbler couldn't be found at Out Skerries, but Shetland did have a rare Citrine Wagtail and a Pallid Harrier. These weren't new birds for Lee and Chris, so we decided to turn the minibus round and come straight back home. Drivers were swapped on the way back and I took my turn lying in the back of the minibus whilst James had on a proper seat.

By Friday 21st September autumn migration was in full swing, and two birds turned up that got the juices flowing. I hastily arranged to get the afternoon off work and then headed first to Suffolk. I got to Landguard at 4:30pm and spent just 10 minutes watching an Isabelline Wheatear. It really had nowhere to hide and wandering around the grassy pastures with its metallic ring. The main feature I noted was the overall sandy upperparts, white eye ring and bold above eye, black on wing and restricted to the alula, whereas the Northern Wheatear has black centres to the median and greater coverts. I felt bad not studying this bird for longer, but there was something even rarer 78 miles to north-west next, at Somersham Gravel Pits – a Red-necked Stint.

I arrived there at 6:20pm and amongst 10 Little Stints was one that could be easily picked out, the promised adult Red-necked Stint, with a distinctive red breast extending to the throat and patches of red on the nape. I enjoyed watching it until dusk. The Isabelline Wheatear was found by Will Brame and only stayed one day; it represented only the 17th record for Britain, whereas the Red-necked Stint did stay the night and was only the 6th for Britain, found by John Oakes.

Those who twitched the Red-necked Stint on the Saturday were in the right place to go on to a 1st winter Pallas's Grasshopper Warbler, only 71 miles away at Blakeney Point. Not expecting to stay the night, I went up on Sunday 23rd and unbelievably it was still present. I saw the bird several times as it was being flushed continually. I was lucky on one occasion as I and another had a good 15-second view away from the main crowd who were searching for it. We decided not to alert them, as it would have created a mass stampede and I would never have seen its strong yellow supercilium, fine black streaks on back, heavy streaking on upper breast, orange rump seen in flight, white edges on some tertials. This felt a bit sneaky, but it was only the third English record and the first twitchable one. Found by Steve Joyner, it stayed 3 days.

Dave Browne and I decided to book a 2-week lads' holiday to Tenerife on 24th September. I mentioned it to Gary (a friend of Steve's from Westerham), not really expecting him to come, but he did. Gary had been to Tenerife before and knew the crack. All three of us were excited as we departed from Gatwick Airport. David was prepared to behave himself if he met any ladies, as he was still seeing Nicki. Gary was the best looking out of the 3 of us, but he never mentioned having a girlfriend so presumably he was single.

When the plane landed in Tenerife, as soon as the doors opened you could feel the heat. The holiday came with a transfer bus that took us to Playa de las Americas. Our apartment had 3 double beds in one large room, bathroom and balcony overlooking the pool.

Our first major purchase was €300 worth of beer and spirits. To keep things fair, we split the cost three ways, so if anybody wanted a drink, they could just help themselves. Not Gary – every time he wanted a drink, he would ask permission.

On our first full day at the apartment we decided to head to the pool. Around the pool I was surprised to see many topless sunbathers. I had no confidence in diving in, but a woman came over and gave me advice on how to dive. I was copying her actions but too scared to make the final leap into the water. I was a novice swimmer and was only capable of doing a couple of lengths before getting knackered with my bad technique. David couldn't swim at all, but I think he was getting fed up watching me standing around with this lady. He ran up to the edge of the pool and threw himself in, luckily, he landed on a Lilo. If he had missed, it might have got ugly as there was no lifeguard to save him. The pool was 8 feet deep.

David was very chatty. He got talking to a gang of guys and invited them back to our apartment for a drink. Why? They all got very drunk (including David) and for a laugh the visitors decided to throw our plastic balcony furniture into the pool.

Later we collected the furniture and no damage was done, but David is clueless at assessing people.

Holidaymakers didn't really go out to the bars till gone 10pm. One night we wandered into Yates and DJ noticed Gary wearing shorts and sandals. The DJ said on the mic 'Nice to see the Germans are in'. Everybody was laughing and somehow the DJ persuaded me and this pretty young girl to get up on the stage. Neither of us had any idea what was going to happen, but it turned out to be a competition between boys and girls. We had to perform various tasks in the club, and the last one to achieve the task would have a forfeit, which was to take off an item of clothing. She got down to wearing just her knickers and I lost the last task and had to take my boxers off and hold them up in the air. The whole experience was fun.

One night Dave and I decided to go to a foam party and Gary decided not to come. Day by day, he was starting to annoy David and me. Gary would always go for an afternoon run, so David and I would have to wait for him to return before we could get ready to go out. Whilst waiting we would sit on the balcony having a nice beer enjoying the last of the sunshine. Once he got back from the afternoon run, he would go straight into the bathroom for an hour and leave no hot water for David and me.

I decided to fly home after a week. David and I landed back at Gatwick on 1st October, whereas Gary stayed.

The day we left for Tenerife, Britain's third Green Heron turned up at Messingham Quarry in Lincolnshire. Sadly, it departed the day before we got back. I could have gone back to work, but wader-mad Kris Duttherridge was keen to see a Sociable Plover at Pett Level. I wanted it for my Sussex list and decided to meet Kris at the railway station. He travelled down from Yorkshire and stayed over at my mum's. We went to Pett on the 1st of October and got good views of the Sociable Plover for 45 minutes hour before it decided to fly off with some Lapwings.

Nearby Dungeness had a 1st winter Isabelline Shrike which we saw. Back home my mum made us both dinner and Kris got into a heavy discussion with her and I then went to bed. On Thursday we had a lazy day and my kind-hearted mum made us both a cooked breakfast, but whilst I was taking a bite of a sausage the pager mega alerted. A Grey Catbird had just been found by Ken Croft in Anglesey. This was another first for Britain and we wouldn't have got to Anglesey till 4pm even if we left immediately. Instead, we went to Cow Gap and saw a Rose-coloured Starling and found a juvenile Montague's Harrier flying low over the fields, then went out to sea at 1pm.

The Grey Catbird was being elusive. It was seen for 5 minutes by Ken Croft. The news was then broadcast and four RSPB guys saw it in an elder briefly before it flew into a dense patch of gorse. more and more people started to arrive, but it was only seen by one lucky observer at dusk. Kris and I probably made the right decision in not going.

On Friday 5th October the Grey Catbird was heard calling in the morning and Kris and I decided to hold fire and go for a Wryneck at Church Norton. We had to wait for it to show, but it did so at 1:15pm and we went on to Pennington marshes for a Grey Phalarope. Then news come through that a sizeable crowd had got to see the catbird perched out in the open. I rang Lee and he told me many of the big listers including Chris Heard and Steve Gantlett had seen it. The message was clear: we had to go.

On Saturday 6th October, Kris and I met 200 birders early morning at South Stack. At 10am a bird flew up from the gorse and dropped straight back down again. Simon King and I saw it and thought it had good features for a Grey Catbird. Andrew Moon and Pete Antrobus also got a decent flight view, and they were of the opinion it was still there. News was given to the pager that the bird was still present. Lee quizzed the observers, and the conclusion was these sightings were not confirmed. By midday, the gorse bush had been flattened by people who were desperate to see this bird. It was never seen again, and never heard to call. This event is now famously known as the Saturday Catbird and an extension to the Saturday sighting was passed by the BBRC. The only good thing about the trip was seeing 4 Choughs. Kris had a good time with me and my mum's hospitality and decided to head back to Yorkshire.

On Monday 8th October I returned to work, as I was going to be busy for 5 days. I had no chance in going quickly for a Rose-breasted Grosbeak on Lundy. This week then became even more unbearable with a Bobolink found at Prawle Point, a Baltimore Oriole in Ireland and on the Friday a Black-faced Bunting on Lundy.

Friday night I was due to go to Brannigans with David and the lads, but told them to have a good time as I was off to Devon. When David got back from Tenerife, Nicki, the love of his life, decided to dump him. She was convinced he had cheated on our on holiday, which she had no proof of, and for the record he certainly didn't. But his tears were quickly forgotten when he got chatting to a single mother called Vanessa.

On Saturday 13th October, when I caught the MS *Odenburgh* at 10am, news came through that there was no sign of the Black-faced Bunting. However, there was a consolation prize waiting on Lundy. I manage to get a 1st winter Common Rosefinch. Other nice birds on the island include 3 Spotted Flycatchers, a Pied Flycatcher, Barred Warbler, 2 Yellow-browed Warblers, a Firecrest and 4 Ring Ouzels. So all in all it wasn't a bad day. We got the *Oldenburgh* back at 6pm and I made my way through the narrow roads to Prawle Point, where I stayed the night in the car. Next morning, I saw a pair of Cirl Buntings and then got great views of the American Bobolink perched on some bracken. Result!

On Saturday 10th November I got a lift with Graham Ryland to Balvicar in Argyll. The bird we were going for had been seen in early November by John Warlow. He believed it to be an egret, which were rare birds in Scotland. Bill Jackson was next to see it after he was tipped off by local gamekeeper Carl Banner that it had shown at Balvicar on the 5th November. Andy Adcock saw photographs and was convinced it was a Snowy Egret.

We arrived at 9am and saw the first-winter Snowy Egret at no more than 30 yards feeding in the water. It had a slightly down-curved short black bill, with yellow bare skin patch surrounding the eye and extending to the base of the upper mandible. Feet yellow with black on the forelegs. Little Egret can be ruled out on leg colour, without even looking at the base of the upper mandible. The frenzied feeding action was also very different from Little Egrets. At 9:15am it flew off and with such a long journey home, we also left. I saw my first Otter feeding opposite the Knipoch Hotel in Argyll and just before leaving Scotland we saw a Great Grey Shrike at Fannyside Muir along with 177 Taiga Bean Geese. The next day we went for the Redhead in Kenfig Pool and saw it between 9:10-10:45am. This bird has subsequently been rejected as a hybrid. The Snowy Egret was a first for Britain and was last seen on 17th September 2002 at Lochar Water in Dumfries & Galloway.

On Saturday 24th November, I decided to go up to East Anglia for the weekend. First stop was to see the main target bird, a first winter drake Baikal Teal that was first spotted on the 18th of November by Will Miles. When we arrived at 11:30am this bird was asleep and occasionally lifting its head. Currently there have been no accepted records of Baikal Teal in Britain and this was potentially a young bird due to the shape of the scapulars. We spent the night at Sheringham Guest Lodge. Next day we saw a White Pelican at Friary Hill and 2 Mealy Redpoll at Titchwell. The Mealy has a much greyer appearance than the Lesser and is very easy to spot with a mixed Redpoll flock. It has a cleaner wing bar, whereas the Lesser has a yellow-brown wing bar. We also saw an adult Red-breasted Goose at Flitcham and ended the day watching a Snowy Owl at Trimley in the company of Kit Britten.

Over Christmas I was planning on meet a Lithuanian girl called Lilita. I originally met her at a place I might have mentioned before – yes, you got it, Brannigans. She was with a few other Lithuanian girls who were just coming to the end of their holiday. I found her a very friendly, happy, smiley girl and managed to meet up with her just before she flew back home. We swapped telephone numbers and email addresses and I spent a quite a few evenings talking to her on the phone. When she was back home, we agreed to meet up over Christmas. I booked a return British Airways flight to Lithuania.

My good friend Eddie Myer was hearing so many good things about her that he decided to fly over on his British Airways concessions to meet her. Eddie was still single, and you could write a book about his unsuccessful efforts to find Mrs Right. Once Eddie was back home, he rang me up and spoke. 'Wow she is a lovely girl, and she has got a great job and I think you could make a nice couple', but my work friends (who had never met her) said 'Garry, you need to be really careful. She

may only really be interested in finding a way to get out of Lithuania, and it may not be real love'.

I was due to fly to Lithuania on the 24th of December, and decided not to go and change the flight to Edinburgh.

On Monday 24th December I landed at Edinburgh Airport, picked up my hold luggage and hire car, drove north and found a nice hotel to stay at in Peterhead. I ate in the hotel and had a few beers. Being Christmas Eve there was a disco in the function room with a bar.

Next day most people would now be opening their presents and nibbling on chocolates, but I was sitting in the Tower Pool Hide enjoying a very distant white morph Snow Goose. Everything from this hide is so distant, but I decided to finally tick one of the 15 Barnacle Geese present. We've got a lot of feral ones in the south and knowing which one is wild is virtually impossible. Scotland gets thousands each winter, so you can't go wrong.

I left at 9:50am and arrived at Burghead at midday. I spent 4 hours looking all over the bay for an American Black Scoter. No sign, plenty of Long-tailed Ducks, Velvet Scoter and Common Scoter and a few Guillemots dying on the beach. Next day was Boxing Day. I arrived at Burghead Bay first thing in the morning and one of the first birds I saw was a drake American Black Scoter, really close in. Seeing its massive orange cob on top of its bill was an amazing feeling. Where was it in the 4 hours I searched yesterday?

It was only 9am, so with my target bird bagged I decided to head north to Castlehill at Dunnet Bay. The journey was horrendous, thick snow along the whole of the A9 and still snowing. I averaged 27 mph for 5½ hours. You really need to have nerves of steel for this sort of trip because any second you could brake too hard or oversteer and be involved in a nasty collision. I did skid about 10 times, but luckily, I got the car back under control. So glad the adult Ivory Gull was there on arrival at 2:30pm. Not a lifer, but a plumage tick. It was sitting on the pier, and I just viewed it from the car for about 20 minutes, wishing that smart phones had been invented by then. I have no pictures of this all-white gull, with short black legs, blue bill with yellow tip and beady black eye. It was originally found by M. Elwell on the 22nd and staying to 26th December. 40th British record. Now it was just the small matter of driving 274 miles in the snow to Kennagcraig.

On Thursday 27th December I hopped on the 7am car ferry to Port Ellen on Islay. I arrived just after 9am and soon found a 1st winter Iceland Gull in the harbour. Wherever you go on Islay in the winter you will not be far away from geese. You will mainly see Greenland White-fronted Geese, Greenland Barnacle Geese and if you are lucky, Canada Goose. Islay gets 50% of the 80,000 worldwide population of Greenland Barnacle Geese each year. Migration starts on the breeding grounds of eastern Greenland, they take a pitstop in Iceland and arrive in Islay late September. Migration is finished by November. The 24,000 Svalbard Barnacle Geese winter from the Solway Firth to the English/Scottish border and the 130,000 Novaya Zemlya Barnacles winter in Netherlands.

The worldwide population of Greenland White-fronted Geese is estimated as 18,800. They breed on the coast fringe of west Greenland and winter exclusively in Ireland and Britain, with Islay getting 50% of this population.

Just up the road from the port I found 3 Bramblings amongst a flock of 700 Chaffinch. My first Lesser Canada Goose was on map co-ordinates NR380590. This was apparently a Parvipes according to the experts, a midsize Canada Goose. I can't tell the difference between these and Todd's.

I was fortunate enough to meet Brett Richards on Islay. He had already sussed out exactly the best place to see the vagrant geese there. But before I went hunting down the geese, I was keen to see a Golden Eagle. I only had to wait one hour, and one majestically flew over the whole of Gruinart flats, and I watched every second till it went out of view. Wow what a bird, what a sight. Just breath-taking.

Brett advised me to go to the south-west corner of Loch Gorm, and after scanning through loads of Barnacle Geese I eventually found the Taverner's Canada Goose at 2:30pm. Taverner's are quite easy to identify as they have a black gular line, also called a chinstrap. These geese have been coming to Islay for several years and are presumed to be wild as they come in with the Greenland Barnacle Geese. It was now time to visit the Bowmore Hotel. This accommodation is real luxury, 5 bedrooms, restaurant, and bar. Just the place to really unwind. There was another birder staying at hotel called Andy.

On Friday 28th December I saw the following birds: 3 Whooper Swans (Bridgend), 1st winter Iceland Gull (Esknish area), Richardson's Canada Goose and 1 lesser (parvipes) Canada Goose (Ballygrant), 1 blue-phase Snow Goose and 1 Merlin (Loch Gruinard Watchpoint), 1 Red-breasted Goose (Kilnave), possible Rough-legged Buzzard (south of A846 near a red house) and approximately 10,000 Greenland Barnacle Geese and, 1,000 Greenland White-fronted Geese from various parts of the island.

As a treat the owner of the hotel took Andy and me for a trip around Loch Indaal in his 4x4. Here we saw 9 Pale-bellied Brent Geese, 16 Whooper Swans, Turnstone, Curlew, Oystercatcher, Bar-tailed Godwits, Ringed Plover, Raven, 2 Great Northern Diver, Red-throated Diver, Black-throated Diver, 700 Scaup, Eider, 210 Common

Scoter, Common Gull, Herring Gull, Robin, Rock Pipit, Pied Wagtail, Fieldfare, Redwing, Shag and Wigeon. Such a wonderful trip.

I left Islay early Saturday morning and made my way back to Edinburgh for the flight back to Gatwick.

SUMMARY - 2001

During the year I travelled 12,302 miles in Britain in the pursuit of new birds and managed to increase my list by 25 BOU species, taking my British Life list to 372 different species. The Official British List now stood at 555 species, and I was up to 67%. There was one addition to the Official British List during the year: Short-billed Dowitcher (1999).

From last year's target, I managed to see two more Scottish species, Black Grouse and Ptarmigan, leaving Capercaillie and Corncrake. This would now become a priority for 2002.

That year I felt I had transitioned from a weekend birder to guy who is has got a degree of flexibility to see mid-week birds. I was never going to able to go during the last week of each month, but with a list of 373 and 182 to go on the British list I felt sure 2002 would give me plenty of opportunities.

My anxiety and depression did not cause me any problems during 2001 and I didn't have to resort to anti-depressants. My life had changed massively in the last year and the excitement of meeting and chatting to different women had been fun. I was sure Miss Wright is out there somewhere, but in the meantime, I had a nice big group of friends who can help me find her.

The most important bird I saw during 2001 was Argyll's Snowy Egret. This was a first for Britain, its normal range being from north-east USA to north-east South America, with vagrants found in the Azores and Iceland.

CHAPTER 4

2002

Scouser Chris had been a party animal for years and had bags of confidence in talking to strangers. Chris had a wonky eye and was overweight, but he knew how to make people belly laugh. He wasn't a fan of Brannigans, but I did manage to get him down there a few times and he met the gang. David was still coming out to Brannigans, but usually with pregnant girlfriend Vanessa in tow. Chris was more of a Cinderella's type.

Cinderella's night club was in Purley and had the biggest dance floor in the UK. It changed its name regularly over the years and I first went there for my 21st birthday party, when it was called Cinderella Rockerfellas. Somehow, they knew my address and sent me a pile of free tickets and a voucher for a free bottle of bubbly. I hired a minibus and a driver for 16 of my Upjohn work colleagues and they helped me celebrate.

Cinderella these days are not keen on letting in gangs of lads, so just before entering the queue we found a female to walk in with. I think Chris liked Cinderella because a ticket entitled everybody to free meal from the hot buffet. This saved him cooking before leaving the house.

Chris often took ecstasy tablets on nights out. I took half a tablet once – on that occasion I couldn't stop smiling and was talking nonsense to everybody I met. The next day my teeth were hurting from all the jaw clenching. I guess I can tick it off my imaginary bucket list, but never again.

On the work front, the finance department agreed that I needed a part-time employee to help process invoices that were moving from Stanwell to Rowfant. Jan on reception knew a lady called Jackie Tester who lived close by in Copthorne and was looking for part-time work. I wasn't used to interviewing people and when Beth from HR and I invited Jackie in for an interview, I made the humongous mistake of offering Jackie the job at the end of the interview. Beth went apoplectic at me and said afterwards she had never felt so embarrassed at an interview. I apologised profusely. A few days later she forgave me, and Jackie accepted the job.

Jackie was an absolute star. She was hard working and got on with the whole Coating Roadstone team and finance department.

On Sunday 17th March I teamed up with Richard Bonser to see an Alpine Accentor at Minsmere RSPB. This species I had previously dipped in St Margaret's in Kent. Typically, these are one-day birds and I was delighted it decided to stay the night. This bird was frequenting the disused chapel. It took nearly four hours to reveal itself, but when it did, I was impressed by its size. I guess I was expecting it to be the size of our British Accentor, the Dunnock, at 14.5cm, but it was a whopping 18cm, the same size as a Hawfinch. During the 4 minutes it was sitting on the chapel I was able to see the white throat patch, black bill with yellow panel on lower mandible, extensive rufous flanks, black median covert strip, grey head and streaky black and grey mantle. Just like the book illustration, and I felt mightily relieved to make up for dipping it before.

On Friday 22nd March it was Scotland time again and Lee was going to start early Saturday morning at Langdon Beck, Co. Durham. We saw 20 Black Grouse and 4 Red Grouse and then got onto a first winter female Hooded Merganser at Newbiggin. This was only two years since the well-twitched bird of Clachan, North Uist. This American duck was originally found on 7th March and stayed to 25th March, becoming the second for Britain. We found it at 8:20am and watched it at close quarters for 10 minutes. There had been many Hooded Mergansers before the 2000 Outer Hebrides individual, but the location and the time of the year made the BOURC decision a whole lot easier. We also managed to see a nearby wintering Siberian Chiffchaff and a Hume's Yellow-browed Warbler.

We left the site at 9:15am and then spent a lot of time looking for a female King Eider at Aberlady bay, but it just couldn't be found. We stayed the night in the usual B&B. On the Sunday I managed to tick a male Capercaillie at Grantown on Spey. It was a flight view, but this time I made sure I stuck to Lee like glue when he was walking through the forest. Other good birds on the trip included a Goshawk, 3 Waxwings, a Great Grey Shrike, a Scottish Crossbill and a Golden Eagle.

Sunday 12th May brought me to RIMAC in Lincolnshire for a Lesser Sandplover. The last individual at Pagham was not identified as Lesser till it had gone. On arrival the pager was announcing it as a Greater Sandplover, but this all changed whilst more and more people were turning up on site. The feature that helped to rule out Greater was the leg colour. The RIMAC bird had short black legs. Greater have longer legs and vary between greenish grey to yellow, depending on which race. The RIMAC bird had a blunt, short, stubby black bill. All greater races have a longer, sharper black bill. The RIMAC bird was only 1cm longer than a Ringed Plover, while the Greater is up to 5cm longer. In flight, the toes of the Greater project beyond the end of the tail, the Lesser are inline. The wing bar on greater is broader on the primaries than the Lesser. I watched this female Lesser Sandplover for 2 hours. This bird was originally found by Michael Tarrant and Barry Clarkson on the 11th May. It stayed until 15th May and was only the 2nd British record.

On Thursday 16th May I got a lift from London-based birder John Archer to Scilly. The *Scillonian* was full of birders and whilst I was eating in the downstairs café all hell was breaking loose. I wandered upstairs to find that 100 or more birders were sure they had just seen a Red-billed Tropicbird fly past the boat. I wandered round asking people what they had seen and when I got to Johnny

Allan, he said it was a Gannet with a short piece of rope trailing behind it. This was broadcast on the pagers, but people still didn't want to believe there had been a mass hallucination onboard. The Red-billed Tropicbird was on everybody's radar since one had been found 2 months prior. Jez Robson, P. Davison and John Pegden had found it on the 29th March, only about 6.5 kilometres east of Scilly. The guys were in the Scillies to see an Alpine Swift that had lingered around Bryher and Tresco between 23rd to 28th May. Sadly, they missed it by a day, but found a bird of lifetime instead. This was only the second accepted record for Britain. I know which one I would have rather seen.

We docked at St. Mary's and made our way to Carn Morval Point near the golf course. A 1st summer Lesser Kestrel was hanging in the wind on arrival at midday. I noted the blue-grey head, plain brick red back with no black streaking, faint black moustachial stripes, slightly rounded wings, heavily spotted underwings and flanks and slightly projecting central tail feathers. It was feeding on beetles and caterpillars by catching them on the ground and eating them in flight. I never saw it perched the whole 3 hours I was there. The diagnostic pale claws and BTO type silver ring in the bird's right food were not seen. We got the *Scillonian* back and on the way home and made a quick stop off at Marazion to see a 1st summer male Citrine Wagtail.

On Saturday 18th May I was trying to see a Great Reed Warbler at Frensham Little Pond when the pager mega'd news of a Lesser-crested Tern at Dawlish Warren. I decided to abandon the Warbler at 11:20am and head to Dawlish. On the journey down some observers were doubting it was a Lesser-crested Tern because it had a white rump and tail, and the pager changed to 'Orange-billed Tern sp'. I carried on and got to Dawlish Warren,

but there was no sign of the tern by the time I arrived. It was originally seen by Paul Marshall and Martin Mc Gill and a small group of beginner birdwatchers from Gloucestershire from the hide with Sandwich Terns. At midday it flew out to sea with the Sandwich Terns and by 12:30pm, 20 birders had re-found it feeding offshore, still with the Sandwich Terns. Our luck was in. At 5:45pm Adrian Webb picked it up feeding offshore. Phew! So I saw the Orange-billed Tern, though very distantly, and most importantly I too could see its long orange bill.

Only 5 minutes later news of another lifer was coming from Lodmoor RSPB. This time an Alpine Swift was found, and it lingered. The drive was only 73 miles and should take just under 2 hours. When I arrived at 8pm many birders were still present, and the Alpine Swift was still on show. I watched it from 8-9pm hawking insects over lakes with plenty of Common Swifts and other hirundines. Up to this point, Alpine Swifts hadn't been twitchable for me - they were generally seen by one observer briefly and miles from Sussex – but today I triumphed.

During all this swift action, the pager mega'd saying that the Orange-billed Tern was in fact an Elegant Tern. This would be a first for Britain but not for Ireland. Ireland had three previous records, in 1982, 1999 and 2001.

Debbie Shorter and Sue Thompson, who ran the Colas canteen, were both very organised women who made sure there was a choice of hot food and salads at lunchtime. They also made sure there was a selection of sandwiches, chocolates, canned drinks, crisps, fruit and cakes every time somebody requested food for a meeting. I often heard the click of a meeting room door and then waited for the food trolley to be wheeled out into corridor by meeting attendants. Being a massive fan of freebies,

I would rush to the trolley before Debbie or Sue arrived and help myself to a delicious cup cake and a can of fizzy pop. Other office scroungers used to visit the corridors after lunchtime to see what scraps were left.

On Friday 21st June, Sue agreed to bring her single friend Kim to Brannigans. I went over for a chat. I could see straight away she was my type. Kim was 36, slim with blonde hair. She lived in Rusper with her two boys, 13-year-old Luke and eight-year-old Andrew. I pulled a few strings to get them access into the VIP lounge and then went back to my friends. I didn't really want to risk inviting her to meet my friends as they could ruin my chances of getting a date.

I decided to have a chat with Sue on Monday and see what Kim thought of me. Sue said 'Yes, she likes you' and gave me her number. I rang Kim and we agreed to meet up at the weekend.

Then Lee Evans rang me wondering if I could be a spare driver for his minibus trip to Scotland. He was going to try and get a Corncrake. I reflected that most of my dates didn't really work out and who's to say Kim and I would be a success? I agreed to go with Lee, then rang Kim and said 'I apologise but I'm desperately needed to drive a minibus to Scotland this weekend. Can we cancel Saturday, and we can make a date when I get back?' She agreed.

That week I got a letter confirming that my marriage had been dissolved by Horsham County Court and I was free to marry again. Rock'n'roll!

On Friday 28th June I met up with Lee and his minibus crew and we headed straight to Skye. We got to Uig early the next morning and soon heard the 'crex crex' call of a Corncrake. We managed to locate where the call was coming from and see it. What a bird! Whatever we saw now would be a bonus. The weekend included: 4 Whinchats, 8 Black Guillemots, Bonxie, summer plumaged Red and Black throated Diver, 2 Twite, Spotted Flycatcher, 2 Golden Eagle, Woodcock, Osprey, 2 Ptarmigan, 2 Wood Warbler, Roseate Tern and juvenile Tawny Owl. But all weekend my mind kept drifting back to the way I'd cancelled the date and whether she really would see me after being stood up.

Back at work I discussed what had happened with Sue. I felt I owed it to her to at least ring Kim and see if the date was still on. What was the worst that could happen? She could only say no.

On 6th July I drove to Rusper to pick Kim up and we finally went on our first date, at a Greek restaurant in Epsom. We both felt very relaxed in each other's company. We talked equally about past relationships and what we both wanted out of life. After the meal, we were both handed plates to smash. I did spend quite a bit of time on a toilet visit and I came clean that I was due to have a minor operation on Thursday. I was in excruciating pain and the pain lasted about an hour. Kim invited me back to hers, as her two kids were at their dad's.

On Sunday my mum asked how the date went. I joked, 'We had a smashing time, and she knows I'm a pain in the arse'. During the week Kim drove over to my mum's and brought her kids.

On Thursday 11th July Kim drove me to East Surrey for my lateral sphincterotomy. This is an operation performed on the internal anal sphincter muscle, one of two muscles that control passages of faeces. The procedure lowers the resting pressure of the sphincter and improves blood to fissure and allows faster healing. In layman's terms, it was now going to easier for me to have a poo.

Over the next few weeks, I introduced Kim to my main non-birding friends, David Browne and Scouser Chris. Chris was now dating Tina, who was living just around the corner from my mum's.

Tina was a similar age to Kim, and it was nice to go out in a mixed group of four.

If Kim was prepared to take me to hospital after knowing me for less than a week I really needed to pull out all the stops and make this relationship work. Time to dump one of my obsessions: chess.

I originally used to play chess against my dad. He was a good player, but as I improved, I noticed he kept making major mistakes by leaving a piece unprotected. As soon as I noticed the mistake, I would take the piece, and he would instantly resign by wiping his hand across the board and knocking over all the pieces. I never got the opportunity to say 'checkmate' to him. I played chess at school and infrequently against friends up to 1998. That year, Zainab suggested I join Crawley Chess Club a go. I did and loved it, and met David Corke, who got me to join Coulsdon Chess Club. I was now playing chess two to three evenings a week and even some weekends I was playing in tournaments. When I was not playing league chess I was playing at Dave Cork's house. He had a BCF grade of 140, which was about 45 points more than mine, but despite this our games were very close.

David was obsessed by chess and was tutoring a 10-year-old girl called Jessie Gilbert. I got paired against her in a tournament when she was 11. Jessie had only played 4 moves and I was in dire straits. My defence was crumbling, and my clock was running down very quickly. Jessie lost interest in our game and after every move she wandered around the room looking at other people's games. This turned out to be my biggest defeat, and to make it worse Jessie was only a third of my age. The same year, she won the Women's World championship at Hastings and was now representing England on the World stage. This win was so significant that Sports Minister Tony Banks commented, 'We are extremely proud of what Jessie Gilbert has achieved in chess and for this country'. Jessie gained a bursary and travelled to New York to study chess with a grandmaster called Edmar Mednis. In 2006, she gained three norms in chess tournaments. Norms are the highest level you can achieve in chess. In 2009, she earned the title of Women's International Master in the Czech Republic. The following day she mysteriously took her life by falling from the 8th floor of Hotel Lave in Pardubice.

I was devastated when I heard this news. It only confirms that playing chess competitively can take over your life. When something becomes unhealthy you need to retract. During my chess career my win rate was 37% in 1998/9, 44% in 1999/2000, 46% in 2000/2001 and improvement was on the cards for 2001/2. My big claim to fame was the occasion I played for Sussex, but I decided enough was enough.

Missing last year's Fea's type Petrel on the *Scillonian* pelagic got the better of me. I and many other booked it for 11th August and did some seawatching at Porthgwarra the day before. During seawatching, the pager announced that it was being cancelled and a male Pallid Harrier was currently being watched in Kent. The bird first reported on Sunday 3rd August to Elmley RSPB staff as a male Hen Harrier. Over the next week John Hunt, Stuart Brown, Barry O'Dowd, Bob Gomes, Andy Stanbury, Dave Belshaw saw a lot of pro-Pallid features. On the 10th August Chris Bradshaw read that Hen Harriers can show the Pallid type primary wedge, but the Pallid Harrier never shows a trailing edge to the underwing. This bird didn't have a trailing edge to the underwing. At 1:30pm, after 5 hours of searching the area in the pouring rain, a pale raptor was seen on the access track to reserve by Gordon Allison. News went out a little later to Birdline Southeast that a Pallid Harrier with a white rump was being watched and broadcast as Probable.

During the afternoon, many Kent birders connected and were all happy it was indeed a Pallid Harrier. I arrived at Elmley in the dark on Sunday morning and parked the car along the access track. I woke up and saw hundreds of cars lining the track. The Pallid Harrier eventually showed sitting on distant fence posts and making short flights. I could see the already mentioned primary wedge and white rump. I hung around most of the day, enjoying the spectacle, and also saw a Long-eared Owl, 4 Little Owls, a Hen Harrier and Marsh Harrier. The Pallid Harrier stayed to 20th August and attracted 5,000 birders during its stay. It was only the 10th record for Britain and the first once twitchable on the mainland.

On Saturday 25th August Kim was invited to the 60th birthday party in Suffolk of Morris, a family member. I drove Kim, Luke and Andrew. Both of Kim's sisters, Tracey and Leanne, came with their respective boyfriends, Sean and Richard. So did Kim's mum. Morris managed to get the keys of a neighbour's house and we all slept in the two houses.

Next day on the way home, a Terek Sandpiper was found in Maldon, Essex. This species I had dipped twice before – could this be third time lucky? Kim was not a good long-distance passenger and really wanted to go home. She allowed me to make the small detour and I watched the wader at 11:45am with Andrew. The good news for Kim was that it decided to fly off after just 20 minutes and we both returned to the car. This was the first time I had been travelling when a lifer was literally just down the road.

Jason Bishop noticed a Turtle Dove in his back garden off Hillside Road, Stromness on 20th November. He didn't see it again to 1st December,

when he felt it might be an Oriental Turtle Dove. Eric Meek, Martin Gray and two other birders visited his house over the next four days. Martin spoke to Jason about broadcasting the news, but before he did this a consultation was held with the Chairman of Stromness, Orkney Council, Hillside residents, the local recorder, the RSPB and the Northern Constabulary. Once Martin reassured people that there would be no entry into private properties, everybody agreed to release the news to Birdline Scotland. This happened at 8pm on the 5th December.

Lee knew about it before the pagers and wanted us to go for it immediately. I drove to Lee's and picked him and Chris Heard up, then on to Staffs for Steve Nuttall. The whole journey should have taken 12½ hours, but it was done in a fraction less than 11 hours. Great tail wind, I'd say!

We managed to contact the Scrabster Northlink Ferry and they agreed they would wait for us to board on foot. When the ferry departed around 7am, 50 other twitchers were on board. One and a half hours later we docked at Stromness, walked off the ferry and followed the trail of twitchers to Hillside Road. The ultra-rare juvenile Oriental Turtle Dove was still present, only the 5th record for Britain since 1950. The last record was seen at Spurn in 1975 by Ron Johns, so everybody needed this bird.

The bird was remarkably like our Eurasian Turtle Dove. I would suggest overall it felt a shade darker than Eurasian with dark centres to the scapulars, tertials and inner wing coverts. Some scapular edges had a mixture of rufous and white. We watched for an hour and then had five hours to kill before the ferry departed, so we had a bite to eat and enjoyed a leisurely stroll around the harbour. We saw a beautiful adult Iceland Gull and an adult Ring-billed Gull, which was now present for its

LESSER SAND PLOVER
Charadrius mongolus
Rimac, Lincolnshire
12th May 2002
GBAGNOL

14th winter. The Ring-billed Gull was originally found on 3rd January 1988 as a first winter. It was last seen in January 2008 and therefore became the longest stayer, at a whopping 20 years.

For Christmas, Kim's parents invited my mum and me over to the farmhouse. I was blown away by how kind they were to also invite my mum. Everybody got on with her and Kim's sister Tracey really made her feel part of the family. This time last year I had been birding in Scotland. Amazing how life can change.

I decided to take Kim away for a week on 28th December. We went to an adult hotel in Benidorm called the Flamingo Beach Resort. No flamingos there apart from a giant one drawn onto the side of the building. In some adult hotels you might witness plenty of romance going on. Certainly not the case here, as the average age of guests was about 70. Kim and I felt very out of place.

SUMMARY - 2002

During that year I travelled 15,644 miles in Britain in the pursuit of new birds and managed to increase my list by 24 BOU species, taking my British life list to 396. The Official British List now stood at 564 species. There were nine additions to the list during the year: Macqueen's Bustard (1962 re-identified), Mourning Dove (1989), Red-billed Tropicbird (2001), Snowy Egret (2001), Hooded Crow (split), Syke's Warbler (split), Slender-billed Curlew (1998), Grey Catbird (2001), Western Olivaceous Warbler (split), Siberian Blue Robin (2000) and removal of Houbara Bustard (1962).

Last year's singular target had been achieved, of seeing the last of the Scottish specialities (Capercaillie and Corncrake), and it was now time to break the British list into bite size chunks:

Target 1 – Getting 400 species in Britain. That should be easy, with only three to get.

Target 2 – Getting all the 263 regulars listed in The Shell Guide to the Birds of Britain and Ireland by James Ferguson-Lees, Ian Willis and J.T.R. Sharrock. I had seen 261, which just left two: the Long-tailed Skua and the Icterine Warbler.

My general target was prioritising vagrants with less than 10 records. Any vagrant with more than 10 records has a high chance of repeating over the long run, whereas less than 10 records are the real blockers.

The flexibility Colas had given me had really seen my British Life List rocket. To have a list of nearly 400 felt amazing, and I felt that 500 might be achievable in my lifetime.

Most people had managed to see the long-staying adult Long-tailed Skua at Farmoor Reservoir in 1995. Others had seen the spring passage en route to northern Scandinavia at Aird an Runair, North Uist. Autumn migration mainly involves difficult-to-identify juveniles on the east coast. My best chance was to get a long stayer at an inland reservoir, which couldn't be many years away. Icterine Warblers seemed to get good numbers in the Shetlands most years. There just didn't seem to be many close to home.

I decided that the most important bird seen during the year was Lincolnshire's Lesser Sand Plover, the third for Britain. It breeds from the Himalayas to north-eastern Siberia, wintering on sandy beaches in East Africa, South Asia and Australasia. The previous two records were from Aberdeenshire in 1991 and the controversial 1997 bird in Pagham Harbour. This was only accepted as Lesser from photographs after bird had left.

I'll never forget 2002, the year my life changed for the better. Kim was undoubtedly the best thing that had ever happened to me, and I really felt I wanted to spend the rest of my life with her.

CHAPTER 5

2003

I started off 2003 in style by seeing my first Rock Bunting close to our hotel in Benidorm on the 1st January. I flew back to the UK on the 3rd and the time was right for me to move in.

Kim was renting a small house. The ground floor had a good size lounge, tiny kitchen with a small square extendable dining table and a compact bathroom. The narrow staircase led upstairs to a small landing with three bedrooms. I hired two men and a van to take my double bed, bedside cabinet, wardrobe and chest of drawers from Crawley to Rusper and followed with the rest of my possessions in my Ford Probe. To get my 2-meter-tall wardrobe up the stairs with two consecutive right turns was comical. In the end the guys had no choice but to dismantle the wardrobe and take it piece by piece into the bedroom. This took several hours and naturally their fee trebled.

Opposite our double bed was an alcove. That made a lovely space to erect three pine shelves and plonk my bird books. I just hoped Kim knew what she was letting herself in for.

The next job was to stop my overhanging feet getting attacked by Kim's cat Daisy. The simple solution would be to stop her coming into our bedroom at night by closing the door, but that was a big no-no. Kim liked to let Daisy roam the house at night. We had to buy a matching pine bed end chest to protect my feet.

I bought Kim a platinum engagement ring on a visit to Brighton Lanes. I suppose I should have done the traditional thing and asked her parents first, but is parent permission important when they've had long term partners?

I didn't get engaged to Zainab – we just got married after living with each other for seven years. Our wedding day involved just four people. My best man was a guy called Winston Gosine who I had known for 10 years. We became friends when we both worked together in the QA department of Upjohn. Zainab invited her best friend Emma, who she had known since school days. The wedding didn't really feel right. We kept the numbers small because Zainab wasn't sure if her mum would come and it was therefore not fair to invite my parents. The only other time I got engaged was to a girl called Tracy, who I met whilst DJ'ing at the Apple Tree, Crawley. Tracy visited one Monday night with her mum, Gill. Our relationship lasted a year and we never tied the knot.

Towards the end of January one of my Brannigans friends needed somewhere to sleep and my kind-hearted mum said he could sleep over for £10 a night. Let's call him Mr. L. One month later, Mr. L couldn't afford the rent and said he was short this month and would pay the following month. Letters addressed to Mr. L were arriving in my mum's letterbox. The following month Mr. L again said he couldn't afford the rent and my mum decided to open one of his letters. The letters were from a debt collector. Mr. L owed nearly £4000 and if not paid in two weeks' time the bailiffs would be paying a visit to my mum's house. Soon as my mum told me this, I told my Mr. L he was no longer welcome to stay. He now owed my mum £150. I rang Scouser Chris and a mutual friend, Ben, who was owed money, and we drove round to Mr. L's girlfriend's house in Croydon. Mr. L was there and said he still couldn't afford to pay. We confiscated his car and threatened to sell it if he didn't pay back my mum and Ben. My mum eventually got her money back, but the nuisance bailiffs' letters continued for several years.

Scouser Chris decided he wanted a fee to help collect the money. Out of my own pocket, I paid this money to his girlfriend Tina and never rang Chris again. Looking back at this now, I should never have asked my mum to help. Mr. L refused always refused to talk about his past life and now I could only assume the worst.

On Saturday 26th April Andrew Lassey said he had seen an adult male Red-breasted Flycatcher, but several features didn't fit. Mist nets were erected, and the Flycatcher was trapped. It showed restricted orange red on chin to upper throat with grey border. It was a Taiga Flycatcher. It was released into cover on South Landing and the news released. At the time this bird was classed as a subspecies of the Red-breasted Flycatcher, but subspecies have the annoying habit of becoming full species. I went, as I didn't want to moan about this in the future. I saw it first light on the Sunday. A few top twitchers didn't go because it was not released where it had been originally found. It stayed to 29th April.

On Monday 5th May I was doing general birdwatching at Cow Gap and my car was parked 2 km away in Dukes Drive, Eastbourne. Nearby at Dungeness, Dave Walker glimpsed an Audouin's Gull that had originally been seen a few days before in the Netherlands. The news was broadcast at 1:40pm and I went into headless chicken mode and took 20 minutes to jog back to my car. No time to study the maps, I needed to get to Dungeness pronto. I then made a catalogue of errors; I headed north along B2103 and went West on the A259. Once I got to Friston and realised, I did a U-turn and headed towards Jevington. I found the A27 at Polegate and turned left towards Lewes. Wrong again. Then I followed the A259 towards Pevensey, Bexhill and then Hastings.

Stress levels were building. The road from Bulverhythe to east of Hastings is four miles long and I crawled with the Bank Holiday traffic and stopped at every pedestrian crossing and red traffic light. The journey was turning into a nightmare, and to make matters worse the Audouin's Gull was very mobile and frequently flying all around Dungeness. I felt it could leave at any stage.

I arrived at Dungeness RSPB reserve at 3:20pm and joined a massive army of birdwatchers who were standing on the embankment overlooking

Burrowes pit between Dennis's hide and Firth hide. At 3:45pm the gull flew to the shingle beach near the new lighthouse and a mass convoy of cars followed it round. Over the next two hours I got fabulous views of the gull. The main feature was a red bill with a black tip. It was smaller than the accompanying Herring Gull, with all black primaries and a black bar covering the length of the upper wing. It was seen by 1,400 birders during the first two days and raised £500 for the bird observatory. This first for Britain was last seen on the Wednesday evening coming into roost.

Until then I had never been to Ireland, but Lee Evans and Chris Heard, who kept a combined list, suggested I should join them for a White-crowned Sparrow at Dursey. It was found by Penny and David Durrell on their feeders close to Dursey Island.

My Ford Probe's steering was very noisy, so I decided to buy a replacement car from Tracey's boyfriend Sean. This time I got a more family-centric Ford Escort. I picked up Lee and Chris and we caught the Fishguard-Rosslare ferry as foot passengers at 2:45am on 22nd May. The Budget car rental desk was shut, but somehow Lee managed to wake up someone to get it opened. We got to the Sparrow site at midday and within 5 minutes the White-crowned Sparrow came to the garden to feed. The bird, native to North America, was tailless, but with black and white striped head and pink bill it was still quite a sight. The bird was last seen on the 27th May and was the first record for Ireland.

Stephen Rosser found an unusual black bird at South Stake on 31st May. Ken Croft arrived on site the next day and confirmed it as a Black Lark, a bird of the open Steppe from the northern Black Sea to southern Ukraine. The mega alert sounded at 6:38pm and I left home at 11pm with four other

Sussex twitchers. The journey north had my Ford Escort swaying from side to side, which I thought was due to wind. To make things worse the amber fuel light had been on for quite a long time. We just limped to an open service station. One of my tyres was virtually flat and the diesel cap wouldn't come off. Thank God we bumped into Mick Frosdick. He managed to cut off the old cap with his pen knife and the service station sold me a universal cap.

Minutes later we arrived at South Stack and made our way to a long line of twitchers. Exactly at 5:30am the Black Lark landed at the edge of the cliff, near some pink flowers. What a feeling – seeing a good-looking first for Britain was a sight for sore eyes. The bird was all black apart from a white bill and a sprinkling of white on the crown an upperparts down to the flanks. It was last seen on 8th June, having got 4,000 admirers over the eight days.

Birdwatching during 2003 also involved doing a Sussex Yearlist rather than a Nationwide Yearlist. I saw my 100th species at Arundel WWT on 25th January, a Firecrest, and by 9th June I got a Roseate Tern, which was my 200th species. This was at Rye Harbour.

The list had been a lot of fun up to now, and it was nice to get a tip-off about a Blue-winged Teal at Icklesham. I was expressly told to go and see it but not to tell anybody about it. I did mention it to one other person, who was not from Sussex. The same day the news hit the pager. I investigated where the news had come from, and it was supposedly from a Norfolk birder who had put the news on Birdline National and this had been picked up by Rare Bird Alert. I was never going to be tipped off about another bird in Sussex after this, my name was dirt.

In 1996, 50+ birders got invited to a private garden to see a Black-and-white Warbler. The news hit bird services on the evening of its second day.

The next morning, I was there with nearly 100 other birders and the warbler was gone. It's unlikely to ever happen again. The competitive Sussex Country listers have now got a very exclusive tick, and the number of birds they get invited to makes their county totally impossible to catch. Suppressions are happening all over the country every day. Suppressions on private land or rare breeding birds you can understand, but suppressions on public land are generally for competitive purposes. When public land suppressors are seen twitching publicly available birds, double standards spring to mind.

Kim and I got married on Saturday 28th June at Crawley Town Hall, and 32 guests watched the ceremony unfold. My best man, David Browne, was standing by me and eventually the music started and in walked the two bridesmaids, Leanne and Tracey, followed by Kim and her dad. Kim looked stunning and I got a lump at the back of my throat and started shaking. We said our vows, signed the register and swapped rings, and Kim was now my wife.

We all left the registry room and walked out of the Town Hall and there stood a horse-drawn carriage. I didn't know who it was for, until Tracy said 'it's for you'. It was an overwhelming and very special surprise from Kim's parents. Kim loved horses and I started crying as Kim climbed into the phaeton first, followed by me and then her youngest son Andrew, who fancied the ride. Geoff Goater managed to get some great video footage of the four horses pulling out of the Town Hall and onto the main road. Crowds of people stopped and clapped, as they watched us clip-clop past all the way through the town centre. We felt like royalty.

The horses took us 3.8 miles to The Gate, a pub on the Rusper road, where they got some much-deserved rest and we both had a Pimms and lemonade. Our wedding photographer, Brian, caught up with at the gate and took some lovely pictures as we supped our drink. 20 minutes later we trotted the final 1.7 miles to Ghyll Manor Hotel. All the wedding guests got from Crawley Town Hall to Ghyll Manor before us and then Brian took loads of pictures with his Hasselblad camera in the garden of Ghyll Manor. Brian was a quirky guy and had a real eye for the ladies, but he did make us all laugh. Kim was an employee of Ghyll Manor, and she had seen many wedding functions there over the years. She is quite a shy girl, and being the centre of attention with all her colleagues must have made the occasion even more daunting.

After photographs, we hung around in the terrace garden till the dinner was ready. For the evening we hired a double-decker bus to take guests from Ghyll Manor to a disco at Warnham Village Hall. Another 50 guests arrived, and the double decker made a return to Rusper just after midnight.

The following day, we had booked to fly from Heathrow to the Seychelles. Being a man, I left packing my suitcase to the day of the flight. Only problem was, I couldn't find my passport. I checked all the obvious places and no sign. If I didn't find it soon, there was no way we were going to get enough time to drive to Heathrow and check-in. Kim and I were getting stressed and began desperately tipping drawer contents onto the bed. We had almost given up when I somehow decided to check my suit pockets hanging in the wardrobe. Hallelujah! I found the passport sitting in the inside jacket pocket.

We rushed to my car, drove straight to the Colas depot of Stawnell Moor and parked the car. I ordered a taxi to take us to Heathrow Terminal three. We waited 20 minutes and the taxi never turned up, so hurriedly got hold of another taxi firm and they managed to get us to the terminal just as the check-in desk closed. We were the last two passengers to board the plane. If looks could kill was certainly the impression we were getting as we walked past seated passengers to get to our seats. Once we got seated, Kim and I could finally breathe a sigh of relief and start to relax.

We flew on a Lauda Airways Boeing 767-300 series to Mahe. The flight was just under 12 hours with an hour stop in Rome. We arrived in the early hours of Monday 30th June and just had enough energy to board a taxi direct to Le Meridien Barbarons Hotel. Then straight to bed.

We stayed there 4 days and then took a 30-minute flight to Bird Island. The only hotel on the island was Bird Island Lodge. There were no TVs or phones there and you could enjoy the peace and quiet of lazing around on a private island. The chalets were hidden from each other by tropical trees. Every night a small gecko living in the chalet roof would come out and reveal itself.

The meals served at the lodge were amazing, especially the Red Snapper. We stayed there for three nights and the bird highlights were 1.3 million Sooty Terns, Crab Plovers, White-tailed Tropicbirds, Fairy Terns and Bridled Terns roosting in the Casuarina trees. One night after dinner we decided to sit in the dark on the beach and watch the Wedge-tailed Shearwaters return to their burrows. It really did feel like paradise.

On the Sunday, we flew to Praslin and stayed in one of the twelve rooms at the Black Parrot Hotel for four nights. Days trips included visits to La Dique and Cousin. At Cousin we saw Magpie Robins and Seychelles Warblers, both species which Birdlife International has brought back from the brink of extinction. We left Praslin on the Thursday 10th July and flew home on an Air Seychelles Boeing 767 via Zurich.

Back home that autumn, I saw a 1st summer Common Yellowthroat at Loop Head in Clare, and then Fair Isle struck a mighty blow. A Savannah Sparrow was found on Neder Taft on Tuesday 14th October by John Walmsley and three days later Alun Bull found a female Siberian Rubythroat at Midway. I was offered a seat on a charter plane on the Sunday and accepted. I left home at 1am and arrived at Kirbymoorside Airport in North Yorkshire at 8am. News then came through that the Rubythroat and the Sparrow were still present. The airport now had three small planes that were going to fly to Fair Isle. Ron Johns, the former number one British Lister, was also at the airport.

We took off at 9:30am in a Piper Pa32 Cherokee Six. This was a single-engine plane, and it took us 2¾ hours to get to Fair Isle. We landed at 12:15pm and got picked up at the airport and taken straight to Nether Taft. We saw the Savannah Sparrow within 15 minutes and noted the white supercilium with yellow fore, the heavily streaked breast and no white on outer tail feathers. This is a feature that rules out the very similar Yellow-browed Bunting.

I then made my way to the Virk to look for the Siberian Rubythroat, but after two hours, I had not managed to see it. I decided to go back and have another look at the Sparrow. During this time Chris Glanfield from Sussex rang me and asked, 'How are you getting on?' I hastily replied 'Not good, I've seen the Sparrow but not managed to see the Rubythroat yet. Some birders have seen both'.

Shortly after the phone call the Siberian Rubythroat was refound and I rushed over, but just missed it. It was then seen again by Ron Johns, who was standing next to me. My eyes were just not quick enough to get on it. The plane was due to go back at 3:30pm, so time was pressing. Then suddenly at 3:15pm it was seen again and to my great relief I got onto it. It was on the ground near the Kirk for a couple of seconds. I noticed the long white supercilium, white moustachial stripe and brown upperparts. It was then flushed, and we noticed the tail and back were the same brown colour and the belly was paler.

We flew back on a Cessna 310, stopping for fuel at Kirkwall, Orkney, and landed in Kirbymoorside at 6pm. The trip felt amazing, certainly a bit of rollercoaster on the Sunday, but to see two quality birds in less than 24 hours at the remote outpost of Fair Isle is the stuff of dreams. Both birds were gone the next day. The Savannah Sparrow was the third record for Britain and the Siberian Rubythroat was the fourth.

My father had always suffered with haemorrhoids, and he was eventually operated due to excruciating pain. This genetic problem was passed down to me and from time to time they caused me quite a lot of discomfort. Come Tuesday 16th December, my haemorrhoids decided to misbehave. I rang up work at 8am and we mutually agreed it was best to avoid working today. Twelve minutes later Mega alert announces a Baltimore Oriole in Oxfordshire and twenty-three minutes later the mega goes off again, this time an American Robin in Cornwall.

Crikey, two new birds turning up and I've got the day off to recuperate. Ian Barnard, who is a self-employed carpenter, rang and was keen to go. I decided to risk it and join him. Just after 2pm we clapped eyes on the Baltimore Oriole, perched in ivy near a seed dispenser in Stowood Close. I was watching it on tiptoe over the garden fence of number 38 for about a minute. Some guys were more organised and brought step ladders with them. These gaudy American birds are yellow-orangey all over with a double white wing bar.

We stood around for an hour with no further sign and decided to push onto Cornwall. We saw

the American Robin, a female, near a sand pit around 8pm. I had dipped this species the previous month in Bardsey with Steve Bacon. Males have black upperparts with a brighter red breast, but the females still look nice with their browner upperparts and dull red breast. The Baltimore Oriole was credited to P. Allen, R. Hurst and D. John and it stayed from 10th December to 16th January. The American Robin was credited to by P.A. Gainey, A.R. Pay and M. Tunmore and it stayed from 14th December 2003 to 2nd February 2004.

I went back to work on the Wednesday and my finance boss Bev called me into her office. She asked, 'How are you feeling now?' I nervously replied, 'Yes I'm feeling better'. 'Oh, that's good' She said, 'Because I had a phone call that somebody saw you in Cornwall yesterday.' I was lost for words but nodded that I had been there. She went on to say, 'I've discussed the matter with HR and on this occasion, I will be issuing you with a verbal warning. Next time it will be a written warning.'

I never got to the bottom of who grassed me up, but only a couple of people knew I was on sick leave. I did see one birder in Cornwall who knew I was sick, and he was rumoured to have done this sort of thing before. I confronted him and he denied it. What do birders get out of grassing other birders up? Twitching is best performed as a group activity; you should be able to trust your friends. News of who is going for what is readily available on the birding grapevine. All it takes is one mischievous individual to hear gossip on the grapevine and you could end up jobless.

SUMMARY – 2003

During 2003, I travelled 7,403 miles in Britain and Ireland in the pursuit of new birds and managed to increase my list by 10 BOU/IRBC species. This took my British and Irish list to 406. The Combined Official List stood at 573 species, of which I was now up to 69.1%. There were zero additions to the Official British List during the year, with the removal of the Magnificent Frigatebird and the addition of the Ascension Frigatebird. Adding Ireland has allowed an extra nine species to the combined List (Griffon Vulture, Bald Eagle, Band-rumped Petrel, Red Fox Sparrow, Blue-winged Warbler, Cackling Goose, Hooded Merganser, Elegant Tern and Zino's/Fea's/Desertas Petrel). More importantly, this region now represents the British Archipelago and ignores man-made political boundaries.

I managed to see 228 different species in Sussex during the year, with a Shorelark at Pett Level on 22nd November being my final bird. Christian Melgar got the highest total with Ian Barnard getting second highest and me in third place. My life list broke the 400 species barrier with the Black Kite from Beachy Head in East Sussex. I could now raise the bar to try and see 500 different species In Britain and Ireland.

I decided that the most important bird I saw during the year was the Savannah Sparrow on Fair Isle. This American bird was only the third record for Britain. Fair Isle had a two-dayer in 1987 and the other record was a 16-dayer in 1982 on Portland. The Portland bird may eventually be split as Ipswich Sparrow. I feel every keen birder/ twitcher needs to make the pilgrimage to Fair Isle at least once in their life. It's responsible for at least 27 British firsts. I feel so privileged that the Sparrow hung around for 6 days until the day I was due to visit. It could have all gone horribly wrong. Getting to these remote islands the same day as rare bird news is disseminated is key if you want a happy life and a big list.

2003 went down as the most memorable year of my life so far. I married the girl of my dreams – and next year we were expecting a baby.

Savannah Sparrow
passerculus sandwichensis
Fair Isle
Neder Taft 19th October 2003
G. BAGNELL

CHAPTER 6

2004

Just as in 2003, Kim and I were abroad for the new year. We flew out on Saturday 27th December 2003 to Tenerife for a week's break, staying at Santa Maria Apartments in Costa Adeje. This was my first-time birding in Tenerife, and a little birdie told me there were a few endemic birds (species found nowhere else) worth seeing. The only one I saw from the apartment was the Canaries Chiffchaff. We splashed out and hired a car to explore the island, and managed to see a gorgeous Blue Chaffinch at Las Lajas. This site also held Canarian Blue Tit, Berthelot's Pipit and Canary. The two Pigeons should be gettable at Erjos. The day we visited we had thick fog and rain. We did see 6 dark pigeons but couldn't pin them down to species level. Our field guide suggested La Gomera was good for pigeons, so we got a boat there, but we failed to see any pigeons whatsoever. We thought we'd give Erjos another go. This time we managed to see 4 Bolles Pigeons with their diagnostic dark tail bands, but sadly no Laurel Pigeons. Then the week was up and it was

time to fly back to reality.

Kim was now 24 weeks pregnant and just about had a bigger belly than me.

My first chance for a new British and Irish bird didn't take long. A Harlequin Duck was mega-alerted on 17th February on the Western Isles, and it could have been there for a month already. I'd never been to any of the Western Isles before and I remember when two females were found on 13th April 1996 on Girvan, Ayrshire. I had just seen a Lesser Scaup at Tyttenhanger, Hertfordshire and got into a queue to see a Spotted Crake at nearby Tringfield Reservoir. Lee Evans was organising the queue and at the same time arranging a car trip that night to see the Harlequins. The twitching seemed frenetic back then, but fast forward 8 years and I was now chomping at the bit.

A lift offer was advertised on the pager and all five spaces were taken, by train driver Mick Frosdick, two birders from Kent, Mark Lopez and his friend Andy Edwards, and Hampshire birder Dan Houghton. Dan Houghton was into local patching and was the finder of the 1996 Nutcracker at Denny Wood. Dan is a reliable field observer, who is well versed in bird call. Most autumns he will spend two weeks searching for rares in Shetland.

I left Rusper on the Thursday evening for the 646-mile journey to Ullapool. We booked spaces for my car and five passengers on Friday's 10:30am Caledonian MacBrayne ferry sailing to Stornoway. During the crossing we saw some nice auks and divers, but we got the very unpleasant news that the Harlequin Duck had flown off with some Wigeon at 11:33am.

We docked at Stornoway at 1pm and found two 1st winter Iceland Gulls and 1 Kumlien Gull. White-winged gulls are rare down south, so this place already felt rare. We decided to head to nearby Coll just in case the Harlequin returned, but before we settled there an American Herring Gull was found by Martin Scott at Tiumpan Head. Being a new bird for all of us and only 28 miles away, we gave it a go. No sign, so it was back to Col for the rest of the daylight. It didn't return, but on Thursday at 1:53pm it flew out to sea and was back the next morning, so we still had a chance for Saturday morning. We headed back to Stornoway for a bite to eat and bumped into Chris Glanfield, Ian Barnard, Steve Gent and John Pegden at the Crown pub. They were all smiling like Cheshire cats as they had managed to see the Harlequin Duck at Col before we arrived. They recommended ordering the duck from the menu. Ha ha.

We spent the night in Stornoway and got back to Col at 7:20am, and to say we were overjoyed to see the Harlequin was an understatement. We had superb views as it was swimming close inshore. It was all over light brown with a distinctive elongated curved head. It had a white spot on the ear covert and a faint white patch below and above the eye.

We left the island at 2:30pm, all on a massive high.

The Harlequin duck stayed to 20th May and became the longest staying individual. It represented only the 9th British record. Their breeding range is North American, Greenland and eastern Russia. The record was submitted by M. Hague, Brian Rabbits and A. Walker.

On 28th March I was sitting on the sofa with Andrew watching Arsenal v Manchester United in the Premier League. We cheered as our footballing god, Thierry Henry, scored a goal to make it 1-0 on the 50th minute. Fortunately, Arsenal drew 1-1 with an 86th minute equaliser from William Saha and Arsenal remained unbeaten for 32 matches and were still top of the Premier League.

Another American duck I needed was found on 11th April at Astley Moss LWT in Greater Manchester. This time it was a drake Bufflehead. Kim was due to deliver in 10 days' time and said, 'Don't even think about going!'

Early on the morning of 21st April she started having contractions at home. I drove her to East Surrey Hospital and at 9am our little girl, Georgie Mae Bagnell, was born. I cut the umbilical cord and we both held our beautiful creation and waited for the doctor to give us the all clear. During his inspection, Georgie started to choke, so he scooped her up and ran off to another room. She had a mucus build up and he quickly cleared her airways. The doctor decided to keep Kim and Georgie in hospital for the night. Kim's mum and sons both visited the newest member of the family. The next day I drove Kim and Georgie home.

Over the next two weeks I took paternity leave. I made sure I could feed, wind and nappy change Georgie and Kim was only allowed to do bits and pieces in the house. I spent hours every day watching the different facial expressions Georgie made. I was spellbound. Night-time Georgie slept well in a Moses basket in our bedroom. To me, life felt complete. I'd always wanted a child, and meeting Kim could only be regarded as fate. Now I was a dad, would I ever have the urge to twitch again? During this exciting time, I heard that the drake Bufflehead had relocated to Pugneys, West Yorkshire, on 12th April and stayed to 22nd April.

I went back to work on the 6th May and by 13th May another American duck had been found in Britain, this time a controversial Cinnamon Teal, found on Lewis. It arrived with a good supporting cast of birds of Nearctic origin and was probably the best chance Britain had at getting a wild one. Previous records of Cinnamon Teal have been placed in Category E (Escape). Cinnamon Teal are found in the extreme south-west of Canada and are rare visitors to the east coast of the United States.

On 18th May I managed to get four tickets to Martin Keown's testimonial match at Highbury, where a star-studded Arsenal XI team played a star-studded England XI. Kim's mum looked after Georgie and I was free to drive Kim, Andrew and his friend Greg to Highbury. Martin Keown was a well-respected Arsenal player who had made 310 premier league appearances over 12 seasons. Kim never made it a secret that she was in love with David Beckham, and I worshipped the ground Thierry Henry, Dennis Bergkamp and Freddie Ljungberg walked on. Our heroes all played, and Arsenal XI won 6-0. José Antonio Reyes scored a hat-trick during the match and to think at age 35 he is no longer with us is incredibly sad. He died on 1st June 2019 between Utrera and Seville when he lost control of his car due to a steering or tyre failure. Police estimate his speed was somewhere between 69 to 81mph. His cousin Jonathan also died in the accident.

On a happier note, more and more twitchers were going for the Cinnamon Teal for insurance purposes. Then our long-lost friend the drake Bufflehead was intermittently found again from 24th May at Croxall Lakes, Staffordshire.

I came out of twitching retirement on 28th May. This time I took Essex butcher John Sawyer and two others on an overnight drive to Inverness Airport. We caught the Saturday morning flight to Stornoway and stayed for the weekend. We saw the Cinnamon Teal at 10am on Loch Tuamister and then enjoyed driving around Lewis admiring summer-plumaged Black-throated, Red-throated and Great Northern Divers with both Scottish eagle species and some dodgy-looking Icelandic Redpolls. I got everybody back for Bank Holiday Monday. Just a quick hello and goodbye to my family, then I drove to Staffordshire. The Bufflehead was bagged at 4:30pm and I ended the day ticking a singing Icterine Warbler at Outney, Suffollk.

The Cinnamon Teal stayed to 16th June. The Bufflehead was the 9th record for Britain and was last seen on 25th June at nearby Clayhanger, West Midlands. Surprisingly another Bufflehead was found on North Uist on 10th May and then on Lewis on the 20th May.

July is normally a safe month to have dinner parties with friends, right? My work friend Angela, who lives in Ardingly, West Sussex with partner Nick, invited Kim and me over to their house for a bite to eat. Nick is an extremely good cook and a natural entertainer. What would you do if you were just about to eat your starter at midday and a Greater Sand Plover was found in Norfolk? This was only the 14th record for Britain and the first since the two-day Lothian bird in 1999. Mum and Dad brought me up to believe honesty is the best policy. I quicky decided to announce, 'I'm really sorry but I hope you don't mind if we leave after dinner as a new bird for my list has just been found in Norfolk'.

I dropped Kim back home at 3:30pm and watched the Greater Sand Plover at a range of 200 metres from Snettisham beach car park at 6:40pm. I felt awful putting birds before friends. Angela and Nick were friendly people and not being birdwatchers they didn't understand what the lure of a new bird to my list meant. In the past we would have hung around chatting, joking and playing games to 10pm. I tried reciprocating a dinner party at Rusper, but on both occasions received last-minute cancellations from Angela. This signalled our friendship was over and since that day I've limited social get-togethers to family members, birdwatchers and people who truly understand my obsession with this hobby.

The Greater Sand Plover was seen briefly on Beacon Ponds, East Yorkshire on Saturday 3rd July and then at Snettisham from 4th to 5th July. Joe Doolan found a Great Knot at Swords Estuary on 25th July. My good friend and top Irish lister Vic Cashera only lived 12 minutes away, and five minutes after he arrived a walker's dog chased all the birds out of the estuary. Thousands of waders were in the air when Vic arrived, and they all landed except the Great Knot. This was Vic's local patch, and he regards missing Ireland 1st and only Great Knot as his worst dip.

Six days later Chris Batty of Rare Bird Alert found the Great Knot at Skippool Creek in Lancashire at 6:50am; it stayed till 9:31am. I arrived in the afternoon and dipped. The bird was refound on 16th August and stayed from 9:37am to 12:23pm, when it was flushed by a helicopter. On 17th August it was seen between 9:31am and 3:01pm. It takes 4 hours and 37 minutes to drive the 270 miles to Skippool and I could have got it at this intertidal site if I had known it was going to linger for 5½ hours. I thought there would be a good chance on the 18th, but I got their first light

and waited all day with no sign. This Great Knot was only the 3rd record for Britain. They breed in the mountains of north-east Siberia and winter as far south as Australia.

On 5th September I took a phone call from Chris Heard whilst sitting in my garden and he asked, "What are you doing about the Purple Martin on Lewis?" I replied, "Sorry Chris, currently doing month end accounts and there's no way they will excuse me. Good luck if you go". Chris ended up going overnight with Lee Evans and catching the ferry next morning. Meanwhile Justin Taylor kindly shares what he did about it:

I had just returned from a trip to Staines to see a distant Pectoral Sandpiper and was at some friends for an afternoon barbecue when a mega alert went off. The news was of an amazing find. A Purple Martin, a first for Britain, had been found at the Butt of Lewis and was showing well around the lighthouse. As rarities go this was massive, but its location could not be much further away and being a hirundine the chances of it staying more than a few hours were slim.

Not knowing quite what to do next, I retired to the loo to think. My phone rang, and it was my mate Andy Horscroft. "What are you doing about it?" he asks. "God knows mate, it'll never stay, it's a Martin, I'll get back to you," I told him.

Whilst at the barbecue I was mulling over the options. Do nothing and hope it's never seen again, or put some plans in place and see what happens? The second option seemed best so I called BA, who quoted £325 day return from Glasgow, I booked two seats and we had until 9pm to pay for them. At least we would know if it had roosted.

That evening I was at my then fiancée's (now wife amazingly) parents for another barbecue. My fiancée's sister then worked in the travel industry, and she said she could get our tickets held without payment until 8am on the Monday morning. This news was fantastic and after another conversation with Andy we decided to go to Glasgow overnight and wait on news. The news was positive. The bird had been seen to roost on the lighthouse, so the twitch for the almost impossible was on.

We left Oxford at 1am and Andy's Focus ST170 made light work of the 360 miles, completing it in just over 5 ½ hours. We arrive at Glasgow airport around 6.30am.

At 7.15am the first news of the day hits the pager that there was no sign of the Martin. Then another update – still no sign by 7.25am. It seemed our gamble had not paid off, but at least we wouldn't have to pay for the tickets.

We decide to wait a little longer, and the next message at 7.30am brought news that the bird was still there around the lighthouse. We had to pay for the tickets by 8am, so within minutes we were in the terminal and the seats were paid for and confirmed. This is where the fun begins!

We wre due for a 9.30am departure but once in the departure lounge we saw that our flight was now scheduled for 10am, thanks to a staffing issue. This did not seem a problem as we were allowed to get on the plane at 9.30am. At 9.45am the engines are fired up and the excitement level increased only for the engines to be run down and shut off. What was going on? Engineers in high-vis jackets appeared and the captain announced that we all had to get off as there was a technical issue.

What a nightmare! time is always immensely valuable with any rarity but with a flying hirundine it's critical. We returned to the departure lounge to hear that the Martin had been flushed by a Sparrowhawk and there had been no sign since 8.50am, nearly an hour! This was getting too much, and Andy went outside for a smoke with some others. Conversations were starting to turn to

getting refunds when the news came through that it had been relocated half a mile down the road at Eoropie, flying over fields near the kirk.

We would have to leave Glasgow soon if we were to have any chance with this bird, and we hear the weather front holding the bird at the site was slipping away SW, being replaced by bright sunny skies.

We were called to board at 10.25am, an hour later than scheduled but luckily we were airborne by 10.35am for the 45-minute flight to Stornoway. We had been chatting to John Hopkins at Glasgow and he had offered us seats in his hire car. Stornoway to Butt of Lewis is about 45 minutes' drive and with no pager service it can be a nervy time, but we had a friend on the mainland giving us updates. It was still there at 11.15am, but now under a sunny sky. It was now 11.30am. Would the bird stick?

So now I'm in the front of the 3 door Micra and John does a great job getting us to Eoropie by 12.15pm. We stop, and I can see birders up the road looking up and with my naked eye I can see the Martin! Andy in the back can't see anything and is shouting "Let me out, Let me out!" We pile out of the car and all clamp our bins on it.

We had made it. After a morning of highs and lows we were watching the Purple Martin, a first for Britain. Occasionally it would disappear, only to reappear over the heads of the small crowd. At one magical moment it landed on the wires, and for a few seconds we were treated to a scope view of it perched.

At 12.45pm, just 30 minutes after we had arrived, the bird started to gain height and was lost in the bright sunlit sky. It had gone.

We decided to check the lighthouse to see if it had gone back there, but to no avail, and when other twitchers started arriving from the ferry crossing at 2.15pm they were greeted with the grim *news that it had departed. From talking to others just 38 non-Island birders had seen it (labelled 'cheque book birders' by one who didn't see it). I'm writing this in September 2022, a cool 18 years later. That bird still holds its status and is becoming a blocker. A cheque well used, I think!*

The Purple Martin was found by Shaun Coyle, Torcuil Grant and Mark Witherall at 2:30pm on Sunday 5th September on Butt of Lewis. They didn't have a field guide between them and decided to ring Tom McKinney for confirmation of the identification. News was put out and Martin Scott became the first twitcher to connect. Only 10 people managed to see it on its first day and this bird became the first record for Britain.

Kim decided to organise a big family holiday in Moraira, Costa Blanca, and we hired a five-bedroom villa with games room and swimming pool from 11th to 18th September. This holiday was a bit of a miracle as Kim persuaded her mum Jen and dad Tarb to go. They rarely ever left their farm. Kim's middle Sister Tracy, Luke, Andrew, Georgie, and my mum came. We flew Monarch from Gatwick to Alicante and hired a minibus for the week. My mum couldn't swim, but it was nice to see her having a daily cool down in the swimming pool. My dad was a good swimmer, and it makes me sad that he never met my family.

I managed to sneak off birdwatching with the minibus a few times. I saw 380 Greater Flamingos at Caple Salt Works, Crag Martin and a Blue Rock Thrush at Penon de Ifac, and my mum and Tarb jumped on the minibus when we went to El Montgo and saw two Black Wheatears.

Georgie was now five months old, and we took her to St. Mary Magdalene's Church in Rusper for her christening. Reverend Nick Flint held his normal Sunday service and performed the christening halfway through the service. The church reserved a couple of benches at the front of the church for our guests. They recommend at least three people to be godparents and we chose Kim's sisters Tracy and Leanne and my friend David Browne. Kim, the godparents and I were invited to bring Georgie to Reverend Nick. The ceremony involved all of us promising to support Georgie for the rest of her life. Reverend Nick used oil to draw a cross on her forehead and then poured water from the font over her head and spoke the words 'I baptise you in the name of the Father, and of the son, and of the Holy Spirit. Amen,' so Georgie was now part of God's family. My friend Eddie Myer videoed the whole ceremony and we all went back to our house for a BBQ after.

An update on David's status. He did have a baby with Vanessa, named Louis, but unfortunately they split up just after my wedding last year. David found new love with Lucy, from Portsmouth. They met through a dating agency, and I must say, Lucy is perfect for David.

I'm not used to doing barbecues for 16 adults in the pouring rain, but that's British weather for you. Eddie and I cooked the food on two barbecues side by side with a large fishing umbrella keeping us both dry.

After food was eaten and everybody had gone, Kim and I settled down on the sofa to watch the video back. We couldn't stop laughing – the whole video looked like it had been filmed by someone on a boat at sea. One second you could see our heads and torsos and the next our legs and feet. Eddie couldn't having been looking through the viewfinder. The whole video was very unsteady and reminded me when I first used the video camera whilst the infrared was switched on.

On Tuesday 28th September a Cream-coloured

Courser was found on St. Agnes at 2:10pm and stayed until 3:46pm, when it was flushed by cows towards the Turk's Head pub. I took the *Scillonian III* across the next morning and the Courser was not seen. I stayed on St. Marys and saw 3 juvenile Buff-breasted Sands at the golf course, then went to the Longstone Heritage Café to see a Death's Head Hawkmoth. Somehow, I left my scope in the café and only realised it was missing when I was back at the quay. I returned to the café and found it still standing there.

I got the *Scillonian* back to Penzance and just before docking news come through that the Courser was now on St. Martins. I stayed the night in Penzance and got to St. Martins at 1pm on the 30th, and within a 15-minute walk I found the Cream-coloured Courser again. This was the 7th for Britain. It was taken into care on the 26th October and died at Mousehole Hospital the next day.

The 7th Western Sandpiper for Britain was found on Brownsea Island on 29th September. I was due to be watching Arsenal play Charlton at Highbury on the 2nd October and so decided to kill two birds with one stone. I drove to Chris Glanfield's house at Angmering and left my car there. Chris then drove Richard Kemp, Steve Gent and me to Sandbanks. We got a boat across to Brownsea at 10am, and for some reason I ran the mile from the boat to the main hide. I saw the Western Sandpiper for about 5 minutes and ran back to the boat.

At that time I wasn't fit and I felt rough during the 3½ hour train journey to Waterloo. A single ticket cost a whopping £57.30. I was just glad that Arsenal had a 4-0 victory and I was able to see Antonio Reyes pass the ball to Thierry Henry and immediately send the ball powerfully into the back, all why he was being held by Charlton defender Jonathan Fortune. At 5pm I walked to the underground platform and was then overtaken by uncontrollable bouts of sickness. I covered a large area of the platform with vomit and commuters were giving me a wide berth as they walked past in disgust. Next day Kim drove me to Chris's to pick the car up.

This Western Sandpiper was found by C. Thain and stayed from 29th September to 15th October. It was admired by 1,600 birders and £3,000 was raised for conservation work.

An American Yellow Warbler was found on 2nd October on Barra in the Outer Hebrides. It was found by Stuart Rivers, one of the Barrabirders. They were formed in 2002 and go to Barra every year with the mission to put Barra on the birding map. This American Yellow Warbler is the 4th for Britain and certainly achieves that.

The earliest I could leave work was Wednesday 6th October. I teamed up with my good friend Steve Nuttall, the late John Taylor from Staffs and Lee Evans. The long drive to Oban wasn't incident free. I let John take over the driving and everything was fine for a couple of hours but then he misjudged a junction, got into a skid and I decided it was time for me to go back to driving duties. We arrived at Oban at 4am and managed a few hours' sleep. The ferry was leaving at 9am and everybody purchased a ticket apart from Lee, who wanted to make sure the warbler was seen before handing over the £22. We got positive news a minute before sailing and Lee just made it.

The crossing took 5 hours and 2 minutes. As soon as we docked, we jumped into a taxi to Brevig. We watched the American Yellow Warbler from 3:45pm - 4:45pm. It was performing a circuit involving three gardens and perched mainly on purple flowered Hebes. We booked a taxi to Aird Mhor, ferry to Eriskay, bus to South Uist and stayed the night at the Borrodale Hotel (01878-700444) at £35 a night and had a few pints with the evening meal. On the Friday morning, we left Lochboisdale at 9:20am and arrived at Oban at 3pm. This was a very exciting twitch and to see this American gem on its last day for £112 each made it even more special.

When you live in Sussex and a good bird turns up on Fair Isle and you can't go, you just pray it does the decent thing and leaves. At 11am on Friday 15th October a Chestnut-eared Bunting was found by Hywel Maggs. The next day it was still there and some expensive charter flights took to the air. Kim has told me on numerous occasions 'We can't afford plane charters'.

During the weekend I had a chat with Lee Evans, who told me he had seen it. He never spends big and his flight cost was probably a quarter of what normal charters cost. He was only prepared to give me the pilot's number if I kept it secret. I got the number and rang up the pilot after work on Monday. He was happy to fly me and two others from Wick onto Fair Isle Tuesday morning.

Superb news, I just needed to find two others. I put an advert out on RBA and quickly arranged to take John Archer and Bob Watts. I picked them both up in my Escort at 9pm at Luton and started the 634-mile journey to Wick. The pilot didn't like to answer his phone, and it took quite a few attempts to get through to him. The pager announced at 8:05am that the Chestnut-eared Bunting was still in an oat crop near the South Lighthouse at Sakadden.

Our pilot landed at Wick at 9:05am and we were airborne at 9:35. Forty minutes later we landed on Fair Isle, and Holly from the observatory whizzed us down to the oat field. We hung around for an hour with no sign of the bunting. Our pilot wanted to go back, and Holly asked Deryk Shaw, the warden, if it was OK to flush the Bunting. Deryk agreed and I managed to flush it. It landed on a nearby raised bit of ground and all 9 twitchers on site managed to get good scope views. I was able to see its chestnut cheek patch and partially hidden chestnut breast band for a good minute before it flew back into the copse and vanished.

We left the site at 11:40am and flew back to Wick. On the journey south we had a fish supper, and I could only manage driving for an hour before I handed over car to Bob to drive. I lay across the back seats with no seat belt on and fell asleep. Bob also fell asleep driving past Blair Atholl on the A9. It was getting dark, and Bob woke up instantly when the car mounted the crash barrier at 70mph. The car bounced off and Bob heroically steered us across the A9, narrowly missing all the oncoming traffic, and prevented the car from flipping. The second barrier we hit eventually brought the car to a halt. There would have been several thousand pounds of crash barrier damage. Nobody was injured, but this could have easily spelled the end to all our twitching careers, even our lives. All three of us were zonked out after a fish supper and we didn't obey the unwritten rule that the front passenger should keep the driver awake with constant chit chat.

I rang Kim up shortly after, and she seemed more concerned about the damage to the car than us. I guess she didn't realise how lucky we were to be alive.

We waited an hour for Green Flag to come to our rescue. They did an amazing job. They changed drivers halfway and the new driver dropped John and Bob back at Luton and took my car to a garage in Rowfant. I was able to walk to work for 9am. The impact of the crash pushed both wheels on the driver's side out of alignment and my garage said the car had to be written off. Bob agreed it was his fault and paid £400 towards the cost of a new car, with John paying £100.

The Chestnut-eared Bunting stayed till the 20th

October and an estimated 120 birders connected.

Being carless forced to me to get a new one in a hurry, so on Monday 25th October I visited Shoreham Car Auctions and came away with a Ford Mondeo. That day an Ovenbird was found in pines at Innisidgen Hill on St. Marys. I got a lift to Penzance from Owen Mitchell, a retired policeman. The journey down Wednesday morning was horrendous. Strong gales and rain battered the car and we really feared the Ovenbird wouldn't make it through the night.

At 8:15am we caught a British International Sikorsky S61 from Penzance and found all 26 seats occupied by birders. Taxis picked us up at the airport and drove us near to Innisdgen. The Ovenbird was found the moment we stepped out of the taxi, and the views were breath-taking. It was walking over birders' feet to feed; the wind was still strong and it got blown over a few times. I watched it to 3pm, as many wandered off to look for a Waxwing. The Ovenbird was found by J.C. Harding and was taken into care the following day and died. It was the 4th record for Britain, with Ireland having 2. The last twitchable one was back in 1990 on Dursey Island, County Cork.

Tom Glass found an unfamiliar Shrike at 11:00am on the 29th October at Kilrenny Common in Fife. The next day the bird was relocated at 9am and tentatively put out as a Woodchat Shrike. Ken Shaw arrived at 10am and wondered why

Ovenbird
Seiurus aurocapilla
St Marys : Trenoweth
27th October 2004

G BAGNELL

it couldn't be a Masked Shrike. Permission was granted to trap the bird and it was confirmed as Masked Shrike at 4:08. I drove up that night and next morning couldn't believe the hundreds of cars that were already parked up. The 1st winter Masked Shrike came out of hiding at 8:15am showing its slim bill, large white wing panel, grey-black back, white forehead, black tail and white coverts. I headed south at 10am and couldn't find the Siberian Stonechat at Redcar. This Masked Shrike was a first for Britain and it stayed till the 14th November.

SUMMARY - 2004

During 2004, I travelled 12,617 miles in Britain and Ireland in the pursuit of new birds and managed to increase my list by 11 BOU/IRBC species. This took my British and Irish list to 417 species. The Combined Official stood at 575, and I was now up to 72.5%. There were two net additions to the Official British List during the year: Audouin's Gull (2003), Black Lark (1984), and Long-tailed Shrike (2000), minus the Western Olivaceous Warbler (1961,1962) which was removed.

Seeing the Icterine Warbler that year put me on 262 of the Shell Guide regulars and just left the Long-tailed Skua.

That year the internet began to revolutionise birding. People could surf the web and find a photograph of a rare bird that had just been found. Surfbirds offered a brilliant birding website with many photographs and birders sharing their personal lists, and Birdforum was a great place to find golden nuggets of information if embarking on a twitch. Lots of birders had begun to keep their own websites, and information was now available to the masses.

For the non-football fans out there, Arsenal now held the longest unbeaten run in English football. Between 16th August 2003 and 16th October 2004, they were unbeaten in 49 games. This run came to an end on 24th October when Manchester United won 2-0 at Old Trafford with goals from Rooney and van Nistelrooy.

I decided the most important bird seen during the year was the Ovenbird on the Scillies. Watching it for six hours pecking at people's feet was so special. I couldn't stop the tears when the news of its death came through.

CHAPTER 7

2005

The site at Rowfant was quite large. Opposite the main building was another building that had a large mechanical workshop. The workshop once employed lots of fitters and they used to play darts in the canteen above it. Sadly, the fitters had gone, and the dartboard hadn't been used since.

Peter Webster from finance was also a member of the Colas Social Club and decided to hold an interdepartmental darts elimination tournament. This was a superb idea, and with it in mind I got a darts board fitted in the kitchen at Rusper. I used to play Andrew at 501 and practise by myself. In one practice game on Sunday 13th February I got my first ever 180 with 3 darts sitting snugly in the treble 20s. This felt amazing and I even took a photograph to celebrate this achievement. I eventually moved down the board to 19s and never went back.

The Colas darts tournament was a big success with over 40 people signing up to represent their departments. That year the finance team comprised Darren Butler, Natalie Wren and me. We even won the tournament. This kickstarted lunchtime darts for anybody who wanted to play.

We always have to be alert for mischievous individuals who might try to cause mass panic with the twitching community by putting out a Belted Kingfisher in say, Staffs, on April 1st. There hasn't been a twitchable BK in Britain since the long-staying Sladesbridge bird of 1979, and many needed it. Every year there seems to be a hoax, but on this occasion, I rang Steve Nuttall and he said, 'Gaz, this bird is 100% pukka'.

The Belted Kingfisher was reported over a canal at midday but flew east towards Shugborough Park at 12:10pm. It was seen until dusk. I decided to save half a day's leave and go up the next day with BBC Sports news supremo John Lees. We left Rusper at 2am and there must have been 1,000+ birders at Shugborough at first light. You didn't need to look at the pager to know whether the BK was still about – all the long faces told the story.

Then news came through that it had been seen at Eastrington ponds at 12:14pm. I've never seen a car park clear so quickly. Dougal Gysi jumped in with us and we headed north-east – for 105 miles. It took 2 hours to get there and we found Westfield Lane blocked with cars parked in all directions. Again, there was no sign of the kingfisher since the earlier report, but we wandered around and saw a nice Garganey as consolation.

By Tuesday the 5th, the BK had moved and was found 372 miles further north on the River Dee at Peterculter, Aberdeenshire. I made my excuses with work and headed up overnight with my National Grid buddy John Benham, plus Ian Barnard and Steve Pink. There was no sign at first light but 30 minutes later at 6:30am it was located 400 yards downstream. Over the next two hours, we watched it with beaming smiles – I hadn't realised it would be the size of a Jackdaw. We had a big greasy fry-up before heading home. My friend John Lees went on Saturday 9th and came home empty handed. It was claimed that day by one lucky observer at 5:45am in the pitch black.

The BK was the 3rd for Britain and found by Roger Broadbent in Shugborough and refound by Katy and Joyce Landsman on the River Dee. Joyce informed two local birdwatchers and Ian Broadbent and Harry Scott saw it that evening. Remarkably, Ian was Roger Broadbent's son.

The spring wasn't over. I managed to see Britain's 2nd Barrow's Goldeneye on the Ythan estuary on 13th May and closer to home was Britain's 8th Trumpeter Finch, found by Lee Woods at Landguard on 21st May.

Terns have been one of my favourite bird families since my childhood encounter with them in Pagham harbour. Seeing 1.3m Sooty Terns on the Seychelles cemented my love for this family. I personally don't think you can see a much better bird in Britain than a Sooty Tern. An adult one was found at Rhosneigr in Anglesey on 5th July and moved to the Skerries by 7th July. I turned to the internet and searched for companies who were prepared to charter boats in NW Wales and found a guy called Aubrey who owned a rigid inflatable boat, RIB for short. Aubrey claimed he could get to the Skerries in 15 minutes from Holyhead, whereas most boats would take almost 40 minutes to get out there.

The Sooty Tern was seen on the 8th and that night Ian Barnard picked up John Lees, Christian Melgar and me. The RIB could take eight, so I offered four spaces to Steve Nuttall, and he quickly filled them. By the time Aubrey got out to the Skerries at 6am there were already ten charter boats searching the group of rocky islands. The Sooty Tern was reported to have roosted on the Skerries from 8:30pm the previous evening and there was a report that it had also flown out to sea. However, there was no sign of it in the morning. Boats had arrived from 5am and searched the island to 2pm. We stayed around the Skerries until 9:45pm. During our time out there we had magnificent views of 2 Roseate Terns, 300+ Arctic Terns, and 100+ Puffins, to name but a few of the highlights.

Back on the mainland, we started our search from Rhosneigr at Ynys Feirig RSPB. The reserve is a long island strip which can be viewed at a range of 1.5 miles. We stayed there 4 hours, but the only good bird was a brunette in a green bathing costume. South Stack had 20+ Chough feeding close on the approach road and it was good to see 6 Black Guillemots at Holyhead Harbour.

Time was getting on and we now thought there was no chance of the Sooty Tern being relocated. We left Anglesey at 6pm and Ian Barnard started the six-hour drive home. At 7pm my mobile rang – it was Mark Lopez excitedly saying that Richard

Bonser had relocated the bird back on the Skerries. Ian turned the car around immediately and drove as fast as possible back to Holyhead.

I was feeling extremely stressed and rang Aubrey to see if we could re-book the RIB. We could, and we'd be back at Holyhead in 30 minutes. I agreed to be there by 8pm. I rang RBA to advertise 4 spaces on our boat. In a 3-minute period we had 10 calls, and I gave them to Andrew Lawson's party from Kent and cancelled the advert with RBA.

Andrew got to our boat before us, and they had to wait 25 painful minutes for us to arrive. We arrived at 7:55pm and by 8:15 we were with three other boatloads of birdwatchers watching the Sooty Tern sitting in a Kittiwake colony. I managed a record shot before we left the tern at 9pm. On the way back we saw another boat chugging its way to the Skerries.

Be careful about booking your boat, as some of the boats are illegal and they are asking up to £35 each per passenger for a 3-hour trip, giving only an hour on the Skerries. We found our boatman the best value for money with a 4-hour trip costing just £150 and able to take 9 people.

The Sooty Tern crossed the Irish Sea to visit nearby Rockabill for a couple of days on 11th July. It was mainly seen at Cemlyn Bay intermittently to 26th Jul and from 7th to 15th August it was seen in County Down. It was last seen at Strumble Head on the 23rd of August. This represented the 13th record for Britain since 1950 and the 2nd for Ireland.

One good tern deserves another... Paul Lee found a Lesser Crested Tern in Norfolk whilst walking his dog and RBA mega-alerted It at 7:23am. The last twitchable Lesser Crested Tern was 'Elsie', which returned to the Farne Islands every summer between 1984 and 1997, and many thought this would remain a big blocker on their lists. I headed to Norfolk with Ian Barnard at 9am on Saturday 16th July with little expectation of seeing the tern, but we both felt it was better to be in Norfolk than Sussex with such a rare bird on the loose. We birded the Norfolk interior and at 4:45pm father and son team Geoff and Alan Clewes saw the tern flying west at Overstrand. My heart was pumping and it felt good that we were in Norfolk and a shame we were an hour away from the coast. We got to Cley at 5:45pm, 11 minutes after Andy Stoddard had seen it. There was a chance it might go to the Blakeney Point Sandwich Tern colony. I walked for an hour and a half each way, but as suspected it was impossible to get views into the 1600-strong colony unless permission was granted.

Ian and I decided to spend the night in Norfolk. We got up Sunday morning around 4:15am and started sea watching at Cromer. At 5:40am my Sussex compatriot Ian 'lucky bugger' Barnard found it flying east; Alan & Geoff Clewes managed to get views as well. But I got into a total panic and ran around like a headless chicken. I ran over to where Ian was sitting, had a scan with my bins and saw three terns. The Lesser Crested Tern was one of them, but when I got to it my scope was pointing into the sun and I just didn't get enough to tick. The other three were celebrating.

Ian spent the rest of the day feeling the way I wanted to feel, but he was quite prepared for a gruelling day for me to see this bird. Later that morning I met a guy called Ben whose local patch was Overstrand. Ian and I teamed up with Ben and we went searching for the tern. Ben had a hunch that it would not go as far as the rocks at Sea Palling.

So off we trek – no sign. Ben had to head back and attend a barbecue and we drove back towards Cromer for maybe a chance of an evening flypast. The bird was seen at Happisburgh between 9:20 and 9:30am. At this stage we were slightly NW of it so we decided to stay put. For the next 2.5 hours pager messages of possible sightings were coming in. Finally we saw the Lesser Crested Tern at Waxham and I could breathe a sigh of relief. We watched it sit on the rocks till 1pm and finally felt ready to go home. The Lesser Crested Tern stayed in East Anglia till 22nd July and represented the 9th record for Britain.

My mum, Kim, Georgie and I were invited to stay at my sister Chantal's home in Verchocq, Northern France. The main purpose of the trip was to attend the first communion of Chantal's eldest boy, Louis. The only time I had met Chantal and husband Yves was when they had visited Folkestone back in 1993. Now I was in a healthy relationship I was looking forward to getting to know her. She had no kids back in 1993, but now she Louis, aged 11, Remi, 9, Henry, 7 and Paul, 6 months old.

The communion was held at Wicquinghem church. Unfortunately the only French I had learned from school was how to say hello, count to 20, order a coffee in a café and a couple of swear words from the naughty kids in the class. None of this came in useful on this occasion, but I felt privileged to be there all the same.

Once the service was finished, the church emptied, and I wandered across to the village hall and thought it would be a nice touch to give Chantal a video of people arriving in the hall before the music starts. I videoed everybody arriving and was saying 'Bonjour' to them and they were smiling at me and saying 'Bonjour' back. I must have been in there 5 minutes, and none of Chantal's or my family had arrived. I carried on videoing, then somebody came up to me and spoke a couple of sentences in French and pointed me towards the door. I wandered to the door and outside were Chantal, mum and Kim. As soon as they saw me,

they burst out laughing. Chantal said, 'You've been videoing the wrong communion, we're all in the building next door!'

I felt like a fool, but after that faux pas we all had a splendid time at Louis' communion. We must have eat seven courses of food, aperitifs, beer and wine. I was getting dragged up to do various French dances by different women and Kim was getting dragged up by different men. We were made to feel so welcome and we were already getting to like the French culture. The three days went quickly. The feeling I got from being with Chantal and her family was the beginning of something special that we both cherish.

Meanwhile, back in Britain, the most frequent American Wood Warbler we get is the Blackpoll Warbler. One was found on St. Agnes on 27th September. I had never seen an American warbler in Britain and Ireland and decided to advertise car spaces on RBA. John Benham replied, and I agreed to pick him after waiting for the match between Liverpool and Chelsea to finish in a disappointing goalless draw. I managed a couple of hours' sleep in the dark car park of Drift Reservoir. We saw a juvenile Long-billed Dowitcher and after that I had a phone call asking if I still had the room to rent in London. I said, 'Sorry you must have the wrong number'. Then I got another call about this flat. I must have got 100 calls during the time I saw the Dowitcher, sailed on the *Scillonian* and got the 12:30 inter-island boat to St. Agnes. These calls were a real nuisance, and I couldn't cancel the advert on Gumtree, so I had no choice but to turn my phone off. I suspect this might have been another birder trying to have a laugh. The rent was a bargain and had the desired effect of me getting thousands of calls. Whoever did it, I'd just like to say 'Thanks for trying to ruin my day'. The

Blackpoll Warbler was ticked off at the parsonage at 12:40pm, with bonus birds including a Baird's Sandpiper on St. Agnes and a Sora on St. Mary's.

The Blackpoll Warbler was found by D. Page and D. Price on the 27th September. It stayed on St. Agnes to 30th September and was relocated on St. Marys from 3rd October to 3rd November. There are 34 records on the British list. During 2005, a further two were found, both one-dayers, one on Skye and the other on South Uist. This bird laid to rest the spring Seaforth bird of 2000 which I had decided to twitch, then changed my mind. Since then, there has only been a 4-day bird in South Uist in 2003, which I decided against going for.

I managed to see a Green Heron in Schull harbour, Cork, with Watford-based train driver Mick Frosdick and ace bird finder Lee Gregory. We saw it on 11th October, and it represented the 1st for Ireland and the 5th for Britain. Great to get this bird back after missing the Messingham Sands bird of 2001 whilst in Tenerife with David and Gary.

On Saturday 29th October, Hurricane Wilma brought two Chimney Swifts to Sherkin Island and one to Cape Clear. The following day one was found at Clonakilty, one at Baltimore and another on the Scilly Isles. A bonus Yellow-rumped Warbler was also found on Cape Clear. Not knowing how long these Swifts were going to stay, I made the decision to head to Ireland as opposed to Scilly.

On Monday 31st October, I teamed up with Mick Frosdick again and got an Easy Jet flight from Gatwick (£104 return) to Cork. We arrived in Cork at 9am, met up with rare bird alert employee Stuart Piner and hired a car. Everybody was buzzing with excitement. Stuart & I were so excited about the trip that neither of us managed to get any sleep the night before.

While driving the car out of the compound Chris Batty informed Stuart Piner that the Myrtle Warbler was still present on Cape Clear. Hoorayyyy!!! Remember that back then, pagers didn't work in Ireland and smartphones hadn't been invented.

On the way to the ferry at Baltimore, we stopped at Connaugh Village and Clonakilty to check for yesterday's Chimney Swifts. Unfortunately, there had been no sign of them at either. Still feeling upbeat, we all decided at this stage that the Myrtle Warbler was the rarer of the two and we would always have another chance to go for the Scillies Chimney Swift if we failed in Ireland. Onwards and upwards!

As we neared Baltimore we heard that there were no Chimney Swifts there either. Well at least we should get a Myrtle Warbler in the bag… Mick spoke to Harry Hussey and found that a special boat charter had been arranged to visit the Cape from Schull. The boat was due to leave at 11:30am and come back around 5:00pm. This seemed like a good option considering that the scheduled service from Baltimore would involve an overnight stay, so we decided to go on the charter.

On arrival in Schull, we met up with the 15 Irish lads and boarded the boat. The journey to the Cape took about 45 minutes. On approaching the harbour, we saw a birder scoping a bird in the harbour. Was it the Warbler? After a 200-metre walk to the birder we found it was a Grey-cheeked Thrush. Wow – and just three metres range.

The 18 birders spent less than a minute with the thrush and proceeded to where the warbler was seen last. Five minutes later I arrived at the site to find some people were pointing and giving scope directions. Adrenaline kicked in. I hastily took my rucksack off my back a little too quickly as all the straps had perished and they snapped with my pent-up energy. I got the scope set up on what everybody was looking at – a flaming Rock

Pipit. The Myrtle Warbler had apparently been on show for 90 minutes from 9am, then had hopped into someone's garden and had not been seen since our arrival on the Island at 12:30. Never mind, I thought, our large group and five birders staying on the Cape would have a good chance to relocate the warbler before our 5pm return. It sadly never showed, but there was a nice Grey Phalarope within a 2-minute walk. We ended the day back with the Grey-cheeked Thrush.

On the boat back to Schull, news broke of 3 Chimney Swifts at Courtmacsherry. At this stage the good news was that our plane was departing Cork on Tuesday back to Gatwick, so at least we had a chance of these reported birds.

Next morning, we spent a good hour looking for the Blue Clearwater sign on the crossroads between Courtmacsherry and Broad Strand. This was the exact point the swifts had been seen the previous night. Eventually we found it. It was in a new housing estate that we must have driven past 5-6 times. But were the birds there? No, so we drove to the beach at Courtmacsherry and had a scan. Stuart Piner shouted out 'I've got them!' I had a mini heart attack, and I couldn't see the birds for love or money as the shakes had kicked in. Mick got them and said, 'Get onto them quickly, they're getting higher and higher – they seem to be leaving.' At this stage, I screamed 'Give me a bloody landmark!' Someone said they were near the telegraph pole. I eventually found the right telegraph pole and hugged Stuart for finding these little beauties with his incredibly sharp eyesight.

We watched the 3 Chimney Swifts for the next 2-3 hours. They were simply amazing with their unusual flight action. They seemed to fly like bats and resembled the shape of a Stealth fighter plane. On occasions, all three birds were in the same telescope field of view. I tried to get some photographs, but because these birds flew so fast, I could only manage shots of white clouds in a blue sky. Then I discovered sports mode on the camera. I practised on a Jackdaw and managed to get a snap of it, then I managed to get a Chimney Swift in the top left-hand corner of the picture. The rest of the day was spent looking for American Golden Plovers and American Wigeon, though we settled for a Lesser Yellowlegs. What a trip – magic! I got home at 11pm Tuesday night.

It was estimated that 10 Chimney Swifts were in this Irish influx. The Courtmacsherry birds found by J. Crowley and Peter Wolstenholme stayed two more days to the 3rd November and brought the Irish records up 17. I would also have been able to twitch the Scillies Chimney Swift at Trenoweth on Monday 31st. It stayed loyal to the site from 8:07am to at least 4pm and was refound on the 2nd of November at the Parsonage on St. Agnes. In 2005 Britain had 6 Chimney Swifts, bringing the total to 19 records. This was the first twitchable one since the 1999 two-dayer at Rame in Cornwall. Our 2005 records of Chimney Swift pale into insignificance if you compare the 112 estimated on the Azores that autumn.

Jim Dowdall found a Myrtle Warbler in Cotter's Garden on the 30th, and it was last seen on the morning of the 31st October. It became the 11th record for Ireland.

Then on 30th November a Brünnich's Guillemot was found by M. Heubeck and R. M. Mellor at Lerwick on Shetland. I was too busy at work to go immediately, and my first available day was Saturday. I decided to charter a return plane from Blackpool to Sumburgh (please don't tell Kim, she's unlikely to read this book...) Advert out on the pager and by Friday all seats were taken. I drove up Friday night with James Hunter and Bob Watts. Mike and Jane Malpass joined us en route, whilst Phil Ball, Ian Kendall, Andrew Self and Anne Lawson met us at the airport.

We flew from Blackpool in the dark and landed at Sumburgh. When we arrived I hired a minibus and drove everybody to Lerwick, including the pilot. We could not see the Brünnich's Guillemot on arrival but an employee at the Ferry terminal said he had seen it on the Bressay side. We decided to check his story out and got the next ferry to Bressay, then walked north up the Bressay Sound and there sitting on the sea was the guillemot. I noticed the white line on the bill and the clean white flanks, whereas the Common Guillemot has black streaking on the white flanks. The white belly extends to a point on the throat where it joins its black head. This feature is blunter in Common Guillemots. This was the 37th record, and it stayed to 20th December.

December was on fire. I saw Britain's 5th American Buff-bellied Pipit at Frampton RSPB on the 13th, found by Paul French. Then I had a 7-day family holiday to Lanzarote, where we saw Houbara Bustards, and I did a boat trip to Fuerteventura, where I saw a Chat, Lesser Short-toed Lark, Black-bellied Sandgrouse and Barbary Partridge. Back home on 29th December I wasted no time in driving overnight with Steve Webb to see a 1st winter male Black-throated Thrush at Stoke St. Gregory, Somerset.

SUMMARY - 2005

During 2005, I travelled 11,842 miles in Britain and Ireland in the pursuit of new birds and managed to increase my list by 16 BOU/IRBC species. This took my British and Irish list to 433. The Combined Official stood at 579 species, and I was now up to 74.8%. There were four additions to the Official British and Irish List during the year: Black Scoter (split), Yellow-legged Gull (split), Purple Martin (2004) and Taiga Flycatcher (split).

I decided that the most important bird seen during the year was the Lesser Crested Tern in Norfolk. Driving four hours for a seabird on the coast is always a risky strategy. I started birding in 1997 and that was the last time Elsie graced our shores, so getting another opportunity to connect with this species was too good to miss. What a rollercoaster of emotions this twitch alone turned out to be.

Lesser Crested Tern
Thalasseus bengalensis
Warham, Norfolk
17th July 2005
G. BAGNELL

CHAPTER 8

2006

The 0.97ha Stanwell Moor Coating plant is only 200 metres from Junction 14 of the M25 and on the 30th March 2004 it ceased operations. The plant was removed in 2004 and after extensive soil testing Colas needed to turn the land back into greenbelt, which meant replacing 0.4m of contaminated soil with subsoil and topsoil and planting hedgerows.

The closure brought good news and bad news. The bad news was that David Browne, Colin, Ginnie, Denise and the plant operatives were all going to made redundant and the good news was that I was safe. It felt like a sketch from 'The Office'. I was only safe because a Management Accountant called Ted Hood was retiring, and because we were both based at head office it was easy for me to learn his roles of accounting for Fibredec and the Plant and Transport division.

The Fibredec process is like surface dressing, but instead of putting a fresh layer on the road they make footpaths with a fibre added to the mix for strengthening. My new manager was a Geordie called Arthur Thompson who visited head office monthly. He was a popular figure at Rowfant and the directors adored him as his contracts never lost money. Arthur was due to retire in a few years and being a workaholic, it would be a hard transition for him.

The Plant and Transport division had workshops at Newcastle, Grantham and Birmingham, where they employed fitters whose sole purpose was to maintain the vehicles owned by Colas. Grantham held a lot of vehicle stock which I had the added responsibility to reconcile. I was expected to attend monthly meetings with site managers to discuss their accounts. Easy peasy. The manager for the division was Gary Condon.

Plane spotting was now a far distant memory for me, but somehow on the 24th February, I got tipped off to go to Heathrow Airport to see an aeroplane that hadn't visited Britain in 26 years, the same time as between the Shugborough and Wadesbridge Belted Kingfishers. The plane was a Libyan Arab Airlines Gulfstream Two, registered

5A-DDS. I drove up like a shot. I found it parked on the fuel farm and the Old Bill pulled up next to me and asked what I was doing. I was sure they were used to plane spotters, but I was so excited. I said, 'Just admiring one of the four remaining Gulfstream Twos that I've never seen before'. One good thing about birding, I've never been dragged away by the police from a twitch.

When a Calandra Lark mega alerted just before 7am on 12th May on the Isle of May, I wasn't sure what to do. The two Johns wanted to go. I had my arm twisted and headed north the moment Hove-based John Lees arrived in Rusper. I swung by Leatherhead to pick up John Benham and then travelled north without really knowing if there were any ways to get across to the island. The 100-seater May Princess (07957 585200) that sailed from Anstruther was undergoing maintenance and no other boats were replacing it. This news stopped most twitchers dead in their tracks. However, the so called 'Georgie Michael of birding' came up trumps. He managed to secure an 8-seater RIB to cross 5 miles of the Firth of forth. We took 4 spaces each with Steve Nuttall jumping in when I passed Staffs.

Today were the FA Cup finals, and we had been listening on the radio to see how John Lees' team, Liverpool, was doing against West Ham. When we arrived at Anstruther at 4:15pm, Liverpool was winning 2-1. 30 minutes later we got on off on the Isle of May and headed towards the lighthouse. There were Eider on the nest throughout the island and you had to be careful where you walked. We saw the Calandra Lark in flight and I made sure I clinched the characteristic dark underwings with white trailing edge. I managed to scope it on the deck at the helipad at 6:49pm, noting the orange legs, large conical bill, black and white collar and short tail. Back at Anstruther at 7:30pm, John heard on the radio that Liverpool was 3-3 with

extra time. They won 3-1 on penalties. To help John celebrate we found a fish and chip shop in Biggar.

It was also the day of the Scottish Cup Final, in which Hearts played Gretna at Hampden Park in Glasgow. This result ended at 1-1 and Hearts won 4-2 on a penalty shootout. Lots of happy Hearts fans were singing in the fish and chip shop and one guy happily handed me a crate of Tennents for the journey home.

The Calandra Lark was found by A. Newell and was the 13th record for Britain. It was successfully twitched on Sunday 14th May, but after that news was withheld for the rest of its stay. It was last seen on Wednesday 17th May.

Tuesday 13th June was my 39th birthday and to celebrate, I twitched a Eurasian Scops Owl in Thrupp, Oxfordshire. I watched it till 1am singing in a Horse Chestnut tree whilst it was spotlamped for a while, giving spectacular views. The bird had probably arrived on 21st April, when locals passed it off as a faulty alarm on a canal boat. The noise persisted and the locals concluded it might be a Scops Owl. Parish councillor David Clarke contacted Ian Lewington (Oxfordshire County recorder) on the evening of the 12th June and Ian went down with Nic Hallam, planning to have a drink at the Boat Inn if it turned out to be a false alarm. They met David Clarke at his house and walked along the canal at Thrupp. As soon as they walked past the pub, they could hear the owl calling. Ian pointed out that it would attract many admirers, but David Clarke was not keen on cars parking in Thrupp village. Eventually they agreed to release the news on 13th June and people were advised to park away from the village and walk in. On 13th June 60 twitchers turned up, but on the 14th the numbers swelled to 450, from all over Britain. It was estimated that between two and four thousand birders visited Thrupp over 17 days. The owl was last heard on 30th June.

A Black-browed Albatross returned to Sula Sgeir on 23rd May, originally discovered during 2005 by Guga hunters. Guga means young Gannet. Every year the Guga hunters visit Sula Sgeir for two weeks and have special permission to kill 2,000 young Gannets for food. This tradition has been going on for more than 60 years, and the hunters sleep in stone dwellings that their ancestors made.

Sula Sgeir is located 40 miles north of the Isle of Lewis and is very difficult to get to. It was possible to go on a 7-day cruise from Aberdeen that passes Sula Sgeir, but it cost nearly £1,000. I decided to ring up some fishing boats and see if they were up for a charter. All my requests were declined, but Simon King managed to find one who was prepared to give it a go. Every week Simon checked with the skipper to see if the forecast weather permitted a sailing, and the first window a sailing looked possible was five weeks later, on 30th June.

Ian Barnard picked me up at half past midnight and drove us to Catford, where we got into John Pedgen's car. John drove to the M6, and Ian and I took it turns to get us to Inverness. John was now suitably refreshed and drove like Michael Schumacher to Ullapool. We had an unsuccessful look for a Bridled Tern that been reported in the Minch.

We got to Kinlochbervie at the same time as the skipper and I couldn't resist a sneak preview of the boat, a 60-foot-long fishing trawler. I had to climb down the steps from the quay to the boat. Once aboard I went straight to the lower deck and found a TV, kettle, fridge, stove, dining table etc. I was really impressed how much could be crammed into a small space. Then I went down a further set of steps to the sleeping area, which had compartments for at least 9 people. To access them, you had to climb through a small opening in the wall and slide into a bunk bed. Each bed had a foam mattress and foam pillow.

Shortly after 7pm Simon King, Ron King and Trevor Every arrived from Hampshire. Geoff Clewes, Matt Mulvey and Dougie Bar arrived 30 minutes later. We loaded the vessel with scopes, picnics and handbags like one big human conveyor belt, with people in various positions all over the boat. The boat left promptly at 8pm, and some birded whilst other watched the Italy v Ukraine match. I watched the last 15 minutes and was starting to yawn, so I went back to the bunk, but I found it impossible to sleep. The boat was pushing me from side to side for the next five and half hours. At 3:30am many birders left their bunks and staggered around, trying to take a step without colliding into others.

At last Sula Sgeir was in sight. It looked like the island where Odysseus meet the Sirens. It was a tall rock 70 metres high and a mile long, covered in early morning mist. Looking at it sent a cold shiver down my spine.

As our boat got closer and closer to the island, we started to see white specks on the cliff, which were tens of thousands of Gannets. I was the first to find the Black-browed Albatross, which was sitting approximately 4m from a vertical cairn on top of the rock. This was the highest ledge on the rock, and it had fewer gannets than other ledges.

I watched the Albatross for the full hour and a half we were at the rock. The boat swayed constantly side to side the whole time we were out there, which prevented me from getting good telescope views. The swell was 2 to 4 metres, so viewing with binoculars was the best option. Views improved as the boat edged closer to the rock. The boat was only 100 metres out at one point. During my binocular views I observed the bird's long bill, eyebrow and long black wings. It was a pleasure to watch it fully extend its wings. The bird seemed to move a whole 360 degrees to get comfortable either by sitting or standing.

In the end, the swaying of the boat got the better of us. Three of us were now vomiting, Matt Mulvey, Duggie Bar and me. Fortunately, I did not have to admire the result for long as it was washed overboard every time the boat dipped.

Trevor gave me two sea-sickness tablets and I retreated to my bed. I went to sleep from 5:30am to 12:30pm, the boat docked at 1pm and I was very glad to reach dry land. That trip was hell, and I swear to you I will never be going to Sula Sgeir again on a fishing boat, even if they get a Yellow-nosed Albatross.

In mid-June, we decided to rent a villa in Malaga for 7 nights with a shared pool. Kim, Andrew, Greg (Andrew's friend), Georgie and my mum were going. Being 6 of us, we rented a minibus. The villa was owned by a Brit but rented out to holidaymakers. All the other people on the complex were English and residents. I don't think they were happy to see us arrive. The very first time we went into the pool, one of the female residents said, 'There are strict pool rules, and nobody is allowed to play ball, use lilos or inflatable toys'. This had not been made clear when we booked, and the same lady kept her beady eye on us all week. Thankfully my two-year-old daughter was allowed to wear armbands.

One day we decided to visit Gibraltar. It was a two-hour drive and when we got to the border we weren't allowed in as we had left the passports in the villa. We visited the picturesque Ronda instead. Ronda has three bridges, each 120 metres tall overlooking the Tajo canyon. If you don't like heights (like me) this is a scary place to go. A few days later we made sure we packed our passports

and this time we entered Gibraltar. There is a cable car to get to the 400-metre summit, but we decided to drive the minibus up. We got about halfway up and then the damn clutch broke. We phoned for help and were told we couldn't be rescued until the very end of the day, so we had to abandon the vehicle on the windy road.

We made our way to the summit, where there were some very sweet baby Barbary macaques. One of them jumped across us and stole Georgie's baseball cap from her head. She screamed and I shouted as I chased after the baby macaque and then a big daddy macaque grabbed me by the scruff of my neck. I froze and didn't know what to do. It felt like a scene from Planet of the Apes. Luckily the baby threw the cap back, but a few minutes later as I was admiring the vista another macaque grabbed my sandwich out of my hand. I was certainly glad to see a replacement minibus at the end of the day.

I did see some new birds for my WP list including Griffon Vulture, Egyptian Vulture, White-rumped Swift, Scrub Robin, Thekla Lark, Short-toed Eagle, Purple Swamp hen and Rock Sparrow.

The last regular species in the Shell guide I needed was the Long-tailed Skua. When a juvenile was found at 5:48pm Saturday 9th September on Queen Mother Reservoir, I thought I was likely to triumph. I got there in 82 minutes and out in the middle of water was a very distant small dark morph skua. The next day I went back and hired a boat to take me for a closer look. This bird hung around to the 17th of September.

On Sunday 8th October, Maurice Hanafin and Seamus Enright visited Kilbaha to try and see a Red-eyed Vireo that Kilian Mullarney had found the previous day. They found the bird and Seamus stayed put to get a photograph whilst Maurice drove 300 metres up the road and stopped at Peter Gibson's farm.

At 4:45pm Maurice heard an unfamiliar sound and saw a golden-coloured warbler. Seamus clinched the ID as a Canada Warbler by thumbing through his Sibley guide. I set off and made my way to First Service Station at Newport to meet up with Ross Newham, Dougal Gysi and John Clements. Ross drove us to Fishguard and we caught the early sailing to Rosslare.

We saw the Canada Warbler just after arriving at 11:30am. I only saw it three times in total, but the last view was the best, lasting 5 minutes. The warbler appeared to be similar size to Chiffchaff, with a bright yellow throat, belly and flanks. It was brown from tail to head with a white vent and eye ring and vertical brown streaks forming a necklace. This warbler was very popular during its six-day stay and there must have been 100 admirers whilst I was there.

Twitching Ireland is getting more popular with the Brits, and it's nice that twitchers are now adopting a British and Irish list and realising how good Ireland is for attracting Yanks (American birds).

The Canada Warbler was the first for Ireland and the 20th different species of American Wood Warbler for Britain and Ireland. Unfortunately, it was not new for the Western Palearctic as the Azores had had one.

Back to work on Tuesday and that evening I was twitching again. This time I drove to Filey and saw the Two-barred Greenish Warbler sub-species at Filey. I made it to the office on Thursday and had a quick catch-up call with Ian Barnard. Whilst on the phone the Mega Alert started bleeping. I read the thrilling words MEGA-ALERT and after a few minutes it read 'MEGA HERMIT THRUSH CO. CORK'.

Sadly, Ian has never been tempted by the lure of Ireland, so I thought it would be interesting to know what Lee had to say about it. I rang him and he said something like this: 'You've got no chance of seeing it... it was only seen briefly by a few birders... it needs to develop a pattern before you can see it!'

I just said 'fine, I'm still going for it, do you want to come? Lee said, 'Possibly, I need to investigate further.'

John Lees would have love to have come to get a grip back on the last one Scilly had in 1993. He just got the Tresco bird in flight as it disappeared into cover, and decided not to count it. But he was on Scilly, so I picked up Essex-based Dave Webb, Mick Frosdick and Lee at junction 7 of the M4. Dave shared an old story about when his 11-year-old son Adrian found a Long-billed Dowitcher at Dungeness. The resident warden did not believe him and refused to check the sighting out. The Dowitcher miraculously then flew into full view of the warden, who said, 'It could be a Short-billed Dowitcher'. No hint of congratulations, but then the Webbs were informed by the reserve staff of a much rarer species in Essex. This was a Cream-coloured Courser which spent four days at Hadleigh in 1984. They both saw it the next day.

We arrived at Fishguard at around 1am and had plenty of time to kill. The day return to Ireland was still a bargain at £19. On the Stena Ferry there are lots of places to sleep. We opted for the bar area. I had a traditional English breakfast for £9 in the restaurant and found our sleeping corner had been nabbed by Richard Bonser and Richard Stephenson. Trying to sleep was close to impossible. Some extremely drunk 40-year-old northern lass was singing a crapella to her 60-year-old shellsuit-wearing lover. I and others asked her to be quiet, but she was gone too far to grasp our request. She looked quite attractive from where we were lying, but a closer inspection revealed she was a BOBFOC (body off Baywatch, face off Crimewatch). I suspected they were going to have a romp, but fortunately for the 57 people in the bar area they both fell asleep, and we all had peace and quiet.

The ferry arrived an hour later than schedule at 7:10am and this hampered our chances of getting to Baltimore for the 11am scheduled Cape Clear boat. We went to the Budget desk to pick up our hire car at 7:25am. We had to wait for it to open, giving us a further 20-minute delay. Mick and Lee's stress levels were starting to build.

The wacky races then got underway for three car crews to get to Baltimore. Lee arrived at 11:40am with gold, Richard Bonser few seconds later collecting silver and Neil Alford got there at midday and took bronze. We had missed the charter boat by an hour, but Neil managed to get another one costing €25 each. We got to Cape Clear at 12:50, and 13 of us got off the boat and started walking towards the Post Office Garden. Lee had arranged a lift with the warden, Steve Wing. He was waiting at the quay for Lee and some Irish lads. Mick and Dave thumbed a lift and the rest of us endured the 20-minute uphill walk from quay.

The Hermit Thrush was sitting on the fence on arrival. We had gorgeous scope views for 4 mins and then it vanished. It was relocated by Neil Alford 30 minutes later nearby. This time we watched in awe for 20 minutes before it flew off. We departed the Cape at 2:20pm and got the 9:15pm ferry back from Rosslare.

I really must go to Cape Clear for a birdwatching holiday one day. The observatory costs €18 a night and only a handful of birders stay on the island. It was one of the few golden weeks this hobby occasionally gives us, seeing three top-class birds in just five days.

John Lees had a nice time on Scilly, but missing these birds must have been hell to watch for his partner Liz.

On Tuesday 7th November, Dave Hopkins discovered what he believed to be a Little Auk swimming close inshore just inside Langstone Rock at Dawlish Warren, Devon. Pictures were uploaded to Dawlish Warren website and a link was put on Birdforum on Friday 10th to see what others made of the photographs. The picture overwhelmingly resembled a Murrelet, either a Marbled Murrelet or the migratory Long-billed. Luckily Kevin Ryland refound it 4 days later, 100 metres offshore from Dawlish. The news was put out at 8:39am. I got to the site at 1:40 to find that this was most definitely the biggest twitch I had ever witnessed. There were already 500 birders lined up the length of the southwest coastal path and pier, and more were arriving ever minute. It was a Long-billed Murrelet, and it was constantly diving when I arrived. Around 2:40pm it stopped diving and drifted further out to sea.

The main feature to separate the Long-billed Murrelet from the Marbled is the amount of white around the neck. Marbled almost have enough white to form a complete collar. The Long-billed Murrelet was seen daily up to Tuesday 14th November. It represented the first record for Britain and the 2nd for the Western Palearctic. The first was a dead bird found on Lake Zürich in Switzerland in December 1997.

On Sunday 19th November I arrived at Holbeach Marsh at 7am and saw a 'lineatus' Black-eared Kite from 7:20am as it flew east towards Wash. I moved the car to a motorcycle scramble track and walked along the sea wall towards the black tower. From there I could see the kite perched in a tree. It then flew back towards my parked car.

Black-eared Kites show an extensive amount of white on the outer underwing primaries, with distinctive barring on the inner primaries. 'Western' Black Kites have very little white, if any at all, and the underwing appears quite dark, with indistinct barring on the inner primaries and reduced white bases to the outer primaries. The wing-formula of Black-eared differs from 'Western' Black Kites. The Black-eared has a broad and squarish wingtip, caused by a long sixth finger. On the 'Western' Black Kite the sixth primary is shorter. This creates a more rounded wingtip and the wing appears narrower on the whole, unlike the deeply splayed fingers of the Black-eared. Finally, Black-eared Kites of this age exhibit a pale rear underbody, whereas Western Black Kites show less contrast.

This Black-eared Kite was originally found on 2nd November and stayed to 13th April 2007, when it moved around the wash to Snettisham RSPB. This was the first record of this form in Britain, although it breeds over a wide area from western Siberia to China and Japan. Unfortunately, it's still a subspecies 16 years later and no rumours of it being split.

SUMMARY – 2006

During 2006, I travelled 8,381 miles in Britain and Ireland in the pursuit of new birds and managed to increase my list by 7 BOU/IRBC species. This took my British and Irish list to 440. The Combined Official total stood at 581 species, so I had now seen three quarters of them. There were two net additions to the Official British and Irish List during the year: Canada Warbler (2006), Rufous-tailed Robin (2004), Masked Shrike (2004) and the removal of the Moustached Warbler (1946).

Birding World had categorised vagrants into eleven divisions back in December 1990. They ranked the rarest (No.1), the Red-necked Nightjar to the White-winged Black Tern (No.258) as the commonest. In those days the combined British & Irish list stood at 533 species. The 1983 Shell Guide listed 263 species as regular. To make the analysis easier, I've added 14 species to the regular list (Little Egret, Purple Heron, White-tailed Eagle, Yellow-legged Gull, Buff-breasted Sandpiper, Pectoral Sandpiper, Sabine's Gull, Ring-billed

Canada Warbler
Cardellina canadensis
Kilbaha, Clare 9th October 2006

G BAGNELL

Gull, Bee-eater, Yellow-browed Warbler, Richards Pipit, Common Redpoll, Common Rosefinch and Hooded Crow) and removed the Savi's Warbler, which has gone back to a BBRC species. Therefore, regulars now numbered 276 (see table below).

So now we had 295 vagrants (581 less 276). My analysis was similar to the *Birding World* division, but my 10 vagrant columns put the species into Non-BBRC, 1 year, 2 year, 3 year, 4 year, 5 year, 10 year, 20 year, lifetime and Category B columns.

The table shows I had now completed the regulars after seeing the Long-tailed Skua this year, and then it went from 95% of the Non BBRC species to seeing 6% of the lifetime birds.

I decided the most important bird seen during the year was my second ever lifetime bird, the beautiful Canada Warbler found in Kilbaha. Everybody loves American wood warblers, don't they? There have now been 20 different species of them, the first being the Black-and-white Warbler in 1936. Then we had 3 in the 50s, 5 in the 60s, 4 in the 70s, 4 in the 80s, 1 in the 90s and 2 in the 2000s. Cape Clear's Blue-winged Warbler in 2000 and this year's Canada really put Ireland in a good position to get the 21st.

2006	Regular	Vagrant	BBRC/ IRBC 1 year	BBRC/ IRBC 2 year	BBRC/ IRBC 3 year	BBRC/ IRBC 4 year	BBRC/ IRBC 5 year	BBRC/ IRBC 10 year	BBRC/ IRBC 20 year	BBRC/ IRBC Lifetime	Cat B	Total
Seen	276	35	78	8	7	5	20	7	2	2	0	440
During	1		1	1	1	1		1		1		7
B&I Total	276	37	91	12	12	13	40	34	25	32	9	581
	100%	95%	86%	67%	58%	38%	50%	21%	8%	6%	0%	75.7%

CHAPTER 9

2007

This was another year that started with a foreign holiday, as we decided to have a cheapish winter sun break. My mum was up for it, and she joined Kim, Georgie and me, Kim's boys staying at her parents' farm. We flew from Gatwick to Marrakech on 20th January, hired a car at the airport and then drove to the Hotel Amine. The hotel was quite run down, and the food was unbelievably disgusting. On a positive note, there were House Bunting and Common Bulbuls in every direction you looked, the staff were pleasant, and we had a roof over our heads.

I decided to go off birding for a couple of days whilst the girls kept themselves busy and booked a tour of the souks. Just as I was leaving Marrakech a police officer flagged me down for speeding and handed me 400 dirhams (£24) fine. I only had 100 dirhams in cash, and he put it in his pocket and waved me on. Can't beat a crooked cooper, can you?

I drove 340km and arrived at Tamri on the 24th. I failed to see Bald Ibises leaving the roost, so I headed over to Cape Rhir to search. I did see two Moussier's Redstarts sitting on a prickly pear cactus, but no Bald Ibis. Just as I was losing the will to live, I showed a Berber a picture of a Bald Ibis and he jumped in my car and took me to the breeding cliffs. Unfortunately, again there were none there. My car got stuck in the sand. The Berber found a spade, but he failed to dig me out. He then asked an elderly sheep herder to help, but still the car would not budge. Then a young guy called Omomar Bilkadi turned up – he was an employee of Birdlife International and was monitoring the Bald Ibises. He managed to get my car out of the sand and better still, showed me 36 Bald Ibises at another site. We returned to the cliffs and he showed me a pair of Barbary Falcons, just as 16 Bald Ibises flew over. Wow! What a sight, what a place.

I left Tamri at 3pm and drove 425km to the Hotel La Perle du Sud (+212 24 88 86 40/41). This was a three-star luxury hotel, and the food was tasty. Next morning, I left the hotel and drove 169km to Tinerhir, where I overshot the

Tagdilt track by 60km and thought I saw a Desert Sparrow on the roadside. I turned the car around and eventually found the Tagdilt track. Here I saw Thick-billed Lark, White-crowned Black Wheatear, lots of Red-rumped Wheatears and a Temminck's Lark, but I had to retreat to my car when a pack of barking wild dogs hurtled towards me. I got back to Marrakech at 9:30pm.

The girls had a terrible time on the tour. They found it hard to keep up with the guide and he was taking them down narrow alleys full of leering men. Towards the end of the holiday my mum misjudged a kerb and fell over onto her arm. It was broken, so we spent the whole day in a Marrakech hospital waiting for it to be put in a cast. The experience in the hospital was awful. There must have been several hundred injured people with missing limbs covered in blood waiting in crowded corridors to be seen. Back in England, my mum's cast was cut off.

On the 12th of January, June Atkinson discovered a Pacific Diver on South Lake at Farnham Gravel Pits on the outskirts of Knaresborough. The gravel pits were owned by private members of Harrogate and District Naturalists' society and being the first for the Western Palearctic, it was decided to suppress the record, but the news was leaked to Yorkshire lister Garry Taylor. He contacted John McLoughlin and Martin Garner on 29th January and they all saw it. The news went out nationally at 10:36am. The following day access was available from midday. I arrived, paid the £10 entrance fee and watched the new bird. It resembled a Black-throated Diver, but the Pacific has a black chinstrap and lacks the white flank patch. I dropped into Bingley to see a wintering American Robin before going home.

At midday on Wednesday 28th February I was feeling poorly at work, so I drove home and went straight to bed. I had some form of flu, and I didn't leave my bed for 48 hours and was too ill to eat. I did get tipped off by Lee Evans that a Glaucous-winged Gull was just about to be mega'd in Camarthenshire. This bird had originally been found on 15th December 2006 by John Saunders at Gloucester landfill. It was cannon-netted and a blue Darvic ring with orange letter was fitted. Not wanting to get a big twitch, the news was held back and not released until January when the bird was long gone. This time Dominic Davidson went looking for an Avocet at Ferryside on 2nd March and found the same Glaucous-winged Gull with the blue ring.

When I arrived at Ferryside at 7am on 3rd March, 30 carloads of birders were already out and about searching. I had a kip for an hour and then joined the search from the car park. I guess there were now 300 twitchers about, and it felt like a dip was on the cards. I visited the café just over the Railway Bridge from Ferryside and enjoyed a full Welsh breakfast and a cup of coffee with a floating anchor pattern.

By 2pm people were getting restless. A few drove to Llys-y-Fran Reservoir in Pembrokeshire to look for Britain's second Pacific Diver, but many people went home. Then the most unlikely thing happened – people started running around and shouting 'The gull has been found!' Essex-based twitcher Les Holiwell got the kudos for finding it. Soon a 200-strong crowd was watching a very distant Glaucous-winged Gull. I saw it, but I couldn't see its blue ring, though I did see enough salient features to rule out Glaucous Gull. I watched the Gull for a further five minutes before it flew out of view. What a relief.

We left the Twyi estuary at 5pm and head for Cornwall, where we were overtaken by a group of birders and one famous passenger called Richard Bonser decided to moon at us. Nice view for my passengers.

We found a vacant B&B in Bodmin at 10:45pm and I ended up sharing a room with top snorer Chris Heard. B&Bs are such a waste of money when you vacate at 5:05am without eating, but seeing a Gyrfalcon in the pouring rain at Stepper Point made it worthwhile. My only waterproof clothing was a hi viz coat. I did get a few dirty looks from other birders wearing it. I watched the Gyr for three hours on a stone fence. It was nice to see a White-billed Diver, Spotted Sandpiper and Central Asian Lesser Whitethroat in Cornwall.

Christian Melgar got so drenched that he decided to travel home trouserless. I even got my naked bottom pinched whilst pulling up my pants in the toilets at Exeter Services. The door lock was broken, so it was probably an accident – I hope.

Kim wanted to go on a city break and suggested visiting Madrid. I thought it sounded perfect as she normally allows me a day to do my own thing. All I could think about was Bustards, Azure-winged Magpies and Spanish Imperial Eagles. She managed to find an apartment in the centre of the city and we booked and went. Just the four us flew to Madrid on Friday 20th April. We hired a car and then the fun began. Trying to find an apartment in a busy capital city with loads of one-way system with non-map readers was a challenge. Thankfully 12-year-old Andrew sussed that we were going around in circles and suggested we needed to park and walk to the apartment. He found a space and Andrew directed me back, but forgot to tell me to stop before I hit a steel post. Bang! The apartment was very pokey with a double bed and a pull-out sofa bed. Certainly I didn't get the view of a Madrid square depicted on the owner's website.

We got the Metro to Plaza De Toros Las Ventas. This is where the bullfighting takes place every Sunday at 7pm. I knew I wasn't going to enjoy it and after the first fight Georgie and left in disgust,

but Kim and Andrew watched all four fights. Bullfighting is a deeply rooted historical tradition, but I do hope it's outlawed in my lifetime.

On the Monday I went birding and headed to Trujillo for dawn. I heard singing Calandra Larks and Quail as the sun was rising. It was a magical place. New birds here included 11 Little Bustards, 1 male Great Bustard and 26 Azure-winged Magpies. Then I drove on to the Parque Nacional de Monfragüe. If you want raptors, this is the place to go. I had spotted 150 Griffon Vultures, 4 Black and 3 Egyptian Vultures before I got to the lookout tower. There were quite a few bird lovers there, and I wish I had investigated the excited individual who started shouting out a few words in Spanish. Later I was talking to an English-speaking guy who explained that the shouting was because a Spanish Imperial Eagle was flying over. Never mind, always next time. I did manage to see a pair of the Eagle Owls before nightfall. I really could have done with Andrew being with me on the way back. Back in Madrid, it took me three hours to find the ruddy apartment.

Wednesday 6th June Richard Hesketh was on Caerlaverock WWT reserve refuelling duties when he caught sight of a wader with long yellow legs. Richard got his scope and went to the Tower hide for a better look. Photographer Brian Morrell was contacted and passed some photographs onto Birdline Scotland, who promptly identified it as a White-tailed Plover.

It was too far north for me to see it on the first day, so I went there the next day for 4:15am, and it was a big relief when I clapped eyes on it from the Avenue Tower hide. It was feeding in a small pool and its strikingly long yellow legs were visible in the half light. Its small white tail was obscured whilst standing but could be seen when it swung its head around for food. It had a white face and a light brown cap on its head. In flight you could see the striking underwing pattern of black tips to all white wings. I departed at 7am and made sure I paid the £4.40 entrance fee.

This was the 5th record for Britain and many twitchers were delighted when it was re-found on the 10th June at Leighton Moss. Here it spent 8 days and my good friend John Lees managed to catch up with it.

Tony Phizacklea was counting young Common Eider ducklings at Walney Island on Thursday 14th June when he heard a Whimbrel call. He had a quick look and noticed it had a dark rump and a dark underwing. The bird was identified as a Hudsonian Whimbrel and the news was broadcast at 9:18pm. The next day the weather was atrocious, and it was not seen again till Saturday 16th between 1:45pm to 2:55pm, when it was flushed by a plane. I had previously missed this species at Goldcliff Lagoons on 6th -7th May 2000 and 3rd-4th May 2002. I arrived on Monday 18th at 6am and an hour and half later I connected. I watched it till 9:10am, noting the dark blue legs, broad white supercilium that joined behind the nape, brown rump, back and auxiliaries. A much whiter throat and head made this stand out from accompanying Eurasian Whimbrel. The bird stayed for 74 days and was last seen on the 19th August.

On Friday 28th September a male Siberian Thrush was found at Hametoun on Foula by P. Gordon. It was feeding in grass fields and hung around till dusk. It was successfully seen by a boatload of Shetland twitchers in the afternoon. I decided to go on the overnight National Express coach to Aberdeen, but got to Aberdeen three hours later than scheduled as the coach broke down en route. It didn't matter anyway, as news came through that the thrush had gone. I spent six hours trudging around Aberdeen with a sleeping bag, scope, tripod, rucksack, big coat and my food & drink bag.

The journey home was a nightmare. The coach was full, and I had to sit opposite a complete moron for 12 hours. He rang at least 15 people on his mobile during the night and told them how he had someone get their fingers cut off by opening a safe. The good thing about the coach is it can cost as little as £26 return if you book in advance.

A Brown Flycatcher was identified by Yorkshire-born Richard Baines and his friend Phil Cunningham on 3rd October at Flamborough at 3pm. They felt like they had won the lottery. Richard is well known to Sussex birders for finding a Black-eared Wheatear in 1988, when he was showing a party of school kids around Bewl Water. Paul Harvey found the first Brown Flycatcher on Fair Isle on 1st July 1992 – it was heard on its second and last day. The BOURC placed this record into Category D due to usual arrival date, indicating it might be an escapee. Since October 2005 it has been illegal to import wild-caught birds into the European Union. This Brown Fly had everything going for it and I had immediate pressure to get the Thursday off work. My finance boss signed off my holiday card.

I left Rusper at 3:30am Thursday morning with Ian Barnard, Christian Melgar and John Lees. We met Chris Heard at Junction 18 on the M25 and today I was using my 40th birthday present from Kim, a satnav, after the Madrid shenanigans. It was probably worth more than my P reg Ford Mondeo. It tried to get me off the M1 at every junction for A/B roads to Flamborough and kept beeping for speed cameras. Maybe I could fix this in the settings, but I was really impressed with it and felt these devices would revolutionize birding.

When I arrived at 9:10am, everybody ran from the car, leaving me to me to lock it up and make my own way to see the flycatcher. About 150 birders were on site and as I arrived someone boomed in a thick Scottish accent, 'Can you f**k off please, your head's in the f**king way!' I was sure I had been there before him, but not wanting to make a scene, I moved to the side. I found out that this was a Glasgow patch birder called Donald Wilson. I met him again years later on Lundy, and this time he didn't swear at me and we had a good chat and bite to eat.

The Brown Flycatcher performed well for me for a continuous 5 minutes just before midday. It was at a range of only 20 metres, and I watched it with bins and marvelled at its massive eye with pale eye ring. This view saved the day as most people were only getting fleeting glimpses. On the way home we saw an Isabelline Shrike at Buckton and a Siberian Stonechat at Spurn. John got a few ticks and had some smelly dog shit attached to the bottom of his Wellington boots – the smell lingered the whole way home. The car developed an annoying rattle, but we managed to get home without calling Green Flag.

The Brown Flycatcher was gone the next day. During the two days it was there £1,600 was donated by visiting birders for St. Catherine's Hospice and Flamborough Bird Observatory.

Darts was becoming very popular at Colas, and I fancied improving my ability by joining a pub team. I found that the nearest darts pub to me was the Fountain Inn at Horsham. On the first night of the league I turned up and met the captain, Geoff Broadbent. Geoff was in his late 50s or early 60s and quite chatty. When he found out I lived near him in Rusper, he let me play that first night. Geoff drank many pints and was reliant on his wife bringing him to the pub and then picking him up at closing time. I was happy to do all the driving to home and away matches, so his wife got her evenings back.

The league, the Mid Sussex 5s, had two divisions. Matches started in October and ran through to April and each league night a team had to bring five players to qualify. Each team played three singles matches, two doubles matches and a 5-man team 1001. I played in the doubles with Geoff and in the 1001 game. It couldn't have turned out any better as our team was victorious on the night. That year the Fountain was in Division 2, but at the end of the season we got promoted to Division 1 for the start of next season.

When news broke of a Rose-breasted Grosbeak on Scilly, I decided to ring Sussex birder Ian Barnard. Ian was enduring his third successive week on Scilly without a tick. He went across late on Tuesday 23rd from St. Mary's to St. Agnes and dipped. He mentioned that only one or two people had seen the bird on the Tuesday, and a load of birders dipped. I decided to leave it to the Thursday and see what happened on the Wednesday. The big talking point on Wednesday was when a fight broke out between two twitchers trying to see the Grosbeak. One of the guys, who I'm not going to name, has already appeared in my story. It's not surprising that this sort of thing was happening at twitches. More and more people were getting into birding and if large bodies of birders congregate in confined spaces, all trying desperately to see an important rarity, tempers begin to fray. Then you've got to deal with pager and mobile phone noise, loud chatting and people pushing and shoving when a bird shows. People might arrive to find that the bird they are after has already been deliberately flushed. Codes of conduct are needed, and pagers can only do so much.

The Grosbeak did show well to the masses on Wednesday morning but failed to show late afternoon. The *Scillonian* was not operating on the Thursday, so I decided to give British International

Helicopters a go. I advertised car spaces and they were quickly taken by Dan Houghton, 17-year-old Ashley Howe and John Benham. Luckily for my passengers the heater had been repaired after being broken for the last 5 months. This was Ashley's first trip with me, and it was nice to hear a youngster's view on twitching. He was extremely keen and I thought he could have a big future in the hobby. He was tall, single, and prepared to drop things and go anywhere. He had already been to Ireland, had lots of birding friends, was not fazed by dipping and could easily get time off work.

During the Journey to Cornwall conversation topics were very varied, but it transpired that none of my passengers had managed to connect with the Brown Flycatcher. I might have slipped it in a few hundred times… sorry to gloat, honest!

We arrived at Penzance at 6am and caught the 8:30am chopper to St. Marys. The news at the airport was that Chris Cappelo had seen the Grosbeak at 8:20am with three other birders. Wonderful news! We jumped into Chris Webb's taxi and caught the 9:15am boat to St. Agnes with around 40 birders, but there was no further sign of the Grosbeak and half the birders decided to leave the island. Then at 1:11pm the pager read 'Rose-breasted Grosbeak 12:40-12:50 near campsite then flew to Troy Town Fields and lost to view'. With that news, the 20+ remaining birders quickly went to Troy Town, but sadly the bird was not seen.

After about an hour searching the general area, I decided to give up and make my way back to the area between Cove Vean and the Post Office. I was hungry and with no sandwiches left in the Post Office, I had to settle for a Boost, Snickers, Flapjack slice, salt 'n' vinegar crisps and packet of Polos. There were boats back to St Mary's at 2:15pm, 3:45pm & 4:30pm. If I got the 2:15pm boat, I would get a chance for the Wilson's Snipe on Lower Moors, but I decided to maximise my chances, stay on St. Agnes and take the 3:45pm crossing, giving us plenty of time to catch the 5pm chopper back to Penzance.

Then more good news came out of the pager – Jonno had relocated the Grosbeak in a weedy field in Troy Town at 2:54pm. At this stage I was not too far away and got to the site at about 3:10. The Rose-breasted Grosbeak was still there. Result! It was feeding on tall stalks of grass for about 10 minutes before it made a short flight to a neighbouring weedy field. I got the 3:45pm boat off and went for a quick shufti at Lower Moors, but there was no sign of the Wilson's Snipe.

The Grosbeak was originally found by P. Read and it stayed to 29th October.

On 27th October I was back at Penzance waiting for the *Scillonian,* this time with Andy Appleton, John Lees and John King. This time we saw a Wilson's Snipe at Lower Moors. It was a very uninspiring bird, but one day it might be declared a full species.

On Thursday 1st November a Mourning Dove was mega'd on North Uist. My thoughts at 1:52pm were that I could not possibly go – I was due to go to the Emirates on the Saturday with a friend to watch Arsenal v Man United.

Plus, I needed to take mum to hospital on Friday for a check-up. They were thinking about fitting an oesophageal stent. My mum had been diagnosed with throat cancer a few weeks after the fall she had in Morocco. She was given chemotherapy and lost her hair and was constantly feeling sick, and she decided to give up on the treatment. The only thing the hospital could now was to fit a hollow tube at the base of the tumour to keep the oesophagus open. It's a hard story to hear. Let' s get back to the twitch.

As the minutes ticked away at work, I started to

think about all the twitchers smiling and gripping me off if they saw the bird. I had a decision to make: should I go tonight and use my last full day of annual leave and pretty much upset the whole family and friends with my decision? How focused would I be at work on the Friday when the pager messages flooded in saying how well the Mourning Dove was showing? I wasn't going to go – it was only a bird…

At 3:56pm the bird got the better of me. I put out a pager message saying 'W. Sussex Lift offer to W. Isles tonight tel. Garry'. My Arsenal friend understood my predicament and agreed to take BOTH tickets off my hands. I got my wife to take my mum to the hospital on Friday. I filled my car and now I just had to sit in the office and watch the clock move slowly minute by minute until it got to 5pm. I ran out of the building to my parked car and got home by 5:30pm. I didn't bother eating the meal Kim had prepared for me (I'm a naughty boy). I got out of my work clothes, got the birding gear on and drove to Leatherhead to meet John Benham. Next stop was to get to Steve Nuttall's off junction 2 of the M54. The last pickup point was Junction 15 on the M6 to meet another 17-year-old, Dan Pointon.

Steve had been with me on 4 twitches and never dipped. This was Dan's first trip with me, and I must say I was quite impressed with his rarity knowledge of dates and places, considering he has only been twitching for two years. We arrived at Uig at 7:15am after narrowly missing two Red Deer standing in the road. There were 40 cars in the car park and many of our elite twitchers were already there. One of the cars had a large section of his bonnet & bumper missing. I hoped it wasn't because of a Red Deer.

Stuart Piner received notification that the Dove was still present, and a big yell rang out around the quay. Shortly after the ticket office opened, and 85 twitchers started panicking as they tried to be first in the queue (the cost was £59 per car + £15 per passenger). The reason for the panic was that somebody spread a rumour that there were only 10 remaining car spaces on the ferry. Just a hoax, as we all got on.

The ferry departed Uig at 9:40am and arrived at Lochmaddie at 11:10am. We enjoyed the £4.90 Scottish Breakfast on the ferry. My car was almost the last to get off, as it was parked on the moveable deck section, so we quickly lost all the cars hurtling at pace to Clachan-a-luib. We lost the pack, so Dan rang a friend for directions. We arrived at the site just after midday, but the weather was not good. It was cold and miserable with horizontal rain. The Mourning Dove was very distant, sitting on a stone, facing away from us, and getting soaking wet. Some birders could not be bothered to wait for better views and raced back to catch the same ferry going back to Uig. The rain eventually stopped, and the remaining twitchers got smashing views of the Dove as it flew and perched on the path.

My crew all splashed out £12 each to stay at the Bunk House in Lochmaddie. That evening three of us went out to the Loch Maddie Hotel for dinner. I had the beef & ale pie (£7.95) and then went back to the Bunkhouse for some late-night birding banter. It was nice to meet Peter Hutchins and his 13-year-old son Jay, who live in Hampshire. Peter could easily be spotted on twitches because he wore shorts all year round and it was nice to see families going on long distance twitches. The next day we caught the 7:30am ferry back to Uig and head home.

This Mourning Dove was found by A MacDonald and stayed to 7th November. It was the 3rd record for Britain.

On Friday 7th December, Ashley Fisher went

to the Hilda Quick hide, Lower Moors, at 2pm in awful light and saw a Grey Heron almost obscured behind a patch of juncus. It had chestnut-coloured carpal joints. Thoughts turned to Great Blue Heron. Bob Flood soon arrived with a camera and the news was broadcast at 2:13pm. The bird stayed till dusk. That evening I drove to Penzance with Chris Heard, Ian Barnard and John Lees.

There were probably 100 twitchers waiting for news at the heliport on Saturday morning. Chris managed to get himself onto the last space on the first chopper going across. News broadcast at 8:23am was not good: no sign of the Great Blue Heron with poor weather conditions. We could all have decided to go back home, but we had come this far, so we decided to get the next chopper across. Once we arrived, we walked to the hides at Lower Moors and just checked it out for ourselves. There was a chance that the heron might fly in at any moment. The other islands had not been checked and with a good army of 70 twitchers we had to stand a chance. Sadly, there was no sign on St. Mary's all day.

We were now stuck on Scilly till at least Monday and had no choice but to find accommodation. We managed to get some rooms at Rose Cottage B&B (01720-422078) for two nights. The highlight of the evening was a tasty beef and ale pie in the Atlantic.

Sunday came, and so did more poor weather. We stayed in the B&B all day, and only went out to eat at the Porthcressa in the evening, this time having a nice steak with a creamy sauce.

Monday brought pleasant weather, and many groups were keen to increase the search to other islands. Tresco was considered to have the best habitat. Many of us chartered a boat there (07917-791962, 07714-152682). Tresco didn't hold the Great Blue Heron on either of their large pools, so it was back to St. Mary's. We made a final check of Lower Moors and then took the chopper back to Penzance. I spent in the region of £270 plus food. It was a pleasant place to dip, but with hindsight would we have done the same thing? I think so.

SUMMARY – 2007

During 2007, I travelled 9,431 miles in Britain and Ireland in the pursuit of new birds and managed to increase my list by 8 BOU/IRBC species. This took my British and Irish list to 448 different species. The Combined Official List now stood at 587 species, and I had seen 76.3% of them. There were six additions to the Official British and Irish List during the year: Long-billed Murrelet (2006), Chestnut-eared Bunting (2004), American Herring Gull (split), Caspian Gull (split), Magnificent Frigatebird (1998) and Olive-tree Warbler (2006).

The 8 lifers in the table above are Long-billed Murrelet (Lifetime), Chestnut-eared Bunting (20-year), Mourning Dove and White-tailed Plover (10-year) , Dark-eyed Junco, Rose-breasted Grosbeak

2007	Regular	Vagrant	BBRC/ IRBC 1 year	BBRC/ IRBC 2 year	BBRC/ IRBC 3 year	BBRC/ IRBC 4 year	BBRC/ IRBC 5 year	BBRC/ IRBC 10 year	BBRC/ IRBC 20 year	BBRC/ IRBC Lifetime	Cat B	Total
Seen	276	36	81	8	7	5	20	9	3	3	0	448
During		1	3					2	1	1		8
B&I Total	276	38	92	12	12	13	40	34	27	34	9	587
	100%	95%	88%	67%	58%	38%	50%	26%	11%	9%	0%	76.3%

and Pechora pipit (1 year) and Caspian Gull being the non-BBRC vagrant.

If you're getting more ticks per year than official additions, you're making progress. I had gone up one percentage point this year, and now needed only 52 for my main target of 500.

I decided that the most important bird seen during the year was the Asian Brown Flycatcher. It was only the second record for Britain, and the fact that it hung around for a second day was a real blessing. Twitching Asian birds is a real dilemma. It's easy for them to build up fat reserves with numerous stops to Britain and be gone the next day. On the other hand, a healthy North American passerine will generally stay longer. Their depleted fat reserves will take a few days to build up before moving on.

Asian Brown Flycatcher
muscicapa dauurica
Flamborough N. Yorkshire
4th October 2007

G. BAGNELL

CHAPTER 10

2008

The year started off in style with a trip to Wimereux in Northern France to see a wintering Wallcreeper. I was getting fed up reading about it on the pager, so on the 27th January I finally cracked and went. I took Britain's top digiscoper, Paul Hacket, with me and we met 25 other birders on site. They were mainly French, with a few Belgian and three from Kent.

Talking about wintering birds, I fancied seeing an American Herring Gull at Nimmo's Pier. I managed to get a return flight from Luton to Shannon for £22 and flew over on 16th February. I was glad to bump into Tom Cluff, who made sure I saw the right bird.

On Friday 6th June at 3:37pm the Pager Mega alerted the news of a Citril Finch on Fair Isle. This being a first for Britain, I felt I needed to go somehow. The elite twitching group who charter planes were out of luck. Fair Isle were forecasting heavy fog for Saturday and the planes wouldn't be able to land. The only option was boats. I spent the whole evening surfing the web for boat numbers and ringing them. It was surprisingly difficult to find a boat, but I found someone who was prepared to sail Sunday night at 7pm to Fair Isle from mainland Shetland. I advertised on the pager 2 car spaces and 10 boat spaces.

I left my house at midnight Friday and picked up Chris Heard, Tony Ford from Scarborough and John Bell from Dundee. We arrived at Aberdeen Harbour at around 4pm on Saturday, after seeing a Whiskered Tern at Loch of Strathbeg. I bought a single Aberdeen to Lerwick Ferry Ticket costing £27.10. When I boarded the ferry I was very surprised not to see any other twitchers. The only other birders on the boat were Clive Byers and one of his friends. The ferry departed soon after 5pm. Clive was an extremely entertaining and interesting guy who was responsible for painting many plates in the Pica Press 'Buntings and Sparrows' book. Chris and Clive had a good catch up talking about the old days and whilst I was happy to have a pint, I'm not sure Clive ever stopped.

When we arrived at Lerwick at around 7:30am,

my boat charter man rang me to say the weather forecast was not looking good for sailing to Fair Isle. I noticed that a guy from Bolts Car Hire had been walking around with a board waiting for one of the ferry passengers. There must have been over 300 people on the ferry. Most passengers could easily get off the ferry within ten minutes. It was now 8:30am and the Bolts Car Hire guy asked us if we knew Clive Byers – we all laughed. I said 'Yes he was definitely on the ferry. He's about five foot tall with ginger hair'.

By 9am the Bolts Car Hire guy was fed up waiting and was just about to leave the ferry terminal when Clive appeared with his friend. The car hire guy handed the keys to Clive and shot off to sort his taxi business. Clive hadn't come to Shetland to twitch the Citril Finch but to show his friend breeding Red-necked Phalaropes on Fetlar. I wonder if he caught the only ferry to Fetlar that day? I don't know, but I do know he set off the car alarm system and the engine was immobilised. Bolts' hire desk was now closed to after midday.

Chris, Tony and I remained in the Ferry terminal to discuss the options for the day, while John was on a mission to get some breakfast. John came back and reported that nowhere was open, but Somerfield would open at 11am. Sussex lister Paul Marten rang me to say the Terek Sandpiper was back in Sussex. I had missed it the previous week when I was in France at Remi's communion, and this would have been a good bird for my Sussex Life list (third record for Sussex). We all ate a Scottish Breakfast at Somerfields and the latte went down a treat.

We couldn't stay carless in Shetland. There was a showy Marsh Warbler at nearby Sumburgh Farm, and we decided to hire a car and go for it. Just as we parked at the farm, I got a text from Fair Isle warden Deryk Shaw saying 'Citril Finch still present but MOBILE'.

We didn't even get out of the car to look at the Marsh Warbler – our focus once again was on getting to Fair Isle. During the next few hours, we begged boat skippers in Scalloway and Lerwick to take us there. Their excuses ranged from too dangerous to too far, weather too bad, could if boat was working, busy tonight etc. Even Good Shepherd, the Sumburgh helicopter and Islander couldn't help. We were so close to the Finch and yet so far.

All this driving about was thirsty work, so I dropped into Sumburgh Airport Café. I got served by a scary looking lady who would have given my four-year-old daughter Georgie nightmares.

Just as I sat down, I noticed nine of Britain's keenest twitchers. There sat Matt Mulvey, Alan Clewes, Chris Batty, Andy Clifton, Stuart Piner, Malcolm Goodman, Paul Chapman, Andrew Holden and Vicky Turner. This elite bunch would have flown direct to Fair Isle on a charter plane if it hadn't been for the fog. Instead, they had spent big and made sure they got to Shetland and connected with a charter boat. They had successfully seen the Citril Finch on Saturday and were now just waiting to fly back home. They deserved it, and so did we now we were on Shetland.

Later that day, Tony heard that his friend Brett Richards had chartered a plane from Blackpool to Fair Isle. Tony rang Brett and asked, 'Any chance you can get your plane to pick us up from Sumburgh and drop us on Fair Isle?' Not sure why, but Brett refused to help.

John Bell conveyed some possible good news from Hugh Harrop. The Council were chartering a plane on Monday morning at 7:10am to fly empty to Fair Isle, pick up some school children and bring them back to Sumburgh. There would be enough spaces for us to fly from Tingwall to Fair Isle, coming back at 11:45am. John asked, 'Do we want to give it a go?' 'Yes!' I shouted. 'We most definitely do, and give Hugh a big thank you for offering it'.

That night we all felt there was a good chance that the clear skies might move the Citril Finch on. Oh, before I forget to mention, we did eventually go and see the very showy and vocal Marsh Warbler at Sumburgh farm and ended the day with fish and chips in Lerwick.

That night we all stayed in a bungalow owned by a lady Chris knew. She made us feel very welcome and served us tea and coffee. Sleeping on her floor was certainly better than the car.

Hugh and his friend met us at Sumburgh Airport on Monday at 6:45am. Airport staff soon arrived, and it was not long before they agreed to take all six of us on the council charter flight. We were charged £56 each for a return flight to Fair Isle.

We landed on Fair Isle at around 7:45am, and as usual Deryk Shaw was waiting for us in the minibus. He took us all to the area where the finch had been seen yesterday and we started searching. We had only a four-hour window to see the bird.

The first two hours passed quickly. Hugh and his friend searched independently and managed several flight views of the finch, but none of my group saw it. Chris was desperate to stop for a coffee, in the only shop on the island. With only two hours remaining, I persuaded him against it.

Then we bumped into an American lady who said she had seen the Citril Finch building a nest further up the road. Non-birders often think rare birds are nesting when they are just feeding.

Chris and I eventually went to investigate and as soon as we did we bumped into Peter Harrison (author of 'Seabirds, an Identification Guide'). He and his entourage had also seen the Citril Finch in flight heading in the general direction of the place where we were talking to the American lady. Thirty minutes go by, then we heard that a couple

who were staying in the Observatory had seen it in a ploughed field for five minutes. We investigated again, but no sign. John Bell heard that it had been seen at Barkland again, but as soon as we arrived it had apparently gone again. Then the assistant warden saw it in another ploughed field. Chris wondered if he had seen it himself or was just relaying the couple's sighting.

It was now 11:30am, and the plane was due to take off in 15 minutes. Considering the difficulty in getting to Fair Isle and knowing the bird was still here, Chris, Tony and I were prepared to miss the plane and make our own way back.

Then at 11:45 Chris shouted out 'I've got it!' We all looked where Chris was pointing, and there was the Citril Finch sitting on a fence next to the ploughed field. Everybody was hugging each other in excitement. John Bell was desperate to catch the plane back and settled for a 20-second binocular view before legging it back to the airport. I carried on watching the finch through the scope for 30 minutes. Then, to our surprise, John Bell came back and said our plane had been delayed because thick fog had just descended at Sumburgh Airport.

Then a charter plane flew over the island. This flight brought in Billy Simpson, John Regan, Malcolm Roxby, Jerry Warne and Mark Sutton. These guys were long established twitchers, and all sat in the top 20. Unusually I had got there before them, but everybody knows getting to Fair Isle isn't easy.

Back at the airport, It was nice to have a chat with the finder of the Citril Finch, an American called Tony Hyndman who had been living on Fair Isle for 18 months with his wife, Liz Musser. They ran a B&B where Tommy made woolly hats.

We departed Fair Isle around 3pm and flew to Tingwall, then drove back to Lerwick and left the hire car for collection. Safely on board the 5:30pm ferry to Aberdeen, we could finally sit back and relax.

Our Citril Finch was last seen on Wednesday 11th June at 5:50pm. Seven years later one visited Burham Overy dunes in Norfolk. This would have been a far easier twitch, but nothing beats seeing a first for Britain on a remote island without the crowds.

On Tuesday 19th August we rented the Villa Sessiz in Ovacik in Turkey. My mum was no longer coming on our holidays. She preferred to stay at home and be within easy reach of the hospital, especially now she had a stent. Whilst in Turkey, I got a call phone call from Matt Mulvey asking what I was going do about a Northern Waterthrush on Cape Clear. I replied, 'Nothing Matt, I'm in Turkey and I'm not back till 2nd September. Good luck if you see it'.

This bird was found by B. Haslam and stayed to 30th August. Ireland was going American warbler crazy. Steve Wing found a Yellow Warbler on Cape Clear from 24-30th August and D. Ballard found another on Three Castles Head on 26-28th August.

Maybe I had picked a bad time to be away. This being our first trip to Turkey, at least I managed to see ten new birds for my WP list including Red-fronted Serin, Krupper's Nuthatch and Ruppell's Warbler. But I would swap all ten for a Northern Waterthrush in Britain.

Thursday 18th September produced an American Redstart at Mizen Head in Cork. The news broke at 6:47pm. The last American Redstart had been 23 years ago, so this motivated me to give it a go. Sussex birder Gordon Beck met me in Rusper and I met Lee Evans and Hampshire's Trevor Ellery en route. The plan was to go as foot passengers on the Fishguard car ferry.

The next day we hired a car in Rosslare. As we were entering Waterford at 8:04am we heard there was no sign of the American Redstart by the lighthouse. Lee wanted something for his bucks, so we headed to Ballycotton to see Baird's and Semipalmated Sandpipers. We headed back to Rosslare and caught the fast foot ferry to Fishguard.

During the journey the Mega alert went off at 4:20pm announcing a Cretzschmar's Bunting at North Ronaldsway, Orkney. I went over to Lee, who was fast asleep, and woke him up. I just showed him my phone message and Lee was glued to his phone for the next five hours. The ferry docked at Fishguard at around 5pm. We walked to the car, and I saw a 'NO PARKING TICKET WARNING' attached to the windscreen wiper. Lee had had them before and told me to ignore it.

At 6pm Lee got a call from his pilot, Charlie, and agreed a flight time and price from Wick. At this stage Charlie had agreed to fly his plane from Kirkwall to Wick on Saturday 20th and pick up Angus Murray, John Sweeney and Dougie Barr for 8:30am, then fly to North Ronaldsway and drop them off. We would fly back to Wick empty, then take the second group of twitchers to North Ronaldsway. Incidentally, the second group was Steve Webb's party, leaving at 10:30am. Then we would return with Angus's party and then take our party of Lee, Chris Heard & me at 12:30pm, then bring back the Steve Webb party. These were all the bookings Charlie had at this time.

Lee got a call from Steve Webb saying he had booked on a different plane from Inverness. Lee immediately rang Charlie back to see if we could now get on the second flight as Steve appeared to be double booked. Charlie then mentioned a fourth plane load for Dan Pointon, John Pegden & Mick Frosdick at 2:30pm and a fifth flight for the Broadbent family.

At 9pm, we got to junction 13 on the M4 and

Trevor kindly drove Gordon back to my house, while I followed Lee back to his place in Little Chalfont. We left Lee's at just after 11pm with the addition of Chris Heard. The drive to Wick was shared between all three of us. We got to Wick at 11am Saturday morning and on arrival we were very surprised to see nine other birders sitting in the airport lounge. One group consisted of Bob Watts, Julian Thomas and Adam Wilson. The second group consisted of John Gregory, Jonathan Williams and Simon Slade and the third was Dan Pointon, John Pegden and Mick Frosdick. We couldn't believe our eyes – the Pointon party was not due at the airport for another 3½ hours. Why were John's and Bob's crews here? It turned out that Bob's party had been given the 10:30am from Steve Webb. They had all arrived at Wick 15 minutes early for their flight, only to find out that the Broadbent party had got to the airport early and taken their flight.

Then John Gregory announced that he had agreed with Charlie that his crew would go next, and that Charlie was operating on a first come, first served basis. Lee disagreed and explained that first come, first served could not work. When people book a flight, they leave their house at a time which will coincide with them arriving at the agreed time to catch the flight. Eventually Lee agreed the order with all birder teams. Julian Thomas' group would go first, Lee's group second, John Pegden third and lastly John Gregory's group.

Then Julian heard that the CAA were inspecting all charter flights onto North Ronaldsway to make sure they had all the paperwork to carry fee-paying passengers. Julian stated that Charlie was not doing any more North Ron flights today. Julian and our group decided to head to Gills Bay for the Pentland car ferry to Orkney and John Pegden needed to be at work on Monday, so he would be heading back.

Whilst waiting at the ferry terminal, we noticed Charlie's plane landing back at Wick. We drove back there and saw him taking John Gregory's party direct to North Ronaldsway! This conflicted with what Julian had told us. I rang John to update him on what I'd seen. We then raced back to Gills Bay and managed to catch the 1:15pm crossing by the skin of our teeth. During the crossing, Bob Watts managed to get a scheduled flight to North Ron at 5pm. Lee, Chris and I booked a scheduled flight there for 9am Sunday. All return bookings were a mixture of dates and times. The main problem with the scheduled services was that islanders could only carry eight people per flight and fly three times a day.

The Pentland Ferry docked at 3pm and we drove straight to Kirkwall Airport to see if there was any standby list. Unfortunately there wasn't. We could only wait and see if all the passengers turned up for the flight. They did – but I had a huge slice of luck. The 5pm flight had two very small children on it. Due to weight allowances, the plane could take an extra adult. I suggested to Lee and Chris that I ought to have the last place, because on 16th September I had driven to Fife for a trapped Collared Flycatcher, which got re-identified as a common Pied Flycatcher. I had then taken my car to Fishguard and got a parking fine. I had dipped the American Redstart and now my car was with us in Orkney. They agreed, and I joined Bob on the flight.

Now let this sink in for a minute. Chris was the third highest lister and Lee was the seventh highest lister and they were both letting the 200th highest lister take the last plane seat. This was only the 4th ever Cretzschmar's Bunting for Britain, and it might be gone tomorrow.

Bob and I landed on North Ronaldway at about 5:15pm. We were driven by Bob Simpson to the Cretzschmar's Bunting site and there it was, showing to a small assembled crowd including Alex Lees, Franko, Ian Wilson, Pete Donnelly, Johnny Allan, John Pegden, Mick Frosdick and Dan Pointon. Yes, you read it right – John Pegden had told me he was heading home.

The bunting stayed feeding in the same area for two hours and Bob and I enjoyed it the whole time. Around 7pm it flew up and perched on a fence, then hopped to the other side. Alex and Franko walked around the long way to re-locate it and failed. Then Adam Wilson and Julian Thomas flew in from Kirkwall. The light was going when they arrived and they missed the bunting by minutes.

We all stayed at the observatory and had very enjoyable meal served up by Kevin and Alison Woodbridge and their staff. I sat back and prayed the Cretzschmar's Bunting would stay the night, for everybody's sake.

On Sunday morning we got the superb news that Julian and Adam had both seen the Bunting. The scheduled flight bringing Lee and Chris landed at 9:24am and then took Franko, Johnny Allan, Bob Watts, Julian Thomas, Adam Wilson and me back to Kirkwall. At Kirkwall, I took Johnny to see a showy summer-plumaged White-billed Diver before we caught the 1:15 ferry back to Gill's Bay.

Lee and Chris hired a taxi from Kirkwall Airport to St. Margaret's Hope ferryport. The ferry's footbridge was up, but we managed to get staff to lower it and let them board. They got back to Gill's Bay at 6:30pm and I started the not very enjoyable journey home.

The whole Wick airport scene could have turned into a massive brawl if Chris and I hadn't calmed it down. Even 14 years later as I write this trip up, I'm still not sure why lies were told. Why did people queue-jump when it was clear Charlie was allocating time slots? Was the CAA message a smoke screen to get rid of Lee, Chris and me whilst they headed back and caught their flights? Whatever the reasons, it exposed a deep-rooted problem with our hobby. For some, the competition to see a bird is more important than friendships. Some say birders will only stop at murder to see a bird.

The Cretzschmar's Bunting was originally found by Pete Donnelly on the 19th September and stayed to the 21st September.

On Thursday 25th September Chris Heard and I headed to Flamborough to see an adult Brown Shrike. There was a nice fall of autumn birds including Red-backed Shrike, Red-breasted Flycatcher, 2 Yellow-browed Warblers, Ring Ouzel and 3 Whinchat. But on the way home, we failed to drop in and see a supposed Red-footed Falcon at Tohill Low nature reserve. The falcon was found on 14th September and stayed to 15th October and only when it was gone was its true identity discovered. It was identified from photographs as an Amur Falcon, and this was the very first record of this species in Britain.

The Brown Shrike was found by A. Allport on the 24th September and stayed to the 25th September. It was only the 6th record for Britain and Ireland.

On Sunday 5th October at 8:34am, RBA mega alerted a Little Blue Heron in Galway. There was not enough time in the day to see the bird the same day by catching the usual ferry, so, the only option was to fly. Ryanair don't advertise their flights online for same day travel – you have to ring a premium rate number (£1 a minute) to make a booking.

I gave Ryanair a ring and they wanted £380 day return. Considering the heron was now there for its 12th day, surely another week wouldn't hurt? I decided to book a day return for Saturday

11th October from Stansted to Shannon for £64. I should have 11 hours in Ireland to see the heron and do a 5-hour round trip to Letterfrack.

That week rare migrants were going mad. On the Tuesday, a Scarlet Tanager was found in Cork. On the Wednesday an Empidonax flycatcher species was found in Cornwall – a first for Britain. That would be two more new birds for me and the earliest day I could twitch was this Saturday. Even if the Tanager stayed till Saturday, it would not be possible to see the two birds in 11 hours. I worked out that I would need 15 hours in Ireland, so I booked a one-way flight from Stansted to Shannon for a further £70 for arrival on Friday night. It felt mad to have to pay for two outbound flights, but in a world where airlines use price discrimination, dynamic pricing, and augmented-pricing structures, what chance did we really have to see a bird on the cheap? Booking advance flights to save money is a gamble. If any birds stayed till Saturday you'd saved £246 and if they were gone you'd lost £134.

On Friday morning the flycatcher had departed Cornwall, but both the Irish birds were still present. I left work on Friday 10th at 5pm and headed towards Stansted Airport with John Lees. En route we made a small detour to pick up Vince Halley-Frame in his trademark Burberry baseball cap. We arrived at Stansted just before 7pm and parked in the mid-term car park (£15.50 per day). We met our fourth member, Tony Vials from Northamptonshire, airside. We picked up a Land Rover (£60 a day with enhanced insurance) from Hertz, left the airport at 11pm and made our way to Garinish Point. Tony saw a sheep in the road and I narrowly swerved round it, waking up Vince and John.

We arrived at 3:30am, but the combination of trumpeting bottoms and Vince's snoring made it a challenge to sleep. We all surfaced at 7:30am and wandered up to a house with a For Sale Sign in the garden, as directed. Here we met Mark Carmody, and he explained the Tanager routine to us all. At 8am Mark located it in a small tree opposite the house. I felt privileged to see this yellow American gem, with ten people on site.

We left at 9am and picked up Ashley Howe at Shannon airport en route, arriving at Letterfrack at 3:20pm. The Little Blue Heron was on show immediately, and it allowed us to photograph it at point-blank range. It had an obvious growth on the back of its neck that could be seen when its neck was fully stretched whilst feeding. After 30 minutes it decided to fly off to a more distant bay, and that was a cue to head back to Shannon Airport.

The real heroes of our hobby are the bird finders, and to meet five of the six Punkbirders (Rob Martin, Richard Moores, Dr. James Gilroy, Jez Bird and Dr. Alex Lees) at Shannon Airport was a pleasant surprise. They'd just come back from birding Inishmore in Galway and stayed

2008	Regular	Vagrant	BBRC/ IRBC 1 year	BBRC/ IRBC 2 year	BBRC/ IRBC 3 year	BBRC/ IRBC 4 year	BBRC/ IRBC 5 year	BBRC/ IRBC 10 year	BBRC/ IRBC 20 year	BBRC/ IRBC Lifetime	Cat B	Total
Seen	276	36	84	8	7	6	22	10	3	4	0	456
During			3			1	2	1		1		8
B&I Total	276	38	92	12	12	14	42	33	29	36	8	592
	100%	95%	91%	67%	58%	43%	52%	30%	10%	11%	0%	77%

LITTLE BLUE HERON
Egretta caerulea
Letterfrack. Galway
11th October 2008
G. BAGNELL

true to form by heading straight to the airport and avoiding the slight detour for the heron.

The Scarlet Tanager was found by Tony Lancaster and Kieran Grace on the 7th October and stayed to 11th October, becoming the 4th record for Ireland. The Little Blue Heron was first identified by Dermot Breen. Originally found on 24th September, it stayed to 22nd October and became the first record for Europe.

On Monday 13th October, Ireland struck again. This time D. McAdams found a Philadelphia Vireo at Kilbaha in Clare. The earliest I could go for it was Wednesday, and I decided to book a return flight to Shannon for £78 and teamed up with John Archer and Bob Watts. Unfortunately, we were a day too late to see the bird.

Now what about Justin Taylor from Oxfordshire? He saw the Scarlet Tanager and Little Blue Heron over a long weekend twitch. Then, whilst sitting in the departure lounge at Shannon Airport, he got a call from Nic Hallam asking 'What are you doing about the Philadelphia Vireo?' Two hours later, Justin saw it.

SUMMARY – 2008

During 2008, I travelled 7,512 miles in Britain and Ireland in pursuit of new birds and managed to increase my list by 8 BOU/IRBC species. This took my British and Irish list to 456 different species. The Combined Official still stood at 592 species, so I had now seen 77% of them. There were five net additions to the Official British and Irish List during the year: Little Blue Heron (2008), Green Warbler (split), Red-throated Thrush (split), Naumann's Thrush (split), Great Blue Heron (2008), Wilson's Snipe (split) and the removal of the Madeiran Storm Petrel.

The 8 lifers in the table above are Little Blue Heron (Lifetime), Cretzschmar's Bunting (10-year), Wilson's Snipe and Scarlet Tanager (5-year), Hooded Merganser (4-year), American Herring Gull, River Warbler and Brown Shrike (1-year).

I decided that the most important bird I had seen during the year was the Little Blue Heron. This was only the fourth for the Western Palearctic, the first three having been in the Azores in 1964, 1997 and 1998. This bird was initially identified as an odd-looking little Egret by Aonghus O'Donail. He had his concerns about the lores and the legs being on the bright side for Little Egret. During the evening of the 3rd October, Dermot Breen was looking through his David Sibley's North American Bird Guide and the image of Little Blue Heron on page 63 looked like their bird. Dermot started kicking himself that it hadn't been nailed sooner, but was so happy when Aonghus and Ger Walshe relocated it the next morning. During the bird's 29-day stay it's estimated that it attracted 500 birders.

CHAPTER 11

2009

2009 was my 10th Year at Colas and every year the business managers seemed to change. No, they weren't getting fired – they were just getting old. That year my manager, David Fairchild, retired, and his role went to a Birmingham-based manager. The related accountancy work was given to Birmingham-based accountant Ish Hussain. I was due to lose my Fibredec accounts at the end of year when Arthur Thompson retired, with my work going to Ish. The old Plant and Transport manager left and was replaced by Trevor Purfield. Trevor, luckily, was Rowfant based, so I managed to keep the accounting responsibility. These changes didn't worry me, but it was of paramount importance to maintain a good working relationship with all managers so they would allow me to shoot off for our feathered friends at a moment's notice. This flexibility had kept me loyal to Colas.

Georgie started swimming lessons from age 4 and we decided to join Crawley Swimming Club rather than nearby Horsham. The reason we chose Crawley over Horsham was two words - Janice

White. Janice worked in the legal department at Colas; she was into birdwatching and played lunchtime darts in the Colas lunchtime league. She had suggested bringing Georgie to Crawley to learn to swim, and Georgie was turning into a good swimmer under her tuition. Janice's daughter wasn't bad either – she won silver in the 1982 Commonwealth Games.

At 1:40pm on Wednesday 4th March a 1st winter Siberian Thrush was seen and then taken into care at the Natural Surroundings NR in Norfolk. It was then placed in a large aviary and it could be viewed by paying £3 as an entry fee. It was released at 3:49pm and flew into cover, where it was seen until dusk.

I arrived at the NR at first light and fell asleep in the car. When I woke at 9am there were hundreds of cars lining the road and approximately 200 individuals looking for the thrush in the reserve. There had been no sign of it, and after reviewing pictures of the bird, problems could be seen with its hind claws. They were far too long for a bird that is used to feeding on the forest floor, and more reminiscent of a bird use to feeding without too much effort. The bird was gone anyway, but whilst in Norfolk I did see a Black-billed Dipper, two Rough-legged Buzzards, two Great Grey Shrikes, a Hen Harrier and 4 Golden Pheasants.

How the Siberian Thrush had got to the Nature Reserve remained a mystery. Apart from the claws, The unusual circumstances included:

(1) Arriving at an unusual time of year.

(2) It was a year with few or no overwintering Siberian Warblers.

(3) The bird had damaged primaries, although it was housed in an aviary for only a short time.

(4) There was little feathering around the bill.

(5) The same finder had made other unusual finds.

I Initially thought that the wintering Belgium Dusky Thrush would explain a Siberian Thrush being found at this time of year, but Chris Heard informed me that the Dusky Thrush is hardier than the Siberian Thrush and the latter enjoys wintering in much more southerly tropical locations.

My P reg Ford Mondeo needed extensive work to get it through the MoT and Rowfant Garage suggested it needed scrapping. This car had never let me down in the 4½ years I had owned it and I managed to get 47 new birds and clock 75,000 road miles in that time. I sold it to Billy Bridge's scrapyard and replaced it with a Y reg Vauxhall Vectra from Lancing car auctions.

During the spring I saw a Collared Flycatcher in Dave Saunders' garden in Southwell. I saw it on the 29th April flycatching from a sycamore to Leylandii with 50 other birders. The next day a Crested Lark was found by Dave Bunney at Dungeness. The news came out late and 60 people connected on the first night, but I missed out by 15 minutes. I stayed overnight in my new car, which had seats that could recline almost to 180 degrees. I had a good night's sleep and four times with 70 others I managed to see the Crested Lark in flight. It was constantly being flushed and always landed out of view on the shingle. I left the site at 6:10am without satisfactory views, so my plan was to come back at the weekend.

A calling Eastern Bonelli's Warbler at Southwell was found on Friday 1st May. I made the unwise choice of waiting till the next day, and dipped. If I had left on getting news from Sussex like Ian Barnard, I would have connected.

The Sunday saw me back at Dungeness from 11:30am to 3:45pm. This time I did manage to see the Crested Lark on the ground three times for 10 seconds or more. I saw its large bill and erect crest and heard flight calls. This bird was estimated to have attracted 2,000 visitors over the eight-day stay. Thirteen years had elapsed since the last record, which Paul Holmes found in Landguard. This was found on the 2nd October and then seen a week later, 9th October, with no one knowing where it was for 7 days.

On Friday 8th at 4:22pm the news broke of a Brown-headed Cowbird on Fair Isle. I spent the afternoon and evening on the phone trying to find a way to get up there. I found the *Good Shepherd* was not sailing on Saturday and was delayed to Sunday. Two scheduled flights were already booked, taking at least 9 twitchers across. Two charter planes left York and one left Blackpool, and one of them made a special pickup from Wick, enabling 19 people to connect.

Tony Ford managed to get a charter plane booked for the Sunday, so I drove up Sunday morning with Chris Heard and Tony Shepherd. News came through at 7:41am that the Brown-headed Cowbird was still present. I felt so happy I punched the air in excitement. Minutes later we arrived at airport and were joined by Tony Forde and Ian Kendall. The pilot wandered over and told us Fair Isle was sunny, but the wind was in the wrong direction for the plane to land. I was not used to this type of news, but this was only my 4th charter. Surely the weather would change?

We thought at one point that the plane was going to fly as the wind speed dropped and the pilot asked Chris and me to fill the wing with fuel, but a last-minute call to Fair Isle prevented our flight from happening. The pilot thought he would be able to land the plane with just two passengers, but he wanted £750 each to make it worthwhile. To accept his offer and whittle our group down to two wasn't fair. The pilot was prepared to fly on Monday. Tony and I decided to go back to work Monday and headed back home at 4pm. Adrian Kettle and Lee Gregory took our places.

Through the grapevine I heard that three twitchers had successfully connected with the Brown-headed Cowbird on Sunday. They went on the ultra-cheap Good Shepherd. I could have been one of them, if only I had stuck to Kim's household rule of not accepting or organising plane charters. The Cowbird was gone on the Monday and the charter plane was cancelled.

During 2009 there were 3 accepted Brown-headed Cowbird records. Northumberland had a male from 25th April to 2nd May and Pembrokeshire had another male from 14th to 15th July. The Northumberland one was not in the public domain till 3rd June and Pembrokeshire was not in public domain till 18th July. Only the Fair Isle bird was truly twitchable. It was found by Steve Davies and was the 3rd British record.

Jonah from Form Films contacted me saying he wanted to make a pilot documentary for the BBC about twitching. If the BBC liked the pilot, they would commission it. I'd never been on TV before and I wanted to do all I could to help.

When a Great Knot was found in Great Yarmouth on Friday 29th May at 6:20pm. I gave Jonah a ring and said a rare bird had just broken in Norfolk and I would probably be going in the early hours of tomorrow morning, did they want to start filming the trailer? Jonah agreed. I advertised a lift on the pager. John Lees and Dan Houghton were first to ring and they didn't mind being involved in the filming.

Jonah and his colleague Jerry got to my house shortly before John and Dan. They started filming there, and the film commenced with Jerry holding the camera and Jonah holding the microphone boom arm. They got some footage of John, Dan and me discussing the Great Knot and looking at a computer whilst Lee Evans rang and got into the filming.

All five of us left my house at 1am. We got to Breydon Water at 5am to hear the news that eight people had seen the bird fly off fifteen minutes before we had arrived. Some guys were 100% sure it was a Great Knot and said this on film, but the bird was never submitted, and others were convinced that a photograph by Brian Small showed it to be too small to be a Great Knot.

At 5:14pm on Thursday 28th May a Collared Pratincole was found at Pagham Harbour. It was not a new bird for me, so I didn't go. It only stayed one night, but then the experts studied Richard Ford's photographs and decided it was the much rarer Oriental Pratincole. Missing a British lifer and a Sussex lifer felt like a double whammy.

My Vectra's engine was intermittently cutting out, which was not something I was prepared to put up with. I handed it to Rowfant garage to diagnose and fix. Kim worked a kilometre from home at Ghyll Manor Hotel, so she agreed to walk to work and lend me her car.

The Oriental Pratincole was relocated at Dungeness on the 3rd June. I caught a lift with John Lees and watched it from 5:13pm as it flew onto a visible section of Denge Marsh. I saw it in flight three times from a five-bar gate with 30 other birders. I saw the rusty coloured underwing, no white trailing edge to upper or underwing, and a very small tail, which appeared 2cm shorter than the primary projection at rest. This latter feature was never nailed at Pagham. I swapped cars and got a lift back with John Benham. Getting this bird back so quickly restored my faith in humanity.

The Kent bird was found by David Roche and was only available for one day. It became the 6th record for Britain.

A Royal Tern was found at 4:45pm at Abersoch, Gwynedd on Monday 15th June. It hung around at about 7:30pm and relocated to Black Rocks Sands at 9:03pm, then stayed to dusk. My car was still in the garage, so I decided to hire a Vauxhall Astra from Alamo Gatwick. I spent the next day from dawn to 8:30pm on site with no sign of the tern. I didn't go hungry – I had a cooked breakfast and ate ice cream on the beach. I finished the day with fish and chips and a can of Coke for less than £5.

Chris Heard rang me at 3pm Saturday and asked, 'Have you looked at your pager recently?' I looked and saw that the Royal Tern was now at Llandudno. I carried on eating my dinner whilst I mulled over what to do. The garage still had my car, but this time Kim was prepared to lend me hers for a long 6-hour twitch as long as I was back Sunday morning to look after Georgie. I cracked, left home, and hurtled towards Wales.

I arrived at 7:40pm, knowing full well that the Royal Tern had last been seen at 6pm disappearing around the Great Orme. There were about 100 people on site, and at 8:10 people starting getting excited. It was back in view, but only for 2 minutes at three quarters of a mile. Steve Webb connected but didn't see enough to tick. It was also seen further west along the headland, by Andrew Lawson.

I rang Kim to see if it was possible to get her mum to babysit Georgie on Sunday whilst she worked. She agreed and I slept in the car at the seafront.

The next day there were 60 twitchers on site, and most of yesterday's lucky 10 had stayed the night. There were a few false alarms during the day and I left empty-handed at 4:30pm.

The Royal Tern was found on 15th June at Abersoch by S. Hugheston-Roberts and re-located by Phill Woollen at Black Rocks. It was found at Llandudno by Alan Davies on 20th June. It became the 5th record for Britain.

On Friday 26th June 2009 we went off on a family holiday in Konakli, Turkey. The villa was owned by a Russian and the pool was chlorinated two or three times a week by a local maintenance guy. During the holiday I got 19 new birds, including Olive Tree Warbler, Pale Scops Owl and Menetries Warbler, but I picked up an ear infection from the badly maintained pool. While we were there I got a phone call from Linda to say that mum had become very poorly with the throat cancer. I was reassured that I didn't have to curtail my holiday and I could ring Linda for daily updates.

Back home on 6th July mum was getting daily visitors from St. Catherine's Hospice nurses. They are wonderful human beings and a real credit to the hospice. Every day, a happy, smiling nurse would visit mum and inject morphine to give her some quality of life. Her brother Ronny insisted I should get a stairlift fitted so she could come downstairs if she wanted. This cost nearly £1,000 and was only used three times before my mum was moved to St

Catherine's on 13th July.

Every day Kim and I would drive over to Crawley and visit my mum, and no birds were going to stop this daily ritual. We didn't want our five-year old daughter to see the way the cancer had distorted her nanny's face. It wasn't that long ago that Georgie and her Nan use to play hide and seek with a white plastic egg. They used to play this game every time we visited my mum, and Georgie use to get so excited when she found the egg.

I finally got my Astra back from the local garage after 8 weeks and one day, Wednesday 15th July, I was billed for some parts and for a reprogrammed charge by Vauxhall. I should have taken it direct to Vauxhall and probably got it back the same day. You certainly live and learn.

August 2nd was a very sad day. It was the day my mum met up with dad in heaven. Who was I going to turn to now if l needed advice?

The funeral took place at Snell's Hatch crematorium a few weeks later. This would be the last time I would see many of mum's family together, so I was determined to make sure we gave her the best send-off possible. I invited mum's three surviving brothers, Ronnie, David and Terry, and her sister Joyce. On Linda's side all her three children with partners and children came. Chantal drove from France with husband Yves and their four boys. Kim's mum and son Andrew came. My best man Dave Browne came with Lucy. Five different families all close to my mum also attended. It was a big crowd and after the funeral we had the wake back at mum's house.

On Wednesday 22nd July at 10:50 in St. Margaret's, a Blue-cheeked Bee-eater was seen from 10:10am-10:20am and heard at 10:30am. I had dipped here three times before with Nutcracker, Alpine Accentor and Dusky Warbler, but then came the deal breaker at 11:51am stating that the Bee-eater was still present. It must be lingering, so I booked leave and cancelled my French lesson.

I left work at 12:05pm and the satnav gave an ETA of 1:30pm. I beat it by 10 minutes and parked near the monument in Granville Road. I couldn't see any birders, so I asked a non-birder for directions to the bird from the café. Bad move. He said 'You need to carry on down the coastal path'. So off I ran down the hill, bumped into some other non-birders and they said no, I should have taken a right just before the monument. When I got to the right-hand turn, some birders were leaving and said it was showing well. I had a quick look through my telescope and saw the bird very distantly through masses of heat haze, perched on the right-hand side of a very distant hawthorn bush. It was 1:30pm.

I carried on walking and running to join 20-25 birders, all scoping the Bee-eater at point blank range. Before I got to the crowd, my phone rang, Lee Evans asking me if I'd seen it. I said, 'Yes, very distantly in heat haze'. When I arrived at the spot the bird had just flown out of view, and was flying low down behind lots of hawthorns. I first saw it with my bins below the skyline. I noted the green underparts, wings and tail with long central spike. It was silhouetted in the sky and joined forces with hirundines. I was able to scope it only when it had passed the monument and café and vanished.

Two further birders arrived after me, Kent-based Gary Howard and Jonathan Lethbridge. The bird was never seen after 1:38pm. I estimate that I watched the Bee-eater in my bins for 1-2 minutes. If I hadn't got lost, I could have scoped it for 14 minutes. I stayed to 5:30pm and watched hundreds of people from all corners of Britain dipping the bird. I suppose I was one of the lucky ones and for once, living in the south-east had paid off.

The Blue-cheeked Bee-Eater was originally

found by Jack Chantler and became the 10th for Britain since 1950.

Kim and I decided to give up the tenancy on the Rusper house and move into my mum's place. Over the weekend of 30-31st August, Andrew, Luke and I hired a van to take all the house contents from Rusper to Tilgate. Our next-door neighbours were Debbie, Chris, Rachel, Sophie and Nicky. Sophie was keen to find out what twitching was all about, so she decided to sleep over at my house and join me Sunday at 5am for a trip to see some juvenile Marsh Terns at Farmoor Reservoir in Oxfordshire. We arrived at 6:30am and all three terns were present. An American Black Tern had not been split from the Black Tern, but it was nice to finally see one after the 2006 dip at Lady Island Lake in Wexford. I sneaked back home by 9:30am and carried on with the move.

The American Black Tern was originally found on the 28th August and stayed to 3rd September. It was found by Ian Lewington and became the third record for Britain.

The move to Crawley was a good reason to leave the Fountain Inn darts team. That year's performance kept us in the top division, and I think our captain had preferred the previous season with easier opponents.

I decided to form a brand-new darts team at the White Knight pub. The landlady was happy to lay on sandwiches and I twisted the arms of Chris Andrews, Peter Webster and Dave Hobbs of Colas to join. The pub advertised and they got the signatures of Kevin Berridge, Gareth Sheldon and Brett Davies. These guys were going to be guaranteed matches, and that just left Chris and me to complete the core group of five and bring Peter or Dave in as necessary.

On Tuesday 22nd September my darts team had just won a crucial darts match in the friendly league at work, and shortly after returning to my desk, the pager was flashing with news of a Sandhilll Crane in South Ronaldsway, Orkney, the first in Britain for 18 years. The bird had been found in Burwick, which is exactly where the John O' Groats passenger ferry docks.

Jonah from Form Films gave me the good news that the BBC had commissioned the documentary and given Lucy Leveugle the job of producing it. I had a chat with Lucy on the phone and she said she wanted to meet me and film me at work. I got permission from the Chief Exec for filming. Lucy filmed me working at my desk and playing darts. I had never seen so many people wanting to play darts as that day. Twenty people were filmed, and they all had to sign consent forms.

I rang Lucy and told her I was going for the Sandhill Crane after work. She already knew about the crane as she had been given an RBA pager to use over the autumn, and she confirmed that she could come.

I offered a lift to John Lees but being midweek, he would not be able to get leave at such short notice. It was John Benham's wedding anniversary, and that ruled him out. Lee Evans didn't want to come as soon as he knew Lucy would be there. He was now refusing to appear in the documentary which he had helped to get commissioned. My next choice was Steve Nuttall. I rang him and mentioned Lucy would be filming, and he had no issue with that and agreed to come.

I left work at 5pm, grabbed a few things from home and made my way north at 5:40. I picked Lucy up at Luton Airport at 7:30pm and Steve Nuttall at 9:30pm. We crossed the Scottish border at 12:10am. Then an hour or so later, Lucy had a funny turn. I came off the motorway and parked up. She was warning me that she might have to go back home as she wasn't feeling good. Twenty or so minutes later, she was feeling better, and she agreed to carry on with the journey. I am not sure if it was a panic attack or a bout of car sickness, but I was so happy she was feeling better. I felt responsible for her and was glad when we arrived at John of Groats at 6:45am.

The ferry departed at 9:00am with 60 twitchers aboard. I sat beside Julian Thomas on the very cramped upper deck. We also had on board the very funny Tim Cleeves, who was responsible for the '98 Slender-billed Curlew at Druridge Bay. He is married to Ann Cleeves OBE, a mystery crime writer who is responsible for writing the TV series 'Vera' and 'Shetland'.

We docked at Burwick at 9:40am and walked for 10 minutes downhill to the crane's favoured site. Just before we got there it had flown out of view, but it didn't take long to find it again. Once it was relocated the 60 twitchers filled up a narrow lane and got great scope views of the Sandhill Crane.

Some people decided to go in front of the queue and kneel for a more stable scope view. I tried to kneel and, in the process, fell down a ditch and landed on my tripod, breaking it in two.

The Sandhill Crane was the 3rd record for Britain and was available from 22nd to the 29th September.

We caught the ferry back at 5:30pm and arrived at John o' Groats at 6:10. I drove to Golspie (approx 1.5 hours south) and found a very nice hotel called the Ben Bhraggie (01408 633 242). The hotel's owner is a very funny Scottish lady named Desiree, and she asked me to 'chill out' at least 25 times whilst eating in her restaurant. The buzz of the Sandhill Crane and the incredible footage Lucy had filmed put me on cloud nine. I had a very nice tomato & basil soup, followed by sirloin steak and banoffee pie with cream, all washed down with a pint of Stella. We all got separate rooms courtesy of

the BBC, and next day we had a cooked breakfast and were gone by 8:50am. I drove Lucy to Inverness Airport and she got a flight back to London. She had stopped filming at the point where we had finished watching the Sandhill Crane. I guess once the twitch had finished, the video footage was a valuable commodity and had to be stored in a safe location as quickly as possible.

Paul Higson received a voice message about a Common Crane near Liddel Loch. He drove there and found it in stubble fields that weren't viewable from the road. Once he had clapped eyes on it, he rang RBA to check that he wasn't going mad. They confirmed that it was a Sandhill Crane. After leaving Orkney it was seen flying over Loch Sarclet, Latheron, Dunbeath, Helmsdale, Brora and Kildary on the 29th September. It was then relocated in Dax, south-west France for a few days up to 12th October.

On Thursday 1st October a Veery was found on Foula and the following day it was still there. Then another Veery was found, this time on Whalsay. Whilst at work, I had a look at the Flybe website to see what the costs would be for a Saturday flight. The cheapest was £295 return, departing Glasgow at 10:30am on Saturday, arriving at Sumburgh at 11:40am. Lucy was busy at the weekend, so I drove up with John Lees, Gordon Beck and Bob Chaukley.

Whilst waiting for our flight at Glasgow I received notification from a Shetland birder that the Veery was still present at Symbister, Whalsay. Just the type of news you want to hear once you've spent big on a bird. The drive from Sumburgh to Laxo is approx 45 minutes and we comfortably connected with the 2pm ferry to Whalsay. The crossing to Symbister took 40 minutes, and the Veery was frequenting gardens within a very short walking distance of the ferry terminal. During my time on Whalsay I saw it about 8 times, with a combined viewing time of 1 minute. At one point it fed on an exposed lawn for 5 seconds. Pure ecstasy! Whilst on Whalsay we also saw a Pechora Pipit, at Skaw.

The Veery on Foula was found by H and J Aalto. It stayed from 1st to the 7th October. The Veery on Whalsay, which was found by A. Seth and stayed from 2nd to 5th October, became the 9th British record.

We stayed the night in a B&B in Lerwick and next morning we saw a Blyth's Reed Warbler at Voe before flying back.

On Tuesday 6th October an Azorean Gull was found at Didcot in Oxfordshire. I decided to go on the Thursday, and Lucy was up for it. I picked her up at Gatwick railway station and we had a nice relaxing journey to Didcot. The pool by the level crossing was hard to find, but once found there were three other birders there. The Azorean Gull had first been spotted by Ewan Urquart at 1:10pm. I rang Lee Evans to say 'I've seen the gull with Steve Whitehouse, Lee Gregory and Steve Griffin and it flew off'. Then Lee arrived and accused people of cheating. Steve Whitehouse strongly objected and the two started shouting at each other and grabbing each other's throats. Lucy witnessed all of this but kept the camera towards the ground. Once it all calmed down, I told her that you rarely see trouble at twitches.

We left to see if the Azorean Gull had returned to its favourite field. Regrettably not, so once it had started to rain, we drove off to Abingdon and found a nice fish and chip restaurant. Just as we had started eating our chocolate pudding, Lucy got a garbled message on her pager about the gull. I quickly rang RBA and they confirmed that Paul Whiteman had seen the gull flying from the tip to its favoured field. We finished the cake and were

on site in 10 minutes. The gull was present, and we stayed watching for an hour. I had a brief chat with Lee whilst Lucy filmed from a distance.

On Wednesday 14th October at 12:48pm, a Cedar Waxwing was found on Inishbofin in Galway by Anthony McGeehan. When the mega alert went off, Lucy quickly agreed to come. I picked her up from Crawley railway station and John Lees arrived at my house at 5:45pm. Lucy did some filming with Georgie running around in her Batman costume and John getting into the car.

I left my house at 6pm and we picked up Ian Evans on route. He didn't know The BBC were filming. The plan was to connect with the 2:30am Holyhead-Dublin Ferry. When we arrived at Holyhead just before 1am, we couldn't find a petrol station that was still open, so we just boarded the ferry. Lucy did a bit of filming of John and me trying to sleep on the ferry. As soon as we got off, we got fuel in the port. Lucy did a lot of filming when we arrived at Claggan harbour at 10:40am.

We had an hour to wait for the boat to Inishbofin. Whilst waiting, several Brits turned up. I received a text from Victor Cashera, who was currently on Inishbofin, saying 'No sign of the Cedar Waxwing'. Victor was one of the 37 Irish birders who had chartered the 8:30am boat. I thought it would still be fun to film the boat crossing, and some people will only call it a dip once you get to site. I was filmed sitting in the pub, where I tried to ask Harry Hussey about the Waxwing. He grunted and walked off whilst Lucy was filming. I thought the pub scene showing an exhausted driver would be a nice touch for the documentary.

We left the Island at 5pm and 30 minutes later we returned to the Irish mainland. I headed to Dublin Airport, where Lucy caught a flight to London.

The Cedar Waxwing was a first winter. It was

the first record for Ireland and was seen only on 14th October.

One of the perks of working for a French-owned company was that we had two French lessons a week. For the last six months my French teacher, Marie, had been planning a day trip to Lille for her French students. On Friday 23rd October, 17 students were due to leave Colas at 9:15am to be taken by minibus to Ashford to connect with the Eurostar to Lille. We were due to spend four hours doing our own thing, then make our way to a restaurant for 6pm and leave Lille at 8pm, getting back to Crawley at 11pm.

It would have been fun to go on the trip to practise the French we had learned, but Chris Heard phoned the night before to inform me of an Eastern Crowned Warbler seen at South Shields. I couldn't believe how bad this bird's timing was. I would just have to reconcile myself to missing it. I eventually got to sleep and when I woke up the first thing I did was reach over for the pager. No messages yet – that was a good sign, it had probably gone. But then at 7:30am I had a message saying 'Eastern Crowned Warbler still present'. What the hell do I do now?

I got dressed. I was too angry and annoyed to have breakfast, so I just made myself a coffee and told my wife the bird was still there. Her female intuition already knew that. I got to work at 8:15am, not wanting to inflict my grumpy mood on my 16 happy-go-lucky colleagues. I informed my boss of my intention not to go to France and asked if I could have leave at exceptionally short notice. Fortunately, she gave me the day off, and I offered to re-imburse the firm for all travel and meal costs incurred on my behalf.

My mood instantly changed into my usual happy-go-lucky self. All I needed to do was point my car north and drive for five hours.

I rang Lucy to inform me that I was going to South Shields. She relayed the information to Wes, who was already on site filming the Craig family and Johnny Allan.

I finally left Crawley at 9am and tried to find South Shields without my satnav (which was in my wife's car). During the northbound journey I got flashed by a mobile speed camera high up on a bridge overlooking the A1. It flashed me and a tailgater doing approx. 90mph.

I arrived at South Shields at 2pm, and Wes filmed me walking to the crowd of twitchers, chatting to Chris Heard and trying to see the Eastern Crowned Warbler. There were 180 birders watching it. After 20 mins or so I got good bin views of the warbler and a little later, I got good scope views. The twitch was well organised. Franko did a good job in keeping birders away from the section of the quarry that directly overlooked the warbler's favoured sycamores.

I left the site at 4:10pm and agreed to give Johnny Allan a lift back to London. It was nice to chat at length with him about Surrey and the Beddington bird scene. Being a 2nd Dan Black Belt in Karate, Johnny can easily be recognised at a twitch wearing his khaki Jacket and smoking a cigar.

The Eastern Crowned Warbler was found by Dougie Holden on the 22nd and stayed until the 24th October. Dougie had decided to surprise his wife by taking a day off work to celebrate their 26th wedding anniversary, but she had plans she couldn't get out of, so instead Dougie went birding at Trow Quarry. There he photographed what he thought was a Yellow-browed Warbler. When County Recorder Mark Newsome saw the pictures on Birdforum, he muttered the words 'Eastern Crowned Warbler'. He says the colour drained from his face and his heart went into overdrive. It was the first record for Britain.

Ultra-keen twitcher Richard Bonser left the Azores to see the warbler immediately, but missed it by a day.

We stayed at Kim's parents' farm for most of November, whilst builders recommended by Sussex birder Paul Marten agreed to fit a new kitchen, bathroom and ceilings, re-plaster the lounge wall, do a full house re-wire and repaint the interior. The work finished on 5th December and to celebrate moving back I headed to Crawley for a KFC takeaway. I parked the car just round the

Blue-cheeked Bee-eater
Merops persicus
St. Margarets Bay. Kent
22nd July 2009

G. BAGNELL

2009	Regular	Vagrant	BBRC/IRBC 1 year	BBRC/IRBC 2 year	BBRC/IRBC 3 year	BBRC/IRBC 4 year	BBRC/IRBC 5 year	BBRC/IRBC 10 year	BBRC/IRBC 20 year	BBRC/IRBC Lifetime	Cat B	Total
Seen	276	36	85	8	7	7	25	14	4	4	0	466
During		1				1	3	4	1			10
B&I Total	276	38	92	12	12	15	42	35	30	37	8	597
	100%	95%	92%	67%	58%	47%	60%	40%	13%	11%	0%	78%

corner in a dark alleyway from KFC. I waited in the pouring rain for 30 minutes whilst 20 people ahead of me got served. Once served I got back to my car at 7:38pm and my car was clamped. Two tough looking guys appeared out of the shadows and said the only way I could get my car back was to pay £135 now or double when the removal truck collected it. I reluctantly paid the money.

SUMMARY – 2009

During 2009, I travelled 7,762 miles in Britain and Ireland in the pursuit of new birds and managed to increase my list by 10 BOU/IRBC species. This took my British and Irish list to 466. The Combined Official stood at 597 species, and I had now seen 78.1% of them. There were five additions to the Official British and Irish List during the year: Baikal Teal (2001), Pacific Diver (2007), Yellow-nosed Albatross (2007), Glaucous-winged Gull (2006) and Asian Brown Flycatcher (1992).

The 10 lifers in the table above are Glaucous-winged Gull (20-year), Oriental Pratincole, Sandhill Crane, Asian Brown Flycatcher and Baikal Teal (10-year), Blue-cheeked Bee-eater, Crested Lark and Veery (5-year), Pacific Diver (4-year) and Collared Flycatcher (1-year).

I decided the most important bird seen during the year was the Blue-cheeked Bee-eater, which was seen by only 60 individuals during its short stay. It certainly wasn't the rarest bird of the year, but very satisfying to see a bird that could have left at any point. Many birds can see France on a clear day from here and this is probably the reason I've dipped in the past. This was the first twitchable one in Britain since the Shetland individual in 1997. It appeared in 'Birding with Bill Oddie' (Season 2 episode 1, 'Shetland'). I saw the three seasons on BBC Two from 21st February to 31st March 2000. Bill is one of the few celebrities I really admire. He has the ability to make birdwatching look very exciting and I'm sure he's planted that seed in many birders' minds with his numerous appearances on TV. I just hope the effort that went into making the documentary will be well received by the watching public.

I do believe that without my known association with Lee Evans I would have never been picked for this documentary. Lee is well known for being the self-appointed judge, jury and executioner. The way he polices the birding scene is everything a documentary maker could hope for.

CHAPTER 12

2010

Kim's youngest boy Andrew had turned sixteen on 20th January and ever since my mum's funeral he seemed to have been spending a lot of time with Rachel next door. Apparently they were only friends… wink wink, nudge nudge. My six-year-old daughter Georgie wasn't into romance yet, but Nicky next door was of similar age and was becoming a regular visitor to our house. He was a really sweet little boy and it was nice for Georgie to have someone her own age who she could play with.

We shared a single driveway leading to two garages. Our back gardens overlooked each other, and you could often see Debbie Hathaway outside smoking a cigarette. It turned out Debbie was a seriously good darts player who regularly won trophies and highest checkout in the Crawley Ladies' League.

The builders were back in January to convert my front lawn into a paved driveway for two cars and a porch, complete with a small bathroom. I really didn't envy them building in the snow.

On the work front I was given the responsibility of looking after the Traffic Management accounts. This involved flying to Newcastle once a month for two to three nights. My new manager was now Dennis Gregg and I must say he was one of nicest managers I had ever had. Due to lack of office space, Dennis got an extra desk put into his office for me to use.

On Saturday 8th May the news of a House Finch broke at 8:30am at Swingates at Lands End. I wanted to go, so I picked Chris Heard up in Maidenhead. We had got as far as Devon when Chris got several phone calls saying yellow variants (as this was) were due to bad diet and this probably indicated it was of captive origin. Chris remarked he had never seen yellow variants in the USA, and we agreed to cut our losses by not driving another 100 miles to see a bird we would never be able to count. I drove Chris back and went home.

The House Finch was last seen in Cornwall on 12th May and was believed to have first been seen on the 3rd May. It was re-found at East Prawle at 12:40pm on 27th June. John Lees was very keen on seeing it after a 'Birding World' article had pushed it as a wild bird. The following day we saw it in a housing estate sitting on roofs and garden fences. Whilst down that way we lucked into two Gull-billed Terns at Topsham. The House Finch was last seen on the 22nd October in front of the Piglet Stores in East Prawle.

On Sunday 15th August a Syke's Warbler was fund at Druridge Bay CP in Northumberland. The next day, I arrived on site at 2:30pm and the bird showed very well for the hour and a half I was there. It was moving between three Hawthorn bushes and one without leaves gave the best views – some scope views were for five or more minutes. I noted its milky brown upperparts and white underparts and long pointed bill, with a supercilium not going past the eye, long tail and short primary projection with dark centres to the tertials. Its call was heard by others and recalled the rattle of the Lesser Whitethroat.

This bird was found by M. Kerby and became the 11th record for Britain. It was only available for two days. I had missed one in Portland on 1st July 2000 whilst dating Louise. Some guys managed to get one on North Ronaldsay between 29th September and 1st October 2003. A Beachy Head one-dayer was found on 31st August 2002. Locals were invited, but the news did not go nationwide until about an hour before dusk. By that time I was enjoying a hot bath.

On Sunday 5th September a House Crow was reported at Cobh in Cork. Then RBA mega'd it the following Sunday at 9:15pm. I was happy to go on the Tuesday, leaving Lee Evans time to see a King Eider in Suffolk first. This also gave John time to arrange work cover and be back by 3am Thursday. Chris Heard didn't mind waiting a day.

On Monday at 8:06am, I got a text from Mark Carmody saying he was watching the Indian House Crow at Kennedy pier, Cobh. That day only 4 British twitchers travelled. The only other British and Irish record was in 1974 and that stayed 2 whole years. It was seen by a 14-year-old boy called Killian Mullarney.

John offered his car for the drive to Fishguard. During the journey it became obvious that it was going to be very difficult to get there in one piece. The wind was buffeting the car constantly and it was consequently drifting between lanes 1, 2 and 3. I pulled into a service station on Junction 36 of the M4 (Shell at Rhondda) and soon discovered it was drifting because each tyre had only 20 PSI instead of 32.

On the ferry we bumped into three birders from the north-east, including Tony Forde. They booked a one-day car return for £170, whilst we had the joy of taking Budget's last available rental car, an uneconomic 7-seater 4x4. We could have taken every birder on the ferry!

We left Rosslare at 7:15am and made our way west to Cobh. At 8:34am Mark Carmody kindly texted me that the House Crow was still present, and John burst into song.

We arrived at Cobh at 11am and saw the crow perched on a small ledge in the square. Here we met three guys from Norfolk and Phil Davis, who now lives in Ireland. This was my 500th UK400 Club species and a big moment for me to wear my bright Orange T-shirt worded 'I've just seen my 500th wild bird in Britain!' Phil refused to take a photograph of me standing next to the UK400 Club chairman, Lee Evans, so John obliged. I feel I must apologise for my T-shirts not mentioning Ireland. The T-shirt was hastily arranged for the twitchers' programme and it would have been a nice moment if the 500th species had been seen whilst filming. I couldn't leave Cobh without an Irish breakfast, and we popped into the hotspots of Ballycotton and Tacumshin Lake before returning.

The Indian House Crow was categorised as a D2 species (those that have arrived through ship or other human assistance) and therefore was not counted on the Irish List. It stayed 685 days and was last seen near Cobh hospital on 21st July 2012. My official British and Irish list were 33 birds short of magical 500 and this bird may never make the countable grade in my lifetime.

On Saturday 25th September Georgie and I were playing a complex school number game with spinners, counters and a numbered grid (1 to 100), and she beat me. Then Kim shouted out 'You've got a text on your phone!' I ambled upstairs and picked up the phone and it read: 'MEGA Norfolk Empidonax flycatcher (probably Alder, Willow or Least) Blakeney Point in Plantation at 1:05pm. Approach with caution'.

My heart started thumping, but Kim started giving me chores I didn't really want right then. I settled for one, dragging a mattress into Georgie's bedroom, as her cousins were staying the night. I then charged up and downstairs several times and left with warm clothes, camera and notebook. I left home at 1:15pm and the first stop was Tesco for a fill up, while calculating an ETA. The walk from Cley to Blakeney Point took 1.5 hours, and the drive was between 3 to 4 hours depending on traffic. My ETA should be at latest 6:45pm, when the bird would be getting ready to roost. If I dipped, I could always stay the night...

I arrived at Cley at 4:30pm, took one step out of the car and almost got blown over. The 3-mile walk was absolutely horrendous. The route to the point was mainly on shingle with a north-westerly gale blowing hail and rain in my face. I felt like a zombie and even considered returning to the car more than once, but the bird was now being considered a Yellow-bellied Flycatcher, a first for the Western Palearctic. I had to keep moving, even if it meant conserving energy by walking backwards every now and then. I was being overtaken by many fit birders and the visibility didn't allow me to recognise birders leaving.

When I got to the point at 5:45pm, most birders were seated, watching from the raised bank and looking down in the compound. When the bird was first called I rushed over and slipped on the mud. My Manfrotto tripod struck me on the side of the head and covered half my head in blood. I must have looked a mess, but I was just delighted to watch this Empidonax species for a whole minute at 5:55pm. I noted the double white wing bar, typical flycatcher upright stance, lemon-coloured throat and belly, and then it hopped right twice and was gone. This bird was not seen again, and the light was gone by 6:30pm. How lucky was I?

During my brief time at the point, I heard that a Northern Parula had been found on Tiree.

I left the point at 6:30pm thoroughly drenched. My waterproof coat had failed big time, the rain had got through to my jumper and T-shirt. I got into my car at 8pm and pulled my wet Nokia mobile phone out of my coat pocket. Nothing was working, so I dismantled it and found the rain had found its way to the battery compartment.

Britain is probably best known for its fish and chips and its pub culture, so when you're wet and hungry where better to stop that at a fish and chip shop? I found one in Fakenham, and the first person I saw was Lee Evans with his friend Alan. Lee said, 'I've been trying to get hold of you, John Bell has reserved you a seat for a boat leaving Oban for Tiree at 9am tomorrow'.

Initially I wasn't interested, but after putting Oban into the satnav, I could see I would have a good chance of catching the 9am boat with three hours spare. I cracked, dosed myself up on Red Bull and left Fakenham at 9:30pm.

The satnav took me through a few back roads, but it eventually got me onto the A1. At Scotch Corner, I turned onto the A66, then to the more familiar M6. I arrived at Oban at 6:30am. I parked up at the Columba Hotel and John arrived there at 7:45 on foot. At 8:13, the people of Oban might have spotted me hugging him. I did it because the pager had just confirmed the best news in the world: the Parula on Tiree was still present for its second day. What a feeling. Before this message, there was every chance that my sleepless night could have become a whole lot worse because I would have to start driving home.

We drove to the ferry terminal and attempted to get the car booked onto the ferry. It was no problem taking it out, but we wouldn't be able to bring it back until Tuesday. This forced us to go as foot passengers (£16.70 return each, where ticket was open for a month).

Oban is full of pay and display car parks, but if you ask John nicely, he can draw you a map showing where there is free parking, only a 20-minute walk from the ferry terminal.

The Ferry departed on time at 9:00am, and John and I tucked into a reasonably priced cooked breakfast. The crossing was due to take 4 hours. During the sailing, John attempted to organise transport from the terminal to the bird and accommodation for the night. Well, bless his cotton socks, he did try. John has got nearly every useful Tiree number stored on his mobile, including Tiree Ring'n'Ride (01879-220419, doesn't operate on a Sunday), car hire from MacLennan Motors (01879-220555, also closed on a Sunday) and John Kennedy Taxis (01879-220419), who didn't answer the phone. John also tried to book us in at the very cheap Millhouse Hostel, which sleeps 16/18 (01879-220435). They were also closed. In the end, Angus Murray at Birdline Scotland offered help. Angus flew onto Tiree with six others on a charter plane. The minibus that chauffeured them around the island was sent to pick us up at the ferryport once they were airborne again.

During the crossing I spotted an immature White-tailed Eagle flying alongside the ferry, what a wonderful sight! This is the way Scotland welcomes its guests.

The ferry docked at 1pm, and 15 minutes later the minibus arrived. The driver whisked us to John Bowler's house (11 miles away), and only charged us £11 for the privilege. John greeted us on arrival and led us into his beautiful house. We took our shoes off, but I must have left a trail of Blakeney sand and shingle from his front door to his living room window.

The Northern Parula was immediately showing just outside his window, feeding low down on a very small Sycamore. John sent out the news and shortly after, his phone started ringing. He must be popular, but it transpired most of the calls were from the President of the UK400 Club asking some very important questions, such as have you seen it yet? Where? When? How? Who's there? What's the bird doing? How much did it cost? Has Bagnell changed his underpants yet?

John Bowler is a very kind guy and it was so nice of him to allow us inside his house to view the bird. He told us he wanted to call his house 'Parula', because he fell in love with the species after seeing one on the Scillies in 1992. His wife Janet said, 'You can only rename it if you find one'. John has now been living on Tiree for 10 years, and now he has found one. The big question is, will Janet really let him rename the house?

We left John's house at 4pm and did some

birding in the general vicinity. Best birds included some Whooper Swans and a Greenland Redpoll. Around 6pm we attempted thumbing a lift. It was an instant success – a car slowed down and stopped. We both jumped in and shared the back seats with a couple of dogs. The driver had a hunch where we might find a vacant B&B in Crossapol. He introduced us to Marion Campbell (01879 220423) and we were in luck, she had two spare bedrooms. The room was perfect and after making and drinking a coffee I was out for the count.

The next morning John and I woke up 7am and tucked into a sumptuous breakfast Marion had prepared for us. We left the B&B at 8am and decided to walk the 3-mile stretch to Scarinish. The ferry arrived at 12:30pm and departed shortly after. I very rarely see any hot totty on Caledonian MacBrayne ferries, but this ferry was full of them. What I thought was going to be a Norfolk day trip turned into a 61 hours and 25 minutes mega tick fest.

The empid was found by James McCallum as he walked the eastern edge of the plantation and Blakeney warden Paul Nichols walked the western edge. It stayed until 27th September and praise must be given to Richard Crossley, who helped the BBRC to identify it as an Alder Flycatcher. It was the second for Britain and a nice clawback for not going for the 2008 Cornish bird.

The Northern Parula was available from 25-29th September and became the 15th record for Britain. The last twitchable one had been a three-dayer on the Scillies in 1992. Scilly also got a one-dayer in 1995.

The news of a Myrtle Warbler broke on Tuesday 5th October just as I got home from work. The earliest I could go was Friday, and if it stayed for the previous average of five days I was in with a chance.

I booked the Friday 6:35am Aer Lingus flight from Gatwick to Cork, returning on Saturday 22:10pm, for John Lees and myself (£165 return). Flying Aer Lingus was a very pleasant experience, with very large, comfortable leather seats, friendly cabin crew, and no extra charges for taking the telescope and tripod onto the plane.

We landed at Cork Airport at 8:15am and hired a car for two days costing €110 from Budget. We stopped off at the Skibbereen Spar shop and ordered tuna and chicken mayo rolls from the deli counter, arriving at Baltimore at 10am. From the free car park at Baltimore, I could see in the distance a couple of birders with scopes slung over their shoulders, waiting on the quay next to the Sherkin Boat & Cape Boat (+ 353-(0)87-9831876). One of the birders turned out to be Dermot Breen, the guy who had positively identified the Little Blue Heron. He had just come from the Cape and predicted that the Myrtle Warbler would not have left last night. He said there had been strong winds and heavy rain all night. John and I got on the 10:30am ferry and 45 minutes later we set foot on the Cape.

Cape Clear has recorded 303 different species of bird, including SEVEN different species of American warbler (Black & White, Blue-winged, Yellow, Myrtle, Blackpoll, American Redstart & Northern Waterthrush). Mary, the taxi driver (+353-(0)86-3836759), was waiting at the quay . She got us to Michaels Vincent's Garden within 4 minutes. The garden is a forest of trees, shrubs and many cats and is almost impenetrable to the human eye.

John Lynch found the Myrtle Warbler on a stone wall overlooking the garden. I also connected and saw it hovering, feeding and preening for at about 5 minutes at 12:45pm. Its beautiful lemon rump could be seen whilst hovering. However, John Lees missed it. If he had used his eyes alone to pinpoint movement rather than his binoculars, he might have seen it. Four hours later, he still hadn't seen it.

At this point, light was fading fast. Steve Wing (Warden) and Jim Dowdall (Ireland joint top lister) had both arrived by car. Steve got permission from Michael Vincent for all of us to enter his garden. Within 5 minutes of going in, Jim had seen his 6th Myrtle Warbler on the Cape, and then John finally saw it too. Hooorraayy! One nice guy on our boat did unfortunately dip it. He had headed back before the warden arrived, as he was desperate to catch the last boat off the island at 4pm.

John and I walked with a spring in our step to the Cape Clear Hostel (+353-(0)28-41968). On arrival we were greeted by an exceedingly handsome Irish gent called Richie Fenlon, who gave us a tour of the hostel. A couple of very nice features in the hostel were a chess board set-up (on a table) in the lounge and a ping-pong table in the dining room. I would have loved to play Richie at chess, but maybe next time. Also staying at the hostel were Harry Hussey and his friend John Lynch. Harry and John prepared a meal there, but John and I decided to join the Irish birders eating at Club Cleire. That night the dish of the night was pizza. I had one with black anchovies, capers and olives and it was absolutely delicious. The food was so good that every seat in the restaurant was taken.

The birders in attendance were Maurice Hanafin, Seamus Enright, Dennis O'Sullivan, Graham Clarke, Brian Lynch, Tony Nagle, Geoff Oliver (a birder who runs a B&B 028 49193 or 087 6197817), Paddy O'Keefe, James McNally, Alan Horan, David O'Connell, Peter Phillips, Victor Cashera, Jim Dowdall, Steve Wing & Mary Gade. After dinner we went upstairs to watch the Ireland v Russia football match, followed by a log call. We ended up drinking beer into the early hours of the morning.

It was good to chat at length with Jim Dowdall, Dennis O'Sullivan, Paddy O'Keefe and Victor Cashera. Tony Nagle ('the pig') is a charming man if you don't mention the Bird Atlas to him, and then there is Eamonn O'Donnell ('Bob'). Try to avoid talking to him about Bobolink or his views on the British and Irish listing scene. If you see him smile, feel very privileged. Such an enjoyable night with great camaraderie. It reminded me of my first trip to the Scilly Isles.

On the Saturday morning John and I got up at 8am. We made our way to kitchen and had some coffee and beans on toast, then strolled over to the observatory. Steve Wing was testing me out on the bird quiz when news broke of a Yellow-breasted Bunting at Dursey Island. This was starting to become one of most wanted birds since the Chinese started eating them.

I managed to get the midday boat off the Cape and we drove nonstop to the Dursey cable car. Owen Foley went across and was going to text us with any news. He texted me at 4pm saying there was no further sign. We headed back to Cork Airport and I got home at 10:15pm on the Saturday.

The Myrtle Warbler was found by Peter Philips and stayed to 13th October. It was the 12th record for Ireland.

The next bird was an American Bittern, which I saw on Saturday 30th October at Trewey Common in Cornwall with Matt Eade and the two Johns. It left the roost at 8:50am and we all managed to get a 15-second view of it as it flew towards some distant ponds. 20 minutes later it took flight again and this time it was mobbed by two Peregrines and some corvids. The aerial displays were filmed, and the Bittern fortunately escaped and landed near some pines. These were the only views I had of it. In flight I could clearly see its jet-black primaries and unmarked brown upper wing covert patches. Others managed to see brown breast streaking through their scopes. Unfortunately, I only had bins as I had left the scope in the car boot.

The American Bittern was identified by Richard Moores. It stayed from 26th to 31st October and became the 41st record for Britain. From 1st November it moved to Walmsley sanctuary and stayed to 6th November.

BBC4 televised the 'Twitchers: A Very British Obsession' documentary at 9pm on 1st November. I flew into Newcastle Airport in the morning, spent 8 hours in the office and checked into the Holiday Inn in at Swalwell around 6pm. I ate at Zizzi in the Metro Centre as fast as possible and got back to reception at the Holiday Inn and asked if there was any chance they could put BBC4 on. Reception said we could, as there was no football on.

Shame they showed me speeding and not wearing a seat belt plus holding a mobile whilst driving, but the film was well made. I knew the guys back at Rowfant were going to be miffed that they hadn't used footage of the darts match.

Andy Warhol said, 'In the future everybody will be world famous for fifteen minutes'. Considering BBC4 had allowed this to be televised in other countries, I guess this was my fifteen minutes of fame. Executive producer Jonah Weston was very keen to get Lee Evans to sign a consent form, as he felt the programme needed Britain's most obsessive twitcher. When Lee finally agreed, they sadly made space by dropping Sue Bryan and Johnny Allan. The real winner of the programme has to be 7-year-old Mya Craig, who twelve years later has become a household name. She has met Bill Oddie, Chris Packham, David Attenborough and Greta Thunberg and had many TV appearances.

She's recently become an author, with her first book called 'Birdgirl'.

I originally started a thread on Birdforum to advertise the Twitchers programme back on 7th August 2009. The thread got 298 messages in 15 months before the programme aired. Then over the next four days it got another 486. Overall, I think Birdforum members liked the programme. Lee Evans got so much stick that the invigilator, Steve Kirk, decided to close the thread down.

Richard Webber wrote a nice article in the Express on 23rd October about Brett Richards, Steve Nuttall and myself. The article in December's 'Birdwatch' by Dominic Mitchell thought it 'focused on the eccentricities of a few rather than many' and David Callahan said 'when your partner sees this documentary, your birding will now look proportionate, reasonable and sane'.

That evening, the programme prompted my mother-in-law Jen to ring me and tell me off for saying 'You forget you've got a family'. My biggest surprise came on the 2nd November when I got stopped by a member of public in Newcastle who said 'Was you on TV last night?' I'm glad I made the programme and I think Lucy Leveugle performed a miracle to make it appeal to the masses.

Next it was back to Ireland for a Northern Harrier, a North American bird, reported at Tacumshin. I left home on Friday 5th November and met up with Paul Holmes, Simon and Rob Chidwick at 8:55pm. We got to Fishguard at 1:30am and teamed up with John Regan and Tony Ford. During the crossing a passenger was taken ill and the ferry doctor was called out, delaying our arrival in Rosslare by an hour.

Anne from Budgets upgraded us to a seven-seater costing €115 and we got to Tacumshin by 8:15am. The Northern Harrier appeared at 1:01pm. I noted the grey-black hood, separated

NORTHERN PARULA
Setophaga americana
Tiree, Argyll
26th October 2010
G. BAXTER

by a white collar, and the rufous underparts extending to the carpal joint on the underwing. This impressive bird, a close relative of the Hen Harrier, was on view for two hours and provided some good flight opportunities for photographers. We watched it in the company of Mike Nolan, Dennis Weir, Killian Mullarney and Kieran Grace. It was nice to see Kieran and ask him about the Yellow-breasted Bunting he had found on Dursey last month.

The Northern Harrier was found by Tom Kilbane on the 28th October and stayed to 24th May 2011. It was the second record for Ireland.

I saw a possible Eastern Yellow Wagtail at Colyton on 12th December. It was viewed from a public footpath to the west side of a treatment works. The wagtail fed on the same filter tank the whole time I was there, and I didn't hear it call. The constant movement of the water jets prevented it from settling, but it did manage to preen a couple of times on the edge of the filter tank. It lacked any yellow plumage and fitted the classic grey and white appearance which often leads to an Eastern Yellow Wagtail being suspected.

The possible Eastern Yellow Wagtail was found by Phil Abbott and Clive Williams on 4th December and stayed to 19th December. A faecal sample and a few feathers dislodged when trapped on 14th December were sent to Aberdeen University for DNA testing. They unambiguously came back as north-eastern clade (species group).

2010	Regular	Vagrant	BBRC/IRBC 1 year	BBRC/IRBC 2 year	BBRC/IRBC 3 year	BBRC/IRBC 4 year	BBRC/IRBC 5 year	BBRC/IRBC 10 year	BBRC/IRBC 20 year	BBRC/IRBC Lifetime	Cat B	Total
Seen	276	36	85	8	10	9	25	15	5	4	0	473
During					3	2		1	1			7
B&I Total	276	38	92	12	12	15	42	36	32	38	8	601
	100%	95%	92%	67%	83%	60%	60%	42%	16%	11%	0%	79%

SUMMARY - 2010

During 2010, I travelled 5,877 miles in Britain and Ireland in the pursuit of new birds and managed to increase my list by 7 BOU/IRBC species. This took my British and Irish list to 473 species. The Combined Official List stood at 601 species, and I had seen 78.7% of them. There were four additions to the Official British and Irish List during the year: Amur Falcon (2008), Tufted Puffin (2009), Eastern Crowned Warbler (2009) and Citril Finch (2008).

The 7 lifers in the table above are Citril Finch (20-year), Eastern Crowned Warbler (10-year), Northern Parula and American Bittern (4-year), Sykes's Warbler, Myrtle Warbler and Northern Harrier (3-year).

There are quite a few talented individuals who run websites. One of my favourites is Mark Laylor, who runs www.gyrcrakes.com. Mark is a Yorkshireman now living on Guernsey. His humour is so on the money and it was nice to see my face being used on a dance routine at the end of the video. The video is called 'Thou shalt always bird' and was also uploaded to YouTube on 14th November. Check it out.

I decided my most important bird seen during the year was the Northern Parula. This bird had not been twitchable in Britain and Ireland for 18 years, but because there had been 18 records in Britain and Ireland since 1950 it averaged out as one every 3 to 4 years. The Jetstream use to bring lots of American birds to the Scillies in the 80s and 90s and since it moved further north, so have the yanks. Many birders love to mention seeing Parula's and Black-billed Cuckoo on Scilly back in the day, and now I had finally seen a Parula this would be like water off a duck's back. John Bowler must have been on cloud nine for finding it, especially as he sourced plants from overseas to build a garden with best bird habitat on the island.

CHAPTER 13

2011

My second attempt at seeing a Slaty-backed Gull at Rainham was on the 17th February. I was on site by 6:30am and there was no sign of it, but at 11:25am the elusive bird appeared, thank god. I got pretty good views of this monster gull. It was the same size as the accompanying GBB Gull, dwarfing Herring & LBB Gulls. Even at distance the size sooty head and large white crescents to the tertials were obvious. It took a while to see the leg colour and to me they appeared pink. I saw the moon on p8, when it outstretched its wings and when in flight I saw the heavy protruding chest. Over 150 connected today, and the only disappointment, was not going to Chipping Norton first thing and seeing a Rufous Turtle Dove.

The Slaty-backed Gull was originally found by Dominic Mitchell at Rainham. It was first seen 13th to 14th January, then 16th to 17th and 20th to 26th February, then at Hanningfield Reservoir on 6th February and Pitsea on 3rd and 19th February.

On 7th March a Velvet Scoter was re-identified as a Stejneger's Scoter at Rossbeigh Kerry by Josh Jones. News broke on Wednesday 9th March at 10:39am whilst I was on the last day of a 3-day visit to Newcastle. At the exact moment the news broke, I was sitting on one of those comfortable plastic chairs with an oval shaped hole in the centre. I quickly finished the paperwork and got back to my desk to consider my options.

Chris Heard was quick on the draw and texted me to find out my travel plans. Lee Evans was currently guiding a group of birders around Morocco and the Western Sahara and was due back later that day. I departed Newcastle Airport around 2:30pm on a Flybe Q400 aircraft. Once back at Gatwick I was greeted at 3:42pm with some good news. Not that the United Kingdom now had three new billionaires (now totalling 32), but that there had been no sign of the White-winged Scoter at Rossbeigh. I now didn't have to decide what to do. On Thursday, the Scoter was seen again, and everybody wanted to fly on Saturday. I bought all four seats on the credit card for £136 each, flying Stansted-Kerry-Stansted.

On Saturday the plan was for John to get to my house for 3:30am, then to pick Chris and Lee from Chaffinch House at 4:30am and be parked at Stansted's long-term car park by 5:30am. The bus should get us to the terminal for 6:00am. This would give us a whole hour before the gate closed for us all to chill out in the Terminal. Nothing could go wrong, right? Wrong! John got lost trying to find my house. He had been before, but maybe needed to come a few more times before it sank in. He had a satnav, but I didn't think Liz had showed him where the on/off button was yet. Anyway, John rang me just before 4:00am to say he had got lost and was parked at the Asda superstore. I drove to Asda and John followed me back to my house. With only half an hour lost, we should still make the flight.

At approx. 6:30am all four of us were queuing by the x-ray machine. Obviously, we all know you can't take liquids and sharp objects through. But Lee had an item of cargo that made the security guards push the panic button and before you can say "STEJNEGERS" he was surrounded by Armed Police. He had a live shotgun cartridge in his jacket pocket. Lee didn't have a shotgun licence – he had found it whilst out looking for pheasants. And before anyone asks, no he wasn't supplementing the declining stock of Lady Amhersts in Beds/Bucks.

After being detained for about half an hour, a message from the Sergeant at the nearby nick was radioed through: "Let the idiot go". Lee, very relieved, was soon repatriated with us all.

In the plane queue we spotted many groups of fellow twitchers, including Kevin McCoy, who was going to join us. Lee managed to get Justin Taylor and his dad to take Kevin and Dave Ellis. The plane landed on time at Kerry (1.5 hours in duration) and as I disembarked, I bumped into Ed

Carty. He told me "The Scoter is still there and showing well".

I hired a car from Hertz for 62 euros per day and we should be in Rossbeigh in 30 minutes. But we were the last group to arrive from the airport, and unfortunately we had missed the scoter by 10 minutes. Kevin McCoy's crew all connected.

Lee suggested we look further up the coastal cul-de-sac road. Other crews did the same thing. Alan Lewis did remarkable well to re-find the scoter in the bay an hour after it flew off from the beach. He allowed me to look through his scope, but my rapidly deteriorating eyesight could only see black dots, and I couldn't decipher anything with this brief view. Lee and Chris, on the other hand, could see the Stejneger's Scoter well enough to tick. John and I hoped it would come in closer. It didn't, and eventually everybody lost it.

During this time John Murphy was instrumental in getting me onto the location where Alan had found the scoter, but thanks to the many small groups of scoters constantly changing shape with constant diving and re-surfacing, it was hard to get a future landmark.

The rain started and crews started retreating to their cars. We decided to seek out a garage and re-fuel our tired bodies. Within half an hour, the rain had stopped, and we went back to the beach for more searching. Whilst chatting to some of the visiting Brits an Irish birder offered us all free coffee from the boot of his car, supplied by a local hotel. It was an absolutely brilliant gesture and it enhanced the already very high sentiments I have for this nation.

Just as I took my last sip of coffee, Lee Gregory received a call from Stuart Elsom that the scoter had been re-located much further up the cul-de-sac. Within 5 minutes we were on site, and I had a quick look through Richard Bayldon telescope (same as mine) and I could now see the Stejneger's Scoter clearly; I could easily make out the diagonal white eye stripe almost reaching the top of its head. The other features were the white secondary panel, on open and closed wings, reddish edge to lower mandible, black knob on bill, heavy bill. Josh Jones had done very well with this re-identification. Once John had seen it well enough, we headed back to the airport via Cromane for a Spoonbill.

Lee and Chris went off to sleep. As John was embarrassed about his early morning gaffe and being late, I thought I would give him a chance to redeem himself by doing a bit of map reading. All I wanted him to do was direct us back to the airport. John took the map, and I followed his instructions. True to form John directed me in completely the wrong direction whilst in the Castlemain area. Lee woke up and was furious at John for getting us lost. He snatched the map off John and directed me back to the airport. I had to drive at breakneck speed to make the plane, and at one stage I even drove into someone's front garden to ask homeowners if we were heading in the right direction. I was just about to get out of the car and ask and Lee shouted out "we haven't got f**king time, just keep f**king driving!"

I drove as fast as I safely could. I managed to overtake a tractor with trailer and other slow-moving vehicles. The gate for the flight was due to close at 5:30pm and we screeched into the terminal building at 5:35, with no time to return the car to the hire company. We dropped it off in the short-term car park opposite the terminal (I left the car keys with lost property) and we legged it towards the x-ray machines. The gate was now officially closed, but they still let us board. I don't think this kindness would have been replicated at a UK airport.

During this period of madness, I left my mobile on the x-ray conveyor belt. John spotted it and returned it to me; I then used it to apologise to Hertz for not filling the car up with unleaded and dumping it inside the carpark. Yet again the Irish employee of Hertz, said "no problem".

Before we boarded the plane, Ed Carty rounded up the twitchers for a group photograph of us all standing next to the plane. The shot included me, Lee Evans, Derek and Justin Taylor, John Lees, David Ellis, Craig Holden, Will Soar, Matt Deans, Lee Gregory and Kevin McCoy. On the flight home it was nice to chat to a woman called Adele who ran a successful hairdressing business in Kerry. She started off the conversation, so Lee and I quizzed her about the intricacies of hairdressing. I celebrated with a packet of peanuts and a bloody Mary for €9.

After disembarking the aircraft, we waited in the nothing-to-declare zone for John to come through. We were all puzzled, as he had been just behind when leaving the plane. After waiting 10 minutes I could see him distantly being escorted by a security guard through the glass pane. He had lost his boarding pass on the plane and security had to escort him through a different security gate.

The Stejngers Scoter, last seen on the 11th April, was a first for Ireland.

I bought an HTC Wildfire Smart Phone on ebay for £180. It was a device that let you email, internet whilst out and about and was going to revolutionise our highly mobile hobby. I set up a Twitter account. It would be interesting how this took off for birding.

On Monday 6th June at 8:36am I was just putting my laptop and sandwich box in the back seat of my Vectra when I heard the liquid sound of a text message hitting my HTC Wildfire. This turned out be a White-throated Robin in Hartlepool. A proper mega, but going for it wouldn't be straightforward, reasons being:

(1) I was due to be at work in 20 minutes.

(2) On Tuesday I was flying to Newcastle for a 3-day work visit.

(3) The White Knight darts team were appearing tonight in a Cup Final.

(4) This would certainly be "real", and not an elaborate hoax involving a stuffed bird and a native branch.

(5) The White-throated Robin is a nocturnal migrant, and there were 12 hours of daylight left. The journey would take 5-6 hours, depending on traffic.

I decided it was worth the risk of going. All I had to do was get permission. I rang up my Newcastle-based manager, Dennis, and he gave me the thumbs up. Then I put lift offers out with RBA and mentioned on Facebook that I was going to Cleveland. I popped into the office to get some files I needed for Newcastle and during the 3-minute office visit my mobile didn't stop ringing. The only confirmed passenger I had before filling up with diesel was Tony Vials, who was going to meet me at M1 junction 15A. On route John Benham wanted picking up from Leatherhead. I rang Lee, and there was no reply. Brendan Glynn wanted picking up from Junction 18 of the M25. Luckily for Lee, his partner Carmel saw my Facebook advert and drove home and woke him up.

The M25 had ground to a halt, and it took me 2.5 hours to get to Junction 18, where Lee and Brendan joined us. Whilst on the M1 it became obvious that we would need to take a detour eventually, as Junction 19-20 was closed. We pick up Tony Vials at 15A at about 12:30pm. We came off the M1 a few junctions up and got back on the M1 about one junction north of the closure.

Many of the phone calls Lee receives have us

all in stitches. A phone call he had to say that the bowling team had just turned up was hilarious. Lee enquired if they could postpone their match to another day, and he was willing to give them money to stop playing. If you know Lee, it's hard enough getting petrol money out of him, let alone him paying money to a bowling party.

Another phone call about a barking dog was also funny. Lee said it would get push the robin on. Chris Heard was already on site and said he had missed it by a few seconds. 10 minutes later Chris rang to say he had now seen the robin, and it was back on the Green. The dog and the bowling party were still in attendance. Lee at this point was apoplectic. I think that's the right word for Lee's condition.

At 3:15pm we arrived in Hartlepool. There must have been 500 twitchers, all with big smiles on their faces. They were smiling because the robin had made a brief appearance at 3:10pm, and then gone missing for the last two hours. I couldn't believe how small the bowling green was, and it was totally surrounded by twitchers and photographers.

Two and quarter hours then passed with no sign of the robin anywhere. Twitchers/photographers were asked to move back and give the bird space to fly in from the corner of the bowling green adjacent to a doctor's garden). They refused to move. I decided to have a chat with Chris Brown (the finder) and see if he would go back into the trapping area and try to push it back onto the bowling green. He said he would, but the crowd would need to be moved back to at least to where an ice cream van was parked, which was about 20 metres. I then asked them to move. 90% of the gathered crowd moved back, but I didn't see a single photographer doing so. This behaviour I find absolutely disgusting. Why are these people so f??king selfish?? They had already got good pictures and they were not prepared to give the rest of the assembled crowd (500-600 at this time) a chance to see the robin.

Chris Brown soon went into the trapping area. He came out to announce that he couldn't see the robin anywhere. Lee suggested we should all independently start searching for the bird in gardens in the vicinity. After 20 minutes of searching I got a call from Simon Chidwick, who announced that the robin was in the doctor's garden. With that news, Lee, Brendan and I ran like lunatics towards the garden. On arrival, a van was parked up on the pavement outside the garden's 10-foot brick wall complete with anti-vandal paint, and a birder was standing on its roof and watching the robin. Lee manages to get on top of the van to get a view of the bird. He watched it for a bit and then gave me his space. I eventually saw the bird and had the pleasure of having Sue Bryan leaning on top of my back. The robin showed well for me on the wooden structure containing the compost heap for about 20 seconds.

The time was now 5:50pm and I was beaming. I got down from the van and gave others a chance to view the bird, then wandered back to the car and devoured my packed lunch. I sent another tweet and a Facebook message announcing the good news. Time was getting on and it was a bit chilly, so I slipped a fleece on and went back to the garden. Now there were TEN ladders and THREE vans in position to give the large crowd a chance to see the robin. I took another look at it for about 5 minutes on and off. The best news was that everybody connected, and we decided to leave at 7:15pm. I arrange for John Benham, who wanted more prolonged views of the robin, to get a lift back with John Lees. I needed to get home as I was flying to Newcastle at 8:30 the next morning.

The White-throated Robin was the 3rd record for Britain. It was found by Chris Brown and stayed from 6-10th June.

I must say that there was no damage to the wall, but one van's windscreen did get smashed by someone standing on the wrong section of the roof. The roof of the van I was standing on did cave in a little bit... I think 10 people on the roof at the same time was just too much.

On the way home we stopped for fuel and a Burger King. After I had dropped off Lee at Little Chalfont I got back onto the M25 and 5 minutes later I hear a loud bang from the front of my car. The car was still moving, so I carried on – maybe I had hit something on the road. But 3-4 minutes later the battery light started flashing. I felt instantly sick, as my breakdown and recovery policy with Green Flag had expired in March and I had forgotten to renew it. Where the M4 connects with the M25 is the exact point where the RED battery light decided to stay on. What should I do? I decided to carry on driving - I was still 40 minutes from home. I got home at 1:20am without recovery, and then the oil light came on. It was looking like my fifth write-off in 12 years. Kim was furious that my twitching was destroying so many cars.

On 12th June an American White-winged Scoter was found at Blackdog, Aberdeenshire. I was hoping there was no rush to get to Aberdeen. I decided to book a flight from Gatwick on Saturday 18th June at 9:25am, returning the next morning. I travelled with John Lees, Kevin McCoy and Neil Howes. Being a frequent Flybe flier, it only cost me £67, whereas the others paid £125. I booked a night's stay at the Ythan Hotel and paid £48 for a day car hire.

I eventually saw the Scoter at 7pm. It had taken me 8 hours to connect. If it wasn't for the large-scale separation of Eider and Scoter, I think I would have dipped. Steve Richards (Staffs), Ian Foster (Newcastle), Justin Lansdell (Norfolk) and Nick Littlewood (Aberdeen) need a medal for trying to get me onto it. The last two were shouting out excellent directions at 7pm to twenty remaining people. Much earlier in the day Tony Davison (Derby) tried to show me it in his scope, but I couldn't decide which one it was.

My Vauxhall Vectra was transported from home to the Colas Garage in Ringmer. Whilst my car was there, they gave me a courtesy car to drive. They had my car for a couple of few weeks and told me it was going to need many things, including a new engine. This was the first time I had used Ringmer and when I got a bill for nearly £500 for use of hire car, parking at Ringmer, charge for mechanical investigation and moving the car to a scrap yard I was furious. I told my boss Dennis at Newcastle about the invoice, and he asked me to get it charged to Colas Newcastle. Dennis offered this because I was regularly work 4½ hours unpaid extra per day whilst in Newcastle. He never got round to paying me overtime and he thought this was the least he could do.

I didn't think – I asked Ringmer to invoice Newcastle. One week later I was called into Associate Financial Director's office. Here I provided a written statement on what had happened with the invoice. Simultaneously Dennis had to provide a written statement to the Colas North director.

A few days went by before were told that our punishment for this 'company fraud' would be a written warning. For the next six months we both had to be on impeccable behaviour or we could both get instant dismissal. If during the 6-month period we kept our noses clean, the written warning was going to be considered served and removed

from our files. The company viewed this as a very serious offence, and we were lucky not to have lost our jobs over it. I should have never got Dennis involved.

On 29th June 2010, Dennis's 18-year-old son Ryan was involved in a collision on the A1 outside Catterick army barracks. The collision happened just after midnight when Ryan was working for his dad on a stationary crash cushion vehicle and an articulated lorry collided. Ryan was catapulted onto the A1 and received serious head injuries, and he died the same day at Newcastle General Infirmary. How Dennis and his wife Linda carried on working for Colas after losing their son I will never know.

On 28th June I bought a 2006 black Peugeot 407 from my favourite auctioneers in Lancing.

Peter Johnson found an interesting wader at Weir Wood on 15th September 2011. He rang me just after 5pm, as he wasn't sure what this bird was. I had taken a half day's leave, predominantly to see a Sabine's Gull at Brighton Marina and a lingering Long-tailed Skua at Dungeness. I was now at Dungeness. We decided over the phone that it was probably a Temminck's Stint and news was put out. I then phoned Nigel Driver and Jake Everitt to see if they could get down there to help nail the identity. Jake went down, but Nigel couldn't make it on the first night.

Jake rang me to confirm that it was a Temminck's Stint. I needed this for my Weir Wood list, so I was praying it was going to stick the night. Fortunately it did, and Nigel saw it first thing and put the news out. I went to Weir Wood during my lunch break on Friday 16th and saw the bird on arrival. It was the same distance as the possible Red-necked Stint I had found earlier in the month. I was letting people look through my scope, as viewing through bins was hopeless. I saw no reason to doubt the identification. The bird was present for the next 3 days. During that time I was birding in Cornwall and Scilly. On Tuesday 20th September, Lee Evans had just seen a Pallid Harrier at Burpham and rang me at work to find out the exact location of the stint. I described how I had seen it between the two rafts, and the next minute he connected. A few minutes later he rang again and told me to get down there, as this bird was either a Least Sand or a Long-toed Stint. I left work at 5pm and looked at the stint with Ian Barnard, Paul Marten, Jake Everett, Nigel Driver, and a few others. Lee Evans' concerns were quickly agreed by all in attendance. Later on Tuesday evening, the news was put out as a possible Least Sandpiper. During Wednesday, many Sussex listers came down, plus Jerry Warne and David Willis. They were the first to confirm it as a Long-toed Stint. At 4:31pm this was mega'd and 70 people managed to connect. I was contemplating going back down for another look, but once I heard that people were trespassing, I avoided it.

The next morning I popped into Weir Wood to get some crowd shots. 110 twitchers made the effort, and it was nice to see so many familiar faces on my local patch. I just wish the stint had stayed for the visitors. The Long-toed Stint was accepted by the BBRC on 1st April 2022. The original description was poor and when a better description was submitted by Andrew Lawson and Richard Bonser with annotated stills by Kilian Mullarney it finally made the grade. This was the 4th record for Britain and Ireland.

On 16th September at 8:16pm, RBA put out a message "Possible Northern Waterthrush reported St. Mary's Lower Moors from ISBG hide at 7:30pm". After a bit of information probing - the finders had a good track record of finding good birds – I then put a lift offer out. Hugh Price and John Lees agreed to come. Then came a flurry of calls from people wondering what was going on.

John Lees got to mine at 11pm and I drove his car his car down to Three Bridges railway station to pick up Hugh. I then drove to Exeter Services, and then John and I took it in turns to get to Drift for some kip.

Once light was up, we got to hide and heard that soft liquidy sound from my phone. I slid the phone lock and read "Vodafone MDS: MEGA Scilly presumed NORTHERN WATERTHRUSH St. Mary's at Lower Moors from ISBG Hide at 7am". To say I felt a wee bit excited is an understatement. I felt like ripping my clothes off and jumping into Drift. I was smiling like a Cheshire cat as we drove to Penzance and waited for the ticket office to open.

Hugh was trying his best to dampen my enthusiasm on this mega-rare warbler. Every time I mention the words 'Northern Waterthrush', Hugh held his finger to his mouth and said "sssshhhh!"

Shortly after 8am the ticket office opened. I felt like chucking the credit card on the counter and saying "Charge what you like". I had missed the last one whilst I was on a family holiday in Turkey.

On the boat there were, surprisingly, very few birders. I spotted Johnathan Lethbridge and David Bradnum and a few Cornish birders who I didn't know. Whilst making plans to have some beers that night in Cornwall with Jonathan, the MEGA alert went off. The message on the pager was garbled, but one thing was for sure, it was on Scilly and the bird's name had the word 'Black' in it. What could it be? Black Lark possibly, no, not a Black & White Warbler. Yes, Black & White Warbler, confirmed by SMS message. Breathe, gather my composure... is this a bloody dream? I certainly hoped not! There had not been a Black & White Warbler in Britain since 1996.

Our boat docked and our taxi took us and

Andrew Holden and Vicky Turner towards Newford Duckpond. No sign of the Solitary Sandpiper, so next stop was Lower Moors for the two Yankie Warblers. From here, we took the trail and soon met Spider and Joe Pinder, who told us which path to take to start searching for the Black & White Warbler. They said that if we heard the tit flock, it should be close. I located the flock within 20 minutes and the guy standing next to me was the first to spot it. I watched in awe as this beautiful buff flanked lady Black & White Warbler fed at close range unconcerned by our presence. I rang the news out and watched this beautiful creature for the whole three minutes it was on view.

Next stop was the ISBG Hide to look for the Northern Waterthrush. We took the wrong patch and spent 30 minutes fighting our way through an 8-foot-high reed bed and prickly bracken. There was no turning back, as we were too far off the beaten track. When we arrived at the ISBG hide, there had not been any sign of the bird since 7am. We waited in the hide and enjoyed a close view of a nearby Pectoral Sandpiper. Then we got a taxi to Newford Duckpond. There was still no sign of the Solitary Sandpiper, but we did see a Bee-eater at Borough Farm.

At 3:05pm, we had a message that Andrew had found the Northern Waterthrush at Lower Moors, close to the Black and White Warbler. We rushed towards Maypole and booked a taxi back to Lower Moors. On arrival, we soon found the right area, a small pool nicely concealed within the woods, but there was no sign by 4pm, so we decided to get the boat back to Penzance. My mood got worse. I was leaving Scilly without the Northern Waterthrush, which was the main reason I had put myself into Cornwall in the first place.

Back on the boat, the plan to spend Sunday birdwatching in Cornwall just didn't appeal any more. I just wanted to go back to Crawley. Everybody agreed that they were happy to head back home immediately. My daughter Georgie had some homework (due to be handed in on the Monday) which I had promised to help her with. Kim was in a bad mood because I hadn't done it before I left, and her son Andrew had girlfriend problems and had failed his first driving test earlier in the day. I rang Kim to give her some good news. I announced. "You'll be pleased to know I'm coming home back tonight, should be home about 2am Sunday".

During the boat trip to Penzance we saw loads of Storm Petrels, Manx Shearwaters, a Bonxie, 2 Sooty Shearwaters, Grey Phalarope etc. I had a look at the pager whilst on the boat – bad move. The Northern Waterthrush was back. It had been seen at 6:38pm and 6:43pm. Why the hell did I leave Scilly?? We were all due at work on Monday. I could have easily got Monday off as leave and by now I would have seen the Northern Waterthrush. Never mind, it's only a bird. I can come back during the week.

At 7:15pm Hugh and I got off the boat before John and then waited for him to disembark. When he finally emerged, he was one of the last people off the boat and didn't look very happy. He had lost his car keys. John's coat had lots of pockets, and we checked each one. We confirmed that he had lost his car keys, and now the nearby fish and chip shop was closed. The RAC wouldn't tow as home as it wasn't a breakdown. The best they could do was send out a locksmith to get the car open and provide a key to start the ignition. This would cost £350.

John rang Liz to give her the news. Whilst all these calls were being made, Hugh and I had a wander around Penzance to find some food outlets. We found another chippy. This one was open, and

I had haddock and chips.

Once we got back to John, there was very good news. Liz had tracked down John's keys. Somebody had found them on Scilly and handed them into the local police station. Only trouble was, we couldn't get back to Scilly till Monday morning. All plane and chopper seats were fully booked for Monday, so the only way to get the keys back was to go on the boat on Monday morning. John decided he was going to stay in Penzance for two nights and get the boat over on Monday. Hugh and I were due back at work on Monday, and John offered to pay the train fare for both of us to get back home. We couldn't let him do that.

We wandered around Penzance looking for a B&B. The first one had a spare room with only a double bed, the second one the same and the third had one room left with twin beds. Bingo. John and I booked it for two nights. Hugh decided to splash out and check into a 3-star hotel on the Penzance Seafront.

Later that evening John and I went out for a beer. We found a pub with a dartboard and a band playing. I beat John 2-1 at darts and John said hello to a female customer whilst at the bar ordering some drinks. She then starting to act like his long-lost friend. She brushed her breasts into him and a few other guys' arms I could see. I carried on playing darts, and when I looked around I couldn't see John. He had disappeared around the corner, and was strutting his dance moves to the music of the band. When he got back to me, we both slipped out of the back door without John's newfound friend realising.

I had a good night sleep in the B&B. I woke before John, got up and put my dirty clothes on for the second day. Once dressed, I John got up and we spent ages looking for his Y-fronts with his wedding tackle swinging around. The breakfast room was full of holidaymakers. After breakfast we hired a car from a company based in Marazion. They delivered it to us within 15 minutes.

We picked up Hugh from the hotel and started birding at Drift. I found the Semipalmated Sandpiper and we also saw a Lesser Yellowlegs. Then I got a phone call from a Sussex birder that a Pallid Harrier had been found near Arundel. This was a new bird for my Sussex list, but I put it to back of my mind and enjoyed seeing two Black Kites 100 yards from Porthgwarra. One of the locals gave us the gen on where to watch, and we got superb views. We ended the day at Pendeen. John hates sea watching, so after an hour he retreated to the car for a sleep. Hugh and I soldiered on and enjoyed a busy seabird spectacular. Hugh saw 3 Long-tailed Skuas that I had missed, but I did manage to find a few Sabine's Gull's, Balearic Shearwaters, Bonxies and Arctic Skuas etc. The temperature was dropping, so we headed back to base.

Later that evening, all three of us went into Penzance for a bite to eat. We started off in an Italian restaurant and ended up staying there till 10pm. Nice food, but the beers were £5 each with an inch of head.

On Sunday night, I just couldn't sleep and kept thinking about the Northern Waterthrush again. John and I left early to fill the car up with fuel, picked up Hugh and left the car at Penzance docks, where the car hire owner was waiting for us. We said our goodbyes and booked the ferry tickets in the travel shop. Then I realised that I had left my telescope caps in the glove compartment. No bother, the car rental brought them back before we sailed. During the cruise we saw a close Leach's Petrel and a few Manx Shearwaters.

The taxi took us to Newford Duckpond. There was still no sign of the Solitary Sandpiper, but we did see Dan Houghton's Blue-winged Teal. I then went to Lower Moors to have another stab at the Northern Waterthrush. I knew exactly where to watch from, so I made my way to the gnat-infested cesspit of a pool. Many people were gathered around the pool, and I sat on a tree stump until my bum was numb. I must have sat quiet for at least 3 hours.

At around 3:30pm my crew decided enough was enough and headed back for the 4pm boat. At this stage of the game, I was quite happy to stay the night. I had about 20 gnat bites all over my face and I got a bit restless and wandered off to a pool where Dave Mac was standing. After 15 minutes I left him and went back to the original pool. Then, would you believe it, Dave Mac whistled us over that he had seen the Northern Waterthrush. I charged over, but I missed it by 20 seconds. At 3.45 he had seen it perched on an ivy-covered branch, just before it dropped into dense leaf cover. I felt we would have a chance at seeing it as although it was feeding in the leaf cover, there were some leafless clear spots.

Then at 4:30pm it flew back to the same branch where Dave Mac had originally nailed it, and I saw the bird at very close quarters in good light with my Leica bins. I could see its long white supercilium, slate-grey mantle and head in the bright sunlight, and some breast streaking, and then the bird was gone. I had the bird for only two seconds perched and a split second as it flew off from the branch towards an area of dense cover. Two other birders to my left also saw the bird well with me. I felt delighted that I had finally connected. Only 12 people saw this elusive bird on the Monday and 90 dipped.

The boat had now departed, and I thought I'd make my way to the airport. Andrew Holden had been on St. Mary's for 3 days and only managed a 5-second view of the Northern Waterthrush. At the airport I saw 4 Buff-breasted Sandpipers and a Woodchat Shrike. Luckily, the helicopter was running late and there was one space left on the 7:15pm departure to Penzance. Mine for £50. Must be fate. I landed as the ferry arrived and was repatriated with John and Hugh at Penzance Heliport.

The Black-and-white Warbler was found by C. Ridgard and stayed from 17th to 21st September, the 16th record for Britain and Ireland. The Northern Waterthrush stayed between 16th September 2011 and 16th April 2012. It was found by J & T.G. Davies and was the 9th record for Britain and Ireland.

On Monday 26th September I went with Neil Bostock for a Semipalmated Plover in Ventry Harbour, Kerry. We went via Fishguard ferry to Ventry. We arrived at midday, and missed the plover by 57 minutes. There was no sign of it for the rest of the day, and I got a speeding ticket and 3 points through in the post.

Between Friday 30th September and Monday 3rd October, I was on a birding holiday in Shetland with Kevin McCoy. The Semipalmated Plover was still in Ireland on Friday 7th October and Kevin and I got the 9pm ferry from Holyhead to Dublin and saw it well between 8:30 and 8:45am on the Saturday. I took some pictures in the pouring rain with a shutter speed of 1/15th of a second. They were better than expected for a handheld digiscoping effort. I got the 4pm ferry back to Holyhead.

The Semipalmated Plover was found by Dan Brown and Rob Martin on the 24th September and stayed until the 15th October. It was the fifth record for Britain and Ireland.

Rob Martin then found a Rufous-tailed Robin at Warham Greens, Norfolk on the 14th October. It was originally found at 3:30pm, but identity was not confirmed to 5:05pm and then the news went

White-throated Robin
Irania gutturalis
Hartlepool, Cleveland
6th June 2011
GARRY BAGNELL

nationwide. The location was initially given on the pager as East Hills, but this was corrected to say Warham Greens by 5:19pm. Rob Martin managed to get a couple of good photographs showing its big black eye with eye ring, pink legs and brown mottling to upper breast.

Kevin McCoy and I arrived at Warham Greens a little after 2am. We were the fourth car in the car park, and we got a bit of sleep before we were woken by the throng of activity. The crowd of birders was up to 300, all waiting anxiously in the darkness. When it got light, the robin was at first nowhere to be seen. The night before 20-60 people had connected. Not everyone was ticking the bird, due to poor light, and some were just getting movements in dense cover.

At 10:15am we decided to go to Stiffkey and have a look for an elusive Bluethroat. We didn't see this bird either, so we cut our losses and headed back home at 12:15pm. I desperately need some brownie points from Kim. She had only seen me for 2 days over the last 3 weeks.

At 2:16pm, just as I was about to sit down at Bishop Stortford Services for a Whopper meal, the pager Mega'd. We sat in the restaurant and read a pager message announcing a Sussex first: an Isabelline Wheatear. This was a lifer for Kevin, and we both decided drive back to my house and then do a car convoy to Crowlink Down. We got on site at 4:45pm. After a quick run from the car park, we soon connected with the bird. Then I fell down a rabbit hole. I landed flat on my face and

2011	Regular	Vagrant	BBRC/ IRBC 1 year	BBRC/ IRBC 2 year	BBRC/ IRBC 3 year	BBRC/ IRBC 4 year	BBRC/ IRBC 5 year	BBRC/ IRBC 10 year	BBRC/ IRBC 20 year	BBRC/ IRBC Lifetime	Cat B	Total
Seen	276	36	86	8	12	10	27	16	6	5	0	482
During		1		2	1	2	1	1	1			9
B&I Total	276	38	92	12	13	15	43	37	33	39	8	606
	100%	95%	93%	67%	92%	67%	63%	43%	18%	13%	0%	79.5%

my tripod landed on my face, which was covered in blood. My front teeth cut through my lips and the bleeding covered my face and T-Shirt. Jack Everett saw the whole accident take place – I apologise for looking so scary. I left at 5:13pm and got home to a grumpy wife.

Rob Martin's Rufous-tailed Robin was the third record for Britain. Previously one had been found dead on North Ronaldsay on 2nd October 2010, followed by one on Fair Isle on 23rd October 2004.

SUMMARY

During 2011, I travelled 4,947 miles in Britain and Ireland in the pursuit of new birds and managed to increase my list by 9 BOU/IRBC species. This took my British and Irish list to 482. The Combined Official stood at 606 species, so I had seen 79.5% of them. There were five additions to the Official British and Irish List during the year: Hudsonian Whimbrel (split), Cabot's Tern (split), Madeiran Storm-petrel (2007), Siberian Stonechat (split) and Stejneger's Scoter (2011).

The 9 lifers in the table above are Stejneger's Scoter (lifetime), White-throated Robin (20-year), Long-toed Stint (10-year), Northern Waterthrush and Siberian Stonechat (5-year), Semipalmated Plover (4-year), Black and White Warbler and Hudsonian Whimbrel (3-year) and Greater Yellowlegs (1-year).

The Long-toed Stint was my 300th BOU species for Sussex. I had taken an interest in the county scene in 2000, and it took me 12 years to hit the landmark. The full county list stood at 403 species, with John Cooper having the highest list with 361.

I decided that the most important bird I had seen during the year was the White-throated Robin, the third record for Britain and Ireland. Previously there had been a female that stayed four days in Skokholm in 1990. Before that was a one-day male on the Calf of Man in 1983. I was blown away by how good looking the male birds were in Turkey. I never thought we would get one over here. The twitch was an incredible experience, and so many builders turned up with ladders to help birders out. I'm not sure where they all came from, but glad I went on #laddergate day.

CHAPTER 14

2012

I've never been into gaming, but buying a Wii for the family was money well spent. The bowling games got very competitive for the whole family. I managed to find a way to hold the Wii controller and release the ball that was giving me perfect strikes most of the time, which has come in very handy when the Browne family visit. We have a good-natured family rivalry, and I don't think the Bagnells have been beaten at the bowling yet.

Georgie and Nicky love playing Sword Play Speed Slice, a great game for seven-year-olds. I still hear that creepy horn sound when the game is almost finished. Andrew and Rachel get competitive on the Mario Kart Wii. I was playing the game a lot last year and wasn't going to bed until after midnight some nights. The feeling on 29th May 2011 when I finally mastered Rainbow Road and unlocked Rosalina in the process felt akin to getting a new British and Irish tick. Georgie's face the next morning when she realised that we had unlocked Rosalina was priceless. To me, life is all about finding small things that bring about happiness.

I found 'The Nature Trail Book of Birdwatching' (ISBN 0 86020 0141 8) by Malcolm Hart at a boot sale and immediately bought it. It brought back fond memories of when my parents first bought it for me from WH. Smiths in 1977 for £1.50. Just flicking through the pages really makes me smile. Page 11 shows you how to make a feeding bell from a matchstick, darning needle and yoghurt pot. I hung one outside my parents' garden with a mixture of breadcrumbs, currants, cooked potato, oatmeal, and fat and after a few days we were getting Blue Tits feeding on it. This book game me my first insights into drawing birds by using circles for head and bodies.

At the back of the book were illustrations of 56 bird species that could all be seen locally. The I-SPY book of birds was the next game changer. It illustrated 140 different species and you had to visit the coast to tick off some of them. I never saw a Hoopoe in it, but I did get an I-SPY certificate and badge when I scored 1000 points. Shame all these old books were thrown away.

Charlie Moores had been producing podcasts for Talking Naturally for over a year now. He co-hosted with the witty Tom McKinney and John Hague, who was well known for running the popular Drunkenbirder website. Together all three make interesting podcasts covering serious conservation issues throughout the world. On rare occasions they have discussed the British twitching scene and invited me on as guest to talk about last year's White-throated Robin twitch. Guys, please keep up the good work and thanks for inviting me onto your show.

A Spanish Sparrow was found by Sue Wilson in her back garden on 3rd December 2011. Sue's partner Mark Larter managed some photographs. On 7th January they travelled to see a Dark-eyed Junco at nearby Hawkwill inclosure. Mark took his camera and showed the sparrow pictures on the back of his camera to some Hampshire locals. They wanted to visit and were invited the next day at 9am. Before the news was released, the police set up areas for parking and the local army base was informed just in case of suspicions of people walking around with cameras. On Tuesday 10th January at 8:45am, the following news was released on the pagers: "Spanish Sparrow Calshot, Hampshire. Male still in hedge along the B3053 inland from the car park this morning; please park only in the beach car park and walk to view."

I left home on Wednesday 11th January at 5:30am and got on site about 7:30. At that stage only 20 people had arrived, and it was still dark. Just after 8:00am the Spanish Sparrow was spotted in a hedge on the B3053 just opposite Calshot Close entrance. The views were good, but the weather was not bright enough for a good picture. I hung around till 11:45am. During this time, the Sparrow showed very well in the hedge just as you entered Calshot Close and I took 60 photographs. It was

nice to meet Keith Betton for the first time. Keith is a media trainer, PR consultant and writer who had seen over 8,000 bird species worldwide. He's the vice president for the African Bird club, County Recorder for Hampshire and a council member for both the RSPB and the BTO. Such a friendly guy – he also arranged for a BBC cameraman to be on site for a piece on the BBC South news.

The Spanish Sparrow was the 8th for Britain, and it stayed to the 23rd March. Most people saw the Cumbrian male that was seen from 13th July 1996 to 13th December 1998.

On Sunday 29th January at 8:29am, news was released of a female Parrot Crossbill seen the previous day at Black Down NT. I left home at 10:20am, and the satnav predicted I would get into the nearby village of Fernhurst at 11:21am. I couldn't find any directions to Blackdown, but I stopped a pedestrian, and he knew exactly where to go. On the A286 I needed to head towards Haslemere, but when you get to the village of Fernhurst you need to go north on the A286 for 2.2 miles and then take a right on a lane called Scotland Lane. This leads you to Tennyson's Lane which leads you, signposted, to Blackdown. There are two car parks at Blackdown. Go to the furthest one. From this carpark there is a footpath into the woods. Head straight on, and eventually you will come to a ridge. You want to be on the other side of the ridge, so you need to take the footpath to the left, which eventually swings to the right, and that is the best place to stop and scan. If you go past the roadside puddle you've gone too far. The walk is only about 15 minutes from the car park.

When I got there I bumped into Dave Cooper, who showed me some photographs he had taken around 10am. I had only waited for about 20 minutes when a flock of Crossbills came flying in our general direction. There must have been almost 80 birds. Some landed on pines close to where we were all standing. The third Crossbill I looked at through the scope had a massive bill, and everybody agreed this was the Parrot Crossbill. The Craig family, Ian Barnard and Simon Buckingham all managed to see it though my scope as it moved between three pines. It was on view for about 30 minutes before the whole flock flew off. The Parrot Crossbill was last seen on the 18th February.

Our house only had a small garden, but Kim and I decided a conservatory would really set it off. My friend Suneil Sudra arranged for us to see his brother's conservatory just around the corner from our house, built by a Crawley-based company called Window Mart. Their owner, Martin, visited our house and took some measurements. After a few days he was back with some professional drawings for a design we could have. The conservatory was going to extend the full length of the house and be 3 .5 meters deep with three exterior doors, roof window and self-cleaning glass. We agreed a price of £18,000.

The builders arrived on 15th May and every day I took a photograph capturing their daily progress. Eleven days later it was finished, and then we had to wait for our electrician friend Jimmy to fit the heated floor. The whole project was finished by 1st July. We added Marks & Spencer conservatory furniture and mounted a TV on the wall, and it was ready to use. Kim and I were really pleased with the finished room space and Kim suggested the garden really needed a patio to use, especially when it was too hot to sit in the conservatory. Watch this space, folks.

On Monday 28th May I arrived at Grantham for a 3-day work visit. I had a feeling in my water that a tick could be on the cards any day now, so along with the work clothes I packed my scope, tripod, bins and credit card. I checked into the Angel & Royal Hotel (according to the literature this is the oldest hotel in Britain), which was only a 10-minute walk to work and after a hard day's graft I visited the Ospreys at Rutland Water.

Next morning whilst tucking into my full English breakfast, the mega alert went off. I picked up the pager and almost collapsed in a heap when I read "MEGA Cleveland ORPHEAN WBLR Hartlepool Headland trapped + ringed + will be released at bowling green at c8:45am". The last twitchable one was back in 1981 when one spent a week on the Scillies.

The waitress brought over some coffee, and I said to her "Can you believe it, a rare bird has just turned up and I'm stuck doing a stock take". Why did I tell her that? She didn't know me – she didn't need to know any of this stuff. Anyway, what could do I do?! I got a phone call from Lee, who was in Suffolk and kindly offered to pick me up en route to Cleveland. I had to decline, as there was no way I was prepared to let work down. On route to work Liz Costa rang me up and offered me a space with John Lees. I refused again.

I got to work at 8:45am and declared to my plant and transport manager Trevor that a rare bird has just been found in Cleveland, but said don't worry, I'm going to start the stock take. A few more phone calls were received by the gentleman in Suffolk and he confirmed that Chris Bell had seen it and it was a Western Orphean Warbler. OK, maybe I should consider going after work today. AA Routemaster suggested it would take 2 hours and 45 minutes to get there. if I finished work at 4pm (work through lunch), I should be at Hartlepool around 6:45pm. The Warbler wouldn't have gone to roost by then and I should get a couple of hours to connect.

Hour by hour the news kept coming through on my little vibrating rectangular block that the Western Orphean Warbler was still present. At 1pm enough was enough – my important work for the day was done and my vibrating toy was becoming a nuisance. I asked boss Trevor if I could leave right now. He said, "Yeah ok, but do you want to tuck into the buffet food first?" I replied, "Thanks Trevor, but I'd rather go immediately just in case it disappears".

Off I went. I arrived at Hartlepool at 3:30pm to find that the Western Orphean Warbler had left the bowling green at 3:20pm. Jeeeessssssussss! I felt sick. All the strings I had to pull to get there, and the Warbler decides to fly off into a vast housing estate with out-of-bounds gardens. To make things worse approx. 2,000 people had probably seen it over the last 6.5 hours. The last thing I wanted to do was talk to fellow birders about what the views were like.

I did bump into Tony Ford and his wife. She thought I looked hungry and handed me a Snickers bar to eat. I had started chomping away at the Snickers bar when someone started shouting and birders started running. I joined the mob. We were heading in a completely different direction from where the warbler had been seen last.

This pursuit became fruitless, and it was becoming apparent that the Western Orphean Warbler was in fact making its way back to the bowling green. At 4:45pm Dave Holman found it there and was shouting out directions. I never managed to connect for the first hour because I don't the difference between holly, privet and rose bushes. Then at 5:45 pm I finally saw the bird through somebody else's scope. All I could see was its head. I repositioned my scope on a different edge of the bowling green and eventually found the correct closed rose bud and saw just the bill of the Western Orphean Warbler. It sat still and largely obscured for the next hour. Then it hopped to the right and I could see its mantle, wings and flanks (not the head or feet) and a few more hops and it vanished. Some people managed to get a full-on side view from their angle as it moved through the assorted hedge.

The next prolonged view occurred around 7pm when it sat in the holly, where I could only see its vent, primaries, and buff-coloured underparts. It stayed on view for an hour. Every now and then it would turn its head to the left and you could get some head features. Around 8pm I started to shiver, as I was only wearing a T-shirt, and headed back to the car. Here I met Merseyside birder Jason Stannage for the first time. He runs the Facebook Rare Bird groups and I thanked him for the selection of sunglasses he had sent me.

This Western Orphean Warbler had a fat score of 0 and a muscle score of 1 and was not seen feeding the whole of Tuesday. It probably then died overnight, as it was not seen the next day.

I got back to the Angel & Royal Hotel at 10:15pm and found that all the restaurants in Grantham were now closed. I settled for a doner kebab and took it back to the hotel bar, where I washed it down with a pint of Stella.

On Saturday 16th June Kim, Georgie and I had to visit Tate Modern to see some artwork that Rusper Primary School had done. Georgie had been sick when they presented it at school and we couldn't resist the opportunity to view it. We don't often go to London, and we had the bonus of seeing the crowds lining the streets for Trooping the Colour. I had never seen this before, and it was nice to finally see our Queen and Prince Philip with the other royals watching the flypast from the Buckingham Palace balcony.

The following week Kim, Georgie and I went on a week's family holiday to Kemer in

Turkey. Georgie was now eight years old, and her holiday became loads more fun when she met a slightly younger girl called Summer Reeves in the swimming pool. Kim and I hit it off with her dad Aaron and his girlfriend Lyndsey Stafford. Aaron was a self-employed floor layer from Plymouth and had split with Summer's mum many moons before, and Lyndsey worked at Plymouth hospital. They were an incredibly good-looking couple. We spent breakfast, lunch, dinner and evening entertainment in their company and the combined group of six made our holiday very special.

During this holiday, on the 22nd June, I hired a car and drove 87 miles to Oymapinar Baraj and met Ozcan Kilic at the dam. Ozcan was a manager and skipper for Vigo tours. I chartered his pleasure boat for Lee Evans, Chris Heard, Kevin McCoy, Bob Graves, Rob Spark, Keith Vinicombe, Yoav Perlman, Amir Balaban, Rony Livine, Rami Mizarchi and myself, and we sailed off around 2am in the pitch black towards Grand Canyon, 14km away. We arrived nearly two hours later, and the skipper killed the engine. All 12 of us remained silent in the pitch black.

We started to hear a Blue Rock Thrush sing and then shapes were beginning to appear all around us. Five minutes later we could clearly see two adult Brown Fish Owls and a juvenile standing on different ledges. This felt surreal. Ozcan let us get a few pictures, although I was worried that the camera shutter noises were going to flush them into the huge canyon. They didn't, and we were soon on our way to check the little canyon before heading back to the dam. Such a fantastic twitch.

I drove back to the hotel to find my family still in bed. To think those birds were only found in 2009. 50 years ago, Brown Fish Owls could be seen in Israel, Iran, Jordan and Lebanon, but because of all the wars, they are now thought to be extinct there.

If you're going to get married, is there a better place than Charles Dicken's birthplace? Saturday 2nd September was David Browne and Lucy Young's big day, and David had selected me to be his best man. This was a real honour for me, as over the past 45 years I could count the number of weddings I've been to one hand and two of them were mine. I think the main reason for my low wedding count is probably because I'm a bit of a geek. I did twenty years of plane spotting, but once you lose the mutual passion you realise you have nothing in common with your fellow spotters and you slowly drift apart. If these guys ever get married, are they going to remember good old days with me, Baggypants? Now I have a more sophisticated hobby in identifying birds and observing what they do, as opposed to just looking for a plane's registration. I know my newfound friendships are based on seeing birds, but I hold more hope of getting a wedding invite one day. I will never lose my interest in birdwatching, but I can see myself losing the passion for twitching the Scottish Islands one day, especially if money gets tight. Anyway, this is getting depressing – let's get back to the wedding.

The wedding was held when Kim, Georgie, Andrew and Rachel were on holiday in the Isle of Wight. Kim, Georgie and I caught the hovercraft to Portsmouth whilst Andrew and his girlfriend Rachel stayed back in the chalet.

David and Lucy chose the beautiful setting of the Guildhall to get married, and hired a function room for their 50 guests. David and I hired wedding outfits from Moss Bros. We had matching tails with claret waistcoats and bright yellow ties. Lucy wore a cream low-cut wedding dress with a tiara and looked sensational. I videoed the whole ceremony and it was only when I sat down at the top table that I handed the video camera to David's friend Steve. My best man speech lasted 12 minutes and I think David and Lucy's dads both enjoyed it. Sadly, neither of them is still with us, but I'm glad they managed to see their children get married.

Watching this video back now, I do regret the way I built up the speech to mention one of our mutual friends being gay, and then my joke about me practising my speech in front of a live audience at an old people's home, and they liked it because they p*ssed themselves. So so wrong. My video is on YouTube. If you search "Garry Bagnell performing a best man's speech" you'll find it. After the meal, the disco started, and my family got the last hovercraft back to the Isle of Wight.

On Monday 24th September, Chris Heard and I drove to Grantown-on-Spey and waited for news of a Magnolia Warbler found the day before on Fair Isle. A charter plane was going to shuttle passengers from Wick to Fair Isle, and we were going to be on the fifth flight. The Magnolia Warbler didn't stay the night. It was found by Will Miles late afternoon and went to roost on Copper Geo on Lerness. It became the second record for Britain.

Johnny Allan, who was filmed for the 2009 twitching programme, got to Fair Isle on the Monday and missed the warbler. This dip was too much for him and he decided to throw the towel in. Ten years later he's still never been seen on another twitch.

From Friday 28th September to 1st October I had a long weekend on Shetland. The best birds seen were Siberian Stonechat, American Buff-bellied Pipit, Spotted Sandpiper and adult Isabelline Shrike.

On Saturday 6th October I booked a Ryan Air flight from Stansted to Shannon with John Lees, Kevin McCoy, Lee Evans, Chris Heard and Joan Thompson. The plan was to twitch the Eastern Kingbird on Inishmore. The early morning fog at Shannon prevented us from landing, so the plane was diverted to Dublin. The Eastern Kingbird was gone, but a Belted Kingfisher was found between Letterfrack and Leenan in Galway. Climping had a Red-breasted Flycatcher, and this was a Sussex tick for me. I decided to get a flight back to Gatwick and successfully twitched the flycatcher, whilst Lee, John and Joan got the Belted Kingfisher and Chris came back.

The Eastern Kingbird was found by my good friend Hugh Delaney and was only available on the 5th October. It was found at midday with news being released by Birdguides at 1:29pm, and became the first record for Britain and Ireland.

Victor Caschera, as mentioned ealier, is one of Ireland's keenest twitcher, living in Dublin. The car journey to Doolin is 3 hours and 7 minutes. The ferry from Doolin to Inishmore goes 5 times a day at 10am, 11am, 1pm, 2:30pm and 5:15pm and takes 35 minutes. There were no spare seats on flights from Connemara to Inishmore. Could Victor get to Inishmore before darkness and see the Eastern Kingbird?

Read what happened below.

Victor was due to go to Cape Clear on Saturday 6th October for two weeks. The weather was looking good, so he decided to go a day earlier. He left Dublin around midday and started driving south west towards Cape Clear. One hour into the journey he got a call about the Eastern Kingbird. Victor quickly realised that if he caught the evening ferry he would arrive in the darkness. Victor rang Connemara airport and asked, "Are there any flights to Inishmore?" The airport said, "Sorry all flights are sold out". Victor asked, "Can you put me on standby?" Airport said, "Plane holds eight people, and we never get cancellations". Victor said, "I'm trying to get to island urgently, can you please put me on standby?"

He proceeded to drive towards the airport just in case. 30 minutes later the airport rang and said, "We've got good news and bad news. The good news is there's been a cancellation. The bad news is the plane is not flying to Inishmore, it's flying to one of the other islands. We can drop you off first, but you will have to pay an extra €50. Is that ok? Victor said yes. The airport said, "You need to be at Connemara Airport by 4pm for a 4:15pm flight. Is that ok?" "Yes," said Victor. He worked out that the earliest he could be at airport was 4:10pm. He drove as fast as possible and arrived 5 minutes earlier. He managed get himself and his gear weighed and off he flew.

When he landed on Inishmore he had two hours of daylight, but no idea where the bird was and there was no phone reception. A taxi driver asked Victor at the airport "Are you a birdwatcher?" Victor replied, "Yes, do you know where the bird is". The taxi driver replied, "Yes, I've just dropped two other birdwatchers up there". Victor jumped into the taxi and was taken to the drop-off point. When he got out of the taxi, he couldn't see anybody. He wondered, do I walk left or right?

One minute later the farmer arrived and asked "Are you looking for the bird?" Victor said "Yes". The farmer said "It's on my land" and opened up his gate. Victor had started walking towards a shed when four birders across the field started shouting and pointing towards the shed roof. Victor walked a few steps back and saw the Eastern Kingbird flycatching on the roof.

Spanish Sparrow
Passer hispaniolensis
Calshot, Hampshire
11th January 2012
GB4GNEL

That is such a gripping story. I thank Vic for sharing it with me.

I had been a customer with Rare Bird Alert for the past 11 years, but now I was hearing rave reviews about how good the Birdguides app was. Josh Jones discussed their application further and I decided on the 27th October to swap information providers. The only downside I could see from Birdguides was that they didn't advertise car, boat or plane spaces. Hopefully this wouldn't cost me a bird one day.

SUMMARY

During 2012, I travelled 2,285 miles in Britain and Ireland in the pursuit of new birds and managed to increase my list by 3 BOU/IRBC species. This took my British and Irish list to 485 different species. The Combined Official stands at 607, so I had seen 79.9% of them. There was one net addition to the Official British and Irish List during the year: Scopoli's Shearwater (split), Eastern Kingbird (2012) and removal of Madeiran Storm Petrel (2007).

The 3 lifers in the table above are Western Orphean Warbler (10-year), Spanish Sparrow (5-year), Parrot Crossbill (Vagrant).

2012 was very low in terms of ticks, but instead I did quite a lot of time with the family, including a long weekend in Edinburgh in September. This included boarding the Royal Yacht Britannia, seeing the two Pandas at the Edinburgh zoo and trying not to be scared on a ghost and ghoul tour. I had never been into fairground rides, but I enjoyed screaming with Georgie as we rode the fast Vampire Ride at Chessington World of Adventures. The icing on the cake was on 25th November when the X-factor live tour hit Brighton. Georgie loves Rylan Clark, I love Ella Henderson and Kim loves David Beckham. But luckily she's married to me, and anyway I don't think David Beckham was there.

I decided the most important bird seen during the year was the Spanish Sparrow. I remember hearing about the Cumbrian one on Birdline Southeast back in 1996. I wasn't convinced there would ever be another twitchable one, so getting a chance to see one locally was just what the doctor ordered.

2012	Regular	Vagrant	BBRC/ IRBC 1 year	BBRC/ IRBC 2 year	BBRC/ IRBC 3 year	BBRC/ IRBC 4 year	BBRC/ IRBC 5 year	BBRC/ IRBC 10 year	BBRC/ IRBC 20 year	BBRC/ IRBC Lifetime	Cat B	Total
Seen	276	37	86	8	12	10	28	17	6	5	0	485
During		1					1	1				3
B&I Total	276	38	92	12	13	15	43	38	33	39	8	607
	100%	97%	93%	67%	92%	67%	65%	45%	18%	13%	0%	79.9%

CHAPTER 15

2013

Colas' financial year started on 1st January, and with a new financial year people's role can change. That year, Colas made the sensible decision to give the traffic management accountancy role to Newcastle based Mick Curry. I was offered either redundancy or an opportunity to apply for a new accountancy role that included working on a joint venture in Portsmouth, combined with my old plant and transport responsibility. I was up against a chap called Mark Higginson. The previous year he had been reporting to me, and his role of Carnsew Quarry accounting was transferred to ISH at Birmingham.

One of us was going to lose their job. We were both interviewed for the role by the Associate Finance Director and HR. We were both point scored and the decision was to be announced a few days later. I really didn't think I 'd have much chance of getting the job after last year's warning, but I tried my best in the interview and was offered the post. I felt sorry for Mark. At least he had a great chance of finding another job as he was an active studier and was only one paper away from being a qualified accountant.

Due to the vast expense of using motor cars, year Mark Reeder and others suggested doing a January foot challenge. I chose to do an area within a 3-mile radius of my Crawley home and reckoned I would see about 60 species. I started the list on 1st January by staying at home in the conservatory. The next day I was flying to Newcastle (sadly my last visit ever) for three days. My next day birding day would be Saturday, but I would need to pick my scope back up from the repair shop in in Selsey first thing.

Over the course of January, I managed to get out birdwatching for five days. The best bird was a Willow Tit on the 19th January at a site I had been tipped off about. Most of my birds were found at Tilgate Park, Pease Pottage, Ifield Mill Pond, Buchan Park, Stublehome Farm, Cowdray Forest, Balcome Road and Loppets playing field. I walked 100km over the month – to get to any of those green spaces you have got to cross Crawley's concrete jungle first. After every walk my legs were aching, but it felt rewarding to see exactly 60 birds and finish in 26th place. I was way behind the winner, Simon Chidwick, who saw 113 species in the 6 miles around Cromer.

On 2nd February I was taking a Colas accountant and a non-birder, Tim Corn, out for a day's birding in West Sussex. I had only been in my car for 25 minutes when a mega alert sounded. A Pine Grosbeak had been found in a garden north of Collafirth Pier on Shetland at 9:59am. I decided to carry on with the day's birding and drive to Aberdeen at midnight with a view to catching the Northlink ferry the following day. Tim and I had a good day, seeing 28 Bewick's Swans, 6 Corn Buntings, 2 Hawfinches, 1 Brambling and a Little Owl.

I left Crawley at midnight, picked John Benham up at the usual place and met Gareth Stamp somewhere on the M5. I dosed myself up on Red Bull and got an upset stomach in the process. Despite stopping at 10 service stations and John's constant chatting, we got to Rattray Head in one piece at midday. We saw a wintering Desert Wheatear, and then popped in McDonalds. We parked on Stell Road near the Petrofrac building and saved the £16 daily charge at Aberdeen NCP.

On the Northlink ferry there were 11 other birders going for the Grosbeak. I had nice chat with a few I knew and watched the Man City v Liverpool match and had some beers. Around midnight, Gareth and I found the cinema floor was dark and quiet enough for us to sleep on. It was hard and uncomfortable and I woke up every time the ferry banged or rolled.

We disembarked at 8am and picked up the hire car. The car cigarette lighter was having difficulty holding the satnav plug in, so we had to keep pushing it back in. To make things worse, we drove to the wrong Collafirth. The locals said we needed to head for North Collafirth, which was 21 miles further north. Then we got a message from Northlink saying that night's crossing had been cancelled due to adverse weather. I felt like screaming.

When we arrived at the right Collafirth, all the birders on the ferry were already there. There was no sign of the Grosbeak and Will Miles (finder of last year's Magnolia Warbler) decided to drive off north and search there. I was thinking about heading south, but instead decided to move the car to where everybody was standing. If the bird was re-found, we could go immediately.

Before you knew it Will Miles drove back and said he has found the bird at nearby Housetter. Everybody ran back to their cars and convoyed behind him to Housetter.

The Pine Grosbeak was still there. We watched this massive finch, the size of a starling, feeding on spruce needles in three different front gardens at point blank range for 50 minutes. At 11:40 we left and birded the Island, then spent the night at the Aurora Guest House (01595-690105). For dinner, we met up with Mark Rayment, Bob Chaukley and Jonathan Holiday at Lerwick's Raba restaurant. We had a nice mild lamb curry and then hung out with Adrian Webb, Dave Webb, Keith Fellows, and Malcolm Oxlade in the lounge bar.

That night I was in bed by 10pm. The following morning, after a cooked breakfast, we rest of the day birding. The best birds of the trip were a Glaucous Gull, 2 Iceland Gulls and 1 Kumlien's Gull. The Northlink ferry was due to depart at 7pm and I got talking to one of the employees, who mentioned that 34 of them had just been made redundant. I knew exactly how they felt. I could have been there if it hadn't been for the point score against Mark. I hoped Northlink wouldn't reduce their daily sailings, as that sailing, costing £52 return, was the only affordable way to see the rare birds Shetland keeps getting.

The Pine Grosbeak was found by Bert Ratter on Tuesday 29th January and became the 8th for Britain.

On 1st April, Colas handed me the keys to a two-year-old Renault Megane. I left my Peugeot 407 parked in the secure car park at Rowfant and transferred scope, bins, maps, sleeping bag, coats, wellies and walking boots to the boot of the Megane and drove it to my new office in Tipner. I was now working in a series of Portakabins in a grass field, powered by a mobile electricity generator. My employer was still Colas but I was seconded to the Colas Volkerfitzpatrick joint venture; for the next 18 months we had a contract with Portsmouth City Council to build two entry and two exit slip roads off the M275 and a park and ride. My new boss was a chap called Phil Parker, who had been given the role of Commercial Manager, seconded from the Colas Portsmouth division. Phil was a family man and a bit younger than me. Straight after introduction, I thought I had better tell him I was a keen twitcher and from time to time I might have to leave on short notice if a rare bird turned up. Phil was totally cool about it – if the work got done then he had no problems authorising leave. He passed this information to Project Director Goodwin Kirk, who immediately started to take the mickey out of my hobby. This banter was perfect – I had been accepted, and was starting to look forward to the next 18 months of working on a building site.

On Thursday 25th April Adam Hutt found a Rock Thrush at Spurn. Phil let me leave immediately. I was nearly 46 years old and this was only the second time I had been given a company car to drive. More importantly, I had also been given a company fuel card. It was now up to me if I wanted to advertise for passengers. That year I was aiming to get 300 on my year list.

It took me 5½ hours to get to Spurn, where I found the Rock Thrush, a female, distant but showing from the Blue Bell car park. It stayed to 26th April and was only the 27th record for Britain. This was the first twitchable bird since one on Bryher in 1996. A one-dayer in Devon in 2004 was only seen briefly and not really twitchable.

On Saturday 27th April I couldn't resist twitching an Eastern Subalpine Warbler at Landguard. I took Sussex-based lister Mick Davis with me.

At 7 am on Saturday 18th May I was woken by Chris Heard, who asked, "Why aren't you at Margate cemetery?" The night before a Dusky Thrush had been mega'd at 11:03pm, but my phone was purposely muted after 9pm. Like a shot, I got out of bed and drove like a bat out of hell to Margate cemetery, arriving at 8:30am. Chris was still there, and he directed me to where the female Dusky Thrush was perched. It was playing hide and seek, but I got my first unobscured view at 9:12am. For the first two hours it was perched in various Sycamores, and it never came to ground level. It stayed in the cemetery the whole time I was there, and it felt bad to 'walk among the tombstones', which was the name of a film I regularly see advertised on Netflix, starring Liam Neeson.

Just after 11am the crowd dwindled, and the thrush got braver and ventured into the open and started feeding on the ground. This was Marcus Lawson's 500th BOU bird and if he had organised it, I could have lent him my orange T-shirt to wear.

I met Georgie Kinnard, only 15 years old, for the first time that day, who also lived in Sussex. He started asking me about the 2009 twitching programme and I could see he was genuinely interested in the twitching scene. I decided to give him and his two mates Luke Dray and Jake Gearty a lift to Reculver to see a female Montagu's Harrier. Luckily the harrier was not too difficult to find as it was getting a constant stream of Dusky Thrush admirers popping into see it before heading home. On the Sunday, my good friend John Lees got back from Canada and headed straight to Margate with several hundred other birders, but the Dusky Thrush had sadly moved on.

Some members of the BBRC were unsure of the Dusky Thrush's purity, so one visited Tring (National History Museum) and compared Dusky Thrush skins. The Kent bird matched the plumage of the north-western breeding range. This was well away from the potential zone of hybridisation with Naumann's Thrush.

The Dusky Thrush was originally found by Steve Tomlinson on 15th May, when he thought it was a Redwing. He photographed it over the next couple of days and sent pictures to the Rarities Committee and Josh Jones, who immediately recognised it as a female Dusky Thrush, and it was mega'd an hour later. Steve had watched this area for 23 years and it was a dream to find a first for Kent. He felt all the hard work over the years had paid off.

The Dusky Thrush stayed to 18th May and an estimated 1,500 birders visited to see it on the Saturday. This was the 10th for Britain, and only Ron Johns and a few others had seen one here before. The last twitchable one was in 1959 at Hartlepool headland.

Kim asked what date best suited me to invite Dave, Lucy and Tamizin over for lunch. I don't see the point inviting friends over in spring or autumn, but generally anything after 10th June signals summer is over and we agreed to meet on Saturday 15th June. Nice food and plenty of alcohol was purchased for the visit. Kim is very houseproud so for the next couple of hours the house was given a proper vacuuming and polish.

Heavy metal fanatic Jonny Rankin meanwhile found a swift with a white rump flying around the hide at Trimley Marshes at 10:47am. Dave and Lucy had probably just left Hampshire. Kim was adamant that she was not allowing me to go for it. I suggested "If I start driving now for it and it disappears, I can do a U-turn and come straight back home?" Kim said no. I knew that the last time one of these was twitchable in Britain was 20 years ago in Cley. I told her this was a once in a lifetime opportunity, but she said, "I don't care, the answer is no, no, no!" I thought, I had known Dave 14 years now and I was sure we were not going to fall out over me not being there.

I left the house with Kim shouting at me. En route Birdguides was still reporting the Pacific Swift as present. I parked the car at Station Road in Trimley at 1pm. It was a 4km walk to the hide and I was overtaken by marathon runner Matt Eade, who ran straight past me. Landguard warden Paul Holmes was the only person being driven there.

When I got to the hide at 1:55pm, it was a big relief when I clapped eyes on the Pacific Swift. I watched it through the scope and could clearly see the white rump. I only stayed five minutes before leaving, saying goodbye to Matthew Deans and Lee Evans, who were sitting on the embankment. On the way I got a phone call from Kim. She had calmed down and asked me for an ETA. I got home at 5pm and David decided to give me a long clap as I entered the house and walked over to greet everyone. I warmed up Kim's signature dish of lasagne and made sure none of our guests ever had an empty glass. I even let David beat me on the Wii at bowling, but let's just keep that between us.

They left around midnight and the next day I took Mick to Trimley. The Pacific Swift appeared between 7:38am to 4pm, but we never managed to see it. The swifts were much higher up in the sky than on the previous day, and it was never going to be easy to identify it from underneath.

This was only the 7th record for Pacific Swift

in Britain and the first twitchable one since 650 birders saw one at Cley on 30th May 1993 between 10:30am to 4:12pm.

I shared my office with Wayne Wiggins, who was Volker's equivalent to Phil Parker. He was a couple years older than me and planning to retire in less than two years. He was buying rental properties in Hull at the same rate as I was adding new birds to my list. Over the last two months he had bought three. Retirement didn't feel like something I would ever do. My private pensions would only pay £200 per month and that wouldn't go far in 2034.

Philip and Goodwin's offices were right next to ours, and we would have discussions sitting at our office desks and shouting questions and answers out to each other. Even with doors shut, there was no sound proofing and when a mega alert sounded at 4:07pm on 25th June. I felt they were about to take the mickey. This time we had a White-throated Needletail that had been seen on Harris, Western Isles for its second day. This was a biggie and I still had an hour to go before I was due home. I walked into Philip's office, and he suggested I should head off straight away.

I left work at 4:15pm, still wearing office attire, and got to Wraysbury at 5:30pm, where I met Bob Watts and Jerry Warne. I booted up my work laptop and my 4G dongle allowed me to book Stornoway next day returns from Inverness. We would depart Inverness at 7:50am with a 7:35pm return. I managed to book a car and picked up Bob Chaukley from Dunstable before heading north.

The next day we watched a singing male Common Rosefinch at Loch Tummel at 4:46am. We didn't stay long because we still had a two-hour drive to Inverness Airport. At the airport there were 20 other birders on the same flight as us. We landed at Stornoway at 8:20am, and got news that the Needletail had been seen at 7:08am at Tarbert. The atmosphere in the car was at fever pitch.

We arrived at Tarbert at 9:20am to find that the 7:08 sighting related to the previous evening – pm, not am. Trying to stay upbeat, we drove to Loch Direcleit, where the bird had last been seen. We parked on the grass verge and started to wander along the A859 overlooking the loch.

An hour went by, and then a birder in a car pulled up and said the bird had been showing flying over the Loch towards Tarbert. At 10:20am we finally saw it speeding effortlessly along the contours of the hillside, changing direction in an instant. The Needletail performed on and off for the next four hours. We had our mouths wide open and were tingling with excitement as the bird flew inches above our heads and made a return pass just over the loch. You could hear the swoosh of air as it flew over your head.

The Needletail finally vanished at 2:42pm, prompting us to head back to the airport. On the way Jerry spotted a Golden Eagle sitting on a distant hill and we even managed to get an earlier flight back to Inverness. We landed there around 5:30pm and heard the joyous news that the Needletail had been relocated at Loch Plocrapol, on Golden Road. This was superb news for the 40 guys who had got onto the island just after 3pm by ferry.

I paid the £8 parking charge and started to head south. Just before 6pm we heard the tragic news that the Needletail had hit a wind turbine and died. The White-throated Needletail was found by Mark Cocker (of 'Tales of a Tribe' fame) with Adam Gretton and stayed between 24th-26th June. It was the 8th record for Britain and was recovered and taken to NMS, Edinburgh.

The tearful drive home was shared between Jerry and me. I got home 36 hours after leaving Tipner. On the Monday, 1st July, a Bridled Tern was found on the Farne Islands. That night I took four Sussex birders, George Kinnard, Jake Gearty, Dan Booker and Mike Booker to Seahouses, where we booked a Billy Shiels boat trip (01665) 720308 to the Farnes. This is a family-run business which has been doing boat trips to the Farnes since 1918. They have 11 boats and do regular cruises to see Grey Seals, tours to Holy Island and diving charters.

When we arrived we were not allowed to set foot on the inner Farnes but could stand on the large concrete jetty with around 20 other birders. The Bridled Tern was sitting on the rocks and occasionally flying with other terns. We could get as close as 10 metres. It was such an impressive place, with Puffins and Arctic Terns everywhere you looked. The boat cost £20 each, and I will go back one day. Maybe we'll get another Aleutian Tern – the only British record spent two days on the Inner Farnes in 1979.

The Bridled Tern was found by Will Scott on 1st July and last seen on 19th August. During this period, it visited the Farnes three times with a total duration of 21 days. It also visited Saltholme, the Isle of May, Fraserburgh, Creswell Pond and East Chevington. It was the 24th for Britain and the first twitchable one since Cemlyn Bay in 1988.

On Friday 5th July an Ascension Island Frigatebird was photographed at Bowmore on Islay at 9am. The next day I caught the ferry to Islay with Chris Heard and Chris Bromley. We spent most of the day at Bowmore, but the bird never came back. I didn't expect to see it, but I was surprised to see 40 other birders making the effort. We got 30 choughs and a female Hen Harrier for our effort and spent the night in a B&B costing £35 each.

The Frigatebird was originally seen by V.V.S. Bonarjee and T.E. Matre, who spotted it out of their hotel window whilst eating breakfast. It was independently seen by Jim Sim at the same time and all three observers managed to get photographs before it was chased off by gulls. This was only the second record for Britain – the first was found on Tiree on 9th July 1953 and died the same day.

The family holiday in 2013 was back to Turkey, but this time we stayed in Bodrum. I hired a car for a couple of days and got a speeding fine whilst I was on my way to Karine peninsula. On 24th July I managed to see 50 very distant Dalmatian Pelicans and a Great White Pelican on a very large expanse of water. There were a few boats dotted about but nobody was willing to take me out for a closer look. Back in Bodrum I was looking at bandannas. David Browne wore one on holiday and avoided burning his head. I copied him by purchasing three different colours with the Nike logo.

During routine Storm Petrel ringing on Fair Isle, two Swinhoe's Storm Petrels were also trapped, the first on 27th July and the second on 7th August. The second bird was getting trapped most nights, and this was the start of people chartering onto Fair Isle and then chartering off the next day.

On Wednesday 14th August I left Crawley at 7:05pm and picked up Hugh Price, Paul Holmes and Vaughan Watkins. We made our first stop 406 miles later at South Lanarkshire Welcome Break. Hugh kindly bought me a latte and then I drove the final 174 miles to Aberdeen Airport. We parked at the Long term carpark and had a couple of hours to kill at the airport. Flybe have a generous rewards programme, and using their credit card and all the points Ide accumulated in flying to Newcastle over the last three years was really making these Shetland flights affordable. This flexible return flight was effectively free apart from the £40 airport tax.

The flight to Sumburgh took an hour; we landed at 11:13am and got a taxi to Grutness, only 2km away. The *Good Shepherd* only sailed to Fair Isle three times a week, normally Tuesday, Thursday and Saturday, and took about 2½ hours, with capacity for 12 passengers. The ship was on the Grutness quay on arrival and was being loaded with food and various supplies by ex-Fair Isle Warden Deryk Shaw. The return trip only cost £30. We had a nice smooth crossing and saw 3 Artic Skua and some Arctic Terns. We docked at 2:54pm and then got chauffeured to the observatory. This gave us a nice opportunity to dump off our bags and do some birding.

On arrival, Fair Isle warden David Parnaby gave us a bit of bad news. The forecast was for heavy rain and there would be no petrel ringing that night (Thursday). The next ringing session could be the following night, depending on the weather forecast. All four of us wandered around, and we found the first winter Citrine Wagtail that had been seen at Barkland. A Western Subalpine Warbler that had originally been found on 20th July at Schoollton was still present but very elusive. We waited a couple of hours to spot it and watched it with ex-Fair Isle warden Nick Riddiford.

This was my first stay at the observatory, which had been rebuilt several times. The first observatory was built in 1948, the second one in 1969, the third in 1989, and this one was built in 2010, costing £4 milion. The building is spacious with a large changing room, library, bar, and restaurant. During the evening we ate a sumptuous Fair Isle lamb dinner cooked by Susan Parnaby and served by her friendly group of staff. Feeling exhausted, I went to bed at 10pm and was sound asleep while others managed to hear the Swinhoe's Petrel calling at sea.

The next day we got up and saw yesterday's Citrine Wagtail and found another one at Da Water with some common migrants. After dinner,

David Parnaby made the announcement that Storm Petrel ringing should be taking place that night. We got to the ringing hut around 11:30pm. The first bird trapped was a Storm Petrel, which was then processed, and I was allowed to release it back into the dark. I felt its warm feet on the palm of my hand for about 30 seconds before it flew off into the darkness. Three more Storm Petrels were trapped, and then at 11:50pm the Swinhoe's Storm Petrel was caught. I took some photographs as it was processed, and then, just like my Storm Petrel, I watched it fly off, this time out of David's hands. What an amazing experience. I feel so privileged to have travelled this far and witnessed such a rare seabird that had decided to linger off Fair Isle. My party of four, plus Alan Lewis and Jon Dunn, would savour that moment for a lifetime. Only 23 birders had successfully connected with this Swinhoe's, and that was to be the last Petrel ringing session until next year. I hope it would return for more people to see.

The next day I took the 7:30am *Good Shepherd* back to Grutness and then departed Sumburgh at 12:50pm back to Aberdeen. I got home Sunday morning at 0:17.

The Swinhoe's Storm-petrel was the 7th for Britain and trapped from 7th August to 3rd September, by K. Lawrence, Will Miles and David Parnaby.

On Thursday 5th September a Yellow-breasted Bunting was found on the tiny island of Brownsman in the Farnes. It was seen again on 6th September, so I decided to head up Friday night, with Christian Melgar, William Bishop and Graham Jepson. However news came through on Saturday at 7:32am that there was no sign of the bird.

Brownsman is not open to the public for landings but has some excellent vantage points that can be achieved from sea level. There is one small cottage on the island which used to be the home of Grace Darling and her family, and bird wardens now live in the cottage over the summer. We hung around most of the day and chatted at length with the incredibly knowledgeable Jimmy Steele, now no longer with us. Jimmy had found the 1999 Newbiggin Black-faced Bunting and was serving on the BOURC. He was sceptical about the Druridge Bay report of a Slender-billed Curlew, but provided sufficiently robust data to prove it was indeed a Slender-billed Curlew and wrote a retraction paper with the same strength as the original ground-breaking article. Whilst we were chatting, he found us a Long-tailed Skua. Such a pleasure to meet him.

The Yellow-breasted Bunting was found by A.Denton and B.Outram and was only the third record in the last five years.

On 14th September a Great Snipe was found in a ditch at the south end of Beacon Lane at Kilnsea. The news broke at 5:23pm and with only a flight view of the rejected Fazakerley bird to my name, I decided to go the next morning at 2am with John Lees, John Benham, and Simon King. We arrived at Beacon Lane at 6:30am and it was suggested that we should all climb into a ditch and wait. They were right, the Great Snipe gave superb views from 6:47am down to a few feet. I left an hour later, and only realised on the way home that my camera had fallen out of my pocket into the ditch.

On Friday 20th September news broke of a Wilson's Warbler on Dursey Island, Cork. It was too late for me to get the 2:45am Fishguard ferry, so I surfed the web for a flight. I couldn't find anything reasonably priced, but Vaughan Watkins found a Ryan Air flight leaving Bristol on Saturday at 8:05am and arriving at Dublin at 9:10, then departing Dublin on the Sunday at 8:20am and getting back to Bristol at 9:25am. It would cost

£210 each. I booked a couple of flights for John Lees and myself.

I left home Saturday morning at 1:15am and picked up Paul Homes and Bob Watts at Wraysbury before meeting Vaughan at Bristol Airport. News came through whilst we were hiring a car that the Wilson's Warbler was still there, in Derek Scott's garden. This news made the 4½ hour journey to Dursey a pleasure. The cable car cost £8 and operated from 9:30am to 7:30pm between 1st March to 31st October and 9:30am to 4:30pm from 1st November to 28th February. Every day it closes for lunch between 1 to 1:30pm. Telephone number (027)73851. These details may have changed, of course.

We were first in the queue for the 1:30pm cable car, but the operator allowed some Irish people to go ahead of us. We got on the second crossing. The cable car can take 6 passengers at a time and takes 8 minutes to get to the island. Once on the other side it takes an hour to walk the 4.6km to the garden. The island is quite steep, with a few sheer drops. For years, I have suffered with vertigo, and I really don't trust myself not to jump. I managed to hitch a ride with a kind lady, and she dropped me near the garden.

Many birders were already lined up there when I arrived. We found the Wilson's Warbler doing quite a long circuit of the various shrubs Derek had planted. I missed it on at least two circuits, so I repositioned myself near the Pittisporum where people were seeing it. Here Bob Watts and I managed to get close views of the bird. This magnificent American yellow gem showed for about 10 seconds as it perched and hopped its way through the Pittisporum. I watched it the whole time through my bins. Once the pressure was off, I went back to where I was originally standing and got at least three more views. It was nice to see the diagnostic black cap and beady black eye.

John Lees eventually got to the garden, and saw it before it got dark. Once it was dark, we all walked the back to the cable car, and because I couldn't see the sheer drop my vertigo was under control.

The Wilson's Warbler was found by Derek Scott on the 18th September and stayed to the 21st. It was the first record for Ireland. Previously Britain had a one-dayer at Rame in 1984.

You don't often see beautiful 21-year-old girls lying on airport concourse floors, but at Dublin airport, passengers were walking around a lovely girl on the floor while her friend stood next to her. It turned out that both were on a show called "The Valley", a Welsh reality TV show that's broadcast on MTV. This was one of my first twitches wearing my blue bandanna, and I was wondering if it was having the Lynx effect on her. Apparently not. Her friend said "She's been shagging for a couple of days and she's exhausted". Yeah, I remember those days... not.

An Eastern Kingbird was found by Anthony McGeehan on Inishbofin on 24th September. The next day I flew with Bob Watts and Graham Jepson from Stansted. We caught the boat to Inishbofin (€25 each), and I managed to dip my second Eastern Kingbird. The best bird we saw was a Common Rosefinch, whilst Adrian Webb managed to briefly find a Blackpoll Warbler.

On Friday 4th October, the time had finally come to take John Lees on his first-ever trip to Fair Isle. I manged to get us cheap Flybe tickets (£45 each) and two nights' accommodation at Tommy Hyman's B&B. Then, just before we left Crawley, a Thick-billed Warbler was found on the Shetland mainland at Geosetter. All past Thick-billed Warblers had only stayed on one day – Fair Isle 1955, Whalsay 1971, Out Skerries 2001 and Fair Isle 2003. The Fair Isle bird was in a totally different part of the island on its 2nd day.

I drove overnight from Crawley and caught the 7am flight from Aberdeen to Sumburgh. By the time we picked up the hire car an hour later, it wasn't looking good. A message came through at 7:50am that there was no sign of the bird. Geosetter is only a 17-minute drive away, so we decided to go up there anyway. I parked the car on the verge next to the single carriageway, where lots of cars were already parked up. We walked to the burn and the first people we bumped into were Kevin McCoy and Gareth Stamp. Gareth said the warbler was still there. Superb news, but why had nobody else seen it?

A few hours went by and still no sign, I decided to cancel the flights and accommodation with Tommy Hyman. Tommy was fine about it and said his son was also at Geosetter trying to see the bird. Hugh Harrop decided to visit John Sinclair, who owned the field. The field was full of non-commercial crop and Hugh and Judd Hunt got permission to do two organised flushes, one at 1pm and another at 4:30. It worked – John and I managed to get a few flight views of the Thick-billed Warbler. I managed to see it fly out of the crop and land for a few seconds on the ground, a large warbler with a beady black eye on a white face, white breast, milky brown upperparts, and a long tail. It was not a totally satisfying view, but better than dipping.

At 2:02pm news came thorough that there had been a Lanceolated Warbler on Fair Isle. This was a bird John and I both needed, and we could have been there if we had managed to see the Thick-billed Warbler first thing.

I tried to ignore the Lanceolated Warbler and booked some accommodation for the night. Lots of places were fully booked, but we did find a 7-bedroom self-catering house on Spiggie for 2 nights. This cost us £160. Over the next three days we managed to see a Rosy Starling, an Eastern Olivaceous Warbler, a Short-toed Lark, a Lapland bunting, a Little Bunting, a Long-eared Owl and an Eastern Subalpine Warbler. The Eastern Subalpine Warbler was on Yell and there I met the late Martin Garner for the first time. Martin explained to me how to identify an Eastern Subalpine Warbler in the field. The features were strictly confidential and were to be published in his next edition of the Birding Frontiers Challenge Series. Martin was such a nice guy and even made me a cup of coffee whilst I was talking to him.

We left Shetland on the Monday at 11:30am and got back on Tuesday. On the slow journey home, we saw a drake Surf Scoter at Blackdog and three Blue-winged Teals at Boultham Mere in Lincolnshire.

The Thick-billed Warbler was found by Dave Fairhurst and Hugh Harrop. That one stayed from 4th-5th October and was only the 5th for Britain.

On Wednesday 23rd October I was working at Tipner when at 1:20pm news was broadcast of a probable Cape May Warbler on Britain's most northerly island, Unst. This was confirmed at 3pm, and with that I booked a couple of days' leave. The year was starting to feel exhausting – so many new birds were turning up, and nearly all in Scotland. Such a good year to have a company car.

I went home and left Crawley at 6pm and drove all the way to Aberdeen alone. I very rarely twitch long distance by myself, but being at short notice nobody else could come. The next day I caught the 9:55am Aberdeen to Sumburgh flight. I hired a car at the airport and was then joined by Tony Forde and John Regan. We had a cooked breakfast on the Yell ferry terminal and arrived at Baltasound on Unst at 3:15pm. The Cape May Warbler was ranging widely over the Island. Luckily at 4pm we saw it in a lone sycamore. It hung around for about 20 minutes at close range. Rather than stay the night on Shetland, I got the 7pm ferry back with Tony and John.

The Cape May Warbler was found by Mike Pennington on the 23rd October and it stayed to 2nd November. It was the second for Britain, the first having been found in Paisley Glen, near Glasgow, on 17th June 1977.

A Caspian Stonechat was first identified at St. Warma's cove on St. Agnes on 21st November. This bird was on its fifth day; it was originally thought to be a Siberian Stonechat. Helena Craig organised a flight from Land's end to Scilly with a *Scillonian* return on 30th November. I drove John Benham, John Lees and Ashley Howe to Land's End and we met Paul Chapman, Vaughan Watkins, Chris Bromley, Chris Goodie and the Craig family at the airport. The trip went smoothly, no weather delay, and the plane took us to St. Mary's. We took a taxi to the quay and then a return boat charter to St. Agnes. The Caspian Stonechat showed well – such a shame it's only a subspecies. The ferry docked in Penzance and ground transport was laid on by Skybus to take us to Land's End. Superbly organised by Helena, and I wish all twitches worked out so well.

SUMMARY

During 2013, I travelled 12,226 miles in Britain and Ireland in the pursuit of new birds and managed to increase my list by 11 BOU/IRBC species. This took my British and Irish list to 496 species. The Combined Official stood at 608 species, which meant I had now seen 81.6% of them. There was one net addition to the Official British and Irish List during the year: - White-winged Scoter (2011), Ruby-crowned Kinglet (2013) and removal of Slender-billed Curlew (1998 Druridge Bay).

The 11 lifers in the table above are Wilson's

2013	Regular	Vagrant	BBRC/IRBC 1 year	BBRC/IRBC 2 year	BBRC/IRBC 3 year	BBRC/IRBC 4 year	BBRC/IRBC 5 year	BBRC/IRBC 10 year	BBRC/IRBC 20 year	BBRC/IRBC Lifetime	Cat B	Total
Seen	276	37	87	10	12	11	32	18	8	5	0	496
During			1	2		1	4	1	2			11
B&I Total	276	38	92	12	13	15	43	39	33	39	8	608
	100%	97%	95%	83%	92%	73%	74%	46%	24%	13%	0%	81.6%

Warbler and Cape May Warbler (20-year), Thick-billed Warbler (10-year), Pine Grosbeak, Pacific Swift, Needle-tailed Swift and Swinhoe's Storm Petrel (5-year), Dusky Thrush (4-year), Rock Thrush & Bridled Tern (2-year) and Great Snipe (1-year).

I managed to see 304 different species in Britain and Ireland during the year. If it hadn't been for my company car, I certainly wouldn't have done it. The company car was going back early next year and then I would face the harsh reality of wearing my own car out again.

This was my fourth time of seeing 300+ British and Irish species in a calendar year. My 300th bird was a Shore Lark, of which I saw three at Great Yarmouth. This magic moment happened when I was photographed wearing my blue bandanna with John Lees – it was published in the *Washington Post*. This picture was used on the back cover.

The 500 species mark was getting awfully close, and seeing four more new birds next year shouldn't be a problem.

I decided the most important bird seen during the year was the White-throated Needletail. Watching the fastest bird in the world for horizontal flight whooshing inches over my head felt like the defining moment of my twitching career. Although unverified, its thought to reach a speed of 170kph (105mph). If Britain ever gets another twitchable one, make sure you see it, as it really is the ultimate twitch.

White-throated Needletail
Hirundapus caudacutus
Harris : Tarbert
Western Isles
26th June 2013
GREENELL

CHAPTER 16

2014

Late in 2013 I made two-day trips to Holland. First trip we saw a Hawk Owl at Zwolle and on the second trip I saw a Pygmy Owl at Lettele. If I had had a crystal ball this could have all waited to 12th January, when we could have seen both owls and a Caspian Plover.

I decided to go back to Holland with John Lees and Alan Lewis and attempt just the Caspian Plover at Colijnsplaat. We all saw the bird distantly in a farmer's field. We wanted better pictures, so we entered the field and got slightly better views before heading back. The farmer then arrived and spotted John. Alan and I had just got our feet back on the tarmac, but he was still in the field. I shouldn't laugh, but this whole scene was comical. The farmer was half John's age and built like Rambo. He was angrily shouting at him and waving his fists. John managed to get past him and tried to apologise in English. The farmer carried on shouting in Dutch and only stopped when John was safely back in the car. We left the site pronto. Alan and I were ready to go to John's defence if things got violent, but

fortunately they didn't. A real scary man, and we didn't see any signs prohibiting access.

On the way back to port we managed to find a Black Woodpecker in Oost Vlaanderen, Belgium by playback of call.

On Saturday 15th February I spent the day looking for a possible Chinese Pond Heron in Saltwood, Kent, with Vaughan Watkins. We spent the whole time sitting in my car on Turnpike Road. The view of this heron was going to be restricted to flight only at this largely suburban site. 30 birders stood outside their cars and chatted most of the day, and at the end of the day we all left empty-handed.

On Sunday, with John Lees, George Kinnard and Dan Houghton, I took the risky strategy of leaving the south-east. We went to County Durham and saw a reported Yellow-rumped Warbler, and in Avon we saw a Red-flanked Bluetail. Luckily, back in Kent there was no sign of the Chinese Pond Heron that day. On the Monday it was seen again. In fact it was seen every day from Monday 17th to

Friday 21st. On Saturday 22nd February, I decided to give it another go. I drove alone to Turnpike Road and sat in the car from 6:23am. 20 birders were in for a treat as the Chinese Pond Heron was found sitting at the top of a tall oak tree from 7:04-7:34am, right next to my car. I managed some video and felt pretty pleased that I had decided to give it another go.

Back home, Georgie was really enjoying her swimming lessons. Every year Crawley Swimming Club would hold time trials 2-3 times a year to gauge how the students were progressing. Georgie's best strokes were 50-metre free and 50-metre breast. When she reached 10 years old in April, if she could get with the county time, she could qualify for the county championships. This was a massive carrot to give a young swimmer. It would certainly make them want to improve their overall fitness and technique.

Crawley Swimming Club regularly holds swimming galas where the coaches pick the best swimmers of the four strokes (free, fly, back and breast) to represent the club. If any parents have good swimmers, they are expected to help at the galas. I had got roped into being a timekeeper in 2013 and on 16th March 2014 I was due to be an official for the first time. We had six clubs competing that afternoon, and five hours later we found that Crawley had got the most points and won the trophy. The kids went mad and jumped into the pool wearing Crawley Swimming Club T-shirts. The proudest moment for me was when Georgie got first in the under-10s 50-metre breaststroke. I was in tears but had to carry on timekeeping. Kim and her mum watched the whole race from the balcony.

Kim and I used to take Georgie for swimming lessons a couple of times per week and some of Georgie's classmates from Rusper were also members. Kim or I use to end by having a big chinwag on the balcony with parents, like Louise's mum Beverley. Georgie and Louise were having fun and at the same time learning a skill that could save their lives one day.

The Chinese Pond Heron, first found on 21st January was found dead on the 25th March. The DNA confirmed the species. It was occasionally feeding on expensive koi carp in the gardens of Saltwood. Rumours were circulating that somebody had probably shot it to safeguard their carp.

On Friday 11th April, a Crag Martin was seen from 8:59am at Flamborough Head. I decided to leave home at 11:45 and pick John Benham up en route to Flamborough. The journey to Flamborough involved taking many diverts, as there were major traffic problems. When I got to the site at 6:46pm, there had had been no further sighting since 12:38. We listened on the radio to the 7:45pm kick off between Arsenal v West Ham (Arsenal won 3-1) and got some fish and chips and a pint of beer at the Martonian Inn. Feeling tired, we stayed the night at the Poplars Motel (01262) 677251 in Bridlington.

The next morning, bright and early, we headed to Bempton to look for a Tawny Pipit. There was no sign, so making sure we got our money's worth, we went back to the motel to have a cooked breakfast. Not wanting to allow the Crag Martin to beat us, we went back to Flamborough and Bempton. By 1pm there had been no further sign, and we both agreed we had wasted enough time and money and needed to throw the towel in and head back.

We just got off the M18 and onto the M1 when news came through that the Crag Martin had just been seen, at 2:38pm at Thornwick. I rang Chris Batty, and he believed the news was accurate.

Yabba dabba doo! We were now 80 miles south of Thornwick and it was time to do a U-turn and head back north. We got to Thornwick Bay at 3:50pm and missed the Crag Martin by a minute. It had been showing well for 72 minutes. Brett Richards had seen it well, but he he said, "Let me see if I can relocate it". Seventeen minutes later, he found it at Flamborough. We got back in the car, and three minutes later we were watching the Crag Martin with Brett. We watched it flying up and down the cliff faces for an hour.

The whole twitch was beginning to feel like a classic roller-coaster ride. Most people wouldn't have turned the car round by 2pm. The bird was on show to 7:20pm and it wouldn't have been twitchable if I had left Crawley at 2:38. I was getting floods of congratulations on Twitter, and it felt like we'd just won gold for the British birdwatching team at the Olympics.

The Crag Martin, found by A. Allport, was the 9th for Britain, and was last seen at 8:13am on Sunday 13th April. It was only the second twitchable one in Britain. Most people had seen the 1999 individual that had spent one day at Pugney's Country Park in West Yorkshire.

On 18th April, the time had finally come to attack the garden. I would say we were unlucky to have such a small garden plot compared to the rest of the house owners on the block. Beverley's husband Jim, who had a tree surgery business and made the occasional patio, popped round and advised on dimensions, materials and tools to use. I hired a 6-yard skip, dug up the crazy paving that led to back of the garden and filled in the garden pond. Then I started to dig 20cm deep over 15 square metres. This was back breaking, and it was nice to get help from Kim's son Andrew. Even David Browne got handed a spade when he thought he

was just round for dinner.

The skip eventually got filled and we then bought sand and cement and a half-price pack of Indian sandstones from Jewsons'. The sandstone had apparently been dropped during unloading and it was a gamble whether there would be enough good slabs to cover the area.

On Saturday 1st June. I took a day's break from making the patio build and took George Kinnard to Morden Bog NNR in Dorset to try and see a Short-toed Eagle. We arrived in the darkness at 4am and then walked onto the heath with churring Nightjars. Many birders had already assembled at the ridge overlooking the tree where the eagle had roosted the previous evening. The shape of the eagle still sitting in the roost tree could be discerned at 4:43am. I couldn't be totally sure if it was even a bird at this stage, but as the light improved, I could see it was indeed a Short-toed Eagle. Initially it resembled an Osprey, but once you could see it had no face mask you knew it was something special, a large raptor with white underparts, brown speckles on upper breast and a short tail. It had taken 15 years for a twitchable Short-toed Eagle to visit Britain since the last one, a Scilly bird.

I didn't really understand the significance of the Short-toed Eagle back then, but now I prioritise firsts and seconds. I managed a few Digiscoped shots and video footage. It was mobbed by Corvids, and at 10:02am it decided to fly off. It was a five-hour wait, but all raptors look better in flight than perched. Once it took off it brought back fond memories of seeing my first one in Southern Spain.

The 500 birders on site really had a good reason to smile. The legendary creature stayed the night and put on a special performance. On the way back we couldn't resist the breeding Black-winged Stilts at Bracklesham Bay.

The Short-toed Eagle was identified by Paul

Morton whilst taking 12 members of the public on a Poole harbour field trip. It was first spotted by a member of the group called Alan King and Paul initially thought it was a Buzzard, but when the view improved and he consulted Collins Field Guide it was clearly a Short-toed Eagle. It was found on Saturday 31st May and left Morden at 10am the next day.

On 16th May the park and ride scheme by Colas and Volkerfitzpatrick in Tipner was very close to completion and my daily attendance was no longer needed. I said goodbye to the JV team and took the company car back to Rowfant. Beverley then managed to provide me with an office-based job. My Peugeot 407 was still parked in the car park and refused to start. Kim suggested we should pass ownership to her son Luke and get another car from the Lancing and Shoreham Car Auctions. This time we came back with a 2006 Vauxhall Astra estate.

On 13th July, 86 days after the first shovel load of earth was placed in the wheelbarrow, we could step out of the conservatory onto a beautiful patio. Kim often told me my DIY skills were lousy. She was brought up on a farm where her dad knew how to fix a tractor, fit a kitchen and bathroom, fit electric sockets and just about everything else you can mention. I am regularly reminded about the day I tried to fit a wooden toilet seat to a porcelain bowl (base). I was having difficulty fitting the screws in the holes at the back of the bowl and gave the screws one gentle tap with the hammer. That should do the trick… it certainly did. I knocked the whole section off and the screw had no hole to go through. I had to go and buy a new toilet.

The whole process of using a whacker plate, cutting slabs with an angle grinder, then positioned the slabs into the mortar base using a spirit level and a finding the exact spot with the rubber mallet was very rewarding and enhanced my DIY CV. Quite a few of the cracked Indian sandstone slabs were not useable, but Jewsons gave me enough to finish the job.

The next day a Great Knot at Breydon Water mega'd at 6:06am. I wonder if this king of waders knew I had just finished the patio? I took the Astra out on its maiden voyage, left Crawley at 8:30am and arrived at midday. I parked in the Asda car park and walked west. The tide starting to fill and at 2:30pm the Great Knot flew onto the mudflats. David Campbell was instrumental in me seeing it quickly in my scope. The bird was always distant, but it was quite diagnostic. This is the only medium sized wader with all-black upperparts extending past the head to the pectoral region. This contrasted nicely with its white belly. The views didn't improve for the half hour I was on site.

The Great Knot was originally found by Peter Allard the previous evening whilst counting Redshanks. News was released locally as Peter didn't want to prevent people missing the World Cup final between Germany v Argentina (in which Germany won 1-0 in extra time). I guess the 29th May 2009 fiasco didn't help his decision. The bird was a 4th for Britain, and it stayed till the 15th July.

On Thursday 21st August I left the family at the hotel in Mallorca and hired a car for the day. First stop was Cap de Formentor, and the winding road all the way to the lighthouse was full of fast cyclists. I managed to overtake them all and then spend some time wandering around this magnificent headland. I managed to see 4 Eleonora's Falcons, 2 Balearic Shearwaters and a Scopoli's Shearwater, all on foot. Albufera National Park was next on the agenda, open from 9am to 6pm. Here there are footpaths, cycle trails, birdwatching hides, and visitor centre. This is another good site for the Eleonora's Falcon. I didn't see any – the highlights were a pair of Red-knobbed Coots plus young, 12 Stone Curlews, 3 Purple Swamphens and a very photographic Moustached Warbler which I watched from the boardwalk. I ended the day at Cuber reservoir, where I saw 2 Booted Eagles, a Black Vulture and a Griffon Vulture but failed to see a Moltoni's Warbler, maybe being too late in the year.

Back at the hotel, Georgie met a girl of similar age called Charlotte, who introduced us to her parents, Mike and Jane Tickle from Warrington. The six of us had a good time, but from experience on previous holidays, Kim wanted to make sure we gave them plenty of space. We left it up to them if they wanted to join us at the pool, bar or restaurant. They were often with us, but Georgie distanced herself from her boring parents and hung with Charlotte for the rest of the holiday.

Once back home it was time to look at secondary schools for Georgie. We visited Holy Trinity in Crawley, Mallais girls school in Horsham and my old school, Thomas Bennett. Kim and I really liked Holy Trinity and Georgie decided to put it down as her first option, Mallais as her second option and Thomas Bennett as her third. A few weeks later we found that she had been given the catchment school, of Thomas Bennett. Her friends Jemima, Louise and Amelia all got Millais. Whereas Georgie's cousin Kian was given Holy Trinity.

I didn't enjoy my time at Thomas Bennett and after reading a private message that the school hadn't improved, we decided to appeal the decision. The appeal failed and Georgie was due to enrol at Thomas Bennett on the 7th September 2015. I'm not sure why they allow open days for schools when you are only really allowed the nearest school.

Autumn was approaching and Kim's attention was now on a lawn that looked like a building site. I managed to build a wall of sleepers separating the patio from the lawn and fitted three small sleeper steps to get onto the so called building site. I hired a rotavator from Jewson's and managed to turn the whole garden flat. Over the next week I was rolling it daily, and got it perfectly flat, ready for the turf.

The day before the turf arrived, I had been advised to water the lawn. Not knowing how much water to use, I used my initiative. Kim arrived home to see that our once perfectly flat surface had been turned into a saturated, uneven bog. She took one look at it and ordered me to fix it, then stormed out of the house and slammed the front door behind her.

The following day at midday the turf arrived, and it took me five hours to lay the rolls, starting at far end of and working back to the sleepers. By the time Kim got home it was looking like a lawn. It was still too boggy to walk on. Kim rarely gives compliments, but as she was not moaning it was probably all right.

Autumn had arrived, and it was time to have a birding holiday in Shetland. This time Andrew Lawson drove James Hanlon, George Kinnard and me there on the 3rd October. Blackdog produced a Surf Scoter, and as we made our way to the Ythan the mega alert went off. Dan Pointon had found a male Siberian Rubythroat at Levenwick, only 3 miles from where we would be staying. Andrew took his car on the Northlink ferry and ordered a four-berth cabin. This was better than the cinema floor but with all the snoring, I wasn't sure it was worth the extra expense.

On Saturday morning we headed straight to Levenwick. The male Siberian Rubythroat was still there, but I only managed a flight view and wanted to hang around for better views. The others went off to see a Pallid Harrier at Tingwall. It rained all day and at 5pm the Siberian Rubythroat showed well in another garden a little further along. I rang the guys, and they came back for it.

On Sunday the wind was SSW and our first stop was Levenwick. The Siberian Rubythroat was seen by the whole group, and we then did some birding in the south. James Hanlon found a Little Bunting at Boddam and then I saw the Pallid Harrier at Tingwall for the first time, plus a small Horneman's Arctic Redpoll at Veensgarth.

Monday was very windy, and I'm not just talking about Andrew Lawson's backside. We headed for a bit of cover at Channerwick. We saw a large grey warbler in flight which turned out to be a Barred Warbler which we had already seen the previous day. It was nice to see a perched Long-eared Owl at Sumburgh. James Hanlon had lost his phone after finding the Little Bunting, so we went back to all of yesterdays sites to see if we could re-find it. No luck, but the best find of the day was a Leach's Petrel 200 yards from the front door of the digs. This was yet again found by James, or shall I change his name "Bird Magnet"? It was even successfully twitched by Hugh Harrop.

On Tuesday the wind was still strong and coming from the south-east. It rained all morning and we managed to see 2 Black Redstarts, Short-eared Owls, 2 Woodcock, 2 Purple Sandpipers and a Fieldfare. I spent the afternoon at Levenwick with Fred Fearn and Becky Nason. I must have watched the male Siberian Rubythroat for 10 minutes in total as it showed well feeding on entrance path to the house.

In the evening a probable Pallas's Grasshopper Warbler was being claimed at Quendale. The pictures on Twitter were poor, but all four of us were under the impression this was more likely to be a Lanceolated Warbler.

On Wednesday we headed straight to Quendale for first light. Nobody else was there, so we walked through the burn and kicked up 5 Reed Warblers, and after about 2 hours we found the Locustella

(grass warbler spp). From the views in flight it was impossible to identify with certainty. Then the bird flew into the open and its identity was confirmed as a Lanceolated Warbler. This was my 500th BOU species. I had finally achieved it, and celebrated by buying everybody a coffee at the Quendale shop. Photographs were taken of me wearing my famous orange T-shirt, with about 10 other birders. Not wanting to sound morbid, but this was a big moment for me, you never know when you're going to go to heaven. Just think about think Tim Lawrence, who died with 497 species.

After coffee we drove to Virkie. James wandered around birding, Andy went to see a moth at Rob Fray's house, whilst George and I stayed in the car and stuffed ourselves with pies. "Bird Magnet" then found a Great Grey Shrike, but he had forgotten his walkie talkie. He came back to the car, and then all four us wandered off and got the shrike.

Thursday turned out to be a big clear-out day with the Siberian Rubythroat departing. We stopped at Voe and I found a Hawfinch, then George called an Olive-backed Pipit in flight. We all saw it well on the ground and then it flew, with a second OBP.

Then news come through of a Western Bonelli's Warbler at Scalloway. When we got there it had not been seen for a while. After a couple of hours I played the Western Bonelli's Warbler call and it responded.

During the evening we met up with 12 other birders and had a curry in Lerwick. James was not convinced that the Bonelli's Warbler was a Western and wanted to go back for a second look. There was now a bit of competition developing over which group could get the most trip ticks. We were in full competition with the boozy birders, consisting of Paul Hawkins, Nick Croft, Tony Brown and Martin Blow.

Great Knot
Calidris tenuirostris
Breydon Water. Norfolk
14th July 2014
G BAGNELL

Friday we were at Scalloway with a playback of Orientalis. The warbler responded and called back. The call was heard by five individuals, including Shetland local Phil Harris, and the bird was put out by RBA as an Eastern Bonelli's Warbler. 40 birders were now on site, including Paul Harvey with some sound recording equipment. The bird was silent for the rest of the day.

It was so nice to meet birding legend Keith Pellow. He found a Caspian Plover on St Agnes in 1984 and was instrumental in identifying a Wilson's Warbler on Rame head in 1985. What a legend!

Last bird of the trip was a Siberian Stonechat at Hoswick, this was my 122nd trip species. Our group total 129 and did we beat the Boozy birders? No, they beat us by just 5 birds with a total of 134.

Even though we lost, we had a brilliant holiday. Thanks to Andrew for organising the trip and doing all the cooking. We took the 7pm ferry back to Aberdeen and dropped into Burnham Norton to see a Steppe Grey Shrike before getting home.

The Eastern Bonelli's was accepted by BBRC and credited to James Hanlon and Phil Harris. Separating Bonelli's Warblers on plumage and bare-part colours is sometimes possible, but the most reliable feature of the Eastern is the sparrow-like "chup chup" call. The Western makes an entirely different sound, resembling the Willow Warbler's "Hooeet" call. Not all Bonelli's Warblers call in the autumn, and 77 have been assigned to the Western/Eastern camp. This Eastern, available from 10-13th October, became only the 7th accepted record.

The two-day Lanceolated Warbler originally

found by Chris Griffin and Phil Woollen was accepted as the 140th record for Britain. Nearly 100 of these records have been seen on Fair Isle alone.

SUMMARY

During 2014, I travelled 2,815 miles in Britain and Ireland in the pursuit of new birds and managed to increase my list by 5 BOU/IRBC species. This took my British and Irish list to 501 species. The Combined Official was still on 608 species (there were no additions to the Official British and Irish List during the year), and I was still on 82.4%.

The 5 lifers in the table above are Short-toed Eagle and Great Knot (10-year), Eastern Bonelli's Warbler (5-year), Crag Martin (4-year) and Lanceolated Warbler (1-year).

My 500th species was the Lanceolated Warbler. What a place and what a bird to hit this important landmark with. Lee Evans keeps a list of the Birders' Life List rankings. He informed me that

I broke into the Top 100 last year with my Cape May Warbler. I thought I had a chance of good chance of getting into the Top 50, but Top 20 was never going to be within reach. The top 20 have seen 90% of the official list and wouldn't dream of missing birds like the Brown-headed Cowbird, Long-tailed Shrike and Purple Martin.

There have been 45 additions to the official list in the last 15 years. If this continued the first person to hit the 600 species barrier would be sometime in 2029. My next target was 550.

I decided the most important bird seen during the year was the Great Knot. This bird had been high on my wants list since dipping the 2004 Skippool Creek bird twice. This bird is probably the best-looking wader Britain gets. Lots of people saw the 1996 Great Knot in Cleveland. It was better known as the "Great Dot". You had to be standing next to someone with a Questar scope to see it well back then.

2014	Regular	Vagrant	BBRC/ IRBC 1 year	BBRC/ IRBC 2 year	BBRC/ IRBC 3 year	BBRC/ IRBC 4 year	BBRC/ IRBC 5 year	BBRC/ IRBC 10 year	BBRC/ IRBC 20 year	BBRC/ IRBC Lifetime	Cat B	Total
Seen	276	37	88	10	12	12	33	20	8	5	0	501
During			1			1	1	2				5
B&I Total	276	38	92	12	13	15	43	39	33	39	8	608
	100%	97%	96%	83%	92%	80%	77%	51%	24%	13%	0%	82.4%

CHAPTER 17

2015

Alan and Natalie Robbins invited Kim, Georgie and me over to their house in Rusper to celebrate the New Year in. They've got a big garden and they had put up a marquee, where a hundred guests were being entertained by a live band. This was the first time I'd been invited to a house party with a cocktail bar. I'm a big fan of cocktails and would have loved to make my way through the cocktail list, but I only had two.

Jimbob and Beverley Smith were there and giving me compliments on how good the patio looked. Jimbob said, "If you ever move you will know exactly how to make the next one". Georgie made a beeline to hang out with her schoolfriends Jemima, Louise and Amelia (Natalie's daughter).

Exactly at midnight I kissed Kim goodnight, and met John Lees and George Kinnard outside. Oh yes, we were off on a twitch. We left Rusper, picked up John Benham at the usual spot in Leatherhead and made our way to Fraisthorpe, East Yorkshire. Five hours later we arrived in the pitch black. This

was obviously a big twitch, as cars were lined up along the grass verge for two miles.

We found a space to park and managed 2½ hours' sleep, then joined the massive crowd looking into the kale field. By 8:12am we could see the head of the Little Bustard popping out of the kale. I did eventually see the top half of the bird, but it was not moving much and just pecking insects off the kale leaves. I waited several hours, but we never managed to see it its magnificent wing pattern. I estimate we must have seen 700 admirers before we headed off to see Jonathan Holliday's Blyth's Pipit at Pugneys. The Little Bustard first was first found on 31st December by Kevin Barnard. He saw it fly south from Wilsthorpe at 8:30am. Tony Dixon received a call from Kevin and quickly got down there with his six-year old, Reuben. Tony managed to relocate it at 11am at Auburn Farm at Fraisthorpe and it was last seen on 1st January at 3:54pm. It became the 27th record for Britain. There were two others in 2014, West Bexington on 18th November and East Guldeford on 30th

December, both untwitchable. The last twitchable bird on the mainland was back in 1996. This was at the Lizard from 24-29th October.

On 8th March Georgie received a message from Crawley Swimming Club that they would like her to represent Crawley in the Sussex championship relays at the Sovereign Centre at Eastbourne. How brilliant is that! Crawley have a squad of over 30 under-11 girls, and they pick my little bundle of joy.

Georgie swam twice in the competition. In the first race she swam 50 metres in the 200-metre freestyle where Crawley came 7th out of 19 teams. Then she swam 50-metre breaststroke in the 200 medley and the race was abandoned because of someone's minor infringement. Such a pity, Georgie achieved 47.1 seconds, which would have been her personal best. This time, being under 48 seconds, would been good enough for her to enter the Sussex championship for 50-metre breaststroke. I am one proud daddy.

On 16th March my 14-year career as a Management Accountant at Colas was due to end, and the Associate Financial Director, Beverley, offered me a choice – take a financial accounting role working for Spurs supporter Darren Butler or take redundancy. Darren was a great guy, but what would my future pay rises be like if Arsenal finished higher in the Premiership? Joking aside, I thought it was time for a new job challenge. I had had some amazing experiences over the last 14 years and there must be a company out that was ready to hire me. It was time to update the CV and inform HR I was taking the redundancy.

The Birmingham, Grantham and Newcastle Plant and Transport staff all got re-allocated to site business managers with a dotted line still to Trevor Purfield. I was required to visit the above locations and train the management accountants on how I managed the fitters' times and how to allocate their costs to vehicles. Trainee Accountant Jade Lavery took on the residue of the Tipner work and managed just the Rowfant overheads for Plant and Transport.

My leaving date was extended to 17th April, as Grantham boss Dave Stannard wanted to tap into my Excel skills to see I could improve the workload of his Finance Manager, Lynne Furmidge.

A job agency lined me up with an interview with Financial Controller Lee Courtney Wheatley at a speaker company called Bower and Wilkins in Worthing. They needed somebody for a few months to learn the roles of two staff who were leaving and train up replacements. Lee was younger than me and his first task at the interview was to leave me to sit an Excel test. Once I had finished it, I had to put my hand up and Lee would return and see If I had passed. Then he would start the formal interview process with him and his boss Martyn. I passed the Excel test and the whole interview process was enjoyable.

On Tuesday 14th April a Great Blue Heron was found at Old Town Bay on St. Mary's. There was no way I could go, and I hoped it would still be there at the weekend, but it vanished and was not seen next day until 7:29pm on Bryher.

On Friday 17th April I had some good news and some bad news. The good news was that I had managed to get the job at Bower & Wilkins and was starting in three days' time. The bad news was that I would have to keep the lunchtime leaving drinks to a bare minimum as I needed to drive in the evening to Bryher. The Great Blue Heron stayed the night there.

I was very impressed that 41 people turned up for my leaving do drinks at Hillside Inn. It was also, very kind of Colas to pick up the bar bill. Leaving dos are sad affairs, but I was allowed to go straight home from the pub.

I left home at 7:30pm and managed to hook up with Hugh Price, John Benham and John Archer. En route we stopped at Exeter Services, where I took a driving break and Hugh bought me a latte. Once we got to Penzance, all four of us crashed out and got an hour's kip. I thought we needed to maximise our time looking for the heron, so we booked a Skybus departure from Land's End at 10:25am. Up to the point of the departure there was no news on the bird and we all prepared ourselves for the worst, but as soon as we touched down it was all systems go: the bird was still on Big Pool by Hell Bay Hotel. Huge sigh of relief.

We took a taxi to the quay and spent £10 on a return boat to Bryher, and by 11:30 we were watching a very stationary Great Blue Heron. It never flew, but it was huge compared to our native grey herons. This Great Blue Heron had a dark greyish and purplish hue to its neck, breast and wings. The head was a similar pattern to our Grey Heron, but it had a gigantic bill. It had been seen eating frogs and fish, but this never happened during my two hours on site.

We came back home on the *Scillonian* at 4:30pm and had fish and chips in Penzance. We got home at 5am on Sunday morning, giving me plenty of time to recover before starting the new job on Monday.

The Great Blue Heron was originally found by Ashley Fisher and Cavell Smith at 6:56pm on 14th April and last seen on 7th May. It became the 2nd record for Britain, with both being found on the Scillies.

It was a 40-minute drive to Bowers and Wilkins, and Lee introduced me to the rest of the team. I was first introduced to Suzanne Page, account assistant to Lee, and I could see straight away that I was going to like her. She spoke her mind and was full of hilarious stories. She was married to Mags, a scaffolder who was covered in tattoos. I'm pretty sure Suzanne was pulling my leg, but said that If anyone gave her hassle, they would be getting a visit from Mags. Believe you me, no one was going to give Suzanne any hassle, she had arms like Arnold Schwarzenegger and I don't think I've ever met a woman as scary as her before.

She lived in a housing estate nearby in Worthing and being a bit of animal lover, she had two pigs roaming around the house and garden, plus a couple of dogs and a macaw.

I remembered working with Martyn Williams many years ago when temping at Rentokil in East Grinstead. Martyn was the financial controller and spends his spare time pedalling the Sussex lanes on his bicycle. He also lived in Crawley, only a couple of miles from my house.

Lee arranged a factory tour where I was shown how the speakers were constructed. On the tour I bumped into Sussex birder Nick Bond, who was shop floor foreman in the woodwork department.

Back in the office I sat next to credit controller Lorraine Shelfer and a South African guy called John Nieuwoudt, who ran the payroll.

On Saturday 26th April I was buying some milk at Tilgate shops when I noticed I had had a missed call from George Kinnard. I rang him back and he asked, "Have you heard about the Hudsonian Godwit in Somerset?" This wasn't good timing for me as I was due to take Georgie to a swimming gala at Horsham. I returned home and Kim agreed to take her. I left home at 9:15am and arrived at midday. The car park at Meare Heath had 120 spaces and I managed to find the last one. The Hudsonian Godwit was still present with Black-tailed Godwits. It was quite easy to spot with its heavily barred belly and smaller size. I'm glad I managed to get a photograph as it raised its wings and revealed its dark auxiliaries. This was the 74th wader species I had seen in Britain – the only ones on the British and Irish list I hadn't seen were now the Caspian Plover, Little Whimbrel and Grey-tailed Tattler. I wouldn't like to place a bet if any of these three ever visit Britain again.

The Hudsonian Godwit was found by Tom Raven during the evening of the 25th April. The news was put out the next morning when he went back to make sure he wasn't hallucinating. This represented the 3rd for Britain. The last one was 27 years before on Slain pools, Collieston.

On 20th June I was offered two return spaces on a boat charter from Penzance to Scilly. I drove down Friday night and met up with Andrew Holden, Vicky Turner and Stuart Piner (plus girlfriend), James Shergold, Vaughan Watkins, Chris Bromley, John Pegden and Mick Frosdick. We were trying to see a Cedar Waxwing that had first been seen by a non-birder on 2nd June at Rosehill. Then 17 days later it was seen in an apple tree on Trench Lane. Our group of ten spent the whole day searching and unsurprisingly failed to re-find it. It was never seen again, and my share of the boat cost was £90. I spent the night sleeping in the Labrador Bay carpark.

Next day at first light I tracked down a singing male Cirl Bunting and as I was passing the New Forest I popped in and saw a Honey Buzzard. I was just about to head home at 10:20am when Hampshire birder Alan Lewis managed found a Terek Sandpiper at Church Norton. After seeing this I finally got home at 3:19pm on Sunday, when Georgie reminded me it was Father's Day by handing me a card. I'm not the model dad. but I'm glad Kim makes up for my shortfalls.

Georgie left Rusper School on 22nd July and parents were invited to a leaver's assembly. All 14 leavers performed "I'm a year six--year-old, get me out of here" and it was opened with Georgie and Jemima acting as Ant and Dec. Rusper School has been a brilliant experience for Georgie, and the head teacher, Mrs Packham, has instilled so much confidence into these children. I really enjoyed going to the annual Christmas plays and watching every single child take part in singing, dancing, acting or talking in in front of over 100 parents.

Georgie and her cousin Kian both got voted by the whole school to be the house captains for Year 6 for blue and red team respectively. Georgie did get upset when her house captain badge was confiscated because she and Ethan stuck fake tattoos on her arm. This punishment was upsetting for Georgie, but luckily Kim managed to get her reinstated after meeting up with Georgie's tutor. Georgie and Kian had been competing against one another throughout their school life. The most competitive day of the year is the annual sports. Every year Georgie had been on the losing team, but this year the blue team won sports day and Georgie collected the trophy.

Bowers and Wilkins decided to extend my contract and invite me to a family day at Worthing Rugby Club. All employees and their families were invited, and B&W really went to town to make this an enjoyable day out. I was made captain of an 8-man team that competed against three other teams in the 'It's a Knockout' competition. My team included John and Lorraine's partner Lee with five others. We weren't the fittest bunch and lost seven out of the eight events including hop racing, human wheel and walking with giant feet. We did win one event where you had to collect water on an obstacle course. The winners were a team of eight young athletic individuals that were brilliant at all the events. None of my team really had a chance, but it was brilliant fun.

Georgie and I had our faces painted and I was fitted with a harness and managed to get halfway up the climbing wall. It was so nice to see so many of the games you would find at a traditional fair. Do you remember swinging a hammer on the high striker, throwing skills on the coconut shy, or hooking a duck to win a cuddly toy? You couldn't get hungry with vans offering pizza, fish and chips and various grilled meats. There was an all-day Ice cream truck and a popular candy floss machine. Everything was free, and this reminded of stories of the staff parties at Richard Branson's house in Oxfordshire.

During August, Kim, Georgie and I went to France for five nights to stay with Chantal and her family. Chantal and Yves had been self-employed since I first met them in 1993. Yves left the stair-making company and he and Chantal bought their first property in Verchocq and rented out one wing of the house. Since then, they had acquired ten more properties in Calais, St. Omer, Herly, Wicquinghem and Verchocq. I've always been impressed with what their combined skills have achieved. Over the last few years, we had been staying in the Chalet de Herly. This property could accommodate 25 people with nine bedrooms (three ensuite), four bathrooms, six toilets, indoor heated swimming pool, jacuzzi, large living room, kitchen, dining room and garden. Their second property in Verchocq could also accommodate 25, with ten bedrooms, five bathrooms, an indoor heated swimming pool, jacuzzi, games room, large living room with bar, large living room and garden.

We were staying at the property they had bought in 2013. They had moved out of their original house and moved to Château de Verchocq, a stately home which used to be owned by the de Pippemont, the de l'Estandart and the de la Pasture families back in the 18th century. During the first World War in May 1917, Winston Churchill lived there for eighteen months. Yves, Chantal, Lous, Remi, Henri and Paul occupied a very small section of the château and the rest was being renovated day and night by Yves to add to their portfolio of rental properties.

This property was the length of four typical detached family homes in length but had five floors and stood in the middle of the countryside with its own private wood. If this property was in England, it would be worth around £5 million. See for yourself at www.chateauverchocq.com.

I'm so proud of what Yves and Chantal have achieved together. They started with nothing and never spent money on foreign holidays but dedicated their lives to investing profits back into buying more properties.

I've worked for 33 years, and I would have nothing to show for it if wasn't for inheriting part of my mum's house back in 2009. Owning a house should be an affordable purchase option for everyone living in the south-east, but with the constant house price rises it has become impossible for most people to get onto the housing ladder. Kim always wanted to be a homeowner, and owning one does add to your mental and physical wellbeing.

Since being with Kim, I've started to shop around when buying expensive goods, but this goes out of the window when we book our family holidays. We never take Georgie out of school for family holidays, so we have to pay double the price a September holiday would cost. If Britain wasn't so wet, maybe we could try holidaying in England.

This year we had booked a week in Paphos, Cyprus from Friday 28th August. Georgie liked the look of the five-star King Evelthon Beach Hotel, and Kim baulked at the price but we booked. The hotel was large, modern, and clean and you could even get rooms with your own private swimming pool attached. I hired a car for the week and decided to leave the family during the night and head to Lake Akrotiri for first light on the Saturday. The lake was 70km away and the Salt Lake was right next to RAF Akrotiri. The lake occupies 14 square kilometres and is considered one the most important wetlands of the eastern Mediterranean. This place has recorded 260 different bird species and is used by thousands of migratory birds each year.

Once daylight appeared, I could see I was in luck. A flock of Demoiselle Cranes could be seen distantly across the lake, so I decided to walk out as close as possible. While I was counting the cranes two other birders approached me. Half expecting them to be locals, I couldn't believe my eyes when they turned out to be British twitchers Andrew Holden and Vicky Turner.

Counting the birds was made difficult by the compactness of the group, the distance and the heat haze. I looked down and noticed that my foot impressions in the salt were much deeper and bigger than Andrew's and Vicky's combined. This made me cast my mind back to when I was connected to a bungee harness for a trampoline experience with Georgie in France. The trampoline owner was struggling to fit the harness around my waist and once I was secure every bounce was hurting my stomach. I retired early whilst Georgie had a great time doing somersaults. Something would have to be done with my weight straight after holiday.

The cranes didn't look like they were going to leave, so I decided to make my way back to the car. Here I met some locals, and it wasn't long before a flock of 52 Honey Buzzards flew high above us.

Around midday, the cranes decided to leave. They got up and starting spiralled higher and higher and just like the Honey Buzzards, went straight over our heads. I counted 96, and consider myself very lucky in picking the only day these magnificent birds spent the night on European soil after leaving their breeding grounds in Russia to fly to their wintering grounds in Chad, Sudan and Ethiopia.

I also noted 1,500 Greater Flamingo, 1 Eleonora's Falcon and 1 Lesser Grey Shrike whilst I was there.

Back at the hotel I met Kim and Georgie hanging around the bar. I was fully clothed and decided to have a piña colada before putting my swimsuit on. The watered-down alcoholic drinks you get in Turkey were nothing like this place. I only managed two drinks before I was totally wasted. I gave cocktails the respect they deserved for the rest of the holiday, but I did manage to see 8 Spur-winged Plover at Paphos Sewage works and 13 Cyprus Wheatears at Praitori (10km from the Troodos mountains) before going home.

7th September was Georgie's first full day at Thomas Bennett secondary school (she had had a couple of induction days during the school holidays). When I attended the school there was no school uniform, but now there was and Georgie looked superb kitted out with blazer/jumper, blue tartan skirt with shirt and tie. She managed to make a friend called Charlie-Anne.

The same day, I decided to install 'Coach to 5k' on my iPhone 4S, bought some neon yellow Nike running shoes, pink water bottle, ear plugs and arm pouch for phone. Just putting my clothes on made me feel fit, but within 9 weeks I was supposed to be able to run for 30 minutes without stopping. The programme required three sessions a week and the first was a combination of walking and bit of light jogging. I probably looked silly running and walking around the playing fields but who cares?

My Astra seemed to have an intermittent

electrical problem that prevented it from starting. This seems to happen every two months. Each time Martyn William came to my rescue and picked me up and took me to Bowers & Wilkins. I mentioned to Martyn that I had started running and he said it wasn't good to run on pavements and I should have a chat with a runner he knew at work. I did this and he suggested padded socks, replacing cotton clothing with nylon, and leaving the water bottle at home on small runs.

On 22nd September I managed to drive my car to work, to hear news of an Empidonax flycatcher species mega'd at 10am in Dungeness. This bird was originally found by ex-Sussex birder Martin Casemore at 9:30am whilst he was seawatching at the fishing boats. Martin knew it was one of the Empidonax species and watched it until 11:25am, when heavy rain pushed it off the beach. He went to the observatory with David Walker and consulted the literature. It was re-found at South View cottage by 12:45pm and some Birdforums experts were now suggesting it was an Acadian Flycatcher, which would be a first for Britain. Chris Batty was the first the first to broadcast the news as 'provisionally' an Acadian Flycatcher and then I asked my boss Lee, "Is there any chance I can book the afternoon off? "Lee quickly replied with a no. I didn't know if he was joking and asked again a bit later, but got the same reply. He was obviously being serious, so my only option was to leave work at 5:30pm and try to get to Dungeness as quickly as possible. I might have sneaked off a bit before 5pm (sorry Lee), but I arrived at Dungeness at 7:45pm. I ran past loads of chatting birders and was told Steve Gantlett was still watching the bird. I caught up with Steve and watched it walking around his and David Walker's feet at 7:50pm. The light was fading fast, but I could easily see it's double wing bar and greenish-yellow underparts. Ten minutes later it flew off into the desert and was never seen again. I was one of the lucky 800 birders who managed to connect, and the next day 2-300 birders dipped.

The next morning at work, Lee quizzed me about what time I had left work and whether I saw the bird. I really wasn't sure how secure my position was going to be if I told the truth and covered up with a couple of white lies. From that moment on, I knew I wouldn't be able to accept a permanent job at Bowers and Wilkins, as it lacked the flexibility our hobby needs.

The autumn was quiet for new birds, but this all changed when a Chestnut Bunting was found on Papa Westray. It was originally found on Monday 19th October and thought to be an usual looking Yellowhammer. The next day it was photographed and by Thursday it was It was identified from photographs and mega'd as a 1st winter Chestnut Bunting. There was no sign of it after Tuesday, but at 2:53pm on Saturday 24th October it was refound. I took a call from the ultra-keen twitcher Mark Rayment, and he managed to find a spare place on his plane charter leaving Wick the next day.

The charter was going to cost circa £250 each and I would be back at work Monday morning. How could I resist such a kind offer? I left Crawley at 8:30pm Saturday and drove to Mark Rayment's house in Dunstable. James Hanlon was already there and at 11pm Ashley Howe arrived and drove all three of us to Wick.

The Chestnut Bunting was seen on the Sunday at 7:28am on the track between Holland Farm and the Knapp of Howar. This early news enabled two charter planes to take twitchers from Yorkshire and Nottingham airports direct to Papa Westray. The planes could then ferry twitchers backwards

CHESTNUT BUNTING
Emberiza rutila
Papa Westray. Orkney
25th October 2015

G. BAGNALL

and forwards between Wick and Papa Westray. Ashley arrived at Wick at 10:30am and forty-five minutes later we were airborne and landed at Papa Westray at 11:35. We had 2 hours 25 minutes on the island, and for two hours we watched the Bunting feeding on the ground from a nearby stone wall. I got home Monday morning at 2:15am and just marvelled at how stress free the whole twitch had been.

Julian Branscombe, who found the Bunting, estimated that 120 birders connected. The Bunting was last seen at 5:36pm on the 29th October. Josh Jones, Andrew Kinghorn and Sam Viles arrived on Papa Westray on the Friday 30th October and gave the island a thorough search but left empty handed.

Summary

During 2015, I travelled 3,571 miles in Britain and Ireland in the pursuit of new birds and managed to increase my list by 4 BOU/IRBC species. This took my British and Irish list to 505. The Combined Official stood at 610 species, and I had seen 82.8% of them. There were two additions to the Official British and Irish List during the year: Alder Flycatcher (2008) and Moltoni's Subalpine Warbler (1894, split).

These 4 lifers in the table above are Alder Flycatcher and Great Blue Heron (20-year), Hudsonian Godwit (10-year) and Little Bustard (2-year).

2015	Regular	Vagrant	BBRC/ IRBC 1 year	BBRC/ IRBC 2 year	BBRC/ IRBC 3 year	BBRC/ IRBC 4 year	BBRC/ IRBC 5 year	BBRC/ IRBC 10 year	BBRC/ IRBC 20 year	BBRC/ IRBC Lifetime	Cat B	Total
Seen	276	37	88	11	12	12	33	21	10	5	0	505
During				1				1	2			4
B&I Total	276	38	92	12	13	15	44	38	34	40	8	610
	100%	97%	96%	92%	92%	80%	75%	55%	29%	13%	0%	83%

I think the most important personal achievement for me was to start running. The feeling of managing to finish the couch to 5k training sessions by the 7th November was incredible. I felt fit, and for the first time in my life I could run for 30 minutes without stopping. I had lost 10 kilos and gone down one trouser size. You can see that my face looks much slimmer when compared to previous Facebook profile shots. I like my new look and I can't imagine life without running now. My first 5k was easily achieved on 9th November with a time of 36 minutes and 24 seconds.

On a less positive note, on 1st November my Vauxhall Astra broke down for the fourth time in a year. This happened whilst at Blashford Lakes in Hampshire watching an Osprey. The telephone conversation with Greenflag wasn't going well. They said I had reached the limit on how many call-outs they could provide, but they would recover me on this occasion. I was towed back to Kim's parents' farm and her son Luke promised to try and diagnose the problem. In the meantime, Martyn kindly took me to work each day. Luke managed to get the car running by fitting a water pump and starter motor. This car had cost me £2,000 in July 2014 and in 16 months I had only driven 22,000 miles. I concluded that it was false economy buying cars from auctions, and I would be better off getting my next car from a second-hand car dealer, with a warranty.

The most important bird seen during the year had to be the Chestnut Bunting. This bird stayed 11 days and was AWOL for 3 of them. Being re-found on a Saturday is a weekend twitcher's dream. During my time at Colas, I would only ask for time off outside the five-day period when the month end accounts were prepared. The various bosses I had at Colas only stopped me once from taking short notice leave, back in 2003 when I was denied the opportunity of seeing a one-day Yellow-breasted Bunting at Portland. Those 14 years with Colas really boosted my life list, and whilst I was grateful for the temporary employment at Bowers & Wilkins and especially for Martyn's help, I really needed to find a company that I could bend over backwards for and expect them to reciprocate.

CHAPTER 18

2016

On Sunday 10th January 2016, news was broadcast of a possible Vega Gull at Duncannon in Wexford. It was present and confirmed the next day and mega alerted. There was no sign on the Tuesday but it was seen again on the Wednesday.

I thought I might stand a chance If I left it to the weekend, and decided to book a flight to Cork leaving Stansted at 8:45am on Saturday 16th and returning at 6:40pm on Sunday 17th. The flight cost was £128.50, and to make matters worse there was no further sign on the Thursday or Friday. There was no chance of getting a refund, so I went anyway. Budget offered me a car for €44 for both days and rather than drive east to Duncannon, I opted to drive west for 78 miles and spend the day at Castletown-Bearhaven. I managed some nice views of a Glaucous-winged Gull, then drove 174 miles and spent the night sleeping in the car at Duncannon.

Next morning, I managed to count 8 Brits and 3 Irish twitchers still searching for the Vega Gull.

Only one individual had a smile on his face, and that was not because he was keeping warm in his campervan. This chap was Steve Gantlett, and he had managed to see and photograph the Vega Gull on its last day, Wednesday 13th. The only Brits who managed to see it were Steve and Neil Alford. I got chatting to one carload including Jerry Warne, Bob Watts and Chris Heard. They had been there for several days and were ready to give up. I hadn't seen Chris for a while, so we had a catchup in a nearby café. Because there had been no sign of the gull for four days I wasn't going to stay much longer either. Back at Cork Airport I ate a Burger and Beer. Nice but not worth €17.

The Vega Gull was found on the 10th January by Irish ornithologist Killian Mullarney, who decided to play it safe and get an expert opinion from gull experts Peter Adriaens and Chris Gibbons. They agreed unequivocally that it was a Vega Gull. This bird became the first record for Ireland and more importantly, the first record for the Western Palearctic.

My book wouldn't feel complete without a proper write up of what happened, so here is Brian McCloskey experience:

On the 10th of January 2016, Mark Stewart and I were birding the Louth Coastline. At 14:42pm a tweet from @WexfordBirdNews reached our phones, it read: "10/1 1440: MEGA putative ad Vega Gull @ Duncannon Hbr. Distinctly diff from EuHerrGull, ID confirmation required/v well photographed (KMull)" Wow! That evening shots emerged online and we were in awe! I had to see this bird. Phone calls were made to sort out the plans for the following morning. Despite having school, the next day, I skived off and headed to Wexford with Donal Foley, Mark Stewart and Dave Fox. Icy conditions meant that we weren't on site for sunrise. We felt with the thousands of Gulls around it may be unlikely to be picked up again, however at 09:30am Victor Caschera struck gold! He was eye to eye with this mega Gull from the Pacific Ocean on the pier at Duncannon Harbour. We gave him a quick ring to hear the update for ourselves. Vic was the only birder there and the only one to connected before it flew off out of sight...crap! This was terrible news. Only one year on from the lads having dipped the Slaty-backed Gull by seconds, this would be equally bad.

Another agonizing 45 minutes praying for positive news before we arrived at Duncannon. As we drove onto the pier, we rolled down the window to Vic to see what the story was, and he said "quick it's in the scope!" I ran to the scope and there it was... Vega Gull, a first for the Western Palearctic. A few birders were already on the pier watching it such as Ger Murray, Gerry O' Neill, John Power, Dennis O' Sullivan, Paul Moore etc. Views at the start were a tad distant as it sat on the rocks just outside the harbour. After a few minutes it flew up onto the mast of a boat and gave amazing views.

This is where most birders got excellent shots. However, the views were to get even better as it flew towards us and dropped into the trailers on the pier, exactly what it did for Killian Mullarney the previous day. Now we just had to wait... after what seemed like a lifetime it hopped up and stood eye to eye with me. As it sat on the trailer it lifted its wings and I just happened to have the camera on it at the time...click...click...click. Wow! The primaries were perfect.

European Gulls moult after the breeding season and therefore it would be totally bonkers for one to be moulting in the middle of January. It is obvious from my shot that p10 was still very worn and p9 was still growing (about three quarters grown), p5 on the Vega Gull had a black sub terminal bar and black even reached as far as p4! Showing a small black spot on the outer web. The dark eye made this bird look rare, the orbital ring was pink/red. The mantle was slightly darker than one would expect on an argenteus and was almost argentatus like, however the extent of black on the primaries ruled out argentatus. The bill was pale yellow with a hint of a greenish tinge and a red gonydeal spot. The legs were pink. The head and neck had a speckled brown shawl almost reminiscent of the Glaucous-winged Gull that I had seen 8 days previous! After noting as much as I could on the bird, I knew Cian Cardiff was on his way with his father but they were nowhere to be seen! I gave him a ring and told him to get up as quick as possible! As luck would have it, they both connected with it...just. Some birders were even luckier in connecting with it in flight for a few precious minutes as it disappeared at 11:30. Not to be seen again for another two days!

Apart from the Vega Gull it was a decent day for gulls. A juv Iceland Gull, Lesser black-backed Gull x Herring Gull hybrid, and a Mediterranean Gull were loafing about the harbour. Yellow-legged *and Glaucous Gulls were present nearby on the beach also.*

Once the Vega Gull disappeared, we tried but failed to refind an adult Caspian Gull that was also in the area. We returned to Duncannon Harbour that evening but also failed miserably to connect with the Vega Gull again. We headed home that evening, thrilled that we had scored with such a rare gull. What a top class find by Killian! Will there ever be another?

I'd just like to thank Brian for providing this. You really cannot beat turning up at a twitch and somebody offering a scope view.

Twitching to me has always been about prioritising my British and Irish list, but whilst I was plane spotting in Madrid Airport back in 1993 I couldn't help but jot down Spotless Starlings sitting on a railing. My WP list now stood at 617 species and should go up a bit after the 18th March when I visit Israel with Lee Evans.

I was due to leave Bower and Wilkins at the end of March, but my boss Lee kindly agreed to pay me up to end of March and I could leave a week before I got to Israel and try to find a job.

Fortunately, this week off coincided with a message from Byron Finance enquiring if I was interested in a Financial Analyst role at Rapiscan in Salfords, near Redhill. I was, and they forwarded my CV to a guy called Philip Moores. Philip liked my CV and offered me an interview on Tuesday 15th March. Byron told me Philip, the Financial Controller, was born in South Africa and was a massive rugby fan. They provided some background information about Rapiscan products.

I genned up on Rapiscan and arrived early for my interview. The first person I met was receptionist Barbara. I instantly felt at ease talking to her. Barbara was chatting to me about Rapiscan and I was telling her about what I was looking for.

If a receptionist is barometer on what the company culture is like, I felt I would certainly fit in.

The interview with Philip went like a dream. I was asked what I knew about Rapiscan and for the rest of interview Philip was generally doing all the talking. The HR lady, Shivanie, briefly popped in to meet me and before I knew it, the interview was over and I was driving home. I don't think Philip found out much about me apart from the fact that I was a birdwatcher and going to Israel on Friday. I knew he was the type of person I could easily work for and later that day the agency rang me and told me Rapiscan would like me to meet the Financial Director the next day.

The Financial Director was Laurie Shelton, and he too made me feel very welcome. He did mention in the interview that he would be leaving in a couple of weeks as the US parents had offered his job to an American employee working at a group company called Spacelabs. This was a difficult message to process, as I felt I was developing a good relationship with Laurie and after the interview I was never going to see him again. I found him an intelligent individual who managed to get me thinking when he asked me "What should be the accounting treatment if you've sold an X-ray machine for $1 million in France and the machine gets dropped during the installation process?"

My answer to this question couldn't have been too far out, as Byron Finance rang me on Thursday and told me that Rapiscan would like to offer me the job with a start date of Tuesday 29th March. Byron Finance told me that the manufacturing experience I had gained from Bowers and Wilkins had really swung the job in my favour. Britain was becoming more and more service orientated and relying on countries in the Far East to do the manufacturing. I accepted the offer and felt relieved that Kim and I could relax about future mortgage payments.

On Friday 18th March, Lee Evans parked his car at my house and Kim drove us to Gatwick. I didn't really know many of Lee's clients apart from Essex-based photographer Paul Rowe. Chris Morgan, who owned a B&B in Sheringham, arrived with his brother-in-law Mike. The last member of the gang was Tom Clarke. Tom was originally from Belfast and now lived in South London.

This was my first birding holiday with Lee Evans, and with no published itinerary it was a bit of a magical mystery tour. We flew with Easy Jet into Tel Aviv and headed north to the Hula valley. Lee had forgotten to organise any accommodation for the first few nights, but luckily Chris and Mike found a vacant property in Khulafa. We all squeezed in with a few of us sleeping on two sofas and the floor for a couple of nights.

The birding at Hula was superb with 3,600 White Storks, 1 Eastern Imperial Eagle and 3 Spotted Eagles. We failed to see a Syrian Serin at Golan Heights and Mount Hermon, but I did find a rare Kurdish Wheatear. An adult Great Black-headed Gull was a nice spot at Newe Ur. We headed south on Sunday and saw a Long-billed Pipit at Mount Gilboa with Fan-tailed Ravens, and Tristram Grackles were the only birds seen at the Dead Sea.

From Monday to Saturday night we thought we were going to stay at the Spring Hostel in Eilat. Lee had stayed there on previous trips but wasn't aware that the owner had put his charges up since the last visit. Lee and the owner had a massive row about this, and we were all asked to leave. Somehow, we managed to calm the owner down by paying him exactly what he wanted. The last thing we wanted was to have no accommodation for the next six nights.

During the rest of the holiday we visited North Beach, K18, K20, K19, K82, IRBCE, Seifim Plain, Holland Park, Yovata, Dolphin Beach, Shezaf Nature reserve, Nizzana and Azuz. Overall, Lee was a good guide who helped me get 38 WP ticks. I was really impressed how effortlessly he knew the bird calls. He even shouted out when a pair of Dunn's Larks flew over. I watched where they landed and left Lee and the group - I managed to re-find them and get a few photographs. We managed to see a vagrant Red-billed Teal at Hatseva, but I wasn't so lucky with a Bateleur at Gal'on. Here we bumped into Richard Bonser, and we all spread out looking for the Bateleur. Richard, Lee and Tom all managed to see it distantly, but I just could get not onto the speck they were watching. I spent a further two hours searching, but Lee needed to sleep.

Jonathan Meyrav was the tourism director of Israeli Ornithological Center and spent 70 days a year guiding visitors. We met him at Eilat Beach, where Mike and I signed up for his coach trip to see Nubian Nightjar and Hume's Tawny Owl. The coach made a brief stop at Shezaf Nature reserve, where we looked for an Arabian Warbler, and as night fell we arrived at Neot Hakkikar. A single Nubian Nightjar showed well with the help of the coaches' headlights. Unfortunately, we weren't so lucky with the Hume's Tawny Owl. We managed to hear two but just couldn't see any with the spotlight.

There were so many good birds seen on that trip, but If I had to pick the best bit it was probably when we saw four MacQueens Bustards at Nizzana and finishing the day watching 6 Crowned Sandgrouse drinking from a water hole in Azuz. One night I thought my luck had changed when somebody got into my bed. It turned out to be one our crew who had had too many sherbets and got his bed mixed up.

We flew back from Tel Aviv on Sunday with Easy Jet. Everything was going well until we tried to land at Gatwick. There was a strong crosswind, and our plane was swaying from side to side, so the pilot decided to take no chances and divert us to East Midlands. Here Easy Jet put us up at the Hilton Hotel and agreed to reimburse four of us the next day for a £280 taxi ride to Gatwick. Easy Jet settled the hotel bill but getting the taxi money back was another story. I wrote 21 emails to customer services, and they replied by asking for a booking reference, after which I got a deathly silence. Sussex birder Matt Eade works for Easy Jet and suggested I write directly to the CEO. I got a reply from the CEO's secretary and on 28th July they send me a cheque for £70.

I started working at Rapisan as a Finance Analyst on Tuesday 29th March. For the first two hours I watched an induction video provided by HR, and then I was introduced to the finance team. The team was quite small with a Financial Accountant, Alan Iu, AP Manager, Gill Smelt, and assistant Christopher Thornton, Credit Controller Pam Amos with assistant Carolyn Froud and a very friendly lady called Maia Parkinson, who had a treasury role. Philip managed to keep my predecessor Simon Jarvis around to train me on Navision accounts and show me my stock responsibilities. In a weeks' time Simon was leaving, and Philip would then train me on fixed and intangible asset responsibilities. During the day I met Philip's boss, Alan Mixer, who was the new Financial Director, and Vice President Gary Martin, both Americans living in the UK with their families. My first day was enjoyable and with such a nice group of people I could quickly tell this job was perfect for me.

Dalmatian Pelicans breed in Turkey, Greece and Albania and vagrants have been accepted seven times in Germany, once in Denmark and twice in France. That year one was first seen in Poland at Stawy Przygodzickie on 6th April, then at a couple more sites before moving to Germany. It was seen at Altfriedländer Teich between 12-13th April, then four more German sites before being re-located on 3rd May at Alsace in France. Birdguides mega'd it on Monday 9th May, when it flew towards Nanjizal. It had belatedly been reported from St. Ives on the Saturday. This bird was seen many times during the day flying over Land's End, Sennen and Trevorian Pool and also on the deck at Skewjack farm. It was also seen Tuesday, Wednesday and Thursday.

I then cracked and decided to go Thursday night with the main man, John Lees. We didn't really know where to start looking, as it had only been seen once the previous day flying over Polgigga, but at 10:20am Paul Chapman kindly rang me to say he was watching it at Skewjack. 10 minutes later we were there, and this beautiful big bird was still high up flying in a massive circle to 10:45am, I guess trying to find a good spot to land. I really didn't know how the BOURC would treat this record, but does it really matter? It was a magnificent bird to see in Britain and a thousand times better than the tatty 2006 escapee Great White Pelican I saw at Bough Beech.

This bird was submitted by Paul Freestone and stayed loyal to England to 20th November. During that time it spent 10 days in the Taw Estuary in Devon and was aged as in its 3rd CY.

There was a Green Warbler at Baltasound on Unst from 14-16th May, and I was toying with idea of flying to Sumburgh on Sunday and coming back on the Monday. Flybe wanted £400 return, and then there was the small matter of £180 of return fuel to Aberdeen. I decided stay to stay at home with Kim and have a Chinese takeaway instead.

The spring got very exciting on Sunday 22nd May when a Black-billed Cuckoo was found at

Bayhead, North Uist. After a couple of days of positive reports I booked two days' leave. John Lees and I left my house at 5:40pm on Tuesday. I had advertised a lift on Twitter and a chap called David Aitken joined us. I was starting to feel hungry and pulled into Oxfordshire services at 8pm. This was my 6th month of being a 5K runner and I had quit the cold turkey option of eating burgers on twitches. I was now convinced that eating a foot-long Italian with tuna, full salad, and south-west sauce was the healthy option.

We arrived at Uig at 7am to find that quite a few cars were already parked up, including one containing Lee Evans. He was full of doom and gloom and said "Yeah, the Black-billed Cuckoo's done a bunk. Ashley Howes has been looking for it all morning and couldn't find it". I instantly felt low and just didn't have the energy to head back, but then at 7:48am we hear that the bird was still in gardens by the A865. I later found out from Ashley that he had had a lie in and only gone out birding after getting breakfast at 7am. I'm not sure where Lee got his story from, but dead on 9am the kiosk opened, and we managed to get our car and 3 passengers return for £96.60.

The ferry left Uig at 9:40am and during the crossing to Lochmaddy we had the usual Razorbill, Puffin, Black Guillemot, Shag etc. We docked at 11:45am and it was a 21-minute drive to the site. We saw the Cuckoo briefly (12:15pm), but then it flew off and disappeared. Fortunately, it was relocated nearly an hour later on a nearby wire mesh fence. Here it occasionally dropped to the ground to feed on caterpillars.

We spent the rest of the day birding the island and saw male Hen Harrier, Short-eared Owl, adult White-tailed Eagle and in the evening, we managed to see two Corncrakes singing in full view at Balranald. Wow, what a place!

We stayed the night at the youth hostel, which only cost £20 a night. The next day we caught the ferry back at 7:30am from Lochmaddy. On the ferry John got chatting to a birder who was after a lift home. John said, "My mate Garry can take you back". I'm used to John being good-natured, but it would have been nice if he had asked me first. I'm not sure what the guy's name was, but he was quite brave to travel all this alone on public transport. We dropped him off at a railway station once back in England.

Richard Levett and Tracey Viney were on a week-long birding holiday when Richard spotted the bird whilst driving on the Paible circular road at 2:25pm. He thought it was an American Cuckoo, then turned the car round and identified it as Black-billed Cuckoo. Steve Duffield was later contacted and put the news out nationally. It stayed for 10 days, to 31st May. It was the 14th record for Britain since 1950 and the first spring record, all the others having been in the autumn and generally only surviving one day. North Ronaldsay had an untwitchable one in 2014, but most twitchers staying in Scilly managed to see one at Trenoweth on 10th October 1990.

25th July. Most fathers would do anything for their children and when Georgie come home from School and say's "Dad there's a brilliant game my friends are playing at school, and we need to get it!" I just handed my iPhone to my 12-year-old. Then she installed an augmented reality (AR) game called "Pokemon Go". She showed me we had a Pokemon in the house. How cool! I then watched her throw a Pokeball at it. She caught it, but some do run away. That evening we walked around our neighbourhood and caught some more Pokemon and I was collecting pokeballs by spinning Pokestops. But just a week later, Georgie decided she was bored with the game, although with my addictive personality I was starting to get into it. I thought it was quite snazzy that there were 151 different Pokemon to collect and if you caught enough of one type, you could evolve it into a different Pokemon. Some evenings after dinner I was keen to play the game, and would wander around Tilgate and end up at the park.

My running skills came in useful when a friend's scanner said there was a Dragonite (a rare dragon Pokemon) at St. Peter's Church. We all started jogging from Palace Pier up Grand Parade. The guys were much younger than me but not as fit. They managed to run to Royal Pavilion, then switched to walking. I proudly ran the whole 0.7 miles nonstop to the church. The Dragonite appeared on my screen, and I threw every single pokeball at it, but failed to catch. To make things worse when my two friends arrived, and they both managed to catch it. The reason we all ran was because Pokemons are only available in the game for a finite time before they disappear, known as despawning. By the time I managed to get some more pokeballs, the Dragonite had despawned.

This game probably appeals to me because it has many similarities to birdwatching. Seeing a new bird is like catching a new Pokemon. Birds and Pokemon appear on a check list. Neither birds or Pokemon are around for long, and like rare birds there are rare Pokemon too.

On 31st July I managed to see a Western Swamphen at Minsmere. The news broke at 2:42pm and by 6:45pm I was watching it behind the south hide, but for only 20 seconds as it walked slowly through the reeds.

It was found when Frank Clark did a day trip to Suffolk from Ashford in Kent. At Minsmere he saw breeding Stone Curlews and managed to see an elusive Citrine Wagtail at Konik field. When he arrived at the pool behind South Hide his heart stopped. Straight in front of him was a large blue bird with pink legs, white rear end and red lobe and bill. He shouted 'Purple Swamphen!' but others present said "No, its a Moorhen". Frank rang news onto his pager, and they refused to broadcast. That all changed when an RSPB employee looked through Frank's scope and radio'd the news out.

The Western Swamphen stayed at Minsmere to 5th August and was next found on Alkborough flats in Lincolnshire from 30th August to 4th January 2017. This species currently sits on Cat E of British List with previous records seen in Cheshire 1971, Co. Durham 1975, Nottingham 1978 and Cumbrian 1997. However, the BOURC may now view this record in better light as this year the species has been found north-west of its French breeding grounds.

We decided to book 10 days at Garcia spa & resorts hotel in Olu Deniz with a company called Lowcostholidays.com. The Brownes booked the same days as us with them. The holiday cost £2,500 for our three. Then on the 16th July I heard on the news that our company had gone bankrupt. The company was not ATOL or ABTA bonded and the insurance we bought didn't cover bankrupt companies. I paid for the holiday on my debit card and my bank told me I needed to try and get my money back using the disputed debit method. The Brownes got all their money back as they purchased via credit card. We didn't know what our chances were of getting our money back and I decided to ring the hotel. The hotel people felt sorry for us and offered the same 10 nights fully inclusive for €1,000. The flights and transfers were unlikely to be cancelled, so we decided to take the risk and pay the €1,000 and go on the holiday.

On Friday 5th August we got a taxi to Gatwick and our EasyJet flight number was displayed on the departure board. As we sat at the gate, we heard over the Tannoy a last-minute call for the Browne family flying to Dalaman. They were never going to show as they had used the money to book another holiday, but we boarded the plane and took off. Not having the Browne family with us was a massive blow and it wouldn't take Georgie long to get bored. We were in luck that we managed to meet a similar-aged couple, Dawn and Darren, who lived in Nantwich, Cheshire. Dawn was the female version of David Browne, very much the person you want to hang out with at a party. She was highly sociable and loved to have a good time. Dawn really took to Georgie, as she reminded her of her daughter Jess, who unfortunately had stayed back home.

We stuck to Dawn and Darren like glue. They wanted to be with us and we wanted to be with them – maybe this was holiday fate. One night we decided to avoid the hotel food and go for a bite to eat in Olu Deniz town centre. After a week of self-service, it was nice to be waited on and choose a nice three-course meal. After dinner I went heavy on the cocktails at a few bars. Dawn and I performed a duet at a karaoke bar, and because her voice was so much better than mine, I decided to refrain from singing and let her carry on. Another bar was full of people in fancy dress dancing on tables to catchy disco tunes. Dawn, Georgie and I walked past, and we all got hoisted up on top of the tables to joint them. Kim and Darren just watched and laughed at the whole spectacle.

Darren was a quiet person like Kim, and the saying that opposites attract is so true. However, Darren helped with the high water slide back at our pool. I must have climbed the steps to the top of the water slide ten times, and because it looked too scary to jump down, I just turned around and walked back down the stairs. When I walked back

up with Darren, he gave me a pep talk and said something like "Do you think Georgie likes having a scared dad?" That was all it needed, I closed my eyes and jumped down the slide. I didn't enjoy the speed I was travelling, but it felt good defeating one of my head gremlins.

By the end of the evening I wasn't walking in a straight line but otherwise felt in control. We got back to my bed and soon as I lay down my head started spinning. I jumped off the bed and just managed to kneel beside the toilet before the volcano erupted. I still felt drunk, but after a good night sleep, I woke up as fresh as a daisy.

I decided to check my bank account on my iPhone and couldn't believe my eyes. There was a £2,500 refund sitting in the account. This holiday certainly had been a low-cost holiday and we were mighty glad we booked with them. David and Lucy are real bargain hunters, and we couldn't wait to see their faces when we told them our holiday only cost €1,000 all in.

We arrived back at Gatwick in the early hours of 16th August and headed home and back to work. During the first day at work a Royal Tern mega'd at 4:07pm in Mayo. I went into Phillips office for a quick chat and he was ok with me booking two days. That evening I left home at 7:30pm with John in tow and headed to Holyhead.

We got to Roonagh Lough at 10am and found out we had missed the Royal Tern by 3 hours. Three other carloads from Britain had also made the pilgrimage. We searched the lough in the pouring rain and decided to retreat to a local hotel for a cooked breakfast. Here I met Brian McCloskey and Mark Stewart for the first time. They both live in Ireland and had missed the bird by 25 minutes. Brian mentioned that he had watched the twitching documentary in 2012 and loved the whole programme. He felt the main characters were nuts, and four years later he now fully understands that all obsessed twitchers go the same way.

We hung around the Lough to 7:30pm, but the best birds were 8 Sandwich Terns and 2 Little Terns. We stayed the night in a local B&B. The next morning there was still no sign of the Royal Tern, so we headed back and caught the 2:15pm ferry. This trip cost £347 for the ferry, £123 B&B with dinner for 2, Diesel £95, Toll €6 and phone charge £6. It worked out at £290 each.

A few days later my worst nightmare came true – the Royal Tern was relocated. Davey Farrar found it at Beale Strand, Kerry on Tuesday 23rd August. Davey had now managed to find four rare terns in Ireland: Royal, Caspian, Gull-billed and Elegant. This bird was the same bird as Mayo as it had the same limp. I wasn't in a rush to throw another £300 at trying to get it, but it now seemed more reliable and had been present every day up to Friday... I cracked. I left home at 6:30pm and met up with Ashley Howes and James Hanlon at Chievely (8:45pm). I picked up Sam Viles from Bristol Parkway railway station and this time drove to Fishguard.

We arrived at Carrigaholt Bay, Clare at 10am... no Royal Tern. A message come through that it had flown south-east at 10:40am. We then drove to various spots where it had previously been seen, but no joy. Two hours later it was spotted the other side of the river, at Littor in Kerry. We needed to get the ferry from Tarbert to Kilmer pronto. The ferry took 20 minutes to cross the Shannon Estuary and cost €28 for a car and 4 passengers.

We parked the car at Littor and started the long walk across the sandy beach to the east. We arrived at 1:45pm and found it the 'Carrotbill' (bright orange beak) was sitting with loads of Sandwich Terns. I managed a few photographs and by 2pm it flew off south-west.

The feeling of seeing the Royal Tern on my fourth attempt was incredible, and we were all buzzing. James Hanlon wanted us to pop round and see his uncle and aunt that lived close by. When we arrived, they made all four of us feel very welcome and immediately asked us to sit down at their dinner table. They cooked us a hot meal and served us some pudding. I've always liked the Irish culture, but this kind gesture to feed three complete strangers really made me want to reciprocate to others. We left with full bellies at 4pm and I drove Ashley's car back to Rosslare for the 9:15pm ferry.

My fascination with numbers had me noting down the associated cost of each lifer I got, as you may have noticed. I add up my share of petrol, hire car, ferry, boats, planes, tolls, donations, and accommodation. I ignore food costs unless they are part and parcel of the accommodation. The Royal Tern had become my most expensive tick. I had spent £70 at Llandudno (2009), £30 Black Rock (2009), £290 Mayo (2016) and now £121 for Kerry, a grand total of £511.

The Royal Tern was first found by Seamus Feeney at Roonagh Lough and during the two days it was present, only 16 people managed to see it. When Davey Farrar refound it on 23rd August it stayed five more days. John Lees got to Kerry one day late, on the 29th. This was the fourth time he had dipped this species in the archipelago. The bird was Ireland's third record. The first was a dead one found on North Bull Island (1954) and the second was in Clonakilty (2009). That one was later seen in Wales.

Many Shetland holidaymakers were having a good autumn, and it hit another level on Sunday 9th October. That day a Siberian Accentor, a first for Britain, was found on Scousburgh (3:26pm). I even got mentioned in a tweet from the Boozy Birders' latest signing, none other than Andrew Lawson. He sent a picture of Paul Hawky and himself smiling with a backdrop of twitchers watching the bird. Good on them. The following day the Accentor was still present, and a Black-faced Bunting joined it on nearby Bressay.

My only therapy was to book a one-way flight with Flybe for to Sumburgh (£179.93). John Lees and I left Crawley Monday night and picked up Vince Halley Frame en route to Aberdeen. We landed at Sumburgh and drove the hire car to Scousbourgh. The Siberian Accentor had sadly gone, but the Black-faced Bunting was still present at place called Gunnista. Vince and John had both seen the '94 Pennington Flash individual but were happy to see another. I managed to see the Bunting four times on either a fence or dung heap and possibly distant twice. The bird was very elusive and mobile over a large area. Each time it perched it was only available for 5 to 10 seconds.

My friend Steve Nuttall asked, "Can I look through your scope Garry?" I replied, "Sorry Steve but I really need to nail the features first". I felt bad saying it, but this bird was seriously difficult to see well, and I probably only scoped it for 30 seconds in total. I noted grey head, black streaks on mantle, white belly, and white outer tail feathers in flight and that was about it. I would have loved to have got a picture of it, but there just wasn't time to position the iPhone on the scope and focus, it would have been gone. Just glad I saw it.

To keep the cost down we got the ferry back to Aberdeen harbour and split a taxi five ways to the airport to pick up my car. My share of the total costs worked out at £300 exactly. I had dipped this species in Newbiggin in 1999 and on Lundy in 2001, but I could now proudly claim I had the Black-faced Bunting on my British and Irish list.

The bird, last seen on 18th October, was originally found by Simon Mitchell, J. England, K. Landon and L. Simpson during the last few hours of their stay on the island. It became the sixth record for Britain.

There had never been a Siberian Accentor before, but four days later a second one was found at Easington. I had run out of paid leave and prayed that it would stay to Saturday. The bird was still there on the Friday and with inclement weather Friday night I should be lucky for Saturday.

I drove up and parked in a field off Easington, then joined the queue in the pitch black. The queue started moving at 6:30am when groups of people were allowed to view the small wood. The Siberian Accentor was still there, and I just had to wait my turn, but I managed some photographs of it feeding on the lichen-covered ground. The light was not brilliant, but the accentor was actively feeding and never paused to look up. After I'd had my fill, I saw a tailless Pallas's Warbler in the hand and wandered around Spurn seeing Dusky Warblers, Shore Lark and a couple of Woodcocks. What an amazing place.

2016 would long be remembered for the Siberian Accentor invasion. Britain went from 0 to 13 records during the year and Europe went from 32 to 232+. These birds were brought over by an intense and extensive high-pressure system over Siberia with long-range easterly vectors providing routes through Russia to the Baltic. This event resembled the 1968 Nutcracker invasion, or better still, before 1908, one of the many Pallas's Sandgrouse eruptions.

Britain's first Siberian Accentor was found on 9th October by Judd Hunt whilst trying to find Snow and Lapland buntings on Mossy Hill. The second was found by L.J. Degnan and stayed from 13th October to 19th October.

During November I dipped an Eyebrowed Thrush at Bolam Country Park on the 5th, but I had

BLACK-BILLED CUCKOO
Coccyzus erythrapthalmus
North Uist: Baghead
Western Isles
25th May 2016
G. RAGNALL

Just after 10am we left the bird and found a nice café in the town centre called the Treebus Tea Room. I had a full English breakfast with a latte, and because I had run 1,109 kms during the year I didn't think a slice of coffee and walnut cake was going to hurt.

The Blue Rock Thrush was first seen by Bridget Jennings on 14th December feeding with Starlings in her back garden. It was last seen in the vicinity up to 4th April and miraculously refound at Beachy Head on 6th April 2017. Its DNA was analysed by Martin Collinson and his finding showed the bird was either a European/African/Middle Eastern form (nominate) or Middle East to Central Asia from (M.S. Longirostris). It was aged at a 2CY+ adult and became the 7th record for Britain. The previous record was a male at Elan Valley, Powys, which was never twitchable. The last twitchable one was a 5-day female at Pendeen, Cornwall in 2000.

Summary

During 2016, I travelled 8,048 miles in Britain and Ireland in the pursuit of new birds and managed to increase my list by 5 BOU/IRBC species. This took my British and Irish list to 510 different species. At the end of the year the Combined Official List stood at 613 species, and I had seen 83.2% of them. There were three additions to the Official British and Irish List during the year: Northern Harrier, Brown Booby and Vega Gull.

The 5 lifers in the table above are Black-faced Bunting (10-year), Daurian Shrike, Royal Tern & Blue Rock Thrush (5-year) and Black-billed Cuckoo (3-year).

I was really pleased I had kept up my running. I started the year with fifty-four 5k runs, then increased the distance to a midpoint between

better luck on 4th December when I saw a Masked Wagtail at Cambrose. That was a beautiful looking bird, but can't go on any list now because it's still a subspecies.

Once December comes you can normally kiss goodbye to any more lifers. However, just after Boxing Day on 27th December a Blue Rock Thrush broke at midday in a housing estate in Stow-on-the-Wold, Gloucestershire. I teamed up with Andrew Lawson, John Lees and John Benham and left home at 5am. We arrived at Fisher's Close at 7:30am and we managed to see the thrush sitting on a roof in the pitch black. I tweeted the news out and the *Daily Express* followed up by interviewing me. The *Daily Mail* paid me £25 for my crowd shots. Many people were not sure if this Blue Rock Thrush was indeed wild, but that didn't deter 200+ birdwatchers from visiting that morning.

2016	Regular	Vagrant	BBRC/ IRBC 1 year	BBRC/ IRBC 2 year	BBRC/ IRBC 3 year	BBRC/ IRBC 4 year	BBRC/ IRBC 5 year	BBRC/ IRBC 10 year	BBRC/ IRBC 20 year	BBRC/ IRBC Lifetime	Cat B	Total
Seen	276	37	88	11	13	12	36	22	10	5	0	510
During					1		3	1				5
B&I Total	276	38	92	12	14	15	44	39	34	41	8	613
	100%	97%	96%	92%	93%	80%	82%	56%	29%	12%	0%	83.2%

5k-10k on fifty-three occasions. Then running 10k became the norm, and I ended up running them fifty-four times. In total I run 1,109km. My fastest 10k was 58 minutes 13 seconds, on 18th November. Before running I used to weigh 16 stone (101 kgs) with a 36" waist, but now I weighed 14 stone (89 kgs) with a 32-34" waist. I felt fit. It was such a shame I had discovered running so late in life.

The most important bird I saw during the year had to be the Black-billed Cuckoo. There had been rarer birds in 2016, but I've had to endure many conversations with similar-aged birders and many older birders about how good Scilly was back in the 80s and 90s. They would soon start reeling off stories about when they saw Parula, Black and White Warbler, Hermit Thrush, Common Nighthawk and Black-billed Cuckoo on Scilly. Many thought the chance of Black-billed Cuckoo wouldn't happen again, but now it had been unblocked, I know people would still talk about the Golden-winged Warbler, the Ancient Murrelet, Red-breasted Nuthatch and Red-throated Thrush etc... Aaaarrrrggghhhh! I felt like screaming.

CHAPTER 19

2017

I'm not a big fan of New Year resolutions but after a 17-year break from studying accountancy I thought I would give it one last go. The main reason for this must be credited to my boss Philip. Philip believed being fully qualified would open future doors for my career. Rapiscan were happy to sponsor me on a home study course and it did still feel like feel like unfinished business. I was on the final level of CIMA exams back in 2000 and all my old exam passes remained credits on the syllabus. The final level was called the Strategic level and had three papers with a case study exam. The hardest paper is known to be F3 Financial Strategy and because I can sit one exam each time, I chose to study this one.

Have you ever heard of touch rugby? I hadn't, until Philip suggested I join him on a training session at Horsham Rugby Club on 30th January. The only downside was I needed some kit. £150 later I owned a pair of boots, socks, shorts, shirt, and mouth guard. The club members were predominantly men with a couple of women, ages ranged from early 20s to mid-50s. Generally, the youngest 6 plus substitutes were against the oldest 6 plus substitutes.

Philip and I started as substitutes for the older team. The idea is to pass a ball backwards to someone to get a ball to the touchline. If a member of the opposing team touches somebody in possession of the ball, the ball is placed on the floor where the touch took place. Defending players walk backwards for 5 metres and game restarts. If the same team gets touched 6 times in a row, possession changes. I cannot believe how tiring this game was. I was using different muscles to the ones used in running and getting subbed off five times kept me alive. I never got to the try line.

I enjoyed the session and went back the following week, but I arrived late due to work and went straight into training match without a warmup. The rain was pouring down and an opposition player collided with me. It felt like I'd been knocked down by a bus. I had sore knees for the rest of the match, and that became my last training session. Running was put on hold for several weeks, and this was a wakeup call for my fragile 50-year-old body.

Georgie had been bullied several times by a boy at Thomas Bennett. Kim kept the school abreast of the incidents and the school bully got expelled for a couple of weeks. Alarm bells were ringing for Kim and me. We needed to find a better school for Georgie, and that could only be achieved by moving. Our house went onto the market, and we started looking at houses in east Crawley in the Worth and Maidenbower districts. This would have given Georgie a chance in going to Hazelwick or Oriel secondary schools. My first wife, Zainab, went to Hazelwick School. She spoke highly of it and mentioned that Gareth Southgate had been a pupil a year below her (just in case you didn't know, Gareth is currently the England Football Manager. He replaced Sam Allardyce after some football scandal the previous year).

We also viewed properties in Horsham. This would have got Georgie reunited with her Rusper schoolfriends in Millais.

Kim, Georgie, and I looked at more than 20 properties. Georgie and I liked a 4-bedroom detached property in Worth. During the viewing I bumped into Martyn Williams from my Bowers and Wilkins days. Considering Worth has a population of 8,388 people living in a 2.1 sq km rectangle, what are the chances of buying a house, four doors away from your old boss?

This house needed a bit of sprucing up, but I loved the massive round table in the garden, big enough to seat King Arthur's twelve knights. Kim wasn't relishing the daily commute of half a kilometre with eight sets of traffic lights. That was my favourite house, until we visited a 3-bedroom detached property in Southwater. The house looked beautiful from outside, with enough off-road spaces for three cars. The estate agent opened the front door and as we entered the hairs on the back of my neck stood up. Each footstep was filling me with more and more excitement, and the estate agent could hear the change in my voice and could see I was very close to tears during the tour. There was no way Worth stood a chance, even if they threw in King Arthur's roundtable as a sweetener.

After the visit, Kim, and I looked into each other's eyes and knew this was the one. We didn't even go straight home – we decided to head straight to the Cubit & West estate agent and put in an offer. The offer was rejected, and the homeowner felt his house needed more time on the market as it had been put on. We didn't want to miss out on our dream house, so we bid the asking price and owner agreed. Gosh! I was now quite emotional, and the tears started flowing. If only my mum could see how happy this house purchase was making the Bagnells feel.

Contracts were exchanged and we were due to be out of Crawley on 3rd March and to move into Southwater the same day. No way were Kim's boys and I capable of doing the move by ourselves, so we hired the professional services of Hellier's Removals and Storage based in Partridge Green (01403-710374). They cleared the house contents in about five hours. I loaded my car with the delicate stuff: guinea pigs, cats, telescope, bins, camera and bird books. Kim drove behind me with Georgie and Helliers followed. The journey to our new home was 12.8 miles. Nothing got broken in the move and Helliers were amazing.

Georgie was offered a place at Millais, but she wasn't in a rush to leave her old school. She decided she would leave at the end of spring term and join at the start of summer term on 24th April. This delay was a slight inconvenience for both Kim and me. For six weeks I had a 2-mile detour to take her to school and Kim had at 9.4-mile detour on the pickup. Georgie's first day at Millais involved walking one minute from the front door to catch the free school bus. Better still, Georgie was in the same tutor group as Jemima, Amelia and Louise. The Fab four were back together.

On Saturday 29th April, Simon Davies was performing the northern census of North Ronaldsay when as he was walking past a house at Garso he heard a strange little 'chup' call. He turned around and saw a starling-sized bird land on some gas bottles outside the house. He racked his brains and concluded it must be some type of blackbird. He had seen Red-winged Blackbirds in Texas and remembered the females were dark and streaky. Canadian observatory staff member Larissa agreed with Simon's identification and Kevin tweeted a back of the camera photo.

The Red-winged Blackbird was present the following day, when 9 charter planes brought twitchers over. I had no option but to wait till the coming Friday when the Rapiscan month end process would be complete. I decided to ring up Loganair on Monday see what availability was like for the weekend. They had three spare seats on the early Saturday afternoon slot and three returns Sunday morning. These tickets would cost £21 return and further £58.50 for 1 night in the observatory. John Benham and Mark Rayment expressed an interest in going and I decided to book these three non-refundable flights.

Andrew Lawson wanted to take my fourth car seat as he was confident he could get on a Saturday morning charter boat. Friday came and the RWB was still present, so I started the drive north with all three passengers. I dropped Andrew off at John o' Groats, where he teamed up with others to get the foot passenger boat to Orkney. Here we noted

a Short-eared Owl. The rest of us got the Pentland ferry from Gills Bay to St. Catherine's.

We docked and drove straight to Kirkwall Airport. Whilst we were at the airport, Andrew sent a message to say that he had seen the Red-winged Blackbird. We just hoped we would be as lucky. It was nice to see a pair of Hen Harriers flying around the airport, but we just had to try and wait calmly for our flight.

Once at North Ronaldsay we were got driven to Garso, and like everybody before us, we only saw the Red-winged Blackbird when it got flushed it from the iris bed. It flew out and sat on a large gas bottle. I managed a couple of photographs during our 2-minute view before it darted straight back into the irises.

Andrew now joined us for a wander around the island. I noted 31 different species, including 4 summer-plumaged Snow Buntings and 10 Wheatears. That evening we ate a nice meal at the observatory, chucked £5 into the tick bucket and had a few beers. On the Sunday I managed to see the RWB again and couldn't resist buying a North Ronaldsay fleece from Alison Duncan in the souvenir shop.

All four of us got the first flight off in the morning and when I arrived at my car, I noticed my car keys were missing. Andrew warned me never to leave car keys in pockets unless they are zipped up. I felt like an idiot. Where could I have left them? I despaired. I rang up Greenflag and they wouldn't be able to get a locksmith out to me till the Monday, and it wasn't going to be cheap. The others didn't want to wait for a locksmith and started making enquiries about hiring a car to get home.

I thought I would just try the observatory and see if anybody had handed them in. Alison answered the phone and said, "Sorry Garry, no they haven't any keys handed in". Few minutes later she rang back and said," Garry, I've just found a set of keys in the shop and I'll pass them to Kevin Woodbridge who will arrange for them to be flown back to Kirkwall". I honestly could have kissed her. The others were relieved that they didn't need to hire a car and we just had to wait four hours for the next inbound flight. The plane landed and the keys were handed to me by Ian Broadbent.

Before I forget to mention it, Kevin Woodbridge was previously the GP on North Ronaldsay and in 2017 he became the North Isles Councillor. It doesn't stop there – he is also the chairman of the Orkney Ferries board, vice-chairman of the Orkney Health and Care committee and a member of the Development and Infrastructure, Monitoring and Audit, Policy and Resources and Planning Committees.

You might remember I mentioned Ian Broadbent's dad, who found the 2005 Shugborough Belted Kingfisher, whereas Ian was responsible for getting news out when he saw it at Peterculter.

Before leaving Orkney, we noted 254 Long-tailed Duck and a summer plumaged White-billed Diver at the Ayre of Cara. Once back on the mainland we stopped for food at Inverness, and stayed the night at a Youth Hostel. A male Pallid Harrier was seen the next day at Dunsop Bridge.

This Red-winged Blackbird became the first accepted record for the Western Palearctic and stayed to 14th May. Britain had 17 records between 1824-85, but these were generally attributed to the bird trade.

I turned 50 on 13th June and with moving house this year we decided to hold a house party. We decided to hire cocktail staff and make sure there was enough alcohol to fill a bath.

On Friday 16th June I was delighted to open the door to see Chantal, Paul, Louis, and girlfriend Marine. Chantal's properties were rented most weekends and Saturday she needed to keep free to give guests the keys and take them through how things work. Chantal and Yves rarely hire cleaners, so Chantal and her boys do the hard graft. This was manageable before the château was purchased. Since then, Chantal had a stroke and lost control of half her body whilst she lay in a hospital bed. She was now back to normal but had to be careful not to overdo things. The château was the straw that broke the Camel's back. Chantal and Yves were now filing for divorce, and this wouldn't be a simple process with all their properties to split.

Later that evening it was nice to see the Brownes arriving for the weekend. The fun began with the sleeping arrangements – Kim had to mastermind how to sleep 10 people in three bedrooms.

The next morning David, Marine and I went on a 6k run. I took them my usual 5k route around Southwater village and where I normally walk back from the Country Park to catch Pokemon, we ran back. We were expecting over 50 guests for the party it was nice that Carolyn from work lent me a few chairs. Some chairs and tables came from Kim's parents' farm. The three-piece conservatory furniture we brought from Crawley was taken out of the second living room and placed in the back garden. In my fatter days I was good at breaking furniture. I had managed to break this three-seater sofa and now Louis with his carpentry skills managed to repair it. I set up a gazebo in the garden and converted the dining room into a cocktail bar, whilst the lounge was cleared of furniture to give indoor space to socialise and queue for the cocktail bar. Kim, Lucy, and Chantal organised the buffet and this was displayed the whole length of the lounge next to the wall. Everything was taking shape; we just had a few last minute errands to buy stuff.

Family guests started to arrive around 3pm and for them I cooked a selection of meats on the BBQ. The cocktail staff arrived at 6pm, but they only brought one large bag of ice. The kitchen was next to the cocktail bar, and this was commandeered for their use. Alan Robbins was next to arrive and he setup the disco underneath the gazebo. My brother-in-law, Richard Grady, brought round a keg of beer. Guests started to flood in from 6:30pm. One thing I like about Rapiscan is that there is no elitism shown by top management – their doors are always open to anybody in the company.

I was honoured that Vice President Gary Martin turn up with his wife. Gary was sadly going to leave Rapiscan in a few weeks to take up a senior post with Delta Airlines in the US. Gary was an incredible human being who knew exactly how to motivate the 150+ employees at Salfords. He had transformed the company and every day as you entered the building you saw a massive picture of the workforce surrounding the 100th RTT machine that the factory made. Note RTT110 was a ground-breaking aviation security technology designed to accurately detect explosive threats and prohibited items, including liquid explosives hidden in suitcases. Gary was to be replaced by Marc Stas, who use to be the Commercial Director. He would be a safe pair of hands to run the company going forward. Marc also came to the party with his wife, as well as Mark Watson, who worked for operations and was responsible for inventory procurement. Mark told me he used to be a professional footballer and was almost a scratch golfer! I never found out which club he played for or if he was telling porkies, but one thing for sure, Mark was an entertaining guy who took a keen interest in my life, and I was delighted he came.

I counted 10 colleagues from Rapiscan. Nobody came from Bowers and Wilkins and only Jade and her partner Gary came from Colas. When I got married, I remember only two birdwatchers had come, so this time round I only invited John Lees, John Benham, Andrew Lawson and George Kinnard to attend. Everybody came apart from George, who had informed me a few days before that he couldn't make it. Georgie invited the fab four and they all came with their parents. Kim's best friend Sue Thompson was also there.

Halfway through the evening the ice had run out and I was too drunk to drive to Broadridge Heath Tesco to get anymore, so one of the bar staff drove me there and back and hopefully nobody realised I had gone. I had originally booked the bar staff from 7pm to 11pm, and at 11 we still had plenty of guests enjoying themselves, so I bunged them fifty quid and they carried on serving to midnight. At the stroke of midnight the bar was closed, the disco was turned off and only a handful of drunken guests had to be kicked out. What an amazing evening, and to have 75 guests was a nice way to celebrate the milestone.

Late on 6th July, the news broke of an Amur Falcon at Poligiga in West Cornwall. There was nothing I could do about it, as once again it was during month end. The earliest I could be there was Saturday morning. I've found twitching raptors the morning after a roost site is pinpointed is a sure-fire way of getting them. Next morning 200 twitchers arrived in the dark and as the sun rose at 6:05am the falcon was still there, a 1st summer female and a second for Britain. It hung around until 9:30am and disappeared in the direction of Nanjizal, never to be seen there again.

Remarkably this bird was re-found at nearby St. Buryan, ten days later on the 17th at 12:35pm. I finished working at 1:15pm and made a beeline to my car. If I drove non-stop to Cornwall, I could be on site by 7pm and be in with a chance. The journey west didn't go well. There had been no sign of it for nearly three hours and the advice from friends on Twitter was to do a U-turn and head home. Something inside me told me to carry on driving, though I was not really expecting to see it, but the Amur Falcon was miraculously relocated at 5:23pm by the substation near St. Buryan. I arrived at 7:10pm and spotted two well-known twitchers, Alan Lewis from Hampshire and Steve Webb from Yorkshire. All three of us watched in awe as the Amur Falcon sat close by in a hedge. I managed a couple of photographs before, at 7:15pm, it flew towards a distant house and I called time.

The Amur Falcon was first found by Cornish birder Mark Wallace on a regular walk after tea down Bosisto Lane. That night a few locals managed to connect. The second time it was spotted by Jean Lawman and confirmed once John Swann and John Ryan arrived on site.

An American Redstart was found at Eoligarry on Barra on Thursday 7th September. Again, I had to hang fire until Friday 5:30pm in order to go. I arranged for John Benham to meet me at Rapiscan, and we headed to Dartford to meet Andrew Lawson. Andrew drove us in his 7-seater to Oban with a breakfast stop on the A74M at Abington Services. Chris Bell arranged to leave his car at Oban and join us.

The idea of leaving their car at Oban also appealed to Adrian Webb. Andrew's car was now filled with the addition of Adrian Webb, Dave Webb, and James Hanlon. Andrew drove all 7 of us onto the ferry and we departed at 1:30pm. The highlights of the crossing to Castlebay were a White-tailed Eagle and Manxie.

We docked at 6:25pm and drove (10 miles) straight to Eoligarry church. All the birders walked around the back of the church and sat on a small hill overlooking the garden, which contained five sycamore trees. We were perhaps a tad distant to be able to see the American Redstart if it showed. We had less than hour before dark and our best chances of connecting were standing at ground level peering over the stone wall.

Then the bird flew into an impenetrable section of the sycamore, and I then got a quick flash of its bright yellow panels on the tail. Over the next 30 minutes I did manage three good views as it performed its circuit around the garden. The view each time was on the nearest sycamore. No further sighting occurred between 7:30pm and 8pm, when it probably went to roost.

We dined at Heathbank Hotel (01871-890266) and celebrated with a few pints before sleeping at Barra Holidays B&B (07908-267265). The next morning, it was lovely to find seven packed lunches prepared by owner Helen sitting by the front door. The ferry departed in the dark at 7:55am, giving nobody a chance of seconds with the redstart. Fourteen happy birders were on the crossing, and I managed to get a group photograph of everybody in the lounge. The picture consisted of our group of seven plus Matt Wilmot, Steve Williams, Cliff Smith, Graham Lawlor, Rob Jones, Richard Baatsen and Mark Ponsford. On the way home, James Hanon came back with us. I got home at 12:30am on 11th September.

The total trip cost was £176 on fuel, £28 foot passenger return on ferry, £132 car return on ferry and £18 B&B, making my share £106. The American Redstart was found by Bruce Taylor and became the 6th record for Britain. It was last seen on 17th September.

Meanwhile, Adam Archer got a bonus from work and decided to spend £500 of it trying to see the American Redstart on Barra. He drove up to Blackpool Airport on Saturday 9th September and met two other twitchers there. The pilot, Robert Murgatroyd, decided it was ok to fly and everybody squeezed into the plane with gear, the heaviest passenger sat in the front with the pilot and the others behind. The plane took off and shortly after crashed into a potato field close to the M62. Fortunately, everybody survived. Adam had a couple of broken ribs and a sore leg. This was his first and last charter flight. After going through this ordeal, I just hope Adam gets another opportunity of seeing an American Redstart in Britain.

I don't think my account of 2017 would be complete without mentioning Sussex birder Kevin McCoy. I first met Kevin at Rainham Marshes when he was trying to see the 2011 Slaty-backed Gull. Since then, we had become good friends. I've always admired his positivity and kindness. He is one of the few birders who has dined at my house, and I have at his. We've had birding holidays together on Shetland. One crazy time we did a 11-hour drive to the south of France, watched a Red-footed Booby for 30 minutes and then jumped back in the car and came home. Kevin often failed to twitch midweek because of his senior position with Chichester County Council. He was the Manager for two leisure centres for 21 years. I was devastated to find out that he had been diagnosed with skin cancer, and was only a couple of years my senior. He retired from the council due to ill health on 31st July 2015 but managed to see his 450th bird on 10th June. This was an Elegant Tern at nearby Pagham Harbour. That was the last new bird Kevin ever got, as the cancer savagely took his life on 9th September. I would like to send my deepest condolences to his wife Karen. RIP Kevin.

On Wednesday 20th September my biggest bogey bird, a Yellow-breasted Bunting, was found on Out Skerries. I was hosting several meetings with many staff over the next 7 days to look at ways of improving our investment in slow-moving inventory, so my only opportunity was a weekend twitch. Ashley Howe, Ian Wells, Andrew Kinghorn and I drove up Friday night with a very clear sky to Aberdeen. On the Saturday morning, an Embraer 145 jet flew us to Sumburgh, but it came as no surprise to find that the bunting had departed. Twitching Out Skerries was only made possible because Alan Lewis arranged for the normal ferry to make a special crossing for us. Instead we had to settle for a Common Crane at Quendale and a flock of 35 Black Guillemots viewed from the ferry in Lerwick harbour.

Alistair Gray is a postman who spends most of his spare time birding at Weir Wood Reservoir and wandering around Sussex. I mentioned on Twitter that I was going to try and see a juvenile Cedar Waxwing on St. Agnes at the weekend. Although he doesn't normally leave Sussex, Alistair was keen to come and do the driving. We travelled down to Newquay on the Friday 6th October. During these journeys you can quite often have some thought-provoking conversations. This time I discovered we had a mutual friend called Lee Beadell. I had only known Lee since 23rd July, having met him when I joined his Horsham Pokemon group. Lee's Pokemon group is a brilliant idea. The group made it possible to battle Pokémon called "Raid Bosses", which was only achievable if you had five or more players to take part.

Alistair decided to have Weir Wood reservoir has his local patch soon after I left Colas. I have managed to see 156 different species there and by 2022, Alistair had clocked up 161. Alistair has found some really scarce birds at Weir Wood including Purple Heron and Temminck's Stint, but his best personal best find happed when he was working with Royal Mail on Crawley Industrial estate. He found an Alpine Swift flying over the car park. This BBRC bird was found on 28th March 2015 and even roosted two nights on the Virgin Atlantic building. I think this is Crawley's rarest bird and I'm so grateful I managed to see it too.

Newquay Airport had our flight to Scilly listed on the departure board as delayed with no time. This instantly put me in a bad mood. There was no way of getting to the *Scillonian* now, we just had to pray it was going to fly. Finally, after 1½ hours of waiting, the aircraft was towed out of the hangar and moved to the terminal building. It was a total relief to be flying just after 10am to St. Marys.

We took a taxi to the quay and took the St. Mary's Boatmen's Association boat to St. Agnes. The Cedar Waxwing, a juvenile, had originally been found at Browarth, but since Wednesday it had moved to St. Warna's Cove. It was almost impossible to see from the coastal path, but could be seen occasionally when it moved around some dense pittosporum (cheesewood). We were eventually rewarded after a 3-hour wait when it showed in the open for 2 minutes before flying off. All 80 visiting birders saw it and to celebrate we had a pint in the Turks Head pub.

On Scilly we saw an Isabelline Wheatear at the airfield and then found that our flight back to Newquay had been cancelled. We had to take the *Scillonian* to Penzance and catch a coach to Newquay.

Will Wagstaff originally found the Cedar Waxwing whilst tour leading on 3rd October. It stayed to 9th October and became the 7th record for Britain. The last twitchable one was back in Nottinghamshire in 1996.

Did you ever think Britain was going to get an adult male Siberian Blue Robin? I didn't, but as soon as the news broke on 8th October, I booked 4 spaces with Loganair to North Ronaldsay. These seats were soon snapped up by John Lees, Sean Cole and Chris Bromley. Sean booked Aberdeen-Kirkwall flights and John and I drove to Sean's and slept in his lounge for 3 hours. Sean drove his car to Aberdeen.

Tom Gale and Lewis Hooper found the Siberian Blue Robin on 8th October flying past them and getting trapped in a derelict building at Southness. The bird couldn't escape the building and as it flapped against the window the decision was to catch it by hand. The bird was caught, when they noticed its cobalt blue upperparts, white belly and pink legs. Only then did they realise the significance of the find, and they both got the shakes. They placed into a bird bag and processed over the next 30 minutes. All 15 members of the observatory saw it including 3 visitors.

The robin had not been seen since being trapped the previous day. This was just as well, because our Loganair flight went technical on its first flight of the day. We had a cooked breakfast at Dyce Farm and drove home empty handed.

This was Britain's 4th Siberian Blue Robin and second for North Ronaldsay and I could now add Siberian Blue Robin (13th) to my dip list. My share of this dip was £81 on flights, £ 45 on fuel and £3 parking.

My Vauxhall Vectra had started playing up a bit. It needed water every time I filled up with diesel. There were no water puddles on the driveway, and local mechanic Dorin diagnosed it as needing a head gasket. This was going to cost around £600. I ummed and ahhed and decided it wasn't worth spending that sort of money on a 12-year-old car. Kim spoke to her son Luke, and he suggested getting a reconditioned engine. Luke was prepared to fit it and he found a similar engine on ebay. I rang up the dealer and he said he would be able to

American Redstart
Setophaga ruticilla
Barra: Eoligarry
Western Isles
9th September 2017
G. BAGNELL

get me the exact engine to fit my car the following day. I agreed and paid him £700 directly into his bank account. The engine didn't come when promised and after chasing him, he then gave me another date and it arrived. The engine was rusty, but Luke fitted it with help from his dad. I picked the car up a week later and it sounded like a Sherman tank. I'd been conned – there was no way this engine had been reconditioned. It had probably just been ripped out of a car sitting in a pool of water from a scrapyard. I bought it outside the ebay marketplace, and I had as much chance of getting my money back as Arsenal winning the Premier League.

When I drove the car to work I found that not only was the engine noisy, the brakes were unresponsive and dangerous. I was not prepared to drive this car for a second longer and said to Luke, "The car's yours". I was back in the all-too-familiar situation of being carless. One thing I knew for sure; I wouldn't be getting my next car from an auction.

Auto Trader was advertising a 2012 Vauxhall Insignia 2.0 litre diesel at the nearby Haven Motor Company at Plumer's Plain, only 7 miles away, and soon as I saw it, I knew this was the car for me. I came back home and informed Kim I had just bought a car for £6,000 and was getting it in a few days. My lady was not happy. 1) She was feeling sick and couldn't come with me. 2) She had

2017	Regular	Vagrant	BBRC/IRBC 1 year	BBRC/IRBC 2 year	BBRC/IRBC 3 year	BBRC/IRBC 4 year	BBRC/IRBC 5 year	BBRC/IRBC 10 year	BBRC/IRBC 20 year	BBRC/IRBC Lifetime	Cat B	Total
Seen	276	38	88	11	13	12	39	22	13	7	0	519
During		1					3		3	2		9
B&I Total	276	38	92	12	14	15	46	38	36	44	8	619
	100%	100%	96%	92%	93%	80%	85%	58%	36%	16%	0%	83.8%

thought I was only going to look at it and 3) It was too big for her to drive.

On 30th November I sat my Financial Strategy exam at London Islington. The exam cost £145 and you got 120 minutes to answer 60 multiple choice questions. I had been studying the syllabus with a company called Kaplan since January and knew it inside out. Howewer I scored only 98 marks out of 150, which meant I had failed by 2 marks. I didn't pace myself well in the exam and didn't even have time to write five "As" on the last 5 questions just to give myself a chance of getting one or two right. I would have got a pass if just one those answers had needed an "A".

While the syllabus was fresh in my mind I took the exam again on 14th December and this time got 97. I had to face facts – my brain was not as fast as it was in 2000 and it was 2-0 to CIMA.

SUMMARY

During 2017, I travelled 6,063 miles in Britain and Ireland in the pursuit of new birds and managed to increase my list by 9 BOU/IRBC species. This took my British and Irish list to 519. The Combined Official stood at 619 species, and I had seen 83.8% of them. There were 6 additions to the Official British and Irish List during the year: Slaty-backed Gull, Yelkouan Shearwater, Chinese Pond Heron, Acadian Flycatcher, Siberian Accentor & Chestnut Bunting.

These 9 lifers in the table above are Acadian Flycatcher and Chestnut Bunting (Life), Slaty-backed Gull, Chinese Pond Heron and Amur Falcon (20-year), Siberian Accentor, American Redstart and Cedar Waxwing (5-year) and Cackling Goose (Vagrant)

That year, the most important bird I had seen during the year had to be the American Redstart. When you get a rare bird on a remote island it's a magical experience that remains with you forever. Above I'm showing this bird in the 20 year+ bracket, but the last twitchable one was in Hampshire in 1985. 37 years have elapsed since then.

CHAPTER 20

2018

Rapiscan does have a canteen, no hot food, just a couple of microwaves and a chocolate bar vending machine. If you prefer something cooked, many go the restaurant at Selco builders' merchants next door. Poor people like me have a packed lunch that is usually all eaten by 10am, and then I take my Georgian work colleague Maia Parkinson for a 2km walk along the A23 to McDonalds. I know how to treat a lady. In fact, we rarely buy anything there, we use it as the marker to turn around and go back to work.

This is a great opportunity for Maia and me to catch up on work gossip and solve the world's problems. On every walk I'm generally multitasking, chatting and simultaneously catching Pokémon on three phones. I am also a member of Salford Pokémon group.

Lee Beadell's Pokémon group had made me valuable friends, including the Burse sisters and trainee accountant Kate Wright. I will never forget the day I was coming back from Crawley with all three girls in my car and Kim rang up and wondered if I could pick Georgie up from Army Cadets. I parked up the car and all three girls got out complete with phones, battery packs and charging cables and walked past Georgie's uniformed friends to go home. Georgie wanted to disown me. She got in my car and said "Dad, don't you ever park up and offload your friends there again. In future, you can only pick me up at the front of the building where nobody can see us".

To get everybody up to speed, Georgie gave up swimming lessons when we moved to Southwater and joined Horsham Army Cadets to keep fit. Last year she went to summer camp at Salisbury and met a similar-aged girl called Lola. They've now become best of friends and during the year they alternate at spending weekends at each other's houses.

The first important bird of the year turned up on Fair Isle on Tuesday 15th May. Why do all the good birds have to be on Fair Isle? This one was a Song Sparrow, and the last twitchable one had been at

Seaforth in 1994. I was hoping it was not going to be seen the following day, but it was. Five charter planes all managed to connect over the next few days.

I managed to leave work at 3:30pm on Thursday 17th May and pick up John Benham from Leatherhead, but then we got stuck at the M25/M40 junction in stationary traffic. We only had two hours spare for the whole journey, so we were pleased to see traffic moving again after twenty minutes. We arrived at Aberdeen city centre, parked the car at the usual spot and got the 3am 727 bus to the airport. Our Loganair flight to Sumburgh departed at 6:30am. I didn't think there was any point in hiring a car – our plan was to get a bus to Lerwick.

This plan looked vastly better when we met a desperate businessman waiting by the bus stop. The bus was running late and he couldn't afford to wait another minute, so he had booked a taxi to Lerwick. We were both offered a space in his taxi and in return we just handed over the £6 joint bus fare. I'm not sure if he expected more for the ride, but I guess his trip was on company expenses. Now he could treat himself to a meal deal.

There was no rush for us to get to Lerwick, and when we arrived, we asked the locals how to get to Tingwall. They said there was a bus from Viking bus station which could probably drop us off nearby. At 12:30pm, news came from Fair Isle that the Song Sparrow had not been seen since 9:30am, when it was at a place called Sheep Cru. Three hours without a sighting was a bit disconcerting, but we had to carry on. We mentioned to our bus driver that John could not walk very far, so he took pity on him and rather than dropping us nearby, he took us all the way to the terminal building. Bless him.

Here we met Rebecca Nason and her partner Phil Harris. They too wanted to see the Song Sparrow and we had a good chat with them in the small Tingwall lounge. I love these tiny airport lounges, there's only enough room for eight people to sit and you have the option to watch TV if you wish.

Graham Lawlor sent me a tweet at 2:30pm saying the Song Sparrow had just been found in the gully. I cannot express how exciting this news was. I couldn't do a conga yet as we hadn't seen the bird, but surely, we now had a chance.

We boarded the 8-seater Islander at 3pm and once landed we decided to followed Phil, as he knew which gulley to go to. Wrong! There were no birders at this gully, but when we arrived at a different gully I could see a birder there looking through a scope. I walked over at 3:40pm and it turned out to be ex-Sussex birder Gordon Beck. He was watching the Song Sparrow and allowed us a quick peep through his scope. I then watched the bird walk to the end gulley. We repositioned ourselves at the end of this gully and I managed to get a digiscope as it sat still with a female Blackcap. By 4pm it was walking back through the gulley towards the observatory and vanished. It was never seen again. How lucky were we?

John and I noted 19 different species on Fair Isle and stayed the night with Kathy Coull and her cats at Upper Leogh (01595-760248). Kathy has quite a small house and provides an evening meal for a set price. John and I had dinner with her and chatted for a couple of hours till my energy levels started falling and I had to make my excuses and go to bed.

The next morning, we caught the *Good Shepherd* at 7:30am and arrived at Grutness at 10:05am. Today it was Pokémon community day and from 11am to 2pm a little fire Pokémon called Charmander was going to spawn all around the world. The phone signal was poor at the southern end of Shetland, and I needed to get a bus to Lerwick. where the signal improves. I managed to catch 4 shiny Charmanders and enough candy to evolve one into a big black shiny Charizard. What a beauty! I met fellow Pokémon players at Lerwick and they added me to the Shetland Pokémon group.

I caught the 7pm ferry back to Aberdeen and finally got home at 5pm on Sunday. This four-day adventure had cost me £345.48 (Flight £107.48, 727 Bus to Aberdeen Airport £3.00, taxi contribution £3.00, bus to Tingwall £1.90, flight to Fair Isle £46.20, B&B £65, bus to Lerwick £2.90, *Good Shepherd* £16.60, Ferry to Aberdeen £34.00, Fuel share £65) plus £41 on food and beer.

The Song Sparrow was found by Richard Cope, who caught it in the plantation trap and instantly recognised it. He'd seen them before at Long Point Bird Observatory, Canada whilst volunteering. This bird was processed at the observatory and released in the observatory garden. It hung around the garden for three days before deciding to wander further afield on the 18th. This was the 4th record for Fair Isle and the 8th for Britain.

When Holly Peek and her friends Andrew and Catherine went to Duncansby Head for an organised sea watch for Orcas, Andrew spotted a small bird perched on a wire fence which neither Catherine or Holly could identify. A back of the camera shot was tweeted out and the responses from Birdguides and Alan Davies both suggested Subalpine Warbler. Birdguides asked for more photos and ID was then clinched as a Moltoni's Warbler. The news was mega alerted on 29th May and that evening I hired a car and picked up John Benham, Mark Rayment and Les Holiwell. The overnight drive was shared with Mark Rayment, and at 7:30am Phil Woollen confirmed that the bird was still present.

We arrived at 9:30am and watched it point blank for the next hour. It was nice to see the salmon pink underparts and hear the wren-like rattle. On the way home I ate haddock and chips at the corner café in Wick, at the exact time when Holly and others were watching an Orca at Duncansby. Was I ever going to see an Orca? I had missed them before in Shetland and still needed to see the Northern Lights as well.

The Moltoni's Warbler stayed from 28th to 30th May and became the 8th for Britain. This recently split species might turn out to be an annual vagrant, as people are becoming familiar with features on spring birds.

On 19th June it was time for the family holiday. Just for a change we decided to go to… yes, Turkey again. I'm not sure Kim knows of any other hot countries. I think she's obsessed with fake clothing and handbags. This time Kim, Georgie and I checked into the Parkim Ayaz Hotel in Gumbet for 7 nights. The hotel was next to a beautiful sandy beach with hundreds of sun loungers and water sports facilities. The best part of the holiday was the animation team, especially the one they called Romeo, although his real name was Muslum Yildiz. Every day he sat down with us at the bar, asked us about life in England and told us about his life in Turkey.

Romeo introduced us to three hotel guests. They happened to be a family comprising a grandmother, mother, and daughter. This was a girls' holiday, and their partners were back in England. Georgie became good friends with the daughter, who was 18, quite pretty and a touch overweight.

One night the animation team arranged a pub/nightclub crawl around Gumbet. Georgie wanted to go, but Kim was only prepared to let her go if I accompanied her. Georgie started begging me to go. How could I not let my 14-year-old daughter go to her first nightclub? We were all given bright orange lanyards with whistles attached for our safety. Romeo led all the party animals on foot from the hotel and at the first club we visited we were treated like VIPs by the doormen. Georgie was hanging out with her friend, mother, and grandmother. I decided to stay sober and watch Georgie like a hawk. I wanted to make sure nobody tried to spike her drinks etc.

The women she was hanging out with were all three maneaters and were flaunting their female bits to all the men they met. One guy looked high on drugs and was trying to whisper something in Georgie's ear, and I saw red and went over to him and asked him to back off.

During the evening, Georgie and her friend went to the toilets. Twenty minutes later they hadn't come out. I started to panic, so I showed a random lady a picture of my daughter and asked if she could spot her inside the ladies. She spotted her and a few minutes later Georgie came out with her friend. I really wasn't enjoying this night out and I kept thinking that if anything bad happened to Georgie, Kim would never forgive me. Georgie was getting loads of male attention and I could only truly relax at the end of the night when we were all heading back to the hotel. I will never take Georgie clubbing again, that's for sure, but her holiday was massively improved by meeting her friend.

On the penultimate day of our holiday Georgie wanted money for some water activities with her friend. They wanted to go on a flyfish, a massive inflatable towed by a speedboat. The girls climbed on the flyfish and with gentle speed the inflatable lifted off the water every few seconds. When the speedboat got faster the flyfish started to fly. This was quite nice to watch, until the imbalance of the girls' weight caused the flyfish to capsize at speed. The speedboat had to come and rescue them. Georgie managed to escape unscathed, but her friend wasn't a good swimmer and came back covered in bruises. I don't expect her holiday insurance would have paid out if she had needed medical treatment. Anyway, it was a nice holiday and I guess some people are wondering why Muslum is called Romeo. He's coined this nickname because each week he falls in love with a different lady guest. To some men this would be a dream gig.

Kim noticed I had started to go to toilet a couple of times each night. I didn't think it fair for her to keep being woken up and decided it was time to contact the doctors to see if there was an underlying reason for it. My doctor said it was probably best to test my blood for PSA. This stands for "prostate-specific antigen", a protein produced by cancerous or non-cancerous tissue in the prostate, a small gland found in men below the bladder.

On 28th August I got the results back and was told my PSA was quite high for a 50-year-old. They sent me paperwork for another blood test in two weeks' time. Again the PSA rose, and they decided to fast-track me for a suspected urological cancer.

My urine was also tested and came back normal, as did my blood count. At the end of September, I met with a urology specialist at East Surrey Hospital, who performed a very unpleasant hand inspection of my bottom and couldn't feel anything wrong. This was reassuring, but the specialist said, "You will only know for sure after an MRI scan, and if necessary, a biopsy".

The MRI showed a shadow over the prostate. This could indicate prostate cancer, so now I needed a biopsy to be totally sure. After my good friend Kevin McCoy had died quickly died from skin cancer the previous year, I felt I just had to do whatever tests the specialists wanted, then forget about potential cancer and instead immerse myself in the hobbies.

On 8th October I managed to charter two boats to carry 20 birders to Lundy for a Green Warbler. This would have been brilliant if it had hung around for a second day. Then on the 14th October many Yorkshire birders celebrated when they saw Britain's first White-rumped Swift from 3:24pm to 6:10pm at Hornsea Mere. I went the next day with Andy Appleton, Jerry Warne and Andrew Lawson and dipped it, along with a couple of hundred others.

The Green Warbler was found by Tim Davis and Tim Jones on 7th October and became the 5th record for Britain. A photograph of it was originally posted as a Greenish Warbler on the Lundy birding blog and this unleashed a Twitter storm, with identification being pinned down in the process. The following day a total of 34 birders dipped using charter boats.

Lesley Catherine Ball found the White-rumped Swift looking out of her bungalow window on the 14th October and put the news on her WhatsApp group as a late Swallow. She changed her mind once she stepped outside her bungalow and noticed a white rump. Later photographs showing white trailing edges to the secondaries nailed the identification.

The best bird of the autumn was probably a Grey Catbird. The news was first broadcast on 15th October at 3:55pm when one was seen north of Treeve Moor House in Trevescan, Cornwall. I hung back for a day but went down for the 17th with Simon King, John Lees and Hugh Price. We arrived at 4:45am under a clear starlit sky. Once daylight was up there was a line of 50 birders staring distantly at a patch of sallows and brambles. The first bird of the day was a Robin, closely followed by a Great Tit, but not a sight or sound of the Catbird. With every minute of daylight, many observers' optimism of bird still being there was dwindling.

Then someone thought they saw a greyish bird zip between the distant brambles. Was that it? Nerves were calmed at 8:03am when a different observer was adamant that he had seen it too. The bird remained mostly hidden for the next twenty minutes, but I got a good view at 8:23am when it perched in full view of a sallow. Eight minutes later I saw it at the top of a bramble bush. Such a relief to finally see a Grey Catbird in Britain.

I managed to see it quite a few times over the next few hours, so whatever I saw in 2001 on the Saturday in gorse on South Stack could be safely ignored. This was the real deal, and it stayed an incredible 15 days to 29th October, enabling every keen twitcher in Britain to see it. The owners of Treeve Moor House kindly opened up their field for birders for the duration of the bird.

The bird was originally found by G. Mitchell and became the second record for Britain.

SUMMARY

During 2018, I travelled 4,579 miles in Britain and Ireland in the pursuit of new birds and managed to increase my list by 9 BOU/IRBC species. This took my British and Irish list to 528. The Combined Official stood at 629 species, so I had now seen 83.9% of them. There were 10 additions to the Official British and Irish List during the year: Tundra Bean Goose, Western Swamphen, Least Tern, Red-footed Booby, Turkestan Shrike, Two-barred Greenish Warbler, Pale-leafed Warbler, Steppe Grey Shrike, Eastern Yellow Wagtail & Red-winged Blackbirds.

The 9 lifers in the table above are Western

2018	Regular	Vagrant	BBRC/ IRBC 1 year	BBRC/ IRBC 2 year	BBRC/ IRBC 3 year	BBRC/ IRBC 4 year	BBRC/ IRBC 5 year	BBRC/ IRBC 10 year	BBRC/ IRBC 20 year	BBRC/ IRBC Lifetime	Cat B	Total
Seen	277	38	88	12	13	12	43	22	15	8	0	528
During	1			1			4		2	1		9
B&I Total	277	38	92	14	13	15	50	37	39	46	8	629
	100%	100%	96%	86%	100%	80%	86%	59%	38%	17%	0%	83.9%

Swamphen (Life), Red-winged Blackbird & Grey Catbird (20-year), Two-barred Warbler, Song Sparrow, Moltoni's Warbler & Elegant Tern (5-year) Eastern Yellow Wagtail (2-year) and Tundra Bean Goose (Regular).

On the 1st January 2018, the BOU decided to adopt the International Ornithological Congress (IOC) World bird list. This is a modern version of the Biological Species Concept with increased emphasis on monophyletic evolutionary lineages (De Queriroz 1998, 1999, Sangster 2014). These additional species would help me reach my goal of 550 a lot sooner. For insurance purposes I did see the Pied Crow at Clevedon on 30th June. I was advised this was unlikely to ever be accepted on the official British list but glad to see all the same.

This year, the most important bird seen during the year must be the Song Sparrow. Seeing this bird during its last 20 minutes on Fair Isle was rather fortuitous. This 24-year blocker might not be as rare as the Grey Catbird, but I'm quite partial to seeing anything new in the Sparrow and Bunting family.

Song Sparrow
Melospiza melodia
Fair Isle, Shetland
18th May 2018
G. BAGNELL

CHAPTER 21

2019

My PSA rose from its lowest reading in 2018 of 4.9 ng/mL to a new high of 7.2 ng/mL on 2ⁿᵈ January. Anything between 7 and 10 is a strong indicator for prostate cancer. Surrey Hospital offered me a prostate biopsy on 11ᵗʰ January, and Kim drove me hospital and waited whilst I had 26 needles inserted into my walnut-sized prostate. When I woke up, Kim was waiting at my bedside. The doctor gave me the all clear and then Kim took me home.

I know we all hate operations, but this biopsy is free and it's moments like this when you get to appreciate how brilliant the NHS is. The first thing I noticed after the operation was that my urine resembled red wine. A week later it was nice to see it turning to rose pink before going back to normal.

On 29ᵗʰ January it was confirmed that they had found adenocarcinoma in 0/12 samples on left side of my prostate but 4/14 on the right, which in English means I did have prostate cancer. There was a bit of good news: my Gleason score was 3+3=6. This meant I had the lowest grade cancer.

I had effectively scored 1 out of a maximum of 5. The specialist gave me literature to explain my four options. I didn't need to decide right then – I could go home and decide what options were best for me. The options were:

Option 1.
Monitor. This involves 4 biopsies a year, an annual MRI scan and a blood test every 6 weeks.

Option 2.
Radiotherapy. I'd be given hormones, followed by 7 weeks of daily treatment excluding weekends.

Option 3.
Surgery to remove the prostate.

Option 4.
Brachytherapy. This meant a visit to Guildford Hospital to get radioactive seeds inserted into prostate, then a few days off work to recover.

Kim and I digested the literature and went back

to meet the specialist face to face. I asked out of interest what he would have gone for. He said, "If I had the non-aggressive cancer like yourself, I would opt for monitoring".

"I wouldn't be able to relax doing nothing, so I'll opt for radiotherapy," I said.

My radiotherapy plan was due to start on the 8th April and because I was relatively young and fit I didn't have to get the hormone treatment – I would only need 4 weeks of treatment (20 sessions).

There are some side effects of radiotherapy including becoming sterile, erectile dysfunction, bladder problems, gastrointestinal issues, secondary cancers near the radiation field and lymphoedema. But I if I did nothing, one thing was for certain – I'd be a goner.

My radiotherapy sessions would all take place at East Surrey Hospital. This is 2.9 miles from work and my bosses, Alan Mixer and Philip Moores, were quite happy for me to start work at 9am and leave at 3:30 for my daily 4pm treatment.

On 2nd November 2018 a Tengmalm's Owl was photographed on a toilet on the lighthouse building of Copinsay in Orkney. The precise location was originally withheld due to the presence of 2,000+ pupping Grey Seals. The location was checked again on the 5th and there was no further sign.

Fast forward to Tuesday 19th February 2019, when another Tengmalm's Owl was found in a garden in Tumblin, Shetland. This bird was seen up to dusk (5:27pm) when it left the garden.

I decided to book leave till Friday and started the journey that night. I took John Lees and Hugh Price with me. The plan was to catch the Wednesday ferry. No rush to get there, so I took my time with three one-hour kips on route. At 7:21 Birdguides announced no sign and I pulled off the M6 and parked up at Preston to wait for more positive news. I calculated that I could still get the Aberdeen ferry if I left Preston by 11am.

The next message from Birdguides was again negative, and at 10am we headed home. But the story didn't end there. The Tengmalm's Owl was found again in the same Tumblin garden at 7:21am on Thursday 21st February. John and Hugh were up for going again. This time I left home at 11pm with John, Hugh and Richard Fairbanks.

There was negative news from Tumblin at 7:47am, but this time I was determined to get to Shetland no matter what. We stopped for a Scottish cooked breakfast at Fenwick's Luncheon and Tearoom in Perth at 11am and got to Aberdeen harbour around 2pm. Here we just sat around in the Northlink Ferry waiting room. Quite a few birders turned up and then I heard rumours of a force 6 south-westerly. That could mean a lumpy crossing. Next up, Hugh decided to go cold turkey on us. He wasn't convinced we were going to see the owl and coupled with not want to leave his poorly wife another night, he went back by train.

We got off at Lerwick and found the hire car and 24 minutes later we arrived at Tumblin. There were plenty of birders there. I got chatting to Richard Bonser, who had spent the night searching Tumblin with friends. He said there was no sight or sound of the owl. This was all feeling like a wasted journey – until 9am, when local birder Phil Harris arrived. He informed the crowd that he was going to seek permission to enter the homeowner's garden. Once he got permission he went down on all fours and crawled through a narrow hole into the small wood and disappeared. 15 minutes later he came back to tell us that the Tengmalm's Owl was sitting in a spruce tree. I immediately relayed the news to Lee Evans by text. He too caught the ferry over, but headed for a Common Rosefinch at Blett first.

Phil kindly set his scope up on the owner's front lawn and a 50-strong crowd queued to look through it. I had a one-minute slot and saw the owl. The view was dark, but if you looked long enough you could just make the bird out. I placed £10 in a collection box for Wastview Day Centre Hansel Fund and asked Richard and John if they were ok if I popped over to Lerwick for a bit. They were quite happy to queue for multiple views of the owl.

I didn't want to mention the reason for leaving, but I wanted to get to Lerwick for 11am to try to catch a newly released Pokémon called Clamperl. Don't ask. It feels sad writing about it now, but I caught quite a few including 3 shinies and got back to Tumblin Road by 1:30pm.

Richard and John were keen to do some birding, so I drove them to see a Common Rosefinch at Blett, a Pied-billed Grebe at Loch of Spiggie and 2 Tundra Bean Geese at Sandwick. We saw some other nice birds including Whooper Swans, Long-tailed Duck and Eider. The evening was spent back at the Tengmalm's Owl site. It started to wake up around 5:50pm and left the roost at 6pm. The views were spectacular. Four people used spotlights, and despite improving the viewing this caused a bitter Twitter storm once pictures were posted. I was powerless to stop anybody and I'm just thankful I didn't miss the return ferry back to Aberdeen. The ferry always has a nice selection of hot food on board, and I settled for the Dark Island steak pie and a bottle of Scapa Flow.

I got home on the Sunday at 5:08pm. The trip cost £120 in fuel, £33 car hire, Shetland fuel £25.14, ferry return £44 each. A four-way split worked out at £88 each.

Owen Merriman photographed the original Tengmalm's Owl on the Orkney toilet. The next bird found was by Erik and Jackie Moar and was seen in their garden on 19th, 21st and 23rd February. It was re-found 2.5km away at Lea Gardens in Bixter and seen intermittently from 25th February to 13th April. David Cooper found it on Unst on 14th April, from where it presumably went back to Scandinavia. Jackie Moar manged to raise £1,500 for her chosen charity. The pellets found indicate that it had eaten 2 Ringed Plover, a Common Redshank, a Chaffinch and two mice. This was the 9th modern record for Britain and the first twitchable record since the 1983 long-staying Spurn bird that got trapped.

A week before I was to undergo radiotherapy, I had to visit to St. Luke's Cancer centre at Guildford Hospital for fiducial markers to be inserted, to act as points of reference in imaging. I never looked up what this procedure involved, and thank God I didn't. I was in a small room lying on a bed with my pants pulled down with two ladies. One was talking to me about birdwatching and the other had gloves on and was inspecting my bottom. When she fired a fiducial marker into the soft tissue around the prostate it made me scream out in pain. The sly specialist carried on asking me questions about birdwatching whilst the second marker was fired in. I laugh now, but it was excruciatingly painful. I know I'm a bit of wimp when it comes to pain, but that was probably the most painful thing medical staff have ever done to me. Not only did I get these permanent gold seeds inserted but two tattoo dots were drawn below my belly button. I was given a bag of goodies to take home.

My first radiotherapy session took place on 8th April. I had to use a daily suppository out of the goodie bag and now had to be drinking 2 litres of water a day. I wasn't allowed to go to the toilet, despite having a full bladder, for 30 minutes before lying on the radiotherapy bed. The fiducial markers and tattoo allow the X-ray operator to zap the precise part of the prostate that has to be targeted. Each session lasted a little over 10 minutes and as soon as finished I rushed to the toilet before getting dressed. My journey home was 22 miles and I believe it or not I needed a further toilet stop before getting home.

Between 11th - 17th April I managed to do four 5K runs. During this time my runs were taking four minutes longer than normal, and after the 17th it became too painful to run. I was really glad no more birds turned up during the spring as I wouldn't have been able to go. It was hard enough going to work, but the weekends gave me sufficient recuperation time before radiotherapy restarted on the Monday.

My running resumed on the 28th May and we then booked a nine-day holiday from 14th August. This time Georgie brought her friend Lola on holiday with us. There will be no prizes on guessing where we went this year. Yep, back to Turkey. This time we stayed at Labranda TMT Bodrum resort.

This was one of the few holidays when we didn't have to befriend another family for Georgie's sake. The resort had very few sun loungers around the pool, so Kim awarded me the daily task of taking 4 beach towels and placing them on 4 sun loungers before sunrise. This worked well most days, until we arrived to find a mother and daughter team were lying on two of the four beds. I said, "These two beds have been reserved." The mother replied, "When we came down there was nothing indicating they were in use".

Kim and I took possession of the two remaining beds, but Georgie and Lola had to search for beds elsewhere. I got talking to the mother and daughter, and it turned out they were from Holland. They both spoke good English, and they said they had seen the two sunbeds from their apartment. Further discussions later unearthed that they had asked hotel staff whose towels were on the beds. The staff had removed the towels and said "They are yours now". They must have had a momentarily lapse of concentration and forgotten who they were talking to.

On our last evening we decided to spend our remaining Turkish lira shopping in Bodrum. The walk to Bodrum was a pleasant twenty-five minutes stroll – you just had to turn right when you got to the beach. That evening Kim and I waited at the beach for Georgie and Lola to make a quick stop at the ladies' toilet before the walk. Kim and I were waiting a good 10 minutes and the girls hadn't arrived. We walked back to the resort and saw them walking towards us. Kim asked what the delay had been. Georgie said she had got talking to a Saudi woman wearing an abaya standing in the pool. This lady had remarked how beautiful she looked and loved the shape of her eyebrows. She asked Georgie, "Where are you both going? Once you're back would you like to join me at the bar? I organise a Shisha pipe".

They became friends on Instagram, but Kim found it a bit suspicious as these women don't normally have conversations with anybody outside their own country. Whilst shopping in Bodrum, Georgie got an Instagram video call from the Saudi lady asking what time she expected to get back.

Once back at the hotel we dropped off our purchases in the room and made our way to the bar. Kim and I sat on a table near the bar whilst Georgie and Lola ordered drinks from an expert cocktail maker, Ramazann Ergün. The girls brought our drinks over and went and sat with the Saudi lady. She was on a table with another Saudi man and woman.

It could only have been ten minutes before Georgie and Lola came to our table and sat down.

Georgie told us she had asked the Saudi man what the women were to him and he had replied, "Just friends". He then asked, "What do you want to drink?" Georgie and Lola both said they were fine and pointed to their drinks. A little bit later he asked them to come back to his room later when their parents were asleep. Ramazann texted Georgie during this chat and said, "Get away from those people, they are dangerous".

We shared the story with our now good friend Ferhat Bektas, the entertainment manager from the hotel. He confirmed that the Saudi women would both have been his wives and they would have been brainwashed to do whatever he wanted. Georgie found loads of pictures on the Saudi women's Instagram account of herself around the pool. Ferhat said the Saudi religion would have forbidden him to approach the girls directly. Kim and I believe the girls narrowly escaped being drugged and/or raped, and who knows if we would have ever seen them again. Georgie and Lola were just 15 years old, and today they had learnt an important life lesson. If the same thing had happened at the start of the holiday, it would have been ruined for sure.

I was so relieved we were flying back to England the following day. This would probably be Georgie's last holiday with us, and I wasn't sure I would want to bring Kim back to Turkey after this.

Two days after getting back from Turkey, there seemed to be a bit of a Brown Booby theme going on. Kent had a probable adult flyby at Swalcliffe, Kent on 19th August and then on the 26th August a possible was seen off Porthmeor Beach in St. Ives. I didn't do anything based on probable, but once it firmed as definite immature at St. Ives between 7:5am to 2:33pm the next day, I decided to act. I headed down that night with John Lees and Christian Melgar, and the first stop was Exeter Services just before midnight. Surprisingly no other birders there and we got to St. Ives by dawn with plenty of sleep.

The chapel at St. Ives had over 60 twitchers searching and there was no sign of the Booby, so I left John and Christian there and wandered over to the nearby lighthouse and met Chris Batty, Dan Pointon, Adam Wilson, Paul Chapman, Matt Wilmot and a few others. Just then, unbelievably Chris shouted out that he had got the booby. He shouted out directions at 7:54am and I eventually saw his bird diving. Adam Wilson managed to get some long-range video footage and a few could see the white belly. Not me, my poor eyesight could only see a bird that was two-thirds of the size of an accompanying immature Gannet. It was diving at a 45-degree angle, whereas gannets dive at closer to 90 degrees. Anyone standing at the Hayle would had stonking views.

Matt Wilmott had his car parked near the lighthouse. I jumped in with him and we drove around to Godrevy and Carbis Bay to search for it, but drew a blank in the heavy rain.

Matt took me back to the chapel, where the rain was the main reason for John, Christian and I to head back home. The journey back was at walking pace on the A30. This was because a lorry had gone through the A30 barrier and taken out 6 cars out in the process. The delay added 4 hours to the journey.

Next morning Michael McKee managed to photograph the Brown Booby at 8:12am in exactly the same spot Chris had claimed it. That day it was watched up to 10:25am between Gwithian and Godrevy. There was no sign on the Friday, but on the Saturday it was remarkably seen again from 9:38am to 12:40pm between Gwithian and St. Ives, and then there was a sighting at 4:23pm when it was 10 miles further round the coast at Pendeen, flying west.

On Sunday 1ˢᵗ September I was back again with John Lees, George Kinnard, David Campbell and his friend Ian. It was a great day to get a sun tan, but sadly no cigar, or Brown Booby for that matter.

Kester Wilson was on the beach with his kids doing bucket and spade activities. He didn't think it was a good idea to be using bins on the beach with bikini-clad women about, but he noticed a bird with an underwing pattern looking unlike any immature gannet. The bird was diving at a shallow angle, and with this view he sent a message on a local WhatsApp group saying "Interesting looking gannet-type bird feeding offshore. Looks a bit like a Brown Booby. Sure it's not, but if anyone's out this way." This find was independently seen at the same time by Phil Snaith. The Kent bird was found by Geoff Burton and became the first for Britain. The St. Ives bird became the second, and the third was found on the 2ⁿᵈ September.

Dave Collins moved to the Lizard in 2017. After they had been watching a Red-backed Shrike in nearby Caerthillian Cove with Mark Pass, Ilya MacLean and Toby Phelps, they all split up in different directions looking for migrants. Dave decided to spend the rest of the day hunting along the clifftops and bushes around Kynance Cove. He walked down a few steps of the cliff and was panic-stricken when he spotted a dark brown bird with no white on the rump. When it banked, he could see a brown breast band contrasting with a white belly, and watched it shallow diving. It was a Brown Booby! The news broke on Birdguides on 2ⁿᵈ September at 10:41am of a 1ˢᵗ summer Brown Booby sitting on the pyramid shaped rocks with European Shags.

I couldn't do anything about it as I was busy with month end. I decided to work long hours for the next four days to try to get five days' work done. Philip was happy to cover the few bits I needed to do on the Friday and allowed me to leave home at 9pm Thursday. I travelled alone to Cornwall and arrived at Kynance Cove car park at 7:45am. The parking meter only took cash and with just two £1 coins in my pocket all I could get was one hour's parking. Two hours would have cost £5, by the way. I walked 1km and watched the Brown Booby on the cliff face till 8:54am. I dashed back to the car park by 9:15am and was very glad to see no fine on the car windscreen. Shame I missed it leaving the rock at 9:22am and starting to dive.

This tick felt so much more satisfying than ticking a bird at 3km range. I went past Ringwood McDonalds and couldn't resist celebrating with a banana milkshake. On the Saturday this bird was searched for all day with no sign, and became another Friday night bunk statistic.

Most of my new birds have involved big effort. I had a sneaky suspicion that getting to see a Northern Ireland Common Nighthawk might be best achieved by flying. Easy-peasy-jet were offering a day return to Belfast for £124.35, departing Gatwick at 6:15am and returning from Belfast at 8:25pm.

On Tuesday 8ᵗʰ October I got up at silly o'clock, drove to Three Bridges and found somewhere to dump the car, then took a 5-minute train journey to Gatwick. Not sure why I got to Gatwick at 4:45am because I had to wait 30 minutes before the gate number was announced. The flight took 1½ hours to get to Belfast International. By 8am I was second in the queue for the car hire. I thought £20 was a bit of bargain for a day's rental, but for this low price they wanted to charge my credit card £1,000 just in case I damaged the car or forgot to bring it back.

The drive to the River Maine at Galgorm only took half an hour. When I arrived there was only one birder, but this quickly swelled to fifteen.

Nobody could spot the Nighthawk, so we decided to split up and search a large area running the length of the river. This proved fruitless and everybody reconvened at the original spot. About 9:10am, Neil Hunt realised that the Nighthawk was in fact sleeping on a dead log a stone's throw from where we were all standing. The photographers all lay on the ground, getting some exceptional views.

The bird was flushed at 10:38am, not by the up-close photographers but by a horse. It was wandering around feeding on grass when its right hoof touched the log. The Nighthawk flew to the nearest tree and went straight back to sleep. During the flight I saw the forked tail and the white wing bars. It was now sitting 4 metres off the ground on an exposed branch of a sycamore tree.

I hung around until the afternoon and decided to leave when the rain started. I drove towards the airport and stopped at the first McDonalds for shelter and a bite to eat. According to Birdguides the bird left the sycamore at 7pm that night and started feeding along the River Maine. Alan Lewis managed to watch it flying around for 10 minutes and somehow managed to get on the same plane back to Gatwick as me. How was this possible? Such a sensational trip, and it only cost £149.35.

The Common Nighthawk, which became the third for Ireland, was originally found by a fisherman and believed to be a European Nightjar. Josh Jones spotted a video of it and immediately realised it was its rarer cousin, so he put the news out on Birdguides. The bird was twitched from 7th October to 17th October and the same bird was photographed on 19th October as it flew along the River Thames towards Richmond Park (12:28-12:33pm). The last twitchable one in Britain was on Bryher from 23rd to 30th October 1999.

November 2000 will long be remembered for the time I agreed to take Geoff Goater to Scotland after finishing his Sunday shift to see a female Steller's Eider at Hopeman Harbour. The only trouble was that it disappeared on the Sunday afternoon. My good friend John Benham had made the sensible decision to drive overnight Friday and see it on the Saturday. The bird was never seen again, and it had taken 20 years for us to get another chance.

Sandra and Don Otter moved to Westray, Orkney in 2011. They have found good birds up there, including a Sharp-tailed Sandpiper at Loch Swartmill in 2012. In 2019 they had found an American Wigeon in the same place, and then on the afternoon of 29th October, Sandra noticed an unusual looking duck there. Don scoped it and saw two white wing bars, and after consulting his Collins Guide, he confirmed his suspicions of it being a Steller's Eider. This bird was seen up to dusk.

I left home on the 29th at 5pm with John Lees, George Kinnard, Hugh Price and Ashley Howe, and the plan was to join forces with Dan Pointon, John Bell, Sam Vials, Al Orton and one of Dan's non-birding friends. Dan and his friend were just about to climb a Munro when the news broke. (Munros are mountains in Scotland over 3000 feet high.)

Our first pitstop was made at Toddington Services at 8:47pm. Meanwhile Dan Pointon flushed what he thought was a Tengmalm's Owl from a fence post on the A897 by Forsinard at 11:55pm. We were tempted to make a slight detour for this, but in end we all agreed to head straight to Scrabster and try to get the owl on the return journey. We arrived at Scrabster at 6:40am and got a couple of hours' kip. The Northlink ferry departed at 8:45am and arrived at Stromness at 10:15am. On the way to Kirkwall, we got a message that the Steller's Eider had been seen at 10:25am at Shapinsay. When all 10 of us got onto the charter boat we decided to check out the

Shapinsay sighting. This was fruitless, and after a bit of investigation it turned out that the Steller's Eider had only been seen by a single observer on a moving ferry. Maybe it was there or maybe it was a genuine mistake.

Either way we decided to waste no more time and head for Westray. There was a bus waiting for us at the quay and the friendly bus driver took us straight to Loch Swartmill. This inland loch had plenty of Wigeon, Tufted Duck and Mallard, but not our target bird. Whilst we were hanging around another car pulled up and out got Don and Sarah Otter. They described how they had found the Steller's the previous day. They were a lovely couple, and it was good to have a long chat with them.

George Kinnard was desperate to go to the loo and charge his phone. There were a few houses nearby and George decided to try his luck and knock on somebody's front door. They kindly let him use their toilet and brought his phone back to him when fully charged.

Bob Watts arrived somehow, and both of us being Arsenal fans, we had plenty to talk about. News then broke of a Pipit that had been on its ninth day in a maize field in Sennen, Cornwall. This was neither a Richard's Pipit nor a Blyth's but the non-migratory Paddyfield Pipit, identified by a sonogram by the Sound approach team in the Netherlands. This would be a first for the Western Palearctic if it was ever accepted.

I personally wasn't interested in the Paddyfield Pipit and thought it might be worth staying until dusk on Westray and then taking up Don Otter's offer of sleeping in his friend's vacant house. Dan's friend wanted to head back to the mainland for the Munro climb, and in the end all 10 of us plus Bob Watts joined Dan on his charter boat back to Kirkwall.

We got back at 3:30pm and started driving towards Stromness. We were sitting in the queue to board the ferry at 3:59pm when we received a message that the Steller's Eider has just been seen by Don Otter back at the loch. Holy moley! We got straight out of the queue and headed back to Kirkwall. Meanwhile Dan's team managed to catch the last scheduled ferry to Westray with only one minute to spare. The Steller's Eider was flushed at 4:22pm by children playing close by in a small boat.

Our crew settled for fish and chips and stayed the night at Orcades Hostel (016856-873745). Next morning, we caught the 7:20am scheduled ferry to Westray. We docked at Rapness ferry terminal and started the 3-mile walk to Loch of Swartmill. During the walk, sharp-eyed George spotted a distant perched Merlin, which we all saw well. Now we just had to stay at the loch for the Steller's Eider to return.

The period between 4pm and 5pm was the most exciting, when various wildfowl arrived to roost, but the Steller's Eider wasn't among them. We took the bus to Rapness and the ferry to Kirkwall, and Orcades Hostel got our custom for the second night.

That evening all the crews met up for a beer in the Kirkwall Hotel. John is teetotal, so one pint later my crew walked around the corner and dined at an Indian restaurant. Lovely lamb jalfrezi and then sweet dreams.

We left Stromness on Friday 1st November at 6:20am and got home at 10:30pm. The extra night in Orkney was only possible because my brilliant boss Philip allowed me to spend the Saturday catching up with Friday's month-end work. My cost share of the trip was petrol £175/5, 2 nights hostel £62, 2 charter boat share £65, bus £6, ferry return £54, ferry Rapness to Kirkwall £5 and M6 toll £1. The grand total was £228 plus £77 on food. The Steller's Eider was so far winning 1-0.

Dan Pointon was convinced that the bird was still about. I believe he completed his Munro and then went straight back to Westray to search for it. This guy has very good instincts. On Wednesday 6th November he managed to find the bird, a first-winter drake, early in the morning by the airport shore. Dan is probably the most driven twitcher Britain has. His income is earned solely from playing online poker based on a formula he learned in university days. He can earn money whenever he wants to and go birding whenever he wants. Not only does he twitch birds, he has found massively rare ones including a Yellow-billed Cuckoo, a Siberian Rubythroat, a Brown Shrike and a Rufous Turtle Dove. I cannot praise this individual enough.

The Steller's Eider had now been around for eight days, but the earliest I could think about going would be after work on Thursday.

On Thursday 7th November I left home at 8pm with the intention of first trying for the Paddyfield Pipit in Cornwall and then driving 837 miles to the top of Scotland for another Orcadian adventure. Would it be possible?

The A24 was full of gritting lorries and John Poyner mentioned on Twitter that there had been snow showers in the Highlands overnight. Glutton for punishment Hugh Price met me at Leatherhead, and then it was on to junction 9 on the M3 for the guy who had cost me the 1999 Steller's Eider, Mr Geoffrey Goater. Geoff had seen the Pipit earlier in the week but being a non-driver he was happy to get a lift. I managed 3 hours' kip at Cheriton Bishop and we arrived at Sennen by 7:05am with light just appearing.

The first bird we could hear was a Robin, but soon there was a bit more light and we managed to see the Paddyfield Pipit, which was tailless, near some stones. It looked like a ball of fluff, very odd looking.

The news from Westray was positive. The Steller's Eider had been seen at 7:51am on the shore north of the airport. I think this might have come from Bob Watts getting it on his second attempt. We stayed watching the Pipit to 9:00am. Then, because Hugh was raving about how good Philps Cornish pasties were, we had to try them. If you've never had these before, you are really missing out. It was full to the brim with big chunks of steak mixed with tasty cheese. Absolutely scrummy.

At 10:45am the atmosphere in the car was ruined when we heard that the Steller's Eider had disappeared. I kept driving and was pleased to hear that a male Blue Rock Thrush had been found at Lamb Holm quarry on Orkney. We would pass this quarry on the drive from St. Margarets to Kirkwall. Nice.

Even better news came at 3:44pm: the Steller's Eider had been relocated on Papa Westray. This news was interpreted differently by Hugh. He didn't want to get all the way to Orkney, splash out another £300 and get absolutely nothing, so he jumped ship at Crewe and took the train home. Hugh's car seat didn't get cold, as ace photographer Graham Jepson joined us. The new crew of three then popped into Toddington Services at 6:50pm. I opted for a Whopper with cheese meal.

During the day I made sure our boat charter was still sailing and ok to go to Papa Westray instead. The boat charter became cheaper when Stuart Butchart and William Bishop were up for sharing costs. We arrived at Gills Bay at 6:45am on the Saturday, and I really needed the 2-hour kip I got in the Cairngorms. Whilst we boarded the Pentland ferry, *Albert*, we found that this was only its 10th journey to Orkney.

The news then came through that the Steller's Eider had just been seen near St. Boniface Church at 9:04am by local birder David Roche. Zip-a-dee-doo-dah! We left at 9:30am, and drove full of adrenaline through the winding roads to reach Lambs Holm. Bingo, the bonus Blue Rock Thrush was still there. We watched it perch and fly around for a couple of minutes and saw it flying and perching in the quarry. We left the quarry at 11:40am and 11 minutes later we were boarding the charter boat.

Stu Butchart is chief scientist for Birdlife International and considering he's a wheelchair user its remarkable how he manages to get on these boats. The pier was only slightly higher than the boat and between us we managed to carry Stuart and his wheelchair across.

The news at 11:57 indicated that there had been no further sign of the Steller's Eider by late morning. But we had come this far, we just had to carry on.

The charter boat left at midday and arrived at Papa Westray at 12:45pm. Getting out of the jetty involved a tall climb on a vertical ladder. Stuart had to be lifted with his wheelchair to the top of the jetty. Waiting for us at the jetty was Jennifer, who runs the observatory and had transport arranged for Stuart and William, who were staying there.

Then Jennifer received a call that the bird was back at St. Bonniface church. Now my adrenaline was pumping again, and I just wanted to get to church as quickly as possible. I hope I wasn't rude to anyone during my outbreak of panic.

When Jennifer pulled up at the church I was still in proper headless chicken mode. I got out of her vehicle and couldn't see anybody. Jennifer pointed in the direction where the bird had last been seen and I ran in that general direction. I could now see George Gay in the distance looking through his scope. When I arrived, I looked through the scope and there in front of me was an eider duck with a square head and double white wing bar. I screamed

"Thank f**k it's still here!"

I watched if for the next two hours. I tried to get closer views by walking across some large stones, but I hadn't realised how slippery green algae is. My walking boots couldn't get a grip and I fell hard on my backside. Luckily I avoided hitting my head and nothing was broken. I gingerly resorted to crawling on all fours to the nearest stone, then setup the scope and handheld my iPhone for a few shots.

George and his friends Dante Shepherd and Simon Davies heard that the *Golden Mariana* (01856-872044) had been hired to take a group of musicians from Papa Westray to Westray that day at 4:25pm. This was fabulous news. All six of us sat in a heated waiting room at Bay of Moclett. The journey to Gill Pier in Pierowall took 25 minutes, then the normal bus (07789-034289) took us to Rapness for the 6:30pm ferry to Kirkwall.

That evening we stayed at the Peedie Hostel (01856-875477) and went for fish and chips again. We left the hostel at 7:30am Sunday and got safely back to the mainland via the Pentland Ferry. I was back in Southwater at 11pm and straight to bed.

This Steller's Eider twitch become a 1-0 win and cost the following: diesel share £222.50/3, Pentland ferry £132/3, Boat Charter £400/5, Hostel £25, Rapness to Kirwall £5, Golden Mariana £5 and bus £2.10. Grand Total of £235 each.

The Steller's Eider became the 11th record since 1950 and stayed until 25th January 2020.

On 13th November I received the following email:

Dear Mr Bagnell,

Re: Behaviour towards Jenifer Foley 9/11/2019

It is with regret that I am emailing you today on behalf of the Papay Development Trust. It has come to my

196

attention through a variety of channels that your behaviour on our island on Saturday 9th November 2019 falls below the expectation what we expect from visitors to our fragile community.

Since 1999, we have worked tirelessly to promote and encourage development through the Papay Development Plan and your behaviour towards Jennifer Foley (Director, Papa Westray Building Preservation Trust) is deemed totally inappropriate. As a consequence we are pursuing a writ through the Crown Office and Procurator Fiscal Service, Sheriff Court Watergate, Kirkwall, Orkney KW15 1PD to ban you indefinitely from all trust land on Papa Westray, Orkney.

If you wish to contact the trust to contest before we direct our solicitors JEP Robertson & Son to act on our behalf, please reply to this email with a statement of intent for your actions on Saturday or use the contact telephone number on our website.

Your faithfully
Julian Branscome
Secretary, Papay Development Trust.

I decided to contact Julian to see if this was a hoax. Julian replied, "Love it, and what did you do to Jennifer?" I explained what I had said above and added, "I also sent her an apology letter just in case I upset her. I didn't think she was upset because she was happy to take a photograph of the six of us in the heated waiting room". Julian then said "If you needed to write a letter of apology, then I'm glad you did. She's great. She works tirelessly to look after visitors on the island. I very much doubt she did, not her style at all."

After this remarkable twitch I agreed with Julian to promote Papa Westray by mentioning that you can book Loganair flights (01856) 872494 to Papa Westray return for £32 and stay on Papa Westray at Beltane House (01857)645321.

This hoax reminded me of the time I got a letter from the MoD in the late 80s when I was spotted climbing a security fence at Biggin Hill Airport. This letter was sent to my home address. I found out it was sent by boss's wife, Yvonne, who

COMMON NIGHTHAWK
Chordeiles minor
Galgorm. Antrim
8th October 2019

G.BAGNELL

overheard me talking about this exploit whilst I was working at Upjohn Pharmaceuticals.

Both were class wind-ups and both initially got me worried. Well done.

SUMMARY

During 2019, I travelled 6,861 miles in Britain and Ireland in the pursuit of new birds and managed to increase my list by 4 BOU/IRBC species. This took my British and Irish list to 532 species. The Combined Official stood at 630, so I had now seen 84.4% of them. There was just one addition to the Official British and Irish List during the year - Least Bittern (2019 in Kerry)

The four lifers in the table above are Brown Booby (10-year), Tengmalm's Owl (5-year), Steller's Eider (4-year) and Common Nighthawk (1-year).

This year, the most important bird seen during the year must be the Common Nighthawk. The simplicity of this twitch and the absence of a twitchable one for 20 years stacked the decks in its favour.

2019	Regular	Vagrant	BBRC/ IRBC 1 year	BBRC/ IRBC 2 year	BBRC/ IRBC 3 year	BBRC/ IRBC 4 year	BBRC/ IRBC 5 year	BBRC/ IRBC 10 year	BBRC/ IRBC 20 year	BBRC/ IRBC Lifetime	Cat B	Total
Seen	277	38	89	12	13	13	44	23	15	8	0	532
During			1			1	1	1				4
B&I Total	277	38	92	14	13	15	50	37	39	47	8	630
	100%	100%	97%	86%	100%	87%	88%	62%	38%	17%	0%	84.4%

CHAPTER 22

2020

The radiotherapy I had last year carries on working in the background. My PSA reading on 1ˢᵗ August 2019 dropped to 4.8 ng/mL and down further on 29ᵗʰ November 2019 to 3.6 ng/mL. The Oncology Department were happy with my progress and suggested it would have dropped faster if I had had the hormone treatment. They will keep monitoring me and believe less than 1.0 ng/mL is achievable. The side effects of erectile dysfunction, bladder problems and gastrointestinal issues are all affecting me now, but on a positive note, I'm now running 50km a month. I'm running 5km at a time now – any more than this would require me visiting the little boys' room.

Certain rare birds that turn up in Europe with near mythical status in Britain have a je ne sais quoi about them. Take the Little Curlew I saw in Schagen, Netherlands on the 18ᵗʰ January 2020. There hasn't been one of these in Britain since 1985, with the previous one in 1982. Seeing it made missing those individuals a bit more bearable. I can't count it on my British and Irish list, but I've now seen it in

a vagrancy context. This trip to Netherlands also allowed me to see a cracking male Dusky Thrush in Belgium before returning home.

The timing of the Little Curlew was fortunate as England entered lockdown on 23ʳᵈ March, with most of Europe having locked down on 18ᵗʰ March. English citizens were only allowed to leave their homes for one hour a day for essentials or exercise.

Rapiscan started home working from Thursday 19th March. My three-bedroom house with its two lounges gave me a perfect opportunity to turn one of them into an office.

The restrictions got a bit easier on 13ᵗʰ May when two people from different households could meet up if a 2-metre separation was maintained. Twitching was made at lot easier from 28ᵗʰ May when groups from 6 different households could meet outdoors.

Lucy Burrell found a Bearded Vulture on the 26th June at 3:40pm as it flew over Windmill Lane, Balsall, West Midlands. This bird had many missing tail feathers and could be tied to a sighting in

Netherlands between 30th May – 13th June and in Belgium on the 20th June. Later that day at around 4:50pm it was seen by Wayne Glossop drifting north over the A50 between Scopton and Foston. Then there was a series of sightings from 30th June to 9th July covering Hassop, Edale, Cressbrook Dale, Big Moor and Margery Hill. On 10th July at 10:20am it dropped into the Upper Derwent Valley and was later found by Dan Pointon on the Cliffs at Howden Edge.

Birdguides announced that the bird was still on the cliffs at 10:41pm. I then started the 4½ hour drive and parked at Strines Inn at 3am with about 15 other cars. I started the trek with others to Crook Clough in the pitch black. The first part of the journey was very tiring as it was uphill. I was wearing my running shoes and the angle of the incline starting to hurt my feet. Robert Pocklington, Paul Baker, John Mercer, John Hewitt and Chris Piner all overtook me during the 6 km walk. This walk would have been impossible for some birders, as one minute you were on nice stepping stones and the next you were knee deep in a bog.

I got to Crook Clough at 4:47am just as daylight was appearing. The Bearded Vulture was still sitting where it had roosted the night before. 43 minutes later it lifted off. It flew towards Black Tor and then came slightly closer and started feeding on a dead sheep. The vulture now had an audience of 70 observers. I was satisfied with my views and because it was quite chilly sitting down, I headed back by myself. The whole experience must rank as one of the best raptor sightings I've ever had in Britain. It was simply breathtaking.

I left at 6:30am and walked 3.6 km to Black Tor, where I turned right instead of left. I only realised my mistake when I arrived at Derwent Reservoir. I did not want to look a fool by U-turning and bumping into people I had said goodbye to earlier, so I continued walking and when I passed the Ladybower Inn, I asked for directions. A kind soul then got his car out of the garage and drove me back to Strines. I calculated that since leaving the vulture I had walked 16.6km in completely the wrong direction.

The only previous Bearded Vulture in the UK was found on 15th May 2016 in Gwent and from 3rd June seen around Devon and Cornwall. BOURC place this individual into Category E.

I only realised that there was a Scopoli's Shearwater lingering in Britain when it was too late. This recent split will be nigh on impossible to ever twitch again in British or Irish Waters. My friend Ewan Urquhart can now tell us his story.

11th August. Mark, my twitching buddy, and I both suffer from anxiety and mild depression, not the ideal combination if you have a mind to go twitching. This often means we are awake in the early hours as sleep eludes us. It was such a night on the 10th August, at 2am, as I scrolled through my messages on my phone. The penultimate one was from Mark, sent at 10pm on the 9th August.

Ring me. I think we need to go to Scotland.

A second message timed an hour later said: Ewan. This bird has been there for two days. Ring me when you get up, please.

I had no idea what Mark was talking about. I somehow knew he would be awake and sent him a text despite the hour. A message came back almost immediately: Am awake call me at any time.

I called and learnt that on the 9th August 2 Cory's Shearwaters had been seen between Hounds Point and South Queensferry in the Firth of Forth near Edinburgh in Scotland and one had a distinctive white patch on its right upper wing. Photos taken of this bird the next day showed it had an underwing extensively white reaching almost to the tip, its bill was slender, and the bird's slighter build compared to its companion pointed to it being a Scopoli's Shearwater, which has been claimed three times in Britain but never officially accepted. So, this was a mega, a potential first for Britain and we needed to be at South Queensferry on 11th August as early as possible.

The upshot of our call was we both left our respective homes in Bedfordshire and Oxfordshire half an hour later. I left a note for my wife on the kitchen table: Gone to Scotland. Rare Bird.

We had arranged to rendezvous at Leicester North Services near the M1. At 4am we met up and in minutes were driving north in Mark's car. In my dazed state I had left my bins behind, but it was too late and anyway my scope was probably more essential.

We drove steadily north. Mark called fellow twitcher Cliff, who was a hundred miles further up the road, and we learned there was a pleasure boat that sailed from South Queensferry and would cruise round the approximate area where the shearwaters had been seen. We booked onto it online en route. Checking the weather, the forecast was grim, predicting low-lying cloud and an increasing threat of rain. Dawn rose and all was well until approaching Newcastle on the A1 we came to a huge jam of cars as three lanes of traffic tried to merge into one. At the very last moment we veered off the motorway and up a slip road that fortuitously took us on another route via the Tyne Tunnel. If we had got caught in the jam it would have been twitch over.

I took over the driving at Berwick and we crossed into Scotland. Road signs appeared stating 'Yellow warning Heavy rain predicted'.

Our marathon journey ended seven hours later at 11am in South Queensferry, and we parked almost under the iconic Forth Railway Bridge. We made for the pleasure boat terminal as Mark called Steve, another twitcher friend, who told us the shearwater was currently flying about in the Firth just off Hound Point, which lay a mile east.

We instantly abandoned the pleasure cruise and drove as far as we could towards Hound Point. The rest would have to be accomplished on foot. Both of us were now like taut strings. The long tiring drive with its emotional rollercoaster of minor triumphs and potential disasters was now over, but now we were confronting a situation which demanded instant decisions and actions, any one of which, if wrong, would precipitate disaster.

We joined another dozen twitchers lined abreast on a pier looking out onto the murky Firth. Surely someone was on the shearwater, but no one could see it even though it had been reported as flying towards the pier from Hound Point. It was decided to walk as fast as we could on the track to Hound Point, but halfway there someone received a call that the shearwater was now coming our way. Instantaneously we about turned on the track and desperately sought the first possible gap in the trees that allowed us onto the adjacent shoreline where we hoped to intercept the bird as it flew up the Firth. Minutes later we were lined up and scoping the sea expectantly for a full 10 minutes, before there came the familiar words from a birder down the line that send you into paroxysms of tension and anxiety: "I can see it. It's flying out to the left, from behind the moored oil tanker."

I looked but could see nothing but the moored oil tanker.

Then more words: "It's flown back behind the oil tanker."

Damn, I had missed it. Not sharp enough. Then it re-appeared but still I failed to get onto it before it was lost to view behind the now familiar tanker. I was advised that when visible the Scopoli's was *far out and just about discernible in the murk, but for the life of me I could not find it.*

My heart sank. Tired, dishevelled, and disconsolate, I contemplated the unpalatable fact that my ageing eyes, lack of sleep and unforeseen incompetence with my scope were continuing to frustrate me at this moment of potential triumph.

Others confirmed their joyous individual discovery of the bird as it continued to appear and disappear behind the oil tanker. Eventually I was the only one who had not seen it. From experience I knew not to panic, to compose myself and try to relax and not let the rising tension make things worse.

The shearwater appeared once more. "It's flying above the red flag," someone said.

Then revelation. I saw it! It was obvious. How had I missed it before? It flew low over the sea, a long-winged, languid, gull-like vision of happiness.

The ultimate horror scenario of having to drive home knowing I had been in the bird's presence but not able to see it was banished forever and now relaxing, with the pressure off, I of course was able to relocate it time and time again.

The bird disappeared and ten minutes later was relocated nearer to the iconic bridge. We made a 400m dash along a rocky seaweedy shoreline and there it was sitting on the sea, closer now and preening, before it rose and flew around, conveniently banking to show the diagnostic underwing pattern. It flew a couple of lazy circles and then steadily flew east and away out into the Firth and was finally lost to view. Although we were not to know it at the time this was the last anyone would see of it. Many birders rushing to join us arrived just too late and dipped. The shearwater had been present in the Firth for just three hours and we had seen it at virtually the last opportunity.

I guess about twenty of us had watched it for ten to fifteen minutes and naturally everyone was jubilant. I called my wife to tell her where we were, mentioning the bridge. "Oh," she said, "that was where Dad flew his Spitfire under the bridge in the war."

The Scopoli's Shearwater became the third record for Britain. It was originally found by D. Gilmore and R. Stonehouse on 21st July at Whitburn, Co. Durham and seen between 9-11th August in Kinghorn Harbour, Fife by J.S. Nadin.

On Tuesday 15th September on Tiree, John Bowler casually opened the curtains to his lounge and spotted a Yellow-bellied Flycatcher in his garden. John was familiar with this species after seeing them in Mexico and Belize.

The next morning, I booked two return foot tickets with Caledonia McBrayne to Tiree for John Lees and myself. I booked the Oban-Tiree crossing on Thursday with a return on Friday. I failed to find any available accommodation on Tiree despite ringing 20 different numbers. The only place available seemed to be the campsite, and this prompted me to visit Argos and purchase a two-man tent.

John and I left Southwater at 5:30pm. We arrived at Oban at 2:48am and slept in the car until 6am. The pay and display car park was too complicated for my simple little brain to operate and I'm so thankful Chris Bell was there to press the right buttons for a £10 two-day parking ticket to drop out.

John and I carried our scopes, roll mat, tent, sleeping bags and rucksack for the 10-minute walk around Oban railway station to the ferry terminal. We had to wear face masks in the terminal building and always keep 2 metres apart. These masks certainly made it quite difficult to identify twitchers. The ferry departed at 7am and at 8:47 we heard the flycatcher was still there. We docked at 11:05am and took a 20-minute minibus ride to John Bowler's house. Here we met Hayley (Tiree ranger) who asked us to wait until John was ready to take our group to see the flycatcher. I clapped eyes on the Yellow-bellied Flycatcher at 11:30am. When John first found the flycatcher, he emailed his RSPB employers for guidance on what to do with a British first. They suggested suppressing the news, as Tiree is a small Island with zero Covid-19 cases and bringing 100 twitchers to the island was bound to bring the disease. But somehow the news was leaked, and when John Bowler was quizzed about it, he confirmed the bird was here.

I managed to get a few digiscoped shots of the flycatcher but had to leave at 1:15pm when John's wife returned home. Matt Wilmott could see I was struggling to carry my gear and offered to drive it to the campsite for me.

One of Matt's passengers, Terry, was telling me to f*ck off when I was watching the flycatcher. Initially I thought I was hearing things, but then he said it again. I decided to bite my lip and try to block his voice whilst watching the bird. He then told me to f*ck off when I was loading my gear into Matt's boot. I'm so glad I didn't react any of this swearing, as I found out that he was in the early stages of Alzheimer's and probably didn't realise what he was saying. Another of Matt's passengers, Steve, had an artificial leg and at times was placing it on the car dash. I just hope all of them had a comfortable night sleeping in a cramped car.

John and I were reunited with our luggage at 3pm. The campsite had ample space to setup the tent, and it also had a shower, toilet, and a couple of pods and bothies. Tents were erected by Chris Bell and his girlfriend Angela, Chris Griffin, Peter Stronach and me. Peter probably had the best

strategy to twitch Tiree. He and Bob Swann had both brought their bicycles and tent onto the ferry. I had a couple of hours to kill and decided to do a run from the campsite to John Bowler's house and back. This turned out to be 9 km long and took me 58 minutes and 13 seconds to complete. I got back by 6pm and dived into the shower.

That evening the plan was for Matt to drive us in small groups to the Tiree Lodge Hotel in Gott Bay for dinner. Our tables were booked for 7:45pm and it was a tasty meal. There was a bit of a scene at the restaurant when Terry lost his camera in the restaurant and accused the restaurant staff of stealing it. The staff found the camera in the lounge area where Terry had originally sat.

After dinner Matt took me and John back to the campsite first. I don't think John had ever camped before and this was not a good time for a 75-year-old lying down to sleep on cold ground in just a sleeping bag. If only we could have booked a warm bothy for him. I on the other hand woke up every hour with a sore back and due to the radiotherapy, I had to make a frequent sorties across the campsite for the toilet.

At 9am the next morning the minibus picked us all up and took us to Scarinish, where we had a socially distanced group photograph outside the ferry terminal, then grabbed a coffee from a young lady at Maclennan Motors' shop (01879) 220555. I found out she was a keen runner, and her mum owned the business.

The ferry arrived at 10:57am and got us to Oban at 3:25pm. The cost worked out £119 each (Diesel £112, Ferry return £42, Campsite £24, Taxi £10, Parking £10 split 2 ways plus £20 donation).

I got a phone call from George Kinnard on the 29th September saying, "Have you heard the news?" I said, "No, what?" He replied, "Tennessee Warbler on Yell, Shetland". I instantly felt sick, as I knew I had just one day to get it before the month end started.

Just after 11am I tried to book a flight at 6:50am Aberdeen to Sumburgh with evening return for £430. I filled in my name, address, 16-digit credit card number, expiry date, CVV and it errored and threw me out. I logged back in, and the flight was now sold out. Loganair confirmed that I hadn't booked anything.

At 12:50pm I heard on WhatsApp that the 6:50am flight now had some availability. The fare had gone up to £484, but I still booked it. Philip gave me permission for leave on the proviso that I was available to work 9am on Thursday. My first stop was Broadbridge Heath Halfords, who fitted a new headlamp bulb in seconds for £16.

I got to Aberdeen Airport around midnight and asked if I could park the night at the Premier Inn Hotel. The guy on reception said he thought that would be £6. This offer was soon declined when he checked with his manager and realised I wasn't a hotel guest. I ended up parking in an industrial estate at Wellheads Terrace (near Emerson building) at 0:45am, then walked 2.8km to the airport terminal building.

Sleeping in the terminal building was difficult at best. The airport floor was being cleaned with an industrial cleaner and the quietest place I could find was a sofa with no arm rests near the closed bar. Around 2:30am a security guy woke me and asked me what time my flight was. So kind!

The plane only had 30 passengers and all the aisle seats were unoccupied, which to me is hardly full. I landed at Sumburgh and managed to share the cost of a car rental with Chris Batty and Paul Ellis. Just as I left the airport a stone flew up and chipped the windscreen.

The journey from Sumburgh to Toft ferry terminal is 49 miles and takes about an hour to drive. At 8:32am we got the news that there had been no sign of the warbler during a brief search, but we still took the 9:15 crossing to Yell. The crossing takes 20 minutes and Burravoe is then 5 miles away. I parked just down the road from the primary school and a houseowner led us to the exact garden where the Tennessee Warbler had been seen the previous day. The homeowner pointed at the sycamore tree where it had last been seen. Right then, we could see a Yellow-browed Warbler at the base of this sycamore in a small pine.

Then at 10:05am Malcolm Roxby, Richard Stephenson, Paul Ellis, Bob Watts and I all saw a Chiffchaff-sized bird fly into the top of the sycamore. I failed to see it move through the tree, but the other 4 guys started following it. Paul shouted out "That's the Tennessee Warbler!" He managed to see its dagger-shaped black bill, white-tipped tertial tips, white vent, and brightly coloured yellow breast.

I was getting more and more frustrated as I couldn't connect with the directions being given. All the other nearby birders (approx 20) failed to see it over the next two hours. I got permission to view this sycamore from another neighbour's garden, but there was still no sign. The Edinburgh flight brought another 20 birders to Burravoe.

Birders were becoming desperate and decided to spread out and check various hedges and gardens towards the coast. The strong gusts were hampering the search and people thought the Tennessee Warbler would be hunkered down somewhere less exposed.

At 2pm I went back to the car for a kip. At 4pm Chris and Paul returned. Most of the twitchers were now watching a showy Olive-backed Pipit on the mainland. On the way to Sumburgh a Siberian Thrush mega'd at Fife, and being powerless to do anything about it I just sat back and ate fish and chips in Lerwick.

We departed Sumburgh at 7:40pm and once back in Aberdeen Chris dropped me at the Emerson building in Wellands Terrace. If only I had known there were two Emerson buildings, aaaarrrrggghhh! I eventually found the right building and located my car at 10:15pm. The maps app on my phone suggested I should be home by 7:45am, but I was severely sleep deprived and got home at 9:37am. I had 4 kip stops and took the expensive M6 toll to save time.

On logging into my work computer I got the rotten news that the Tennessee Warbler had been seen at 9:55am at Burravoe in better weather and showed for the rest of the day.

This Tennessee Warbler cost: Diesel £120, Flight £484, Car Hire £34/3, unleaded fuel £15/3, ferry £26/3, toll £4.70 & windscreen charge £150/3. My share worked out at £683.70.

The next few days of work became unbearable, especially on Friday 2nd October when an Eyebrowed Thrush was found on North Ronaldsay. Now there were two ticks in Scotland plus the Tennessee Warbler that I wanted to get a better view of. My weekend was free, but I had the further constraint of having to be back at work on Monday 5th October.

I left home Friday at 6:56pm and headed back north. I got to Kilminning in Fife at 4am Saturday, parked in a car park and slept. When I woke at 7am, there were many more cars there. The light was improving and a few birds starting flittering about. At 7:39am a guy drove around and said the Siberian Thrush was currently showing in the other car park. I didn't know there was another car park. The other one had three cars in it, and I asked one of the guys if he had seen the bird. He replied, "Yes, it was in the dark patch of whitethorn. I saw it in exactly the same place yesterday morning".

The crowd really started to build, and the bird was possibly seen in flight at 10:14am, but the rain soon got heavier, and people retreated to their cars. I stood out in the rain with my scope and a big brolly covering me. At 12:20pm, I saw the Siberian Thrush, a first-winter bird, for about 30 seconds on and off. It was feeding on the berries with two Song Thrushes. The views were good, but the Siberian was never fully visible. The first feature I saw was its speckled underparts, then it moved up a little and I could see the bold supercilium and white facial pattern and black bill. Then it dropped down again, and you could see its lower parts, and then the next time it moved up I could see its head. It was quite near the top of the whitethorn at this stage, so I shouted out "I've got it!" and people starting shouting for directions. Sadly the 30 birders now in attendance didn't see it. The main problem was that they were all sitting in their, cars and because the bird was buried deep in the whitethorn with just a few gaps, you needed to be at the right angle to see it.

The next time I saw it was 5:19pm along with John Pegden and Dave Woodhouse, sitting in different cars. This time it was seen much lower down and facing me. The supercilium made it look like it was wearing a cap on its head. The view was just 5 seconds in total. At 5:40pm I got my 3rd view, and again it was head on. This time I managed to get it in the scope and could see black breast spots, quite a few of them forming a dark line just above the breast. Then it did a quick 180-degree turn and jumped straight back into cover. This view lasted 20 seconds. I had seen the bird for less than a minute over the course of a day, so it must rank as one of the most elusive birds I've ever encountered.

Dave drove John and me to Crail's Fish Bar & Café, where we all ate fish and chips before getting a couple of pints in the Golf Hotel. Then all three of us positioned our cars close to where we had last seen the Siberian Thrush and went to sleep.

Next morning many more cars start arriving and everybody parked nicely in a row until the whole car park became full. Then "Mr Happy" arrived. He parked his black Nissan D40 Navara with Truckman Grand hardtop on the grass between the rowan bushes the Siberian Thrush favoured and the parked cars.

John Pegden tried to have a calm conversation with him. I heard John say, "We've been here all night, waiting patiently to see the bird first thing in the morning and you turn up late. You're going to ruin my visit by parking your truck here". The man agreed to move back 3 metres in total, which was pretty pathetic in the scheme of things.

The Siberian Thrush didn't show at first light, surprise surprise, and during the morning the crowd swelled to 70 observers. The weather was now dry, so if it showed people would be in for a treat. At 9am a Sparrowhawk went through and took a thrush-sized bird. Nobody could see what species it was, but if flew off with it in its talons. Luckily for the crowd, the Siberian Thrush was still alive, and it was seen by a few people at 9:08am. I missed it. There was another sighting at 10:20am and I missed it again. I did watch it move through the rowans about 6 feet off the ground and saw its head side on through the scope for 15-20 seconds. Some others had it briefly before in the same vicinity. I last saw it fly down at 12:00pm.

I left Fife at 12:30pm and had to be happy with my 5/6 views over a two-day period. It just made me wonder how Ken Shaw had managed to find this bird in the first place. Before I forget to mention it, there was a nice showy Common Rosefinch seen here. I got home at 8:45pm, having spent £106 on diesel.

The next day, Monday 5th October, I woke up at 8am and my first task of the day was to check Birdguides for any news of the Eyebrowed Thrush on North Ron. No news yet, but I estimated that I could get to North Ronaldsay on Wednesday, so with positive news, I took the risk and booked non-refundable flights.

On the Tuesday the Eyebrowed Thrush was still present, but the Siberian Thrush had gone. I left home at 3pm with John Lees and made my third trip to Scotland in a week. I was gliding around the M25 and just as we joined the M40 John Lees announced that the Tennessee Warbler was back on Yell (3:53pm). This time it had moved 20 miles from the very south of Yell to the north, at Breckon.

At 4:30pm another mega alert went off. This time it was another Tennessee Warbler, found at Inishboffin, Galway. We drove into Scrabster at 3:31am, having narrowly missed hitting two Red Deer on the A9. When the alarm woke me up at 5:30am there was no sign of life at Scrabster. I wander around in the dark, and it didn't look like we would be departing at 6:30am. I checked my ticket and it said Stromness to Scrabster. Shit! I'd booked it the wrong way round.

By 7:30am I had changed the tickets and we drove onto the ferry and sat in the canteen. John was in the queue for food at 8:24am when the Tennessee Warbler was reported back at Cullivoe. I rushed over to tell him, and immediately we booked Thursday 9:05am flights from Kirkwall to Sumburgh. £278.92 went on the credit card. Now that we were flying on to Sumburgh, we needed to plan how to get my car off Orkney. The ferry from Shetland to Orkney only operates on Wednesday and Friday and that meant we would need a hire car on Shetland for two days. I rang my usual car hire company, who said they could only give me my old car with a cracked windscreen.

The following news on Birdguides put me into a tizz:

9:15am No further sign of Cullivoe Tennessee Warbler.

10:02am Eyebrowed Thrush not seen on North Ronaldsway.

How low can you go on these trips? I had waited 5 days to go for the Eyebrowed Thrush and then picked the day it decided to leave.

Just as we got off the ferry, we read "10:33am Eyebrowed Thrush on Brae, Shetland Mainland". I was now thinking we should cancel our North Ron flight and see if we could get an earlier flight to Sumburgh. Then I heard that the Inishboffin Tennessee Warbler was showing, but Ireland was now closed due to Covid restrictions.

We arrive at Kirkwall at 10:45am. We couldn't get a refund on our North Ron flights, but we managed to change our Kirkwall flight to leave Sumburgh today at 2pm.

At 11:08am we read that the first-winter male Eyebrowed Thrush was still at North Ron and my mood improved. Logainair must really love me, as I had to move the Kirkwall flight back to the original day. We departed at 1:35pm and 15 minutes later we had landed and were waiting for the hold luggage. The seven birders on the flight were John Pegden, Al Orton, Malc Curtin, Ewan Urquhart, Mark Rayment, John and me. John Pegden spotted the Eyebrowed Thrush at 2:25pm, whilst we heard that another had been found on Fetlar.

We watched the Eyebrowed Thrush for 2 hours before flying into Kirkwall at 5:54pm. That evening the two Johns, Malc and I ate at the Kirkwall Hotel. I treated myself to soup of the day, steak and sticky toffee pudding with a pint of Tennants.

During dinner we debated what John and I should do about the Tennessee Warbler. Al suggested I should speak to Chris Griffin. I rang him, and he reckoned the Tennessee Warbler had gone midmorning with lots of migrants. Decision made – I was cancelling tomorrow's flight to Sumburgh and requesting a refund.

We left Kirkwall harbour at 11:45pm and arrived at Aberdeen 7am Thursday.

The bird cost us £224.82 each (£240.17 return ferry with car, £72 North Ron flights, £134.47 diesel, and £3 Kirkwall parking). Loganair did refund the Sumburgh flight after 3 days.

The Tennessee Warbler was found by Dougie Preston and became the 5th record for Britain. It was seen on Burravoe from 27th September to 4th October, and the same bird presumably relocated to Breckon from 5th to 7th October.

The 1st CY female Siberian Thrush was found by Ken Shaw on 30th September and was last seen on 5th October. It was only the 13th record for Britain.

The North Ronaldsay Eyebrowed Thrush was found by Dante Shepherd on 2nd October. It remained to 8th October and became the 24th record for Britain.

On Saturday 17th October, I woke up at 9am to find I had two missed calls. The messages were from John Lees and Christian Melgar talking about some type of rare robin in Norfolk. Turned out it was a Rufous-tailed Scrub Robin. It was clear I needed to get dressed and out of bed pronto. I had breakfast and at 9:40am Liz, John and Christian arrived. We arrived at Stiffkey at 1:30pm. Car spaces were appearing as birders were leaving, and I parked near Luke Nash and Harry Witts' car. They said I would need wellingtons as it was high tide. I put my wellies on and jogged 250m to the crowds. My timing was impeccable. the robin just came out of a bush and sat in a hole where it was visible at 1:44pm, staying for 5 minutes. Views were good and Mike Edgecombe remarked that this was the first time it had showed in over an hour.

The police were now on site and making sure people were practising social distancing. By 3pm we had more then enough views and decided to feed our bellies at a Swaffham fish and chip shop. As soon as we got inside, the heavens opened.

This was the first twitchable Rufous-tailed Scrub Robin since 2nd September 1963, when Richard Richardson received the news on a postcard about one at a Skegness holiday camp. Ron Johns had gone for it with Richard at the weekend. A campus security guy wouldn't let either of them into the campus and they had to make do with wandering around the security fence. They failed to see it. The bird would have been there, as it was seen by others on Monday 9th September. It was great news that Ron had finally managed to get a 57-year-old grip back. Sadly, Richard Richardson never saw it as he died in 1977.

John Reeves found the Rufous-tailed Scrub Robin on 17th October and it hung around for five days. It became the 6th record for Britain since 1950 and it was estimated that 2,000 people managed to see it.

On Tuesday 20th October some high-profile birders were discussing the identification of a Brown Shrike at Johnny Brown's Common in Yorkshire and saying it could possibly be the much rarer Red-tailed Shrike. By 2pm when I joined the crowd watching it, the consensus had swung firmly back to Brown Shrike. I had a cunning plan. I still needed Stejnger's Stonechat for my British and Irish list and if it all went wrong with the Shrike (as it had) I could then descend on South Gare for the possible Stonechat.

South Gare is 88 miles further north, and I arrived at 4:30pm whilst Chris Bell was giving me phone directions where to see it from. He said "You need to drive past the steel works and as soon as you spot a fly-tipped fridge freezer, pull over.

The Stonechat has been frequenting the dried-up reed bed".

I had a good wander about and couldn't see the Stonechat on this side of the reed bed. I managed to cross a sand bar to get to the other side, but I still couldn't see the bird. Unbeknown to me John Dunnett was watching it in the fading light at 5:45pm from the side my car was parked on. John is a local and was responsible for identifying a Long-toed Stint at Salthome, Cleveland, in 1982. What a legend!

The light was virtually all gone now, so I decided to drive to Redcar for some mangé. Locals advised that you couldn't go wrong with a fast food joint called Marco's 2. This establishment does kebabs, fish and chips, burgers etc. I chose a half-pounder and chips for £5.50 and let me tell you, you can go wrong. All the chips were horrid and had to be chucked in the bin. My only option was to drive to Tesco and get a midnight feast.

I parked the car back at South Gare and cracked open a bottle of Budweiser with some nibbles before bed. That night from 9:30pm to 00:30am I had four visits from different police patrol vehicles. Each time they shone a torch into my car and asked if I was all right." I wasn't prepared to stay there a moment longer, so as soon as the police disappeared, I drove my car with its one working headlamp towards Redcar, where I finally found somewhere dark and quiet to sleep. I only woke up when my alarm went off.

I was back at South Gare at first light. I set the scope up and saw the presumed Stejnger's Stonechat briefly in the reed bed. Ian Foster later arrived, and it was nice to have a chat as the Stonechat started showing again. I told him about my police visits and he laughed and told me South Gare was a well-known dogging site.

Before driving back, I took Ian's recommendation

to stop at the first garage I could find. Here the garage owner asked his young enthusiastic car mechanic, who I later discovered had ADHD, to fit my headlamp. Halfords generally have fitters with nimble fingers who can unclip an old bulb and replace it with a new one in a minute. Today, this friendly mechanic decided to take my bumper off and every conceivable screw near the headlamp. I watched him for 30 minutes and he did successfully fit the new bulb, and only charged £10. Bargain.

I would have got home a lot earlier if Peter Afrey hadn't found another presumed Stejnger's Stonechat at Medmerry, Sussex. I got to Medmerry at 5pm and stayed watching the bird till dusk. This individual didn't seem as dark as the Cleveland bird and a poo sample was collected earlier in the day by Matt Eades for DNA testing

The South Gare Stonechat DNA results came back as a 1st year CY male Stejneger's Stonechat. It was available from 17th-30th October and became the 10th record for Britain. No DNA was found in the Medmerry sample.

On Sunday 25th October an Indigo Bunting mega'd on St. Agnes whilst I was watching Tony Cook's Dusky Warbler in Bewbush, Crawley. That night, I left home at 8:22pm with my old and faithful friend John Lees and we parked up at Marazion at 2:33am and slept. I wasn't confident that the Indigo Bunting would stay the night, so I was pleasantly surprised when it was reported at 7:36am. I drove the short distance to Penzance Heliport and bumped into John Sawyer with his new lady love. John had thrown the towel in on British twitching, and was only there for a romantic week on Scilly's. He did admit that once he arrived on St. Mary's he would take the first boat to St. Agnes. I watched them take off on a Sloane Augusta 109 helicopter for the first flight of the day.

Later Ashley Howe, Kevin Hale, Oli Mockridge and David Viles arrived for our flight. David was the father of impressively knowledgeable Birdguide employee Sam Viles. Our helicopter departed at 11am and landed at Tresco at 11:20.

The previous evening, I got everything organised by booking a boat direct to St. Agnes with Tresco Boat Association, but on arrival we had some bad news. Our boat had been cancelled for a last-minute VIP party, and they had no other boats available. This could have potentially ruined the trip. I'm so thankful for the guy at the helicopter desk who contacted Joe Pinder, who diverted an outbound St. Mary's boat to pick us up at Tresco before reaching St. Agnes. What a hero!

I jogged all the way to New Grimsby quay and got stopped by a security man. He said, "Sorry, you are not allowed to wait on the quay. Can you please sit in the waiting room." I was sweaty from the run and the last place I wanted to sit was in a waiting room full of people. I just stood outside it. Then I understood why I hadn't been allowed on the quay. Some very familiar faces were disembarking from a recently arrived boat – Prince William, Princess Kate, Prince George, Princess Charlotte and Prince Louis, with a bodyguard. They got into fancy cars at the bottom of the quay and drove past me on their way to Dolphin House. Typical – the future King of England was the VIP who pulled rank by pinching our boat.

Joe Pinder's boat arrived at 12:32pm with Mark Telfer and his wife on board. They had both been staying on Bryher and the only way they could get to St. Agnes was to go to St. Mary's first. We docked at St. Agnes at 1pm, and Ashley and I jogged to a big bonfire by a big pool. On arrival the Indigo Bunting was being watched by birding biker Gary Prescott, Higgo, and John Sawyer. Yay, John made it. The bird was only a few feet away and constantly feeding. There was a piece of

Indigo Bunting
passerina cyanea
Isle of Scilly: St Agnes
26th October 2020

GARRY BAGNALL

bracken attached to its body that it hadn't manage to dislodge since being blown over at 8am. John Sawyer explained how lucky we were. The bunting was originally seen at 11:05am when it flew into a hedge and hid for 94 minutes, and it had only just come to feed, at 12:39pm. We watched it until 1:55pm, when it walked out of view. We tried to relocate it but failed.

Mission accomplished, all six of us were ready to catch the 2:15pm boat back to St Mary's. Just as the scheduled Kingfisher boat arrived, off jumped Steve Gantlett, Dan Pointon and John Pegden. We told them the bunting hadn't been seen for 20 minutes but they were bound to re-find it. At St.

Marys we ate a delicious meat pasty and failed to see a nearby Nightingale.

The *Scillonian* arrived late at 3:45pm, with around 20 miserable-looking birders on board. It departed at 4:10pm. We got into Penzance at 6:57pm, and because of the social distancing protocol it took 30 minutes for everybody to disembark. Ashley drove me and John back to the heliport, but it was in complete darkness and the gates were padlocked. The 24-hour security number was rung and then my phone went dead. I had to climb over the fence and start my car to get the phone charging before ringing them back. When I told them we were locked in at the heliport they said they would send someone over to unlock us, but couldn't give us a time. 30 minutes later somebody arrived, and we got home at 1:19am on Tuesday.

The Indigo Bunting was found by L.R. Cross and became the third record for Britain. Ashley and I were the last birders to see it, although the next day 30 birders continued the search.

The last twitchable Indigo Bunting was on Ramsey Island from 18th-26th October 1996. Ireland had one on Cape Clear from 9th-19th October 1985.

SUMMARY

During 2020, I travelled 7,644 miles in Britain and Ireland in the pursuit of new birds and managed to increase my list by 9 BOU/IRBC species. This took my British and Irish list to 541 species. The Combined Official stood at 635 species, and I had seen 85.2% of them. There were 5 additions to the Official British and Irish List during the year: Falcated Duck (1986), White-rumped Swift (2018), Dalmatian Pelican (2016), Eastern Orphean Warbler (2017), Hudsonian Whimbrel (Split 1955), Eastern Black-eared Wheatear (Split) and removal of Steppe Grey Shrike.

The 9 lifers in the table above are Dalmatian Pelican (Lifetime), White-winged Scoter, Tennessee Warbler & Indigo Bunting (10-year), Falcated Duck, Rufous Bush Chat & Stejneger's Stonechat (5-year), Siberian Thrush (4-year) and Eyebrowed Thrush (2-year).

Covid-19 had certainly made birdwatching difficult. By the end of 2020 the global deaths were reported at 1,813,188 with a further 1.2 million that didn't get officially reported. Covid was the main reason Britain's Ruby-crowned Kinglet was suppressed on Barra. It was found by Ian Ricketts on 12th November and lingered until 19th November.

On a more positive note, I'm not sure if anybody has noticed, but I was now only 9 birds away from my target of 550.

The most important bird seen during 2020 had to be the Indigo Bunting. Any birds from the 1996 era that I could have seen if I was not a plane spotter were the most valuable, to me even more important than a first.

2020	Regular	Vagrant	BBRC/IRBC 1 year	BBRC/IRBC 2 year	BBRC/IRBC 3 year	BBRC/IRBC 4 year	BBRC/IRBC 5 year	BBRC/IRBC 10 year	BBRC/IRBC 20 year	BBRC/IRBC Lifetime	Cat B	Total
Seen	277	38	89	13	13	14	47	26	15	9	0	541
During				1		1	3	3		1		9
B&I Total	277	38	92	13	14	15	52	37	39	50	8	635
	100%	100%	97%	100%	93%	93%	90%	70%	38%	18%	0%	85.2%

CHAPTER 23

2021

The year started with Rapiscan keeping non-essential office staff working from home, which improved the work-life balance of many people. My daily commute was a 45-mile round trip and not driving freed up 90 minutes per day. Lunchbreaks last year got me taking my bins for a daily walk around Southwater Country Park and Stakers Lake. This January I decided to have another go at listing birds seen on foot. In January 2013 I managed to see 60 different species on foot in Crawley, so it would be interesting how Southwater fared.

My January footlist got off to a good start on Saturday 2nd with 22 different species seen at the two lakes. The wintering flock now had 34 Tufted Ducks. On 10th January the footlist moved to 38 different species as I wandered a larger area, including farmland. I was particularly pleased to find one day a female Gadwall at Stakers Lake and a flyover Little Egret. By Saturday 16th I was up to 50 species. New birds for the region including 2 Egyptian Geese and Meadow Pipit and finch numbers were up to 60 Siskins and 3 Lesser Redpolls at the Country Park.

Over the next week, new species were drying up. I managed to add 6 more, which including 93 Fieldfare at Stammerham Farm, Jay, Stock Dove, Canada Goose, Kingfisher and Pheasant. I pushed the boat out on the 30th by walking 7km to the Knepp estate. This place got the list moving with Great White Egret, 8 Pochard, Teal, 4 Snipe, Shoveler, Wigeon and Skylark. I finished the month on 63 species with Southwater getting a resounding victory over Crawley's total.

Covid brought about big changes to both the girls in my life. Georgie had left Millais the previous year and started a travel and tourism course at Collier's College in September 2020. Due to Covid Georgie rarely attended school. She missed out on her prom and her exam grades were estimated based on her teacher's assessment.

In March 2019, Kim took a gamble by leaving Ghyll Manor Hotel. She had worked there has a housekeeper for 23 years, but now she decided to join Schroders in North Horsham as an office cleaner. Schroders kept their offices open throughout Covid and for their employees' safety they wanted their empty offices deep cleaned every Sunday. This work was quoted by an outside firm and then given to a daytime cleaning team for the same price. Kim jumped at the chance of earning treble time. The extra cash paid for a corner sofa, Italian porcelain, patio slabs, patio furniture and a gazebo, with spare cash in the bank.

It also allowed us to purchase an important addition to the family. Kim, Georgie, and I had concluded that our house desperately needed a four-legged friend to keep us all sane in the crazy world we were living in. I had worked at home for nearly a year, with no plans for an office return. There had never been a better time to get a dog.

The girls did plenty of research of what breed would best suit the family. They wanted a dog that was chilled out, not too big, rarely barked, got on with cats and didn't need loads of exercise. These requirements were best matched by a Cavachon, a King Charles Spaniel crossed with a Bichon Frise. Georgie found a breeder in Crystal Palace, but she could only chose a puppy from the litter based on what could be seen on WhatsApp, as Covid restrictions prevented any home visits. The girls named the dog Barney and on the 20th February all three of us met our 8-week old Puppy in the flesh for the first time. The breeders carried two puppies out of their house and brought them into their back garden for their respective owners. Both puppies looked adorable, and when Barney was handed to Georgie, all three of us got emotional. The breeders allowed us to meet Barney's mother and suggested it would be nice to have a dog family reunion one day.

Barney settled into our home very nicely. He slept in a metal crate overnight in my office and during the working week he slept on the three-piece suite behind my desk.

From 11th February a Northern Mockingbird was found hanging around an Exmouth garden, but lockdown rules prevented anybody driving long distance to see it. Step one of the government road map allowed people to leave home for non-essential travel from the 29th March, and most twitchers then saw the legally. However, the roadmap didn't allow for foreign travel, so a wintering Double-crested Cormorant on Carrig Island, Kerry, in Ireland was still out of bounds. There was a brief window to travel to Ireland before Christmas 2020, which I will write about in the next chapter.

April 7th marked the last day the Northern Mockingbird was seen in Exmouth, but it was miraculously found the next day in Pulborough village at 11am. This is just 9 miles (13km) as the crow flies from my house. Barney was now 15 weeks old, and I wasn't prepared to leave him and shoot off for a new bird. I casually waited for Kim to leave Schroders and be home at 3:30pm. I parked up in a housing estate at 3:57pm and had a 3-minute walk to join an admiring crowd of 40 birders. The bird was showing down to 10 metres away as it sat in low scrub. It did fly to a nearby kiddies' playground for a couple of minutes, but soon returned to the scrub. I watched it for 90 minutes nonstop and didn't see it feed once.

It was nice to chat to the many birders present, including my Pokémon buddy Lee Beadell, who works in Horsham but lives in Pulborough. Lee has missed many good birds in Sussex, so he wasn't prepared to miss this one.

This started when Chris Biddle posted an image of a bird on Twitter asking if it could be a Northern Mockingbird. It was first seen in January and became the third record for Britain. The first accepted record was on 30th August 1982 in Saltash, Cornwall, and the second was on Horsey Island, Essex, from 17th to 23rd May 1988.

Christine Lindsay next spotted the new bird in her garden on 7th April. She photographed it and sent a picture of it to Liam Curson, who instantly recognised it as a Northern Mockingbird. The news was quickly broadcast. Christine's bird only stayed one day, but the story didn't end there. It was found in another private garden from 6th to 9th May in Newbiggin, Northumberland.

Straight after the Northern Mockingbird excitement I was back in the garden preparing the ground for a new patio. Kim and I chose the smooth Marshall Symphony range of porcelain slabs. They were treble the cost of Indian sandstone, but they shouldn't discolour over time. The patio was finished by 15th September with lots of help from my stepson Andrew and his cousin Leah. The total cost of material and plant came to £3,166 and we could have easily spent a further £6,000 on labour if we had called in professionals. I don't think we did a bad job, but I did regret allowing Barney to run riot in the garden, destroying string lines used for marking out the patio. The patio at the bottom of the garden is 6.09m long x 3.65m wide and looks ok if you don't look too hard, but the one outside the house is 9.15m long x 1.3m wide and has a kink at the midpoint where I changed the angle slabs were being laid so they didn't touch the house. I now can't stop myself looking at other people's patios to see if they are straighter than mine. I easily get depressed when I see miles of perfectly straight tiles on airport concourses. Aaarrrgghhhhh! I need help!

April 2021 was an important month for Georgie. She turned 17 on 21st April, and she was so excited about having her first driving lesson. Not only was she driving, she got her first part-time job, working as a waitress at the Queen's Head pub in Barns Green.

Has anybody heard of an American punk rock band called The Offspring? I hadn't, but the cheeky devils decided to use the Washington Post picture of John Lees and me on one of their YouTube videos. This band has sold 40 million records worldwide, making them one of the best-selling punk rock bands in history.

Spring 2021 was quiet in Britain until the 8th June, when all hell broke loose. David Price was staying on the Old Lighthouse on Lundy and was checking his moth trap when he heard a bird sing on a stone wall nearby. The song went *tst-tst-tst-tst-tst* and was unfamiliar to David. When he saw the bird, he thought it might be a Radde's Warbler. However, the bird moved into Millcombe valley and warden Dean Jones took a photograph that was passed to Tim Jones, who shared it on Twitter.

Cliff Smith now recounts what happens next. I'd like to thank Cliff for this write up:

I was working from home that day when a message came through on a twitchers' WhatsApp group at about 10:30am with a photo of a Dusky Warbler on Lundy. They were querying the ID.

This was quickly followed up by someone else suggesting Sulphur-bellied Warbler. This was when panic mode kicked in. Suddenly I was checking my work diary for any upcoming meetings for the next couple of days. Oldenburg sailings were checked, and not sailing or fully booked was the consensus, and there was a message on the group that someone had managed to charter a boat for the following morning at 5am for 12 passengers at £50 a head. the WhatsApp group burst into a flurry of messages with circa 40 people asking for a seat. Unfortunately I wasn't one of the lucky 12! What followed on the group were further confirmations of other charters going over the next two days and a clamour for seats. I managed to book a seat for the following day. Sorted, back to work!

About 12:30pm my phone rang, and I could see it was a friend of mine, a very keen twitcher. Answered call and the first thing he said was could I get to Ilfracombe by 6pm? Yes, why? Well, it seems he had managed to book a diving boat to get us across to Lundy that evening for a couple of hours, again for 12 people at £60 a head. I immediately said yes and hung up saying "I'll see you later."

I used Google Maps to check journey time from home to Ilfracombe – two and a half hours, allowing for traffic and parking etc. I thought I'd allow three hours, then back to the laptop and work. I couldn't concentrate. What if there was a road closure, what if I had a puncture? Sod it, I'm leaving now! I was on the road by 1pm. Five hours allowed for a two-and-a-half-hour journey seemed about right!

An hour or so into the journey a WhatsApp message popped up on the display of the car (thank goodness for Apple play) asking if anyone could get to Ilfracombe by 4pm as a spare seat on a charter had become available. A quick check of the satnav suggested I could make it with 15 minutes to spare, so I replied saying yes and it was duly confirmed that I had the space. I let the organizer of the 6pm charter know my plans and said I'd pay my way on that boat if they couldn't fill my now vacant seat. Game on!

Pin drops had been sent on the group for best parking etc. and I got there in good time to see several friends getting ready in the car park. We were making our way to the quay when I realised two boats were about to leave at 4pm. A few mates on the other boat waved and smiled happily as they pulled away from the quay!

Our boat was still three short of the required 12 passengers, and a few quick calls confirmed people were either running late or had dropped out. A quick vote was taken, and we decided to leave on time and share the costs among those who were on the boat, now about £90 a head! We cast off and left the harbour, chasing the other boat which had left circa 10 minutes before us. Journey time to Lundy was about an hour and a half, and we asked the skipper to get his foot down. We were slowly catching the other boat and about a mile or so from Lundy we crept past them, exchanging the requisite hand gestures!

We docked at the pier on Lundy and disembarked in a heap of chubby birders and optics to see the next challenge of the route uphill to Millcombe Valley, where the bird was last seen. Some ran, some walked fast and some just contemplated the slog uphill by having a couple of fags!

On arriving as a sweaty mess at the large white house, there followed some confusion, as nobody knew the bird's last location and none of the birders on the island were in sight. We stood around vaguely staring at trees until a birder appeared on the track leading further uphill towards the pub. He advised us that the bird had last been seen about an hour before in the shrubs and trees behind the white house. We spread out, by now about 20 strong, looking and listening and checking every slightest movement.

I picked up a bird that looked right behind the house, on some wire cages surrounding some saplings. It was in the company of a couple of chiffchaffs. I quietly called those nearest to me. The bird was quite distant and moving right towards another couple of caged saplings and general brambles and undergrowth, but nobody could get on the bird to confirm the ID.

Circa 20 minutes later the bird was picked up on call by another of the guys on our boat. We all gathered on a narrow path looking down into the undergrowth about 75 yards away. The bird eventually came into view and its ID was agreed by all. The cameras started clattering away, and even I took a couple of exceptionally bad photos with an old bridge camera. Time to get the news out that the bird was still there for the people on the 6pm boats (now three boats had been arranged for them).

I took a back of camera photo with my phone and sprinted up the hill to get a signal to tweet out the news to the services and send a WhatsApp message to the group, as I knew there were about another 20 members on the evening boats. Once I had done that it was back down the hill to enjoy the bird, which was very actively feeding and mobile. A small group of us watched it for another half hour before deciding a celebratory drink was in order, so we slowly walked up the hill to the pub to enjoy a refreshing beer or two. We could see the other three boats arriving, so we decided to go back down to help ensure everyone connected.

The other birders on the last boats arrived in various states of distress after climbing the hill.

The bird had become slightly more elusive and was now sticking to the tree canopy, although we had earlier enjoyed views of it feeding in the open on the quarry face. But thankfully everyone had connected, and it was a happy band of birders that headed back to Ilfracombe that evening for a fish supper at the local chippy. The only downside of the whole experience was not all the boats were filled (60 seats), and it was thought that only about 48 had managed to get to Ilfracombe on time (I had to pay for both of my seats).

That day I was hosting a Teams meeting at 2pm, and all I could do was get a charter a boat for the next morning. Normally I would advertise my boat spaces on Twitter, but on this occasion, all twelve spaces were taken without a single tweet. The boat company wanted a bank transfer that day, which meant I had to collect the money before leaving home.

I left home at midnight with John Lees and got to Ilfracombe quay at 6am. One of the charter boat reps on the quay told me that a birder had turned up yesterday just after 6pm and said, "Here's a thousand pounds, take me to Lundy". This story didn't surprise me. To some individuals there is no limit to what they are prepared to spend on seeing a bird.

We left the quay at 8am, but the RIB had too many heavy crashes and bangs for John's liking. He didn't want to come back on it. During the crossing Steve Nuttall said his friend Steve Richards has mentioned on WhatsApp group that he had just found the bird on Lundy. Once we docked, I rushed to the gathered twitchers and asked where the warbler was. Everybody looked glum. I said Steve Richards had apparently found it. Josh Jones calmly told me that Steve had found a Subalpine Warbler, but the Sulphur-belled Warbler hadn't been seen.

The Sulphur-belled Warbler looked like it had gone, and when I set my telescope up, I found that the crashing and banging it had received from the RIB was preventing it from focusing. What a downer. I consoled myself by going to the Marisco Tavern for a bite to eat with Scotsman Donald Wilson. After lunch I indicated to the charter boat that we were happy to come back as soon as possible. John in the meantime wandered over to the captain of the MS *Oldenburg* and asked if he could go back with them. The captain said, "You could if we weren't full". John had no choice but to come back with us. This time sat he sat at the back of the RIB instead of the front. The crossing was much calmer. The highlight on the trip must have been hearing my favourite childhood song on Radio 2 "Puff the Magic Dragon".

The Sulphur-belled Warbler would become the first record for Britain if the BOURC decided to accept it.

On 14th June at 11:53am, an adult Egyptian Vulture flew over Peninnis Head. It spent the next two hours on Tresco and was last seen at 2:40pm flying low over St. Mary's golf course. The next day 40 twitchers chartered boats from Penzance, but failed to catch up with it.

Ireland's Double-crested Cormorant disappeared on 30th May, but Ireland was keeping a very high standard when news came of a male Least Tern found at Portrane point, Dublin, on the 19th June. It was the second for Britain and Ireland and second for the Western Palearctic.

I was pleased to read that Ireland was allowing international travel from 19th July. The conditions for entry were proof of Covid vaccination and a passenger locator form. The expensive PCR (polymerase chain reaction) test had been dropped. The Least Tern was still present on the 18th July, so I booked an 8:55am Ryan Air flight from Gatwick to Dublin for the next day. The Budget car hire desk was permanently shut in Dublin's international terminal, so security walked me to an open desk in the second terminal. The drive to the Brook pub at Portrane took 20 minutes and it was a further 20 minutes' walk along the beach to the tern colony. Here it was kind of Vic Caschera and Brian McCloskey to help me look for the tern. All three of us searched from 11:30am to dusk. Sadly, we didn't get a sniff of the Least Tern, but we did make a four-legged friend in the process. The terrier-type dog must have followed us around

for four hours until at 5pm its owner come back for it. All three of us ate at the Brook and I decided to sleep the night in the car.

Next morning, again there was no sign of the Least Tern between 6-6:30am. There was a report of the Egyptian Vulture being seen at Avoca, Wicklow the previous day. I decided to spend the day at Avoca with the remote possibility that the Vulture might decide to re-appear. Several hours were spent chatting to Hugh Delaney and Des Higgins with no sign of the bird. I drove back to the usual Budget car hire desk on the Dublin perimeter, and this too was closed. The sign on the gate read, "All rental cars need returning to airport car park". I flew home and only realised when I got home that I had left my power bank in the hire car. Budget Car hire rang me the next day, but not about the power bank. An angry operative said "You've left the car interior covered in sand and it's not acceptable. We have no choice but to charge you €68.10 for a valet". I said, "There was no cleaning facility in the unlit car park, and no operative to hand the car keys back to either". That will be the last time I use Budget.

By the way, they said they had found my power bank but it wasn't until I had been chasing them for a few weeks that they sent it to me. When the parcel arrived it was a car holder for a Motorola phone, certainly not mine, and it went straight in the garbage bin.

This trip costs were: Car rental €140, valet €68.10, petrol €20, Accommodation not used €21, Toll €6, Train fare £12.20, Flight £70, Passenger locator form £27. Totaling £174 plus £40 for my lost phone charger.

Whilst I was over in Ireland Vic asked if I had seen the Black-browed Albatross at Bempton. I hadn't and Vic and Brian said I should go and see it. That seed grew and grew in my head and flowered on the 30th August, when I went for it. The albatross was first seen at Bempton on the 28th June this year. Since then many thousands of tourists have seen it, and it has appeared on Springwatch. I felt confident of seeing it, especially when it was seen the previous day at 3:40pm. I hung around at the famous Staple Newk watch point and watched 13,000 Gannets, but there were zero Albatrosses.

Once the rain set in, I cut my losses and visited the National Railway Museum in York. I've never been there, and I couldn't believe it was free to enter. I did see some wonderful trains and rolling stock. This brought back fond memories of the times I used to drive trains on my model railway with my late father. I was disappointed not to see the Flying Scotsman there, as this was one of the best presents my late dad ever bought me. I found out that the Flying Scotsman was being worked on in Crewe and hopefully one day I will get to see it in real life. I made a small diversion on the way home to see a White-tailed Plover at Blacktoft Sands.

I didn't have to wait long for my next chance of seeing the Black-browed Albatross. on Thursday 9th September at 1pm, a Green Warbler was trapped and ringed by Mark Thomas.

The next day I put out a tweet at 7:07am and asked for an update on it. Dawn Erskine replied 6 minutes later saying it was still there. John and Liz Costa arrived at my house at 8:10am and we started the journey north in the rush hour. The journey took 5 hours and 45 minutes, mainly because of an accident on the M1, when we temporarily came off the M1 at junction 28 and headed to Mansfield.

It was 25 minutes before I got my first brief view of the Green Warbler, and I didn't see the wingbar. The next time it appeared was 4:05pm, when it showed for over a minute by some crab apples. I also enjoyed this view in the scope, when I made sure I saw the yellow super and throat and the white belly, and this time I saw its faint wing bar and leg ring. The whole time I was waiting to see the warbler I was conscious that others were enjoying the Albatross at Staple Newk. I wasn't prepared to wait another hour for the Green Warbler to show, I decided to head to Staple Newk. En route I met a guy sitting on a park bench who informed me I had just missed the Albatross; it had gone out to sea.

Nearly an hour went by, and then Toby Carter called me over and asked me to look at a distant speck sitting on the sea through his scope. He thought it might be the Albatross. At 6:10pm the Albatross flew towards us and did a close fly-past before landing on Staple Newk. My god, this whole experience was so enthralling, and it wasn't even a tick.

I bumped into a lady outside the RSPB building who was writing a poem about the albatross. She recorded our conversation about my experience, and to witness this passion in her enhanced the whole trip for me. That twitch probably ranks as one of the best I've ever been on. The albatross views were sensational, far superior to what I saw on Sula Sgeir. On the way home we celebrated with fish and chips at Howden Fish Bar.

The Green Warbler was found by Mark Thomas and became the 10th record for Britain. It stayed from 9th to 14th September.

On 27th October at 6:32pm news broke of a Varied Thrush in Papa Westray. I was unfazed about it after missing the Sulphur-bellied Warbler and just couldn't be bothered with a 12-hour drive and the hassle of trying to get onto a charter boat. Later that evening Andrew Lawson rang me and said, "I'm going tomorrow night, we've got a boat charter booked for Friday and there's a space if you want it?" I initially said no and thanked him for the offer, but during the evening I looked at the

1982 monochrome type picture in Collins "Rare Birds in Britain & Ireland" and then read the write up by Chris Wormwell about his successful twitch, which ended with the words "Pity there won't be another." I rang Andrew back and said, "If there's still a space I'd like to go". The space was confirmed after he checked with Mark Rayment.

The next day the Varied Thrush was still there, so it was all systems go. I finished work at 4:30pm and agreed to meet Andrew at Dartford. Long delays were being advertised towards Dartford and this could have jeopardized the trip if Andrew waited for me instead. We agreed that I would drive clockwise around the M25 and rendezvous near Alconbury on A1M. We arrived at Gills Bay at 7:15am, having admired a perched Barn Owl on route.

I was interviewed by Rob Flett on BBC Radio Orkney about the twitch and then got the pleasant news that Georgie had only gone and passed her driving theory test. This brilliant news coupled with hearing that the Varied Thrush was still present, was all I needed for a superb trip. We took the 9:30am Pentland Ferry's *Alfred* to St. Margaret's Hope and departed on the charter boat at 11:40am. The 11-man team consisted of Adrian Webb, Les Holiwell, Andrew Lawson, Mark Rayment, Ewan Urquhart, Steve Nuttall, Adam Archer, Andrew Tongue, Martin Davis, Gordon Beck and me. Stefan McElwee was due to be on the boat, but his flight was delayed on Shetland and Mark agreed with the skipper to pick him up later. I noticed Gordon loitering around the harbour and in the end he grabbed Stefan's place.

The sailing to Papa Westray was under cover and we arrived at 1:15pm. Here we met a bus that took us straight to the links, taking about 15 minutes. On arrival there was already a big crowd and no sign of the Varied Thrush. I chatted to

Simon King, who said it had been showing well earlier but had disappeared just before we arrived.

An hour went by and still no sign. Steve Nuttall decided to use his initiative and knock on the door of Sue and Tony Curtis to see if they minded checking out the compound in their back garden. Tony then walked into this walled area and within a minute out flew the Varied Thrush and landed on the lawn. The 40 birders got stonking views as it fed on worms on the front garden. Not the best weather for photographs, as rain was persistent.

Mark Rayment had had a whip round and handed David Roche (the finder) a bottle of Scotch. On site there was a collection bucket and David Roche organised a Gofundme page. These donations totaled £795 and were split between Bird Conservation Nepal and a local charity.

By 4pm the rain had got heavier, and I decided to start walking back towards the charter boat. Martin decided to join me. It wasn't long before the minibus swung by to pick us both up and take us to the quay, and the charter boat returned us to Kirkwall. This trip had been planned to a T, and the ten of us were booked into Ardconnel B&B (01856-876786) in Kirkwall. Andrew drove there, and we managed to grab a modern-looking room with double and single beds, WC with shower and coffee-making facilities. Some of the other lads weren't so quick at choosing their rooms and had to share double beds. Ooops!

The lovely owner, Teresa, drove us first to the off-licence for booze and then on to the Indian Garden restaurant in Kirkwall. The restaurant doesn't serve alcohol but encourages customers to bring their own. We had a group photo taken of our crew plus four others in the restaurant (Chris Waring, Paul Baker, Phil Locker and the very talented bird artist Phil Jones). I opted for my usual Lamb Jalfrezi and once we finished eating Teresa picked us up and took us back to the B&B, where she served us a nightcap of rhubarb gin. Teresa was amazing, and I will certainly be staying with her again in Orkney.

We left the B&B at 6am Saturday morning to catch the 7:30am Pentland Ferry and I was home by 11:45pm. My share of the trip was £261.50 (£82.50 fuel, £54 Gill Bay ferry, £50 charter boat, £10 minibus, £50 B&B and £15 donations).

The Varied Thrush was found by David Roche and became the 2nd for Britain. He found it on 28th November and it stayed to 1st November. The only other record is a monochrome bird that spent 10 days in Nanquidno, Cornwall, in November 1982.

This bird gave me the inspiration to set up the Casual Twitchers WhatsApp group. My group isn't designed for the hardcore twitchers, who are already well connected and generally get to see all the difficult birds that visit our shores. I just wanted to give others the opportunities to visit these difficult islands and see these birds for themselves in real life and not just in magazines. The group now has 200+ members and the admin function is shared between Wayne Glossop, Fiona McClean, Jason Stannage and me. We have members all over Britain. Group members share their sightings, photos, videos, maps, viewing tips and parking, answer questions and most importantly make friends. We have a separate group for sharing lifts. The group was formed on 31st October, a bit too late to help others see the Varied Thrush.

Wayne Glossop was instrumental in helping many people see a wintering Belted Kingfisher. This bird was originally found on the River Ribble at Brockholes LWT and was present from 28th November to 7th December 2021. This site was very much hit and miss. Then Wayne's fishing contacts tipped him off that it had been seen at a private fishing lake next to the River Darwen in Samlesbury. We paid a farmer £10 to access his land so that we could see the kingfisher feeding on the river. Between 20th December 2021 and 19th April 2022 it had over a thousand admirers.

Fiona McClean has been another amazing addition to the team with her local knowledge of Scottish specialties. We now have 20 women members in the group and with Fiona's help this is area we wish to expand on.

Jason Stannage runs many successful rare bird Facebook groups. He has a wealth of bird knowledge and is very experienced in dealing with admin issues that crop up from time to time.

Paul Herrieven is not part of the admin group but has helped the group with merchandising, which I will mention in the next chapter.

SUMMARY

During 2021, I travelled 2,691 miles in Britain and Ireland in the pursuit of new birds and managed to increase my list by 4 BOU/IRBC species. This took my British and Irish list to 545 different species.

2021	Regular	Vagrant	BBRC/ IRBC 1 year	BBRC/ IRBC 2 year	BBRC/ IRBC 3 year	BBRC/ IRBC 4 year	BBRC/ IRBC 5 year	BBRC/ IRBC 10 year	BBRC/ IRBC 20 year	BBRC/ IRBC Lifetime	Cat B	Total
Seen	277	38	90	13	13	14	48	26	17	9	0	545
During			1				1		2			4
B&I Total	277	38	93	13	14	15	52	37	40	49	8	636
	100%	100%	97%	100%	93%	93%	92%	70%	43%	18%	0%	85.7%

The Combined Official stands at 636, so I have seen 85.7% of them. There was one addition to the Official British and Irish List during the year – Eastern Subalpine Warbler (split).

The 4 lifers in the table above are Varied Thrush & Northern Mockingbird (20-year), Green Warbler (5-year), Eastern Subalpine Warbler (1-year).

I was now only 5 birds away from my target of 550 and felt I should get there in the next couple of years. Would 600 be possible?

The most important bird seen during the year had to be the Varied Thrush, the first one for 39 years. Many thought this bird would never repeat, but it has.

Varied Thrush
Ixoreus naevius
Papa Westray · Orkney
29th October 2021

G. BAGNELL

CHAPTER 24

2022

One Casual Twitchers member suggested we should have a pin or badge to recognise each other in the field. We were fortunate to have Paul Herrieven as a group member because he was running a company called "Birding Pins". Paul was selling mugs, pins, T-shirts, key rings and bags all depicting rare birds that have visited Britain.

Our first task was to get a group emblem. I decided to run a Twitter poll on 29th January and asked if our club emblem should be the Black-browed Albatross, Belted Kingfisher, Varied Thrush, or not a bird. Surprisingly we got 192 votes and the share of votes were 32.8%, 18.2%, 11.5% and 37.5% respectively. The non-bird won it. Our member Chris Holt suggested binoculars, and then Paul and his Chinese design team did their magic and made one hundred pins. The emblem allowed T-shirts, mugs, and bags to be created. Paul gave all merchandise profit back to the group and by end of February we had raised £206.

The drawings contained in this book all started life on the 21st January 2022. Over the next 14 weeks, I drew twenty-four birds in my spare time using Faber-Castell Polychromos pencils. Early on, Steph Murphy suggested ditching my scratch pad and using hot pressed 300g/m2 paper. Steph gave me drawing tips and videos on techniques, and I really started getting into my artistic journey.

When news of an American Robin was found in Hill Road in Eastbourne, I arrived next day at 7:30am with Barney in tow for his first twitch. The bird showed well, and it was nice to meet Fiona McLean for the first time. She had driven overnight from Glasgow by herself. Barney even managed to appear in a photograph used for the local newspapers, showing 50+ twitchers all looking at the American Robin with Barney looking directly at the photographer. Knowing Barney, he thought he was going to get a treat. He didn't get one from the photographer but he did from Fiona.

Loads of the Casual Twitchers visited the American visitor during its 20-day stay and Charlie Peverett set up a GoFundMe page for it.

All donations went to Eastbourne Food Bank, which supports people around the city who are struggling to feed themselves and their families. Charlie managed to raise £2,865 including Casual Twitchers' first donation of £115.

On Valentine's Day a Double-crested Cormorant was found at Doon Lough in Leitrim. Good chance it was it was the same 1st summer bird found by Seamus Enright on Carrig Island.

Prime Minister Michael Martin allowed travel between Irish counties on the 18th December 2020 to facilitate a "different but special" Christmas. Ireland allowed shops, restaurants, gyms and pubs to serve food on same date. This news prompted me to book a night at Castle View Hotel on Carrig Island, which is run by a friendly chap called Garrett, who now owns half of Carrig Island and made his last mortgage payment in December 2020. I arrived late afternoon and for dinner he suggested I drove to the Listowel Arms Hotel. There I had potato and leek soup for starter and ribeye steak for main and it was a culinary delight. Straight after the meal I was back at the hotel to sleep.

Next morning, I left the hotel at 7:30am and arrived at the Cormorant roost in the dark. As soon as light appeared I systematically started checking 300 Cormorants and by 8:50am all of them had left the roost. No DCC on this occasion, but I did see five juveniles. At 10:30am I went back to the hotel for a cooked breakfast and then decided to explore Carrig Island. I took the right fork outside the hotel and passed the causeway road and eventually came to a dead end.

I decided to leave the hire car there and try to walk around the island. I had to climb through brambles, bogs, shingle beaches and long grass fields and didn't find a single Cormorant. When I got back to the Hotel, Garrett's dog decided to walk with me to my car. I was thinking about putting the dog in the car and driving it back to the hotel, but I'm glad I didn't.

I started reversing the car down the single carriageway with a stone wall to my left and a 2-metre sheer drop to my right. The road had no straight sections, just continuous bends for about 1km. I'm not a big fan of reversing and for some reason I decided to stop and open the car door. My god, the car was perilously close to the drop-off. My back tyre was half on the gravel road and half in the drop, like the 1969 *Italian Job* film with the bus overhanging the ravine. If I reversed one more inch, the hire car would fall into the ditch and roll over.

My heart was racing, and I felt scared. I gently put the car into first gear and the front wheel started spinning but did get back onto the tarmac. Phew, what a relief!

When I had calmed down, I decided to search for the Double-crested Cormorant at Saleem Pier. I walked as far right as I could along the bank of the Ballyline river, flushing waders left, right and centre. Then I stayed at the intersection of the river Shannon with the Ballyline and patiently waited for the Cormorants to arrive.

At 3:30pm about 10 Cormorants stopped for a bathe with many flying to the distant roost site. I left and decided to drive back to the roost site. I did see a juvenile Cormorant with a bright gular (throat skin) land in the roost trees in the dying light for about three seconds.

After getting back home, I found that other people had been reviewing the roost on the opposite side of the river near the graveyard. My viewing was from farmland with an acute angle that only showed part of the roost. Never mind, let's fast forward to Tuesday 15th February 2022.

I left home at 5:10pm with John Lees and

Liz Costa. The driving conditions were pleasant, but the wind turned gusty as soon as we entered Anglesey. Lee Gregory was waiting for us at the fish and chip shop in Holyhead. Irish travel relaxed its entry requirements by wanting passenger locator forms and Covid vaccination proof but not the expensive PCR test. Neither were asked for by authorities at Holyhead or Dublin and the only thing they wanted to see was my driving licence.

As soon as we arrived at Doon Lough at 9:08am, Lee spotted the Double-crested Cormorant fishing. It was a second winter bird. Finding the DCC on Carrig island had been like finding a needle in a haystack, but the one on Doon Lough was more like spotting a goldfish in a bowl. The DCC seemed very settled, hanging out with three ordinary Great Cormorants in the little lough. The lough had 6 posts sticking out of the water and when the DCC was not feeding it was sitting on a post, even pushing other Cormorants off to get its desired post. The bird had a rounded head with a bright orange gular, whereas the Great Cormorant has a squarish head with a pale yellow gular. The site has enough space for 6 cars and is only two hours 40 minutes' drive from Dublin.

From Doon Lough we drove to Ballygilgan and found a Lesser Snow Goose with 20 Greenland Whitefronts. We failed to find a Lesser Canada Goose at Ballintemple despite searching through 1,000 Barnacle Geese. We slept at the Bailey (090-645-5846) in Athlone. Liz negotiated a good deal with manager Paidi and we felt safe with a Garda building opposite. I got my own bedroom, and the others got a twin room. I was happy to eat here and for dinner I celebrated with goats' cheese starter, roast leg of Kildare lamb and some sticky toffee pudding. I finally got round to drinking my first pint of Irish Guinness. Why has it taken me so long to sample this delicious ale? Sleeping wasn't easy as my room was directly above the bar and the pub was full of noisy youngsters drinking till closing time.

The next morning, we saw a Northern Harrier at Lough Boora and then spent time looking for a Grey-bellied Brent in Dublin. Brian McCluskey gave me 4-5 pins of where the GBB have been recently seen and at the second location we struck gold. I had seen a GBB before in Norfolk but viewing geese wandering around grass fields in a housing estate needs to be experienced to believed. Totally surreal. We left Dublin at 2:40pm and got home at 1:30am on Friday.

The 2022 trip cost £533 ferry split 4 ways, tolls €19.20/4, Irish fuel €60.00, B&B €150/4 and British fuel £92/3. My share worked out as £218.31. If you combine both DCC trips, the bird had cost me £582.94 plus food.

The 1st winter Double-crested Cormorant was found by Seamus Enright on Carrig Island on the 25th October 2020 and was last seen on 30th May 2021. If this bird gets accepted, it will become the 2nd record for Ireland.

The 2nd winter Double-crested Cormorant was found by bird artist Robert Vaughan on 14th February 2022 and hung around until 16th April 2022. This bird obviously liked the salmon the lake had to offer, as it was back on 15th September 2022.

Brian McCluskey rang on the 26th February to inform me that the adult Egyptian Vulture was back at Lough Funshinagh, Roscommon. I left home that evening at 5:16pm with John. Our first stop was at Oxford services, where I watched an angry customer punching a Perspex screen because he was waiting too long for his KFC meal. I felt sorry for the KFC staff and the queuing customers were too frightened to look this angry man directly in the eye. I had never seen anything like it before.

I took the same route to Ireland as last time.

We got off the Dublin ferry at 5:30am and arrived at Lough Funshinagh at 7:08. Always a good sign when you arrive at a site and see a big crowd all looking through their scopes in the same direction. Yep, they were all watching the Egyptian Vulture, distantly roosting in a tree from the previous night. It only stayed 12 minutes before it flew up high and away but appeared to drop.

John Coveney and Hugh Delaney just missed it, so they were both delighted when it was relocated at 8:08am. We followed John's car and this time the views of the vulture feeding on a sheep carcass were breath-taking. Seeing a European Vulture in the British archipelago is the stuff of dreams. I just hope this EV helps to get the 1999 Booted Eagle accepted. John and I both felt it was mission accomplished and celebrated with a cooked breakfast at the Perfect Day Café in Dublin. We were buzzing and ready to get the 2:45pm ferry back to Wales.

The Egyptian Vulture was originally found by Conor Henry on 31st December 2021 at Roscommon. He found it at same place on 26th February and it stayed to 12th March 2022. The same bird was seen on Scilly last year (14th June). It moved to Dunfanaghy New Lake, Donegal, between 14th and 15th July with miscellaneous sightings in Mayo and Wicklow.

There are only two accepted records of Egyptian Vulture in Britain – one immature shot in 1825 at Kilve, Somerset, and another shot at Pelden, Essex in 1868. Ireland had never had one before.

On 3rd March, Georgie and I attended my half-brother Jack's funeral in Snell Hatch, Crawley. Channel 5 made a documentary called "Cause of Death" and it was aired on 2nd November at 9pm. My half-sisters Sasha Paine and Leanne Harris were heavily featured in the making of this programme. There was video footage of Jack acting erratically before he jumped off a 15-foot bridge on 24th January at 9:15am in Preston. He landed in a shallow river, walked forward, then threw himself back. Three passers-by saw the incident and managed to get him out of the river and perform CPR. He was quickly admitted to Royal Preston Hospital, but died an hour later. As soon as it was proved that there was no third-party involvement the police walked away and allowed the radiologist to determine the cause of death. The radiologist could find no fractures and only a little bit of water at back of the synesis (nose), so he suggested a post-mortem. Professor Tim Dawson, Consultant in Neuropathology, performed an invasive post-mortem. The Coroner, Dr. James Adeley, mentioned that Jack suffered from schizophrenia and was prescribed Olanzapine for it. The toxicology report confirmed he had not taken his medication for over a week and there were traces of cocaine.

The inquest diagnosed cause of death as sudden cardiac arrest with cold water immersion and cocaine intoxication. Such a tragic way for a 31-year-old man to end his life. RIP Jack.

Do you remember I mentioned I wanted to see the Flying Scotsman? Well, on the 17th March I drove Kim, John and Liz up to Canterbury West. We parked in the multi-storey car park at 12:50pm and found that we had missed the arrival of the Flying Scotsman by 20 minutes. Its arrival time and the route taken from London Victoria were shrouded in secrecy. When I got to platform 2, I couldn't believe my eyes. There were a thousand steam train fans waiting at the end of the platform looking at a row of Pullman coaches. Clouds of smoke, but no Scotsman.

A rumour on the platform started circulating that the Flying Scotsman needed to decouple from the Pullmans and take water before its journey through the Kent countryside. They were right, but we had to wait an hour before we could see it. It reversed under the signal box and got quite close as it went up a siding to get water. I went alone to the end of the platform and couldn't stop crying when I finally clapped eyes on this beautiful steam engine. One day, I intend to buy myself a Hornby OO gauge model of it and keep it boxed in a display cabinet. I guess I have this emotional attachment because it reminds me of my happy times with Dad. He left me in this crazy world 23 years ago and at times I still feel like a lost little boy without him. John, Liz and Kim didn't see my tears as I left them in the middle of fans on the platform.

The Flying Scotsman took all four of us on a journey through the Kent countryside. We sat in a Pullman first class carriage being served champagne, coffee, scones and chocolates. It's an experience I will never forget. Throughout the journey there were thousands of people waving to us from different parts of the Kent countryside. The engine was pulling 11 Pullman carriages and left a trail of smoke as it chugged away.

The Flying Scotsman was originally built in Doncaster in 1923 and cost £7,944. It was the first locomotive to reach 100mph and spent time in both America and Australia.

We only made one stop, when everybody was allowed to leave their carriage and walk along the platform to photograph the engine. The journey back to Canterbury West involved a diesel pulling us all back, including the Scotsman.

On 9th May, Georgie drove me to Burgess Hill for her driving test. The 30-minute drive to the test centre was smooth, but when she practised reverse parking, I had to shout "stop!" and pull up her handbrake. She would have hit the car behind. Not a good look to turn up at the test centre with a big dent.

She realised her error and managed to park safely and then drove to the test centre. When her driving examiner came out, he seemed friendly and asked her for her provisional driving licence and to lead him to her car. I don't remember my driving examiners being friendly forty years ago.

I waited for 40 minutes before I saw her driving back into the test centre. Her facial expression didn't look good, but it changed when she was told she had passed. On the way home, I drove, and we were both buzzing. She even decided to keep the test secret from work and her boyfriend Josh.

In March Georgie started working four days a week in a nursery in Horsham town centre, and in May she passed her Travel and Tourism coursework. Naturally, she no longer wanted to catch the bus to work and from the 10th May I was officially carless. Georgie took Kim's Polo and Kim took my Insignia.

On 26th May at 11:52am, an Eleonora's Falcon was found at Sandwich Bay. I couldn't do anything about it and was quite relieved when it was seen at Stodmarsh in the afternoon. The next day was Georgie's day off and the Eleonora's Falcon was seen at Worth Marshes, close to Sandwich Bay. I didn't do anything when I heard the news at 9:55am, but when I heard at 10:48 that it was sitting on a post, it was game on. Georgie drove me to Kim's office and at 11:30am I was in my car driving to Kent. I arrived at Worth Marshes at 1:15. I was not sure where to go and ended up parking in a farmer's field off Goretop Lane. I walked towards the railway line, and was soon sweating like a pig and hyperventilating. Then another birder told me, "You can see it from here, but you'll be better off watching from Great Wood".

I followed this guy car to where everybody else had parked, and at 1:40pm I was with 40+ twitchers standing by a wooden gate. Five minutes later Gary Howard got a phone call saying the Eleonora's Falcon was coming our way, and it did. Absolute magic – I watched it non-stop catching insects from 1:45-2:33pm. To see a brown falcon with long wings, brown moustachial stripe, dark brown underwing coverts, heavily streaked belly felt like being in Majorca. I failed to see the Red-footed Falcon but decided to head home and get back to work.

The Eleonora's Falcon was originally found by Robin Stokes and Andrew Edwards on the 26th May and it stayed until 10:27am on 4th June. Previously there had been 8 accepted records with the last one being a typical flyby found by ex-Crawley birder Mick Davis in Winterton, Norfolk on 20th August 2020.

The best news of the summer came on the 3rd June at 8pm from Vic Caschera and Brian McCloskey, who both told me that the Least Tern was back at Portrane, Dublin. I had been monitoring the Little Tern's situation in Britain, and with no positive news by the end of May I really thought my chance of seeing one this year was over. I heard the Portrane Tern site had been destroyed over the winter, but this only meant the Little Terns would move to another colony.

There wasn't enough time to get a ferry, so I thought it best to leave it till next weekend. I mentioned my plans on Twitter and Richard Sparks was up for going. I left home Friday 10th June at 5:50pm with John, Liz and Richard, and got to Holyhead with plenty of time to spare before the 2:15am ferry. The Least Tern had been seen every day at Portrane since the news broke. Can you believe the day we decide to go there was no sign? But then at 9:22pm a message came saying the Least Tern had been seen briefly in the colony. I investigated this news whilst sitting in my car in the Holyhead carpark and found that the wardens

had not heard it call today; the sighting had been by two German visitors who had seen it at 3pm for 10 seconds flying south along the beach. I wasn't feeling too confident now, and with low expectations I fell straight to sleep on the ferry.

We arrived at Portrane at 6:30am and very soon met wardens Paul Lynch and Brian Carruthers. I really enjoyed chatting to Paul, who was responsible for discovering this colony in the first place. He originally found three pairs of Little Terns there and today this this colony numbers fifteen breeding pairs. Ever since finding this colony Paul and other volunteers have fenced off the area and tried to keep the predators away. A fox was responsible for eating 15 eggs the previous week, but being early in the season the birds should lay again.

Paul shared with me the sad story that his wife had died aged 29, leaving him two sons to bring up. Paul did this whilst devoting his weekends to protecting the terns. I watched him scare away a hovering Kestrel with a hand horn.

Paul and Brian had no luck asking a couple walking their large dog to put it on a lead as they walked past the colony. The dog ran into the colony and owners just didn't give a shit and swore back at the wardens in reply. On this occasion no damage was done but it wasn't nice to witness the rudeness from irresponsible dog owners.

That day there was no sign of the Least Tern at Portrane and Brian McCloskey helped us by searching the Baltray tern colony for it. During the day we met David Fox, Luke Geraty and his dad, Bob Watts, Ross Newham and the two Germans from Friday, who came back. Nobody managed to see the Least Tern at either site and my crew were ready to admit defeat.

I drove us back to Dublin and parked up at the ferry terminal. I was curious how much Stena line would charge for changing departure by one day.

When they told me €20, I went back to the car and told the crew. I rang Brian and Vic and they both indicated that it was worth staying longer, as we knew it would come back at some point.

My crew left the decision up to me, and I decided to stay the night. I drove back to Portrane and all three of them shot in for fish and chips whilst I tried to find digs. There was availability with Dublin hotels, but they were charging €200 a night each. I rang over 50 B&Bs. They were all apologising and saying they were full, but one gave me some more numbers to try. I wasn't expecting much joy. The first place I rang was fully booked, but the second one answered, "We've just received a cancellation for two rooms, do you want them"? I didn't even ask the price and said, "Yes, definitely". This was Lolaido House in Skerries, (01)8492585.

I joined the crew in the fish and chip shop and told them the good news and Liz said, "For that, what do you want to eat? I'm buying". The B&B was wonderful and that evening we left John there whilst Liz, Richard and I drove to Skerries sea front and knocked back some Guinness at Joe May's pub. The quay were advertising boat trips to see Rockabill Island, which is famous for Roseate Terns, and let's not forget the 2005 Anglesey Sooty Tern spent the night there.

At 7am the next morning we arrived at the same time as Paul. It could only have been five minutes before Paul said, "I can hear the Least Tern, look, it's over the colony". I could have kissed him. I ran to the beach and watched the bird from 7:08am. It was carrying a sand eel and displaying to a female Little Tern. He tried his best to woo her for 40 minutes, but she wasn't having it. She must have known he was a different species.

The arrival of Judd Hunt, Phil Bristow, and Alex Bevan was impeccable. They all stood with our group and enjoyed the spectacle. It was certainly good to pick out the grey rump, light yellow bill with black line on upper mandible, muddy coloured legs, and disyllabic call. What a fantastic bird.

After 8am there was no sign, and by 10am we were all ready for the cooked breakfast at the B&B. Later that day we saw a Small Blue butterfly at Portrane and went to North Bull, where we saw a Cuckoo and a Marsh Fritillary butterfly. These two butterflies are quite rare and we celebrated our success at a café in Dublin called Insomnia. I really pushed the boat out – I had a latte and a slice of carrot cake. We took the 8:30pm ferry back and I got home at 6:45am to realise that it was my 55th birthday.

Trip cost: ferry £439/4, diesel £140, B&B €45 each, tolls €6, which worked out at £184.50 each. If you do go, please donate generously to wardens. These guys are doing a tremendous job and they desperately need an electric fence.

The Least Tern was originally identified by Niall Keogh and became the first for Ireland. Britain's only ever Least Tern visited Rye every summer from 1984 to 1992.

On 27th June a Red-tailed Shrike was seen at Staple Newk viewpoint, Bempton Cliff, for a couple of hours in the afternoon. The next day it was re-found at 2:21pm on Cliff Lane. By midday on the 29th I was itching to go and left at 1pm with John, Liz and Hugh Price. During the journey up north it didn't look promising, as the Shrike went missing at 1:47pm. When we arrived at Bridlington by 7:30pm it still hadn't been seen again, so we got food at Busy Bees fish & chips. There was no point in heading home, and we found a reasonably priced room for John and Liz at Winston House. They stayed there whilst Hugh and I decided to check Cliff Lane. As soon as we arrived, somebody found the Shrike feeding very distantly in a hedge at 8:55pm. It was too late to go and pick up John and

Liz, as it would have been dark by the time we got them here. Once it was dark, Hugh and I smooth-talked our way into members-only Flamborough Victoria Club CIU. I had a Guinness nightcap and spent the night sleeping in the car near John's B&B.

Next morning, we all went for the Shrike at first light. There was no sign of it, so I used my initiative and walked to Wandale Farm to search last night's bush at close quarters. I managed amazing views of the Red-tailed at 8:35am and then asked the house owner, Will, if he minded others seeing the Shrike. Initially he wasn't interested, but once he realised he could charge £10 a head and all his family had to do was put up with people walking past their house night and day, he agreed.

John and Liz had missed their breakfast at the digs and with Liz being a diabetic she urgently needed to eat. We found a nice place called the Secret Garden Café at Driffield and had a cooked breakfast. It took 5 hours to get home.

The Red-tailed Shrike (also known as the Turkestan Shrike) was found by Trevor Charlton at Staple Newk and re-found the next day by Ian and Karen Howard. The shrike stayed 62 days and was last seen on 27th August. There have only been 6 accepted records. The others were originally accepted as Isabelline Shrikes, and since the Daurian/Turkestan split the BOURC and BBRC have only managed to ascertain adult birds to one of the two species.

On 13th July Casual Twitchers had sufficient merchandise profit to make Its second donation. This time Martin Collinson got £100 from us for his "Genetic identification of birds - The Aberdeen forensic wildlife laboratory" GoFundMe account. Martin set a target of reaching £10,000 and as I write they are at £3,171.

Birdfair was back this year, and I went for the first time. It was held from 15-17th July at Rutland Showground. I hung out with Fiona McLean for the whole three days, and it was nice to meet 30 different Casual members. Each day we did a team photo and I manged to tick off 12 members I had never met before: Samantha Haworth, Paul Herrieven, Karen Jayne, Holly Page, Peter Roseveare, Oliver Slessor, Ryan Walsh, Dean Reeves, Peter Robinson, Michael Stocker, Pat Douglass and Paul Sung. Overall, I enjoyed my first Birdfair, but I was sad that Bill Oddie wasn't well enough to attend.

Meeting Swedish birding legend Gunnar Engblom was a bonus. Gunnar is in a band called Guran Guran and is a marathon runner. He ran a very popular birding website and now lives in Peru and works as a tour guide.

The easiest first-for-Britain twitch I can remember happened on the 7th August 2022, for a Cape Gull. I left home at midday with John, Liz and Matt Palmer. The northbound car journey was a little unpleasant with my air conditioning system broken, meaning all four windows had to be left open with 28°C outside temperature. As we arrived, Matt read out information on Casual Twitchers about where best to park. By 3pm, we could see the gull sitting distantly on Grafham Water. It didn't take long for it to fly to the edge of the reservoir, which enabled us to grill the features. I could see its thick bill, black eye, size in between Greater Black-backed Gull and Lesser Black-backed Gull, large mirror on P10 and greyish legs. The Cape Gull spent plenty of time eating trout on the water's edge. I must say this was a remarkable find; I don't think I would have given it a second look at Pagham Harbour. That day the reservoir had 1,000 visitors and I managed to sell the remaining pins. It decided to fly at 5:30pm, and that was our cue to leave.

Richard Patient first picked out the Cape Gull

by its leg colour, a feature he had learned from his experience with the species at Simon's Town, South Africa, in 2008. The bird was last seen at 5:40pm flying off the railings near the water tower on 10th August.

Over the last couple of years Kim and I had avoided having family holidays abroad, but in 2022 we did manage a long weekend trip to France. We went in July to meet my sister Chantal and her new man, Patrick, who live in a beautiful house next to the beach in Hardelot.

Talking about sisters, Barney also has a sister. Not a real one, but on the 26th August we bought home "Pepper", a Cavapoo, which is a King Charles Spaniel and Poodle cross. Barney took a few days to accept her, but now they are inseparable in the house.

On 16th September we stayed at a three-bedroom dog friendly cottage called Chaplands in Beaford, Devon. This was a wonderful base for Kim, Tracey, Georgie, Josh, and me to relax. The cottage was decorated to a high spec inside and the dogs loved the acre of garden they had to play in. Most evenings I would get lost walking Barney and we'd end up in the Globe Inn drinking Light Bulb. During the week the family did manage to leave Beaford and visit Torquay, Bideford, and Becky Falls. The day the girls went to Bideford I went in the opposite direction to Bere Ferrers and admired a Roller and Osprey combo. It was a brilliant holiday, and for next year we've already booked another dog friendly cottage in Cornwall. If I had a crystal ball, I would see Kim and me plus dogs living in the South West with a good local pub in retirement. I just wonder if I'll still be doing all the crazy drives for birds.

On 10th October I tried to see a Yellow-browed Bunting that had been trapped and ringed at Sandwich Bird Observatory by head ringer Ian Hunter. The bird was trapped at 11am in an area known as the White House. It was released at 11:30am to an audience of 20 lucky people, including three local birders. I had a great time chatting to warden Stephan Walton and decided to spend the night at the observatory, in case the Bunting was re-trapped in the morning. The Crispin Inn was the place to eat, and I chose delicious sausage and garlic mash, washed down with a pint of Neck Oil IPA. There was no sign the next day, but this dip prompted me to nip over to Holland on the 23rd October and see a 1st winter male in Donderen, Drenthe.

If the Kent individual gets accepted, it will become the 6th record for Britain. The last twitchable one was on Hoy, Orkney, in 1998.

My views of the Tennessee Warbler will haunt me to my grave. As soon as I had the opportunity to see another one in Skokholm, I booked four seats on the *Dale Princess*, which was due to leave Martins Haven at midday on 13th October. I drove overnight with Andrew Lawson and Trevor Ellery, and Amy Schwartz was going to meet us at the quay. There was a slight problem: the bird had not been seen by 9:28am and the boat was cancelled. All three of us consoled ourselves by getting a coffee at Morrisons at Haverfordwest and within half an hour we headed home. We had just gone past the M5 junction on the M4 at 1:12 when Andrew announced that a Blackburnian Warbler had just been found on Bryher. All three of us took a deep breath and hastily re-arranged Friday's plans. I turned the car around and headed down the M5. The beauty of having phone-savvy people in the car was that I could carry on driving whilst everything else got booked. Andrew booked day returns on tomorrow's *Scillonian*, whilst Trevor managed to get three spaces on a boat charter to

Egyptian Vulture
Neophron percnopterus
Lough Funshinagh. Roscommon
27th February 2022
G.BRENNAL

Bryher. First stop was Hayle, where we managed to do some birdwatching. Andrew and Trevor located two Lesser Yellowlegs and got busy trying to photograph them whilst I was mesmerised watching a dreadlocked woman strutting her yoga moves in front of her little dog in the creek. The Hayle fish and chip shop filled a hole and then I took Andrew and Trevor to Helston Premier Inn whilst I slept in the car.

Next morning at 7am we drove to Penzance and parked at the seafront. There were birders walking to the quay from all directions. Paul Chapman and Julian Thomas managed to get the last flight across to Scilly yesterday and arrived at Brhyer a fraction too late to see the Blackburnian Warbler. They spent the night on Bryher and at 7:56am they managed to find it in Popplestone Fields. This was just the kind of news the 302 passengers (mainly birders) on the *Scillonian* wanted to hear.

We left Penzance at 9:15am. I got chatting to a various individuals and it was interesting to find out that Pete Hutchings used to be Trevor Ellery's YOC leader. Pete has normally got his son Jay with him, but today Jay was taking his driving test.

The *Scillonian* moored right next to the charter boat. Five minutes later, I was on the boat with Simon King, Ashley Howe, Graham Jepson, Sam Viles, Andrew Kinghorn, Richard Bonser, Ian Wells, Kevin Hale, and the ex-YOC leader. We arrived on Bryher at 12:20pm and within a 10-minute walk we met a group of birders. They hadn't seen the Blackburnian Warbler for a while, but fortunately, it only took 35 minutes to find. Soon all the passengers on the *Scillonian* had arrived and seen the bird.

It was nice to see John and Liz on Bryher. Liz hadn't seen the Blackburnian because her bins were broken, so she took John's bins and I was on a mission for her to see it. It became my 14th species of American Wood Warbler seen in Britain and Ireland. Once you find a Blackburnian, you can generally follow it feeding high up in the pittosporum and elders for long periods.

I met the finder, John Judge, whose local patch is Draycote Water in Warwickshire. John goes to the Scillies every autumn, and he has singlehandedly put Scilly back on the rarity map. It was good to meet local Robert Lambert and family, plus Ashley Fisher with his dog.

We left Bryher at 3:40pm and boarded the *Scillonian* at 4pm. It was all perfectly organised, with no stress. On the other hand, John and Liz left Bryer at 3:05pm on a small boat and due to low tides they were transferred to a larger one midchannel called the *Britannia*. They then had to sail all the way around Bryher before heading across to St. Mary's. *The Scillonian*, with 340 passengers on board, waited for the *Britannia* to arrive before departing. When I bumped into Pete Hutchins I found out that Jay had narrowly failed his driving test. Bad luck Jay. I finally got home 2 am Saturday with a stop at Exeter.

Trip cost: diesel £162.50, *Scillonian* £105/3, Raptor £20 each. My share £111.

If the Blackburnian Warbler is accepted, it becomes the 4th record for Britain and the first ever twitchable individual. It stayed 17 days to 29th October.

SUMMARY

During 2022, I travelled 4,572 miles in Britain and Ireland in the pursuit of new birds and managed to increase my list by 8 BOU/IRBC species. This took my British and Irish list to 553. The Combined Official stands at 640 species, which means I've now seen 86.4% of them. There were 4 additions to the Official British and Irish List during the year: South Polar Skua (1996), White-chinned Petrel (2020), Yellow-bellied Flycatcher (2020) & Ross's Goose (1970).

The 8 lifers in the table above are Egyptian Vulture & Yellow-belled Flycatcher (Life), Double-crested Cormorant & Least Tern (20-year), Blackburnian Warbler (10-year), Turkestan Shrike & Eleonora's Falcon (5-year), Ross's Goose (2-year)

So - my target of 550 has been achieved. As this is the last chapter about bird sightings I will share the totals on my other lists. I've seen 331 species in Sussex, 388 species in the south-east, 491 species in England and 671 in the Western Palearctic. The world list is something I don't care about.

This year, the most important sighting must be the Egyptian Vulture. This bird was found in the British Isles last year, but before that you have to roll the clocks back 154 years to find a record of the last one. I just hope the British and Irish rarity committees now accept it onto Category A and I can keep it on my list.

2022	Regular	Vagrant	BBRC/IRBC 1 year	BBRC/IRBC 2 year	BBRC/IRBC 3 year	BBRC/IRBC 4 year	BBRC/IRBC 5 year	BBRC/IRBC 10 year	BBRC/IRBC 20 year	BBRC/IRBC Lifetime	Cat B	Total
Seen	277	38	90	14	13	14	50	27	19	11	0	553
During				1			2	1	2	2		8
B&I Total	277	38	93	14	14	15	52	39	40	50	8	640
	100%	100%	97%	100%	93%	93%	96%	69%	48%	22%	0%	86.4%

CHAPTER 25

Summing Up

Time for the final chapter. I now want to give my readers some interesting statistics, starting with birding milestones.

I started birdwatching from age 10 to 14 (1977-81) with my friends Paul Cook and Mushaq Ahmed. During this time, I saw 134 different bird species. I didn't keep a notebook, but I remember seeing most of these birds in Crawley, Arundel and Pagham harbour and getting ticks galore when I visited Minsmere, the RSPB flagship reserve.

I then had an eleven-year break from birdwatching before, in 1992 when I was 25, I got myself a notebook and started keeping a year list. I was keen to see 200 different species and I ended the

year on 201, and saw all the 134 from early years again. Getting such a big year list was massively helped by listening to the recorded telephone news service of Birdline Southeast (1992-98). I restricted myself to only twitch the Southeast, plus the occasional Crawley & Horsham RSPB field trip. Birdwatching had always played second fiddle to aviation, but during July 1999 I was ready to purely focus on birds.

The table above shows that my success rate in seeing new birds has gone from 97% to 72% over the last 24 years. I drove nearly 200,000 miles and spent £23.6k in the process. For a bit of fun, I decided to use RPI to convert the total

No of Species	Mileage	No. of twitches	No. of dips	Success %	Cost	Boats	Planes	Days	Years
200	4,067.0	31	1	97%	£177.40	0	0	5,658	15.5
300	14,923.2	60	5	92%	£849.44	1	0	2,694	7.4
400	41,746.6	81	10	88%	£2,299.62	4	0	838	2.3
500	83,864.2	138	34	75%	£10,672.79	29	21	3,933	10.8
550	54,218.6	74	21	72%	£9,653.28	17	20	3,296	9.0
Total	198,819.6	384	71	82%	£23,652.54	51	41	16,419	45.0

spending figure of £24k into today's money and was shocked to see it rose to £34.3k. That's a big number, but it would double if you combined it with the depreciation of the 8 cars used to see these birds. This includes- sold (1), written off (1) and scrapped (6). My current Vauxhall Insignia is entering its 6th year of ownership and coping with the high mileage the hobby expects. This is much better than the average 2-year car lifecycle.

Table 1 (below) shows the breakdown by country for my 553 different accepted species.

My success rate in Eire is only 50% and close to perfect in England where I can get to most sites same day.

I ran a Twitter poll on the 8th November 2022 to see which band my followers belong to. I managed to get 401 votes with 18% seeing 500+ species, 37% 400-499, 29% 300-399 and 16% less than 300. The biggest group of people voted for the 400-499 range. This is not unsurprisingly as it's where I spent 10.8 years of my twitching career. Very encouraging to see 45% of the vote being less than 399 species. This group of people will get most benefit by joining the Casual Twitcher group, where they can make the necessary friends to help push and motivate them to reach the next milestone.

Tables 2 & 3 (below) show which counties I added the most species between 1999 to 2022 and comparing it to best counties since breaking the 500 barrier (2013).

Table 1

Country	Mileage	No. of birds	Twitches	No. of Dips	% Success	Cost	Boats	Planes
England	100,665.2	330	281	38	86%	£8,202.97	15	6
Wales	8,797.6	9	15	6	60%	£524.67	1	-
Scotland	74,089.4	62	62	13	79%	£10,211.15	22	18
Northern Ireland	60.6	1	1	0	100%	£149.00	0	1
Eire	17,804.4	17	30	15	50%	£4,922.41	15	16
Total	201,417.2	553	389	72	81%	£24,010.20	53	41

Table 2

Nationwide from 1999		
1	YORKSHIRE	24
2	SCILLY	23
3	NORFOLK	22
4	SUFFOLK	19
5	CORNWALL	17
6	SHETLAND	17
7	KENT	16
8	DEVON	15
9	SUSSEX	13
10	DORSET	12

Table 3

Since breaking 500		
1	SHETLAND	9
2	YORKSHIRE	6
3	ORKNEY	5
4	CORNWALL	4
5	SCILLY	4
6	KENT	3
7	OUTER HEBRIDES	3
8	NORFOLK	2
9	SUFFOLK	2

Table 3 (opposite) shows the 9 best counties to live if you don't like driving. Sadly, Sussex no longer features here but fortunately Kent still pulls in the birds.

I've managed to dip 72 times before in Britain and Ireland, but over the years you get another chance to heal some of these dipping wounds. My net dip list is now only 12 species. My most annoying dip is the Yellow-breasted Bunting, which I've missed five times in Britain. I was just too late to see Portland '03, Dursey Island '10, Brownsman '13, Blakeney Point '13 and Out Skerries '17. Considering there's been 231 records in Britain and the Chinese enjoy eating them maybe I need to take the next record Britain and Ireland gets more seriously.

I asked people on Twitter in October 2017 how many people keep a dip list. I was surprised to get 61 different people saying they keep one. The biggest was held by Graham Megson, who had dipped 21 times, with James Hanlon taking silver with 20 dips. Bronze was shared 4 ways on 19 dips by Mick Frosdick, Lee Fuller, David Johnstone and Andy Appleton.

Table 4 (below) shows I've only missed 16 twitchable birds in the last 24 years.

Want to hear my feeble excuses for why I didn't see them? Here goes: The seven-day Cape Clear Blue-winged Warbler was not on my radar back then; people told me not to worry about Ireland as they don't count. The four-day Cape Clear Redhead wasn't attempted because I saw the Kenfig Redhead in 2001, but later this was rejected. The Western Black-eared Wheatear on Scilly stayed four days but wasn't considered a full species in 2010. The Scilly Eastern Orphean Warbler identity wasn't confirmed until the Saturday, which meant waiting to Monday, by which time it had gone. The others were down to work constraints, Covid restrictions or not being focused enough. However most Top listers would not dream of missing so many birds.

Note the numbers Table 5 (overleaf) are purely estimates and may not represent their true total. The 1987 ranking above is taken from an early issue of *Twitching* magazine. In 2022 there isn't a public ranking of listers following the combined official lists of Britain and Ireland and the totals here are estimates based upon rankings published by the UK400 Club, totals entered on Bubo.org, and hearsay. It is likely that the totals here differ from their personal totals, but it gives a feel for the current top ten.

Interestingly, only Chris Heard and Steve Webb feature in both tables.

Table 4

No.	Name	Year	No.	Name	Year
1	Sulphur-bellied Warbler	2021	9	Vega Gull	2016
2	Cabot's Tern	2020	10	Western Black-eared Wheatear	2010
3	Philadelphia Vireo	2020	11	Brown-headed Cowbird	2009
4	Scopolli's Shearwater	2020	12	Caspian Plover	2008
5	Yelkouan Shearwater	2020	13	Purple Martin	2004
6	Yellow-breasted Bunting	2018	14	Redhead	2003
7	Eastern Orphean Warbler	2017	15	Long-tailed Shrike	2000
8	Eastern Kingbird	2016	16	Blue-winged Warbler	2000

Table 5

	Top 10 ranking of listers for Britain and Ireland					
	November 2022				**1987**	
Rank	*Lister*	*Total*	*Rank*	*Lister*		*Total*
1	*Steve Gantlett*	590	1	*Ron Johns*		463
2	*Steve Webb*	588	2	*Chris Heard*		450
3	*Chris Heard*	584	3	*Steve Webb*		448
3	*John Regan*	584	4	*Steve Whitehouse*		445
5	*Brett Richards*	581	5	*Dave Holman*		444
6	*John Hewitt*	580	6	*Steve Broyd*		440
7	*Paul Chapman*	578	7	*Pete Milford*		439
7	*Malcolm Roxby*	578	8	*Edwin Welland*		438
9	*Lee Evans*	577	8	*Eric Phillips*		438
10	*Bill Simpson*	576	10	*Dave Willis*		436

Table 6

	Twitchable misses between 1985 to 1998						
No.	*Name*	*Days*	*Records*	*No.*	*Name*	*Days*	*Records*
1	*Red-breasted Nuthatch*	206	1	11	*Little Curlew*	19	2
2	*Yellow-breasted Bunting*	139	38	12	*Pallas's Sandgrouse*	17	1
3	*Ancient Murrelet*	130	3	13	*Philadelphia Vireo*	17	2
3	*Golden-winged Warbler*	77	1	14	*W. Black-eared Wheatear*	13	3
5	*Nutcracker*	73	5	15	*Red-throated Thrush*	9	1
6	*Great Bustard*	61	5	16	*Yellow-browed Bunting*	8	3
7	*Naumann's Thrush*	56	2	17	*Yellow-throated Vireo*	8	1
7	*Redhead*	41	2	18	*Tree Swallow*	5	1
9	*Grey-tailed Tatler*	31	1	19	*Yellow-bellied Sapsucker*	4	1
10	*Ruppell's Warbler*	22	2	20	*Lark Sparrow*	3	1

Table 6 (above) shows twitchable birds I need that people saw in Britain and Ireland between 1985 to 1998. I've shown the number of days present and number of bird records. I've ignored one-day birds.

I know many people could see more birds if they wanted to. But If I hadn't discovered planes and stayed true to birding, there is a reasonable chance I could have 20 more birds on my list. Therefore 553 + 20 + Kelp Gull acceptance + Blue-winged Warbler = 575. This is only one bird below the estimated total to get into the current Top 10.

I don't have any ambition now to get into the

Top 10. I've missed too many birds to take this competition seriously. I much prefer taking a more casual approach to adding to my list.

Anybody aspiring to get into the Top 10 needs to be prepared for a minimum of 40 years hardcore twitching. I look forward to seeing our three keenest twitchers, Dan Pointon, Chris Batty and Richard Bonser, joining this elite table one day.

That's the end of the book – I hope you've enjoyed it. You can find me on Twitter @ **garrybagnell** and Facebook. Good luck everybody, just go and enjoy the buzz of seeing new birds and visiting remote parts of Britain and Ireland, and don't forget to thank the real stars of the hobby, the finders.

APPENDIX

A word about chartering aircraft

Rare birds turn up everywhere, but especially on islands, where arranging transport is difficult at short notice. As a result, some serious twitchers will consider a charter to get there quickly. I am setting out here what I mean by the use of the word "charter" in this book. I am not normally meaning a "commercial charter", so the word is not being used in any technical sense. It does not imply anyone is making a profit. The legislation relating to owners of boats and planes carrying passengers, especially for money, is complex.

Sometimes companies like Skybus, Loganair, British International Helicopters or smaller diving and fishing charter companies will arrange a commercial charter for twitchers to see a bird. But most of the time, I am referring to cost-sharing arrangements where it suits the owner or the operator of the boat or plane to undertake a trip.

Just like someone getting into a cab on the journey home after a night out, the twitcher is dependent on the pilot or owner for all of the legalities, insurance, etc. Over the years, some birders have obtained pilot's licences and some have friends who own planes or were pilots. Sometimes, a plane could be hired by grouping together as a club and a pilot would be available to help maybe through friends of friends or contacts.

It's a complex area. But the most important thing to remember is that the twitcher is dependent on others. They have no idea what sits behind the calculations or the costs or the legal technicalities. They take on trust others to deal with those. The legislation has changed many times over the years, bringing even more technical issues. Clearly, regardless of the arrangements, these trips are expensive and they come at a risk. All will have read of high profile light aircraft disasters in football relating to a Chelsea director, the Leicester City owner and a Cardiff player.

Twitchers are not immune from these risks and many of their locations are challenging, particularly on small islands with grass strips and often in interesting weather conditions. Such trips are not to be taken lightly, and stories of delays and technical issues are relatively frequent. Indeed, later in the book, I refer to an issue relating to an American Redstart twitch. That pilot was imprisoned for seven offences following a crash:

- recklessly endangering the safety of persons in an aircraft;

- recklessly endangering the safety of persons or property;

- conducting a public transport flight without an Air Operators Certificate;

- acting as pilot without holding an appropriate licence;

- flying outside the aircraft's flight manual limitations;

- flying without insurance; and

- flying without the POH (Pilot's Operating Handbook).

In particular, it was alleged that the pilot had failed to disclose to his insurers that planes that he operated had been involved in three fatal accidents in the preceding years.

Complete list of birds seen to date in Britain and Ireland

No.	Species	Date	Location	Class
1	Red-legged Partridge		Pre notebooks (77-81)	Reg
2	Grey Partridge		Pre notebooks (77-81)	Reg
3	Pheasant		Pre notebooks (77-81)	Reg
4	Brent Goose		Pre notebooks (77-81)	Reg
5	Canada Goose		Pre notebooks (77-81)	Reg
6	Greylag Goose		Pre notebooks (77-81)	Reg
7	White-fronted Goose		Pre notebooks (77-81)	Reg
8	Mute Swan		Pre notebooks (77-81)	Reg
9	Shelduck		Pre notebooks (77-81)	Reg
10	Mandarin Duck		Pre notebooks (77-81)	Reg
11	Garganey		Pre notebooks (77-81)	Reg
12	Shoveler		Pre notebooks (77-81)	Reg
13	Gadwall		Pre notebooks (77-81)	Reg
14	Wigeon		Pre notebooks (77-81)	Reg
15	Mallard		Pre notebooks (77-81)	Reg
16	Pintail		Pre notebooks (77-81)	Reg
17	Teal		Pre notebooks (77-81)	Reg
18	Red-crested Pochard		Pre notebooks (77-81)	Reg
19	Pochard		Pre notebooks (77-81)	Reg
20	Tufted Duck		Pre notebooks (77-81)	Reg
21	Common Scoter		Pre notebooks (77-81)	Reg
22	Goldeneye		Pre notebooks (77-81)	Reg
23	Smew		Pre notebooks (77-81)	Reg
24	Red-breasted Merganser		Pre notebooks (77-81)	Reg
25	Swift		Pre notebooks (77-81)	Reg
26	Cuckoo		Pre notebooks (77-81)	Reg

No.	Species	Date	Location	Class
27	Stock Dove		Pre notebooks (77-81)	Reg
28	Woodpigeon		Pre notebooks (77-81)	Reg
29	Turtle Dove		Pre notebooks (77-81)	Reg
30	Collared Dove		Pre notebooks (77-81)	Reg
31	Moorhen		Pre notebooks (77-81)	Reg
32	Coot		Pre notebooks (77-81)	Reg
33	Little Grebe		Pre notebooks (77-81)	Reg
34	Great Crested Grebe		Pre notebooks (77-81)	Reg
35	Oystercatcher		Pre notebooks (77-81)	Reg
36	Avocet		Pre notebooks (77-81)	Reg
37	Lapwing		Pre notebooks (77-81)	Reg
38	Golden Plover		Pre notebooks (77-81)	Reg
39	Grey Plover		Pre notebooks (77-81)	Reg
40	Ringed Plover		Pre notebooks (77-81)	Reg
41	Little Ringed Plover		Pre notebooks (77-81)	Reg
42	Whimbrel		Pre notebooks (77-81)	Reg
43	Curlew		Pre notebooks (77-81)	Reg
44	Bar-tailed Godwit		Pre notebooks (77-81)	Reg
45	Black-tailed Godwit		Pre notebooks (77-81)	Reg
46	Turnstone		Pre notebooks (77-81)	Reg
47	Knot		Pre notebooks (77-81)	Reg
48	Ruff		Pre notebooks (77-81)	Reg
49	Curlew Sandpiper		Pre notebooks (77-81)	Reg
50	Sanderling		Pre notebooks (77-81)	Reg
51	Dunlin		Pre notebooks (77-81)	Reg
52	Little Stint		Pre notebooks (77-81)	Reg
53	Snipe		Pre notebooks (77-81)	Reg
54	Common Sandpiper		Pre notebooks (77-81)	Reg
55	Green Sandpiper		Pre notebooks (77-81)	Reg
56	Redshank		Pre notebooks (77-81)	Reg
57	Spotted Redshank		Pre notebooks (77-81)	Reg
58	Greenshank		Pre notebooks (77-81)	Reg
59	Black-headed Gull		Pre notebooks (77-81)	Reg
60	Common Gull		Pre notebooks (77-81)	Reg
61	Great Black-backed Gull		Pre notebooks (77-81)	Reg
62	Herring Gull		Pre notebooks (77-81)	Reg
63	Lesser Black-backed Gull		Pre notebooks (77-81)	Reg
64	Sandwich Tern		Pre notebooks (77-81)	Reg
65	Little Tern		Pre notebooks (77-81)	Reg
66	Common Tern		Pre notebooks (77-81)	Reg
67	Cormorant		Pre notebooks (77-81)	Reg
68	Grey Heron		Pre notebooks (77-81)	Reg
69	Sparrowhawk		Pre notebooks (77-81)	Reg
70	Marsh Harrier		Pre notebooks (77-81)	Reg

No.	Species	Date	Location	Class
71	Hen Harrier		Pre notebooks (77-81)	Reg
72	Short-eared Owl		Pre notebooks (77-81)	Reg
73	Kingfisher		Pre notebooks (77-81)	Reg
74	Lesser Spotted Woodpecker		Pre notebooks (77-81)	Reg
75	Great Spotted Woodpecker		Pre notebooks (77-81)	Reg
76	Green Woodpecker		Pre notebooks (77-81)	Reg
77	Kestrel		Pre notebooks (77-81)	Reg
78	Jay		Pre notebooks (77-81)	Reg
79	Magpie		Pre notebooks (77-81)	Reg
80	Jackdaw		Pre notebooks (77-81)	Reg
81	Rook		Pre notebooks (77-81)	Reg
82	Carrion Crow		Pre notebooks (77-81)	Reg
83	Coal Tit		Pre notebooks (77-81)	Reg
84	Marsh Tit		Pre notebooks (77-81)	Reg
85	Willow Tit		Pre notebooks (77-81)	Reg
86	Blue Tit		Pre notebooks (77-81)	Reg
87	Great Tit		Pre notebooks (77-81)	Reg
88	Bearded Tit		Pre notebooks (77-81)	Reg
89	Skylark		Pre notebooks (77-81)	Reg
90	Sand Martin		Pre notebooks (77-81)	Reg
91	Swallow		Pre notebooks (77-81)	Reg
92	House Martin		Pre notebooks (77-81)	Reg
93	Long-tailed Tit		Pre notebooks (77-81)	Reg
94	Willow Warbler		Pre notebooks (77-81)	Reg
95	Chiffchaff		Pre notebooks (77-81)	Reg
96	Sedge Warbler		Pre notebooks (77-81)	Reg
97	Reed Warbler		Pre notebooks (77-81)	Reg
98	Blackcap		Pre notebooks (77-81)	Reg
99	Lesser Whitethroat		Pre notebooks (77-81)	Reg
100	Whitethroat		Pre notebooks (77-81)	Reg
101	Goldcrest		Pre notebooks (77-81)	Reg
102	Wren		Pre notebooks (77-81)	Reg
103	Nuthatch		Pre notebooks (77-81)	Reg
104	Treecreeper		Pre notebooks (77-81)	Reg
105	Starling		Pre notebooks (77-81)	Reg
106	Blackbird		Pre notebooks (77-81)	Reg
107	Fieldfare		Pre notebooks (77-81)	Reg
108	Redwing		Pre notebooks (77-81)	Reg
109	Song Thrush		Pre notebooks (77-81)	Reg
110	Mistle Thrush		Pre notebooks (77-81)	Reg
111	Spotted Flycatcher		Pre notebooks (77-81)	Reg
112	Robin		Pre notebooks (77-81)	Reg
113	Nightingale		Pre notebooks (77-81)	Reg
114	Redstart		Pre notebooks (77-81)	Reg

No.	Species	Date	Location	Class
115	Whinchat		Pre notebooks (77-81)	Reg
116	Stonechat		Pre notebooks (77-81)	Reg
117	Wheatear		Pre notebooks (77-81)	Reg
118	House Sparrow		Pre notebooks (77-81)	Reg
119	Tree Sparrow		Pre notebooks (77-81)	Reg
120	Dunnock		Pre notebooks (77-81)	Reg
121	Yellow Wagtail		Pre notebooks (77-81)	Reg
122	Grey Wagtail		Pre notebooks (77-81)	Reg
123	Pied Wagtail		Pre notebooks (77-81)	Reg
124	Meadow Pipit		Pre notebooks (77-81)	Reg
125	Tree Pipit		Pre notebooks (77-81)	Reg
126	Rock Pipit		Pre notebooks (77-81)	Reg
127	Chaffinch		Pre notebooks (77-81)	Reg
128	Bullfinch		Pre notebooks (77-81)	Reg
129	Greenfinch		Pre notebooks (77-81)	Reg
130	Linnet		Pre notebooks (77-81)	Reg
131	Lesser Redpoll		Pre notebooks (77-81)	Reg
132	Goldfinch		Pre notebooks (77-81)	Reg
133	Yellowhammer		Pre notebooks (77-81)	Reg
134	Reed Bunting		Pre notebooks (77-81)	Reg
135	Barn Owl	11/04/1992	W.SUSSEX, Selsey Area	Reg
136	Red Kite	18/04/1992	CEREDIGION, Tregaron	Reg
137	Buzzard	18/04/1992	CEREDIGION, Tregaron	Reg
138	Raven	18/04/1992	CEREDIGION, Tregaron	Reg
139	Grasshopper Warbler	26/04/1992	KENT, Stodmarsh	Reg
140	Kittiwake	02/05/1992	E.SUSSEX,Splash Point	Reg
141	Black-throated Diver	02/05/1992	E.SUSSEX, Splash Point	Reg
142	Fulmar	02/05/1992	E.SUSSEX, Birling Gap	Reg
143	Gannet	02/05/1992	E.SUSSEX, Birling Gap	Reg
144	Slavonian Grebe	03/05/1992	W.SUSSEX, Selsey Bill	Reg
145	Red-rumped Swallow	03/05/1992	W.SUSSEX, Selsey Bill	Vag
146	Osprey	16/05/1992	KENT, Bough Beech	Reg
147	Little Owl	16/05/1992	KENT, Bough Beech	Reg
148	Garden Warbler	16/05/1992	SURREY, Redhill	Reg
149	Wood Warbler	21/05/1992	Location witheld	Reg
150	Little Gull	24/05/1992	SUFFOLK, Minsmere R.S.P.B	Reg
151	Bittern	24/05/1992	SUFFOLK, Minsmere R.S.P.B	Reg
152	Mediterranean Gull	31/05/1992	KENT, Dungeness R.S.P.B.	Reg
153	Arctic Tern	31/05/1992	KENT, Dungeness R.S.P.B	Reg
154	Honey-buzzard	31/05/1992	KENT, Dungeness R.S.P.B.	Reg
155	Hobby	31/05/1992	KENT, Dungeness R.S.P.B.	Reg
156	Woodcock	01/06/1992	KENT, Bough Beech	Reg
157	Roseate Tern	14/06/1992	KENT, Dungeness R.S.P.B	Reg
158	Dartford Warbler	21/06/1992	Location withheld	Reg
159	Nightjar	26/06/1992	W.SUSSEX, Heyshott Common	Reg

No.	Species	Date	Location	Class
160	Red-necked Grebe	09/08/1992	KENT, Dungeness R.S.P.B.	Reg
161	Black-necked Grebe	09/08/1992	KENT, Dungeness R.S.P.B	Reg
162	Scaup	22/08/1992	KENT, Elmley R.S.P.B.	Reg
163	Peregrine	22/08/1992	KENT, Elmley R.S.P.B.	Reg
164	Red-necked Phalarope	31/08/1992	W.SUSSEX, Siddlesham Ferry	Reg
165	Wood Sandpiper	31/08/1992	W.SUSSEX, Selsey Bill	Reg
166	Black Tern	31/08/1992	W.SUSSEX, Ivy Lake	Reg
167	White-winged Black Tern	01/09/1992	E.SUSSEX, Rye Harbour	Vag
168	Spoonbill	09/09/1992	KENT, Bough Beech	Reg
169	Corn Bunting	20/09/1992	KENT, St. Margarets	Reg
170	Glaucous Gull	26/09/1992	W.SUSSEX, Selsey Bill	Reg
171	Arctic Skua	26/09/1992	W.SUSSEX, Selsey Bill	Reg
172	Pied Flycatcher	26/09/1992	W.SUSSEX, Selsey Bill	Reg
173	Razorbill	03/10/1992	E.SUSSEX, Brighton Marina	Reg
174	Black Redstart	03/10/1992	E.SUSSEX, Brighton Marina	Reg
175	Jack Snipe	10/10/1992	E.SUSSEX, Rye Harbour	Reg
176	Merlin	10/10/1992	E.SUSSEX, Rye Harbour	Reg
177	Common Guillemot	11/10/1992	E.SUSSEX, Newhaven Tidemi	Reg
178	Bewick's Swan	17/10/1992	KENT, Dungeness R.S.P.B.	Reg
179	Ruddy Duck	17/10/1992	KENT, Dungeness R.S.P.B.	Reg
180	Yellow-browed Warbler	17/10/1992	E.SUSSEX, Belle Tout Wood	Reg
181	Firecrest	17/10/1992	KENT, Dungeness R.S.P.B.	Reg
182	Siskin	26/10/1992	W.SUSSEX, Ifield Mill Pond	Reg
183	Woodlark	30/10/1992	SURREY, Frensham	Reg
184	Little Egret	07/11/1992	W.SUSSEX, Thorney Island	Reg
185	Great Grey Shrike	09/11/1992	SURREY, Thursley Common	Reg
186	Brambling	19/11/1992	W.SUSSEX, Weir Wood Reser	Reg
187	Goosander	23/11/1992	BERKS, Wraysbury	Reg
188	Ring-billed Gull	23/11/1992	LONDON, Rockingham Recreation Center	Reg
189	Ring-necked Parakeet	23/11/1992	BERKS, Winsor	Reg
190	Shag	05/12/1992	E.SUSSEX, Brighton Marina	Reg
191	Whooper Swan	07/12/1992	CAMBS, Welney W.W.T.	Reg
192	Eider	08/12/1992	NORFOLK, Hunstanton	Reg
193	Velvet Scoter	08/12/1992	NORFOLK, Hunstanton	Reg
194	Water Rail	08/12/1992	NORFOLK, Snettisham R.S.P	Reg
195	Purple Sandpiper	08/12/1992	NORFOLK, Heacham	Reg
196	Pink-footed Goose	09/12/1992	NORFOLK, Holkham	Reg
197	Egyptian Goose	09/12/1992	NORFOLK, Holkham	Reg
198	Shore Lark	09/12/1992	NORFOLK, Titchwell R.S.P.	Reg
199	Twite	09/12/1992	NORFOLK, Titchwell R.S.P.	Reg
200	Snow Bunting	09/12/1992	NORFOLK, Titchwell R.S.P.	Reg
201	Hawfinch	28/12/1992	KENT, Bedgebury	Reg
202	Red-throated Diver	31/12/1992	E.SUSSEX, Scotney G.P.	Reg
203	Great Northern Diver	31/12/1992	KENT, Dungeness R.S.P.B.	Reg
204	Buff-breasted Sandpiper	21/09/1993	W.SUSSEX, Siddlesham	Reg

No.	Species	Date	Location	Class
205	Wryneck	21/09/1993	W.SUSSEX, Selsey Bill	Reg
206	Crossbill	17/12/1993	W.SUSSEX, Cowdray Forest	Reg
207	Long-tailed Duck	11/01/1994	KENT, Dungeness R.S.P.B.	Reg
208	Little Bunting	15/01/1994	W.SUSSEX, Ifield Church	Vag
209	Waxwing	25/02/1996	W.SUSSEX, Broadfield	Reg
210	Great White Egret	02/03/1996	E.SUSSEX, Horseye Level	Vag
211	Ring-necked Duck	10/03/1996	W.SUSSEX, Warnham Pond	Vag
212	Purple Heron	06/04/1996	E.SUSSEX, Pevensey Levels	Reg
213	Lesser Scaup	13/04/1996	HERTS, Tyttenhanger Gravel Pits	Vag
214	Spotted Crake	13/04/1996	HERTS, Tringfield Reservo	Reg
215	Bluethroat	14/04/1996	ESSEX, Bradwell	Reg
216	American Coot	21/04/1996	KENT, Stodmarsh	5yr
217	Cetti's Warbler	25/05/1996	KENT, New Hythe	Reg
218	Marsh Warbler	25/05/1996	Location witheld	Reg
219	Little Bittern	01/06/1996	SURREY, Epsom Stew Ponds	1yr
220	Great Reed Warbler	01/06/1996	KENT, Elmley	1yr
221	Stone-curlew	09/06/1996	NORFOLK, Weeting Heath	Reg
222	Montagu's Harrier	09/06/1996	Location witheld	Reg
223	Red-backed Shrike	09/06/1996	SUFFOLK, Dunwich Heath	Reg
224	Golden Oriole	09/06/1996	Location witheld	Reg
225	Serin	09/06/1996	NORFOLK, Gaywood Hall Drive	Reg
226	White-rumped Sandpiper	17/08/1996	HANTS, Farlington Marshes	Vag
227	Grey Phalarope	30/10/1996	SURREY, Staines Reservoir	Reg
228	Ferruginous Duck	05/01/1997	KENT, New Hythe	1yr
229	Long-eared Owl	05/01/1997	KENT, New Hythe	Reg
230	Pied-billed Grebe	16/03/1997	LONDON, South Norwood Lake	1yr
231	Penduline Tit	16/03/1997	KENT, New Hythe	Vag
232	Little Crake	29/03/1997	KENT, Bough Beech Reservoir	1yr
233	Pallas's Warbler	19/10/1997	KENT, North Foreland	Vag
234	Barred Warbler	25/10/1997	W.SUSSEX, Selsey Bill	Reg
235	Rough-legged Buzzard	02/11/1997	KENT, Harty Marshes	Reg
236	Long-billed Dowitcher	09/11/1997	KENT, Elmley	1yr
237	Desert Wheatear	09/11/1997	KENT, Reculver	1yr
238	Hume's Warbler	16/11/1997	E.SUSSEX, Sheepcoate valley	1yr
239	Little Auk	28/12/1997	KENT, Stonar Lake	Reg
240	Taiga Bean Goose	29/12/1997	NORFOLK, Cantley	Reg
241	Baillon's Crake	13/07/1999	KENT, Groove Ferry	2yr
242	Cirl Bunting	30/08/1999	DEVON, Prawle Point	Reg
243	Pectoral Sandpiper	03/09/1999	W.SUSSEX, Weir Wood Reser	Reg
244	Leach's Petrel	18/09/1999	W.SUSSEX, Shoreham Beach	Reg
245	Crane	26/09/1999	NORFOLK, Dunnings Mill	Reg
246	Blyth's Pipit	26/09/1999	NORFOLK, Happisburg	2yr
247	Dotterel	01/10/1999	KENT, Dymchurch	Reg
248	Wilson's Phalarope	10/10/1999	E.YORKS, Blacktoft Sands	1yr
249	Red-breasted Flycatcher	13/10/1999	KENT, St. Margarets	Reg

No.	Species	Date	Location	Class
250	Temminck's Stint	15/10/1999	HANTS, Titchfield Haven	Reg
251	Yellow-billed Cuckoo	16/10/1999	SCILLY, Tresco	1yr
252	Upland Sandpiper	16/10/1999	SCILLY, St. Mary's: Airfield	1yr
253	Short-toed Lark	16/10/1999	SCILLY, St. Marys: Airfield	Vag
254	Radde's Warbler	16/10/1999	SCILLY, St. Mary's: Watermill	Vag
255	Richard's Pipit	16/10/1999	SCILLY, St. Mary's Airfield	Reg
256	White's Thrush	17/10/1999	SCILLY, St. Agnes	1yr
257	Manx Shearwater	18/10/1999	At sea, Penzance to SCILLY	Reg
258	Ring Ouzel	18/10/1999	SCILLY, St. Mary's: Penninis	Reg
259	Red-flanked Bluetail	19/10/1999	CORNWALL, Rame Head	Vag
260	Dipper	19/10/1999	DORSET, River Bovey	Reg
261	Dusky Warbler	23/10/1999	SUFFOLK, Corton	Vag
262	Paddyfield Warbler	26/10/1999	ESSEX, Lee Valley	1yr
263	Tawny Owl	30/10/1999	LONDON, Regents Park	Reg
264	Blue-winged Teal	31/10/1999	ESSEX, Hanningfield Reservoir	1yr
265	Pallid Swift	31/10/1999	SUFFOLK, Sizewell	1yr
266	White-tailed Eagle	31/10/1999	SUFFOLK, Cove Bottom	Reg
267	Pacific Golden Plover	06/11/1999	CORNWALL, Helston	1yr
268	American Golden Plover	07/11/1999	HANTS, Normandy Marshes	Vag
269	Goshawk	13/11/1999	Location Witheld	Reg
270	Canvasback	14/11/1999	ESSEX, Abberton Reservoir	10yr
271	Forster's Tern	05/12/1999	ESSEX, Old Hall Marshes	3yr
272	Ivory Gull	16/12/1999	SUFFOLK, Aldeburgh	1yr
273	Chough	26/12/1999	ANGLESSEY, South Stack R.S.P.B.	Reg
274	American Wigeon	27/12/1999	CEREDIGION, Cors caron	Vag
275	Cattle Egret	02/01/2000	E.SUSSEX, Henfield	Vag
276	Red-breasted Goose	08/01/2000	SUFFOLK, Waldringfield	Vag
277	Pomarine Skua	08/01/2000	SUFFOLK, Sizewell Beach	Reg
278	Black Duck	09/01/2000	CORNWALL, Stithians	1yr
279	King Eider	09/01/2000	CORNWALL, Mounts Bay Marazion	1yr
280	Iceland Gull	09/01/2000	DEVON, Bideford	Reg
281	Lady Amherst's Pheasant	21/01/2000	BUCKS, Buttermilk Wood Wo	Reg
282	Water Pipit	21/01/2000	ESSEX, Rainham Marshes	Reg
283	Golden Pheasant	22/01/2000	NORFOLK, Waylands Wood	Reg
284	Black-winged Stilt	22/01/2000	NORFOLK, Titchwell	Vag
285	Sora	23/01/2000	DEVON, Stover country park	3yr
286	Lapland Bunting	30/01/2000	E.YORKS, Aldeborough	Reg
287	Gyr Falcon	09/03/2000	CORNWALL, Cape CORNWALL	1yr
288	Franklin's Gull	20/03/2000	SOMERSET, Cheddar Reservoir	1yr
289	Bonaparte's Gull	20/03/2000	DEVON, Teign Estuary	1yr
290	White Stork	30/03/2000	SURREY, Burpham Court Farm	Reg
291	Great Spotted Cuckoo	10/04/2000	HANTS, Pennington Marshes	1yr
292	Marsh Sandpiper	11/04/2000	DORSET, Standpit Marsh	1yr
293	Rose-coloured Starling	20/04/2000	N.YORKS, Ripon	Vag
294	Tawny Pipit	20/04/2000	E.YORKS, Easington: Sammy	1yr

No.	Species	Date	Location	Class
295	Western Subalpine Warbler	21/04/2000	W.SUSSEX, Beach Head	Vag
296	Night-heron	25/04/2000	GLOUCS, Slimbridge W.W.T.	Vag
297	Kentish Plover	25/04/2000	DORSET, Ferrybridge	Reg
298	Ortolan Bunting	04/05/2000	SURREY, QE2 Reservoir	Reg
299	Slender-billed Gull	05/05/2000	NORFOLK, Cley Arnolds Marsh	5yr
300	Asian Desert Warbler	08/05/2000	E.YORKS, Spurn	5yr
301	Puffin	08/05/2000	N.YORKS, Filey Car-nays	Reg
302	Woodchat Shrike	09/05/2000	E.SUSSEX, Coombe Haven	Vag
303	Lesser Yellowlegs	09/05/2000	DORSET, East Fleet: Butterstreet	1yr
304	Fan-tailed Warbler	20/05/2000	DORSET, Hengisbury Head	5yr
305	Broad-billed Sandpiper	20/05/2000	DEVON, Dawlish Warren	1yr
306	Western Bonelli's Warbler	29/05/2000	SUFFOLK, Landguard	1yr
307	Red-footed Falcon	29/05/2000	HANTS, Budleigh New Forest	Vag
308	Black Guillemot	03/06/2000	HIGHLAND, Isle of Skye: Kyle of Lochalshe	Reg
309	Golden Eagle	03/06/2000	HIGHLAND, Isle of Skye: Kyleakin	Reg
310	Rock Dove	03/06/2000	HIGHLAND, Isle of Skye: Linicro	Reg
311	Scottish Crossbill	04/06/2000	HIGHLAND, Grantown Forest	Reg
312	Crested Tit	04/06/2000	HIGHLAND, Moremore Picnic	Reg
313	Red Grouse	04/06/2000	DEESIDE, Glenshee	Reg
314	Squacco Heron	10/06/2000	E.SUSSEX, Pett Levels	1yr
315	Quail	11/06/2000	KENT, Sandwich Bay	Reg
316	Blyth's Reed Warbler	18/06/2000	HIGHLAND, Nigg Ferry	Vag
317	Black-headed Bunting	25/06/2000	GWYNEDD, Aber Dysynni	1yr
318	Eastern Black-eared Wheatear	26/06/2000	DORSET,Upton Heath	5yr
319	Roller	28/07/2000	CO.DURHAM, East Boldon	1yr
320	Melodious Warbler	01/08/2000	DORSET, Portland: Quarry	Reg
321	Caspian Tern	03/08/2000	CLEVELAND, Seaton Snook	1yr
322	Aquatic Warbler	11/08/2000	CORNWALL, Marazion Marsh	1yr
323	Semipalmated Sandpiper	11/08/2000	E.SUSSEX, Rye Harbour	1yr
324	Hoopoe	15/08/2000	LONDON, KGV Reservoir	Reg
325	Black-winged Pratincole	18/08/2000	CUMBRIA, Skinburness	1yr
326	Great Skua	20/08/2000	At sea, Sicillonian Pelagic	Reg
327	Sooty Shearwater	20/08/2000	At sea, Sicillonian Pelagic	Reg
328	Sabine's Gull	20/08/2000	At sea, Sicillonian Pelagic	Reg
329	Storm Petrel	20/08/2000	At sea, Sicillonian Pelagic	Reg
330	Great Shearwater	20/08/2000	At sea, Sicillonian Pelagic	Reg
331	Wilson's Petrel	20/08/2000	At sea, Sicillonian Pelagic	Vag
332	Balearic Shearwater	21/08/2000	CORNWALL, Porthgwarra	Reg
333	Cory's Shearwater	22/08/2000	CORNWALL, Porthgwarra	Reg
334	Booted Warbler	28/08/2000	E.YORKS, Spurn	1yr
335	Greenish Warbler	28/08/2000	E.YORKS, Spurn	Vag
336	Arctic Warbler	02/09/2000	E.YORKS, Spurn	1yr
337	Eastern Olivaceous Warbler	17/09/2000	ABERDEENSHIRE, Collieston	2yr
338	Solitary Sandpiper	23/09/2000	SCILLY, St. Mary's: Carn Friars	1yr
339	Cliff Swallow	30/09/2000	DORSET, Portland: Le Verne	5yr

No.	Species	Date	Location	Class
340	Green-winged Teal	14/04/1996	KENT, Stodmarsh	Vag
341	Red-eyed Vireo	01/10/2000	CORNWALL, Kenidjack valley	1yr
342	Rustic Bunting	07/10/2000	NORFOLK, Stiffkey	1yr
343	Swainson's Thrush	15/10/2000	SCILLY, St. Mary's: Porthloo	1yr
344	Spectacled Warbler	16/10/2000	SCILLY, Tresco	5yr
345	Surf Scoter	21/10/2000	WORCS, Droitwich	Vag
346	Sociable Lapwing	22/10/2000	SUFFOLK,Blythburg	1yr
347	Pied Wheatear	19/11/2000	LINCS, Gilbrater Point	1yr
348	Laughing Gull	13/01/2001	WILTS, Swindon sewage works	1yr
349	Short-toed Treecreeper	28/03/2001	KENT, Dungeness	1yr
350	Black Grouse	13/04/2001	PERTHSHIRE, Braco Moor	Reg
351	Ptarmigan	13/04/2001	DEESIDE, Glenshee	Reg
352	Iberian Chiffchaff	15/04/2001	KENT, Dungeness: Long pit	1yr
353	Thrush Nightingale	13/05/2001	E.YORKS, Spurn	1yr
354	Savi's Warbler	16/05/2001	NORFOLK, Thornham	1yr
355	Little Swift	26/05/2001	NOTTS, Netherfields ash lagoons	2yr
356	Collared Pratincole	26/05/2001	W.SUSSEX, Siddlesham	1yr
357	Marmora's Warbler	30/05/2001	SUFFOLK, Sizewell	10yr
358	Sharp-tailed Sandpiper	30/08/2001	KENT, Grove Ferry	1yr
359	Baird's Sandpiper	12/09/2001	SOMERSET, Blagdon Lake	1yr
360	Red-necked Stint	21/09/2001	CAMBS, Somersham	5yr
361	Isabelline Wheatear	21/09/2001	SUFFOLK, Landguard	1yr
362	Pallas's Grasshopper Warbler	23/09/2001	NORFOLK, Blakeney	1yr
363	Short-billed Dowitcher	24/10/1999	CLEVELAND, Greatham Creek	10yr
364	Common Rosefinch	13/10/2001	DEVON, Lundy	Reg
365	Bobolink	14/10/2001	DEVON, Prawle Point	1yr
366	Sardinian Warbler	19/10/2001	SOMERSET, Brean Down	1yr
367	Snowy Owl	24/10/2001	SUFFOLK, Landguard	1yr
368	Whiskered Tern	31/10/2001	BUCKS, Willen Lake	1yr
369	Gull-billed Tern	17/11/2001	NORFOLK, Titchwell	1yr
370	Common Redpoll	25/11/2001	NORFOLK, Titchwell R.S.P.	Reg
371	Arctic Redpoll	22/12/2001	NORFOLK, Titchwell R.S.P.	Vag
372	Snow Goose	25/12/2001	ABERDEENSHIRE, Loch of Strathbeg	Reg
373	Barnacle Goose	25/12/2001	ABERDEENSHIRE, Loch of St	Reg
374	Ross's Gull	29/01/2002	DEVON, Plymm Estuary	1yr
375	Olive-backed Pipit	03/02/2002	NORFOLK, Lynford	Vag
376	Alpine Accentor	17/03/2002	SUFFOLK, Minsmere	3yr
377	Capercaillie	24/03/2002	HIGHLAND, Grantown on spey	Reg
378	Lesser Sand Plover	12/05/2002	LINCS, Rimac	10yr
379	Lesser Kestrel	16/05/2002	SCILLY, St. Marys: Penninis	5yr
380	Citrine Wagtail	16/05/2002	CORNWALL, Marazion Marsh	Vag
381	Alpine Swift	18/05/2002	DORSET, Lodmoor R.S.P.B.	Vag
382	Least Sandpiper	24/05/2002	STAFFS, Drayton Bassett	1yr
383	Lesser Grey Shrike	26/05/2002	DEVON, Dawlish warren	1yr
384	Black Stork	28/05/2002	NORFOLK, Great Ryburgh	1yr

No.	Species	Date	Location	Class
385	Bee-eater	04/06/2002	CO.DURHAM, Bishop Middle	Reg
386	Spotted Sandpiper	20/06/2002	CO.DURHAM, Derwent Reservoir	1yr
387	Corncrake	29/06/2002	HIGHLAND, Isle of Skye: Uig	Reg
388	Stilt Sandpiper	21/07/2002	HANTS, Pennington Marshes	1yr
389	Pallid Harrier	11/08/2002	KENT, Elmley	1yr
390	Terek Sandpiper	25/08/2002	ESSEX, Maldon	1yr
391	Glossy Ibis	07/09/2002	DEVON, Budleigh Salterton	Vag
392	Snowy Egret	10/11/2001	ARGYLL, Balvicar	Life
393	Hooded Crow	03/06/2000	HIGHLAND, Inverness	Reg
394	White-throated Sparrow	25/10/2002	N.YORKS, Flamboro: Old fall	1yr
395	Rufous Turtle Dove	06/12/2002	ORKNEY, Stromness	5yr
396	Two-barred Crossbill	14/12/2002	NORFOLK, Sandringham	1yr
397	L.White-fronted Goose	16/02/2003	GLOUCS, Slimbridge	1yr
398	Red-throated Pipit	03/05/2003	DEVON, Northan Burrows	1yr
399	White-crowned Sparrow	22/05/2003	CORK, Dursey	5yr
400	Black Kite	03/08/2003	E.SUSSEX, Beachy Head	Vag
401	Common Yellowthroat	04/10/2003	CLARE, Loop Head	5yr
402	Grey-cheeked Thrush	14/10/2003	SCILLY, Tresco	1yr
403	Siberian Rubythroat	19/10/2003	SHETLAND, Fair Isle	4yr
404	Savannah Sparrow	19/10/2003	SHETLAND, Fair Isle	20yr
405	Baltimore Oriole	16/12/2003	OXON, Headingford	2yr
406	American Robin	16/12/2003	CORNWALL, Godrevy	2yr
407	Harlequin Duck	21/02/2004	WESTERN ISLES, Lewis: Col	4yr
408	Pine Bunting	29/02/2004	NORFOLK, Choseley	1yr
409	Bufflehead	31/05/2004	STAFFS, Croxall Gravel Pits	3yr
410	Icterine Warbler	31/05/2004	SUFFOLK, Outney Common	Reg
411	Greater Sand Plover	04/07/2004	NORFOLK, Snettisham	2yr
412	Cream-coloured Courser	30/09/2004	SCILLY, St. Martins	5yr
413	Black Lark	02/06/2003	ANGLESSEY, South Stack	20yr
414	Audouin's Gull	05/05/2003	KENT, Dungeness	5yr
415	Western Sandpiper	02/10/2004	DORSET, Brownsea Island	5yr
416	Yellow Warbler	07/10/2004	WESTERN ISLES, Barra	5yr
417	Ovenbird	27/10/2004	SCILLY, St. Mary's: Trenoweth	5yr
418	Killdeer	08/01/2005	WESTERN ISLES, North Uist	1yr
419	White-billed Diver	23/04/2005	WESTERN ISLES, Lewis: Skiggersta	Vag
420	Belted Kingfisher	07/05/2005	ABERDEENSHIRE, Peterculter	5yr
421	Barrow's Goldeneye	14/05/2005	ABERDEENSHIRE, Ythan Estuary	10yr
422	Trumpeter Finch	21/05/2005	SUFFOLK, Landguard	4yr
423	Sooty Tern	09/07/2005	ANGLESSEY, Skerries	3yr
424	Lesser Crested Tern	17/07/2005	NORFOLK, Waxham	5yr
425	Blackpoll Warbler	28/09/2005	SCILLY, St. Agnes	1yr
426	Black Scoter	26/12/2001	MORAY, Burghead Bay	4yr
427	Yellow-legged Gull	28/06/2000	SURREY, Staines Reservoir	Reg
428	Taiga Flycatcher	27/04/2003	N.YORKS, Flamboro: South landing	10yr
429	Green Heron	12/10/2005	CORK, Schull Harbour	5yr

No.	Species	Date	Location	Class
430	Chimney Swift	01/11/2005	CORK, Courtmacsherry	3yr
431	Brünnich's Guillemot	03/12/2005	SHETLAND, Bressay	1yr
432	Buff-bellied Pipit	13/12/2005	LINCS, Frampton	1yr
433	Black-throated Thrush	30/12/2005	SOMERSET, Curload	1yr
434	Masked Shrike	31/10/2004	FIFE, Kilrenny common	10yr
435	Calandra Lark	13/05/2006	FIFE, Isle of May	3yr
436	Black-browed Albatross	01/06/2006	WESTERN ISLES, Sula Sgeir	2yr
437	Scops Owl	13/06/2006	OXON, Thrupp	1yr
438	Long-tailed Skua	09/09/2006	BERKS, Queen Mother Reser	Reg
439	Canada Warbler	09/10/2006	CLARE, Kilbaha	Life
440	Hermit Thrush	20/10/2006	CORK, Cape Clear	4yr
441	Long-billed Murrelet	11/11/2006	DEVON, Dawlish	Life
442	Chestnut-eared Bunting	19/10/2004	SHETLAND, Fair Isle	20yr
443	White-tailed Plover	07/06/2007	D&G, Caerlaverock	10yr
444	Dark-eyed Junco	14/07/2007	NORFOLK, Langham	1yr
445	Rose-breasted Grosbeak	25/10/2007	SCILLY, St. Agnes	1yr
446	Caspian Gull	31/12/2001	BEDS, Whipsnade Zoo	Vag
447	Mourning Dove	02/11/2007	WESTERN ISLES, North Uist	10yr
448	Pechora Pipit	21/11/2007	PEMBROKESHIRE, Goodwick moor	1yr
449	American Herring Gull	16/02/2008	GALWAY, Galway Harbour	1yr
450	River Warbler	30/05/2008	E.SUSSEX, Beachy Head	1yr
451	Cretzschmar's Bunting	20/09/2008	ORKNEY, North Ronaldsway	10yr
452	Brown Shrike	25/09/2008	N.YORKS, Flamboro	1yr
453	Wilson's Snipe	27/10/2007	SCILLY, St. Mary's: Lower Moors	5yr
454	Hooded Merganser	23/03/2002	CO.DURHAM, Newbiggin	4yr
455	Scarlet Tanager	11/10/2008	CORK, Garinish Point	5yr
456	Little Blue Heron	11/10/2008	GALWAY, Letterfrack	Life
457	Collared Flycatcher	29/04/2009	DORSET, Portland	1yr
458	Crested Lark	03/05/2009	KENT, Dungeness	5yr
459	Oriental Pratincole	03/06/2009	KENT, Dungeness	10yr
460	Blue-cheeked Bee-eater	22/07/2009	KENT, St. Margarets Bay	5yr
461	Sandhill Crane	23/09/2009	ORKNEY, South Ronaldsway	10yr
462	Baikal Teal	24/11/2001	SUFFOLK, Minsmere	10yr
463	Glaucous-winged Gull	03/03/2007	CAMARTHEN, Tywn Estuary	20yr
464	Pacific Diver	30/01/2007	N.YORKS, Knaresborough	4yr
465	Asian Brown Flycatcher	04/10/2007	E.YORKS, Flamboro Head	10yr
466	Veery	03/10/2009	SHETLAND, Whalsay	5yr
467	Sykes's Warbler	16/08/2010	NORTHUMBERLAND, Druridge	3yr
468	Northern Parula	26/09/2010	ARGYLL, Tiree	4yr
469	Eastern Crowned Warbler	25/10/2009	CO.DURHAM, South Shields	10yr
470	Citril Finch	09/06/2008	SHETLAND, Fair Isle	20yr
471	Yellow-rumped Warbler	08/10/2010	CORK, Cape Clear	3yr
472	American Bittern	30/10/2010	CORNWALL, Trewey Common	4yr
473	Northern Harrier	06/11/2010	WEXFORD, Tacumshin	3yr
474	Stejneger's Scoter	11/03/2011	KERRY, Rossbeigh	Life

No.	Species	Date	Location	Class
475	White-throated Robin	06/06/2011	CLEVELAND, Hartlepool	20yr
476	Greater Yellowlegs	13/09/2011	CORNWALL, Wadebridge	1yr
477	Long-toed Stint	16/09/2011	W.SUSSEX, Weir Wood	10yr
478	Black-and-white Warbler	17/09/2011	SCILLY, St. Mary's: Lower Moors	3yr
479	Northern Waterthrush	19/09/2011	SCILLY, St. Mary's: Lower Moors	5yr
480	Hudsonian Whimbrel	19/06/2007	CUMBRIA, Walney Island	3yr
481	Siberian Stonechat	04/10/2007	E.YORKS, Spurn	5yr
482	Semipalmated Plover	08/10/2011	KERRY, Ventry	4yr
483	Spanish Sparrow	11/01/2012	HANTS, Calshot	5yr
484	Parrot Crossbill	29/01/2012	W.SUSSEX, Blackdown	Vag
485	Western Orphean Warbler	29/05/2012	CLEVELAND, Hartlepool	10yr
486	Pine Grosbeak	04/02/2013	SHETLAND, Housetter	5yr
487	Rock Thrush	25/04/2013	E.YORKS, Spurn	2yr
488	Dusky Thrush	18/05/2013	KENT, Margate Cementary	4yr
489	Pacific Swift	15/06/2013	SUFFOLK, Trimley Marshes	5yr
490	Needle-tailed Swift	26/06/2013	WESTERN ISLES, Harris: Tarbert	5yr
491	Bridled Tern	02/07/2013	NORTHUMBERLAND, Inner Farne	2yr
492	Swinhoe's Petrel	16/08/2013	SHETLAND, Fair Isle	5yr
493	Great Snipe	15/09/2013	E.YORKS, Kilnsea	1yr
494	Wilson's Warbler	21/09/2013	CORK, Dursey Island	20yr
495	Thick-billed Warbler	05/10/2013	SHETLAND, Geosetter	10yr
496	Cape May Warbler	24/10/2013	SHETLAND, Unst: Baltasound	20yr
497	Crag Martin	12/04/2014	N.YORKS, flamboro: north landing	4yr
498	Short-toed Eagle	01/06/2014	DORSET, Morden Bog	10yr
499	Great Knot	14/07/2014	NORFOLK, Breydon water	10yr
500	Lanceolated Warbler	08/10/2014	SHETLAND, Quendale	1yr
501	Eastern Bonelli's Warbler	10/10/2014	SHETLAND, Scalloway	5yr
502	Alder Flycatcher	25/09/2010	NORFOLK, Blakeney Point	20yr
503	Little Bustard	01/01/2015	E. YORKS, Wilsthorpe	2yr
504	Great Blue Heron	18/04/2015	SCILLY, Bryher	20yr
505	Hudsonian Godwit	25/04/2015	SOMERSET, Meare Heath	10yr
506	Daurian Shrike	01/10/2012	SHETLAND, Toab	5yr
507	Black-billed Cuckoo	25/05/2016	WESTERN ISLES, North Uist	3yr
508	Royal Tern	27/08/2016	KERRY, Littor	5yr
509	Black-faced Bunting	11/10/2016	SHETLAND, Bressay, Gunnista	10yr
510	Blue Rock Thrush	28/12/2016	GLOUCS, Stow on the Wold	5yr
511	Cackling Goose	28/12/2001	ARGYLL, Islay: Ballygrant	Vag
512	Slaty-backed Gull	17/02/2011	LONDON, Rainham	20yr
513	Chinese Pond Heron	22/02/2014	KENT, Saltwood	20yr
514	Acadian Flycatcher	22/09/2015	KENT, Dungeness	Life
515	Siberian Accentor	15/10/2016	E.YORKS, Easington	5yr
516	Chestnut Bunting	25/10/2015	ORKNEY, Papa Westray	Life
517	Amur Falcon	17/07/2017	CORNWALL, St Buryan	20yr
518	American Redstart	09/09/2017	WESTERN ISLES, Barra, Eoligarry	5yr
519	Cedar Waxwing	07/10/2017	SCILLY, St. Agnes: St Warna's Cove	5yr

No.	Species	Date	Location	Class
520	Tundra Bean Goose	08/01/2000	SUFFOLK, North Warren R.S.P.B.	Reg
521	Western Swamphen	31/07/2016	SUFFOLK, Minsmere	Life
522	Two-barred Warbler	18/10/2006	N.YORKS, Filey	5yr
523	Eastern Yellow Wagtail	12/12/2010	DEVON, Colyford	2yr
524	Song Sparrow	18/05/2018	SHETLAND, Fair Isle: Gulley	5yr
525	Moltoni's Subalpine Warbler	30/05/2018	HIGHLAND, Duncansby Head	5yr
526	Elegant Tern	18/05/2002	DEVON, Dawlish Warren	5yr
527	Red-winged Blackbird	06/05/2017	ORKNEY, North Ronaldsway	20yr
528	Grey Catbird	17/10/2018	CORNWALL, Trevescan	20yr
529	Tengmalm's Owl	23/02/2019	SHETLAND, Bixter	5yr
530	Brown Booby	06/09/2019	CORNWALL, Kynance Cove	10yr
531	Common Nighthawk	08/10/2019	ANTRIM, River Maine Galgorm	1yr
532	Steller's Eider	09/11/2019	ORKNEY, Papa Westray	4yr
533	Falcated Duck	20/12/2008	DEVON, Exminster Marshes	5yr
534	Dalmatian Pelican	13/05/2016	CORNWALL, Tretheway	Life
535	White-winged Scoter	11/06/2018	ABERDEENSHIRE, Murcar	10yr
536	Tennessee Warbler	30/09/2020	SHETLAND, Yell	10yr
537	Siberian Thrush	03/10/2020	FIFE, Kilminning	4yr
538	Eyebrowed Thrush	07/10/2020	ORKNEY, North Ronaldsway	2yr
539	Rufous Bush Chat	17/10/2020	NORFOLK,Stiffkey	5yr
540	Stejneger's Stonechat	21/10/2020	CLEVELAND, South Gare	5yr
541	Indigo Bunting	26/10/2020	SCILLY, St Agnes	10yr
542	Eastern Subalpine Warbler	27/04/2013	SUFFOLK, Landguard	1yr
543	Northern Mockingbird	08/04/2021	W.SUSSEX, Pulborough	20yr
544	Green Warbler	10/09/2021	E.YORKS, Buckton	5yr
545	Varied Thrush	29/10/2021	ORKNEY, Papa Westray	20yr
546	Yellow-bellied Flycatcher	17/09/2020	ARGYLL, Tiree	Life
547	Ross's Goose	17/11/2001	NORFOLK, Wighton	2yr
548	Double-crested Cormorant	27/02/2022	LEITRIM, Doon Laugh	20yr
549	Egyptian Vulture	27/02/2022	ROSCOMMON, Lough Funshinagh	Life
550	Eleonora's Falcon	27/05/2022	KENT, Worth Marshes	5yr
551	Least Tern	12/06/2022	DUBLIN, Portrane	20yr
552	Turkestan Shrike	24/06/2022	E.YORKS, Bempton	5yr
553	Blackburnian Warbler	14/10/2022	SCILLY, Bryher	10yr

BIRDS NOT SEEN

1-yr birds
554 Barolo Shearwater
555 Yellow-breasted Bunting
556 Zino's/Fea's/Des Petrel
3-yr birds
557 Great Bustard
4-yr birds
558 Nutcracker
5-yr birds
559 Yelkouan Shearwater
560 W. Black-eared Wheatear
10-yr birds
561 American Purple Gallinule
562 Brown-headed Cowbird
563 Caspian Plover
564 Pallas's Reed Bunting
565 Pallas's Sandgrouse
566 Red-billed Tropicbird
567 Rufous-tailed Robin
568 Rüppell's Warbler
569 Scopoli's Shearwater
570 Siberian Blue Robin
571 Wallcreeper
572 Yellow-browed Bunting
20-yr birds
573 Allen's Gallinule
574 American Kestrel
575 Ascension Frigatebird
576 Bimaculated Lark
577 Cabot's Tern
578 Chestnut-sided Warbler
579 Eastern Kingbird
580 Evening Grosbeak
581 Grey-tailed Tattler
582 Hooded Warbler
583 Lark Sparrow
584 Little Whimbrel
585 Magnificent Frigatebird
586 Magnolia Warbler
587 Naumann's Thrush
588 Philadelphia Vireo
589 Redhead

590 Rock Bunting
591 Ruby-crowned Kinglet
592 Tree Swallow
593 Yellow-bellied Sapsucker
Lifetime birds
594 Aleutian Tern
595 Ancient Murrelet
596 Yellow-nosed Albatross
597 Bald Eagle
598 Bay-breasted Warbler
599 Black-capped Petrel
600 Blue-winged Warbler
601 Brown Thrasher
602 Bulwer's Petrel
603 Eastern Orphean Warbler
604 Eastern Phoebe
605 Eastern Towhee
606 Egyptian Nightjar
607 Golden-winged Warbler
608 Hawk Owl
609 Least Bittern
610 Long-tailed Shrike
611 Macqueen's Bustard
612 M. Short-toed Lark
613 Moussier's Redstart
614 Olive-tree Warbler
615 Pale-legged Leaf Warbler
616 Purple Martin
617 Red Fox Sparrow
618 Red-breasted Nuthatch
619 Red-footed Booby
620 Red-throated Thrush
621 Rock Sparrow
622 South Polar Skua
623 Summer Tanager
624 Tufted Puffin
625 Vega Gull
626 White-chinned Petrel
627 W-crowned B. Wheatear
628 White-rumped Swift
629 White-winged Lark
630 Wood Thrush
631 Yellow-throated Vireo

Category B birds

632 Band-rumped Storm Petrel

633 Eskimo Curlew

634 Great Auk

635 Great Black-headed Gull

636 Griffon Vulture

637 Red-necked Nightjar

638 Ruddy Shelduck

639 Spotted Eagle

640 White-faced Storm Petrel